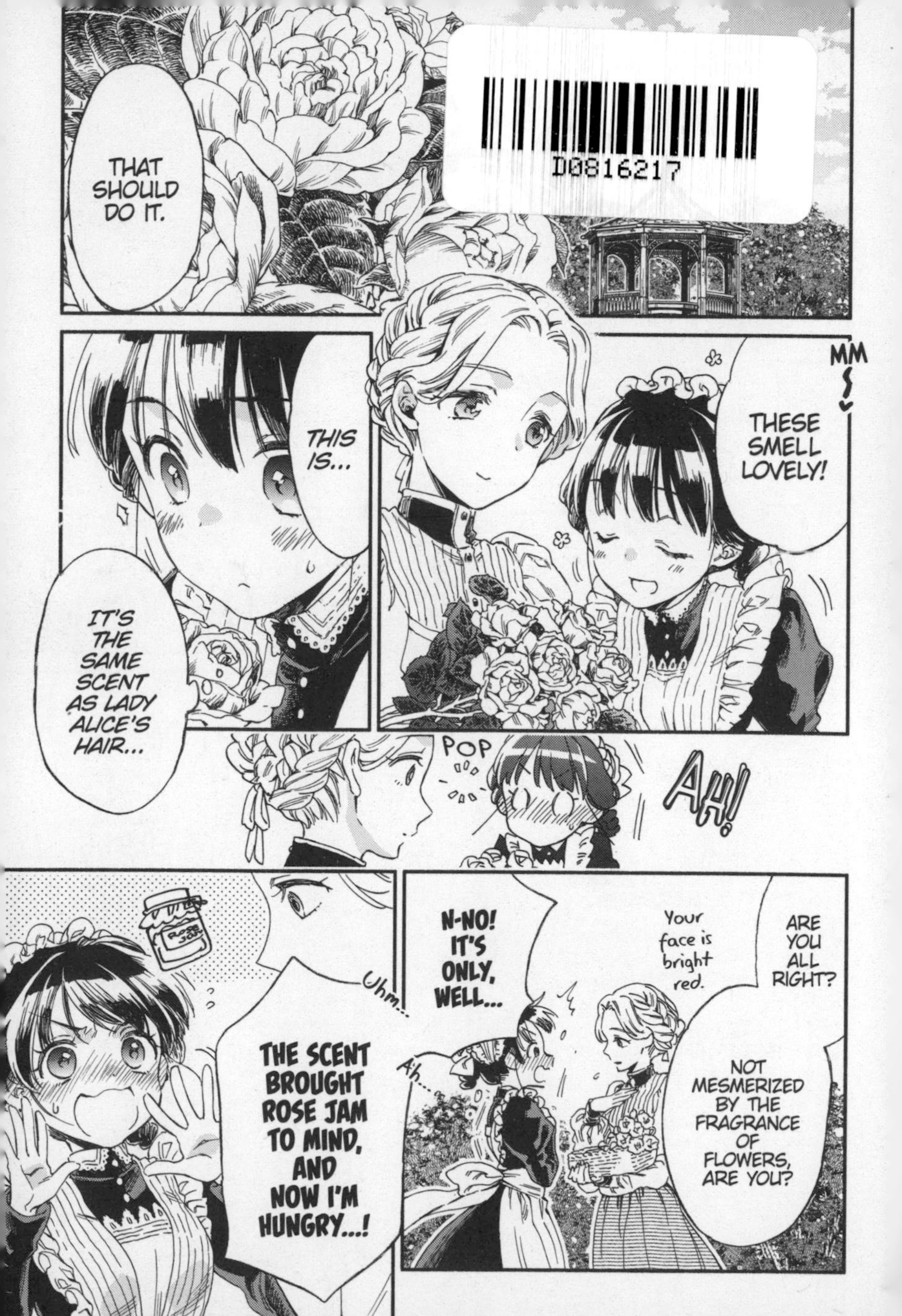
THAT SHOULD DO IT.
MM~
THESE SMELL LOVELY!
THIS IS...
IT'S THE SAME SCENT AS LADY ALICE'S HAIR...
AH!
POP
ARE YOU ALL RIGHT?
Your face is bright red.
NOT MESMERIZED BY THE FRAGRANCE OF FLOWERS, ARE YOU?
N-NO! IT'S ONLY, WELL...
Ah...
Uhm...
THE SCENT BROUGHT ROSE JAM TO MIND, AND NOW I'M HUNGRY...!
ROSE JAM

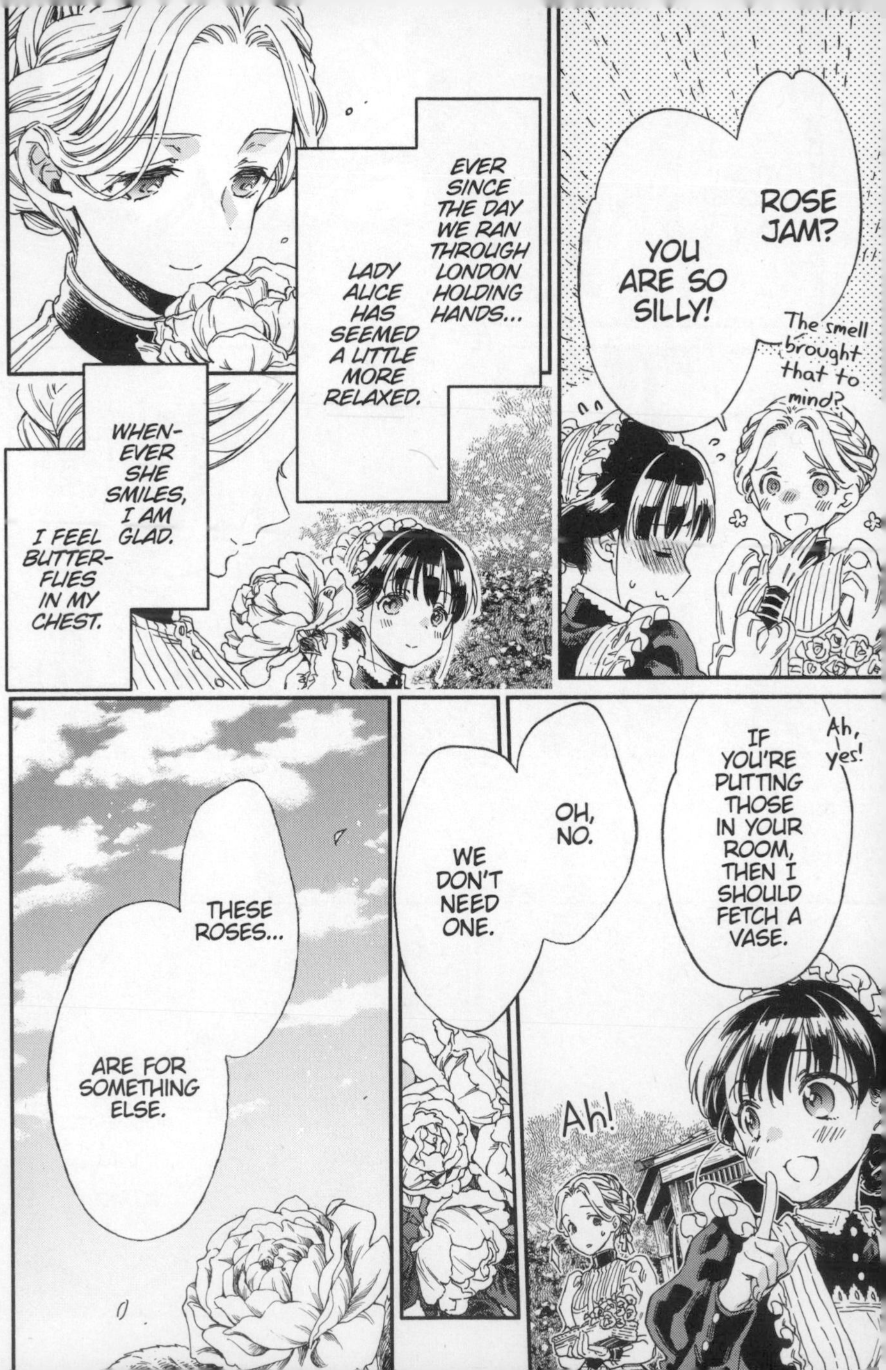
ROSE JAM?
YOU ARE SO SILLY!
The smell brought that to mind?
EVER SINCE THE DAY WE RAN THROUGH LONDON HOLDING HANDS...
LADY ALICE HAS SEEMED A LITTLE MORE RELAXED.
WHEN-EVER SHE SMILES, I AM GLAD.
I FEEL BUTTER-FLIES IN MY CHEST.
Ah, yes!
IF YOU'RE PUTTING THOSE IN YOUR ROOM, THEN I SHOULD FETCH A VASE.
Ah!
OH, NO.
WE DON'T NEED ONE.
THESE ROSES...
ARE FOR SOMETHING ELSE.

{ Chapter 6 }

A Rose Burned Before a Grave

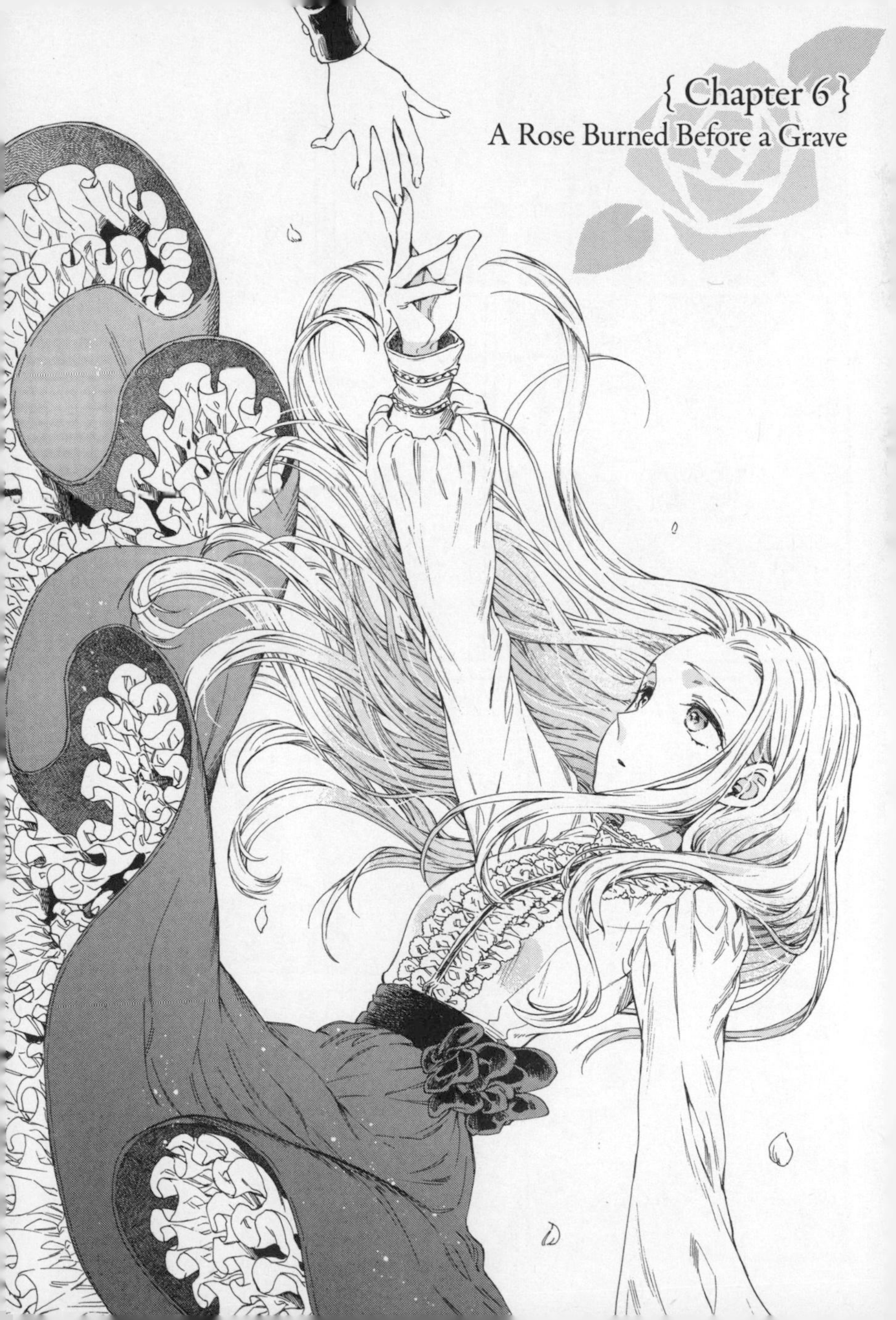

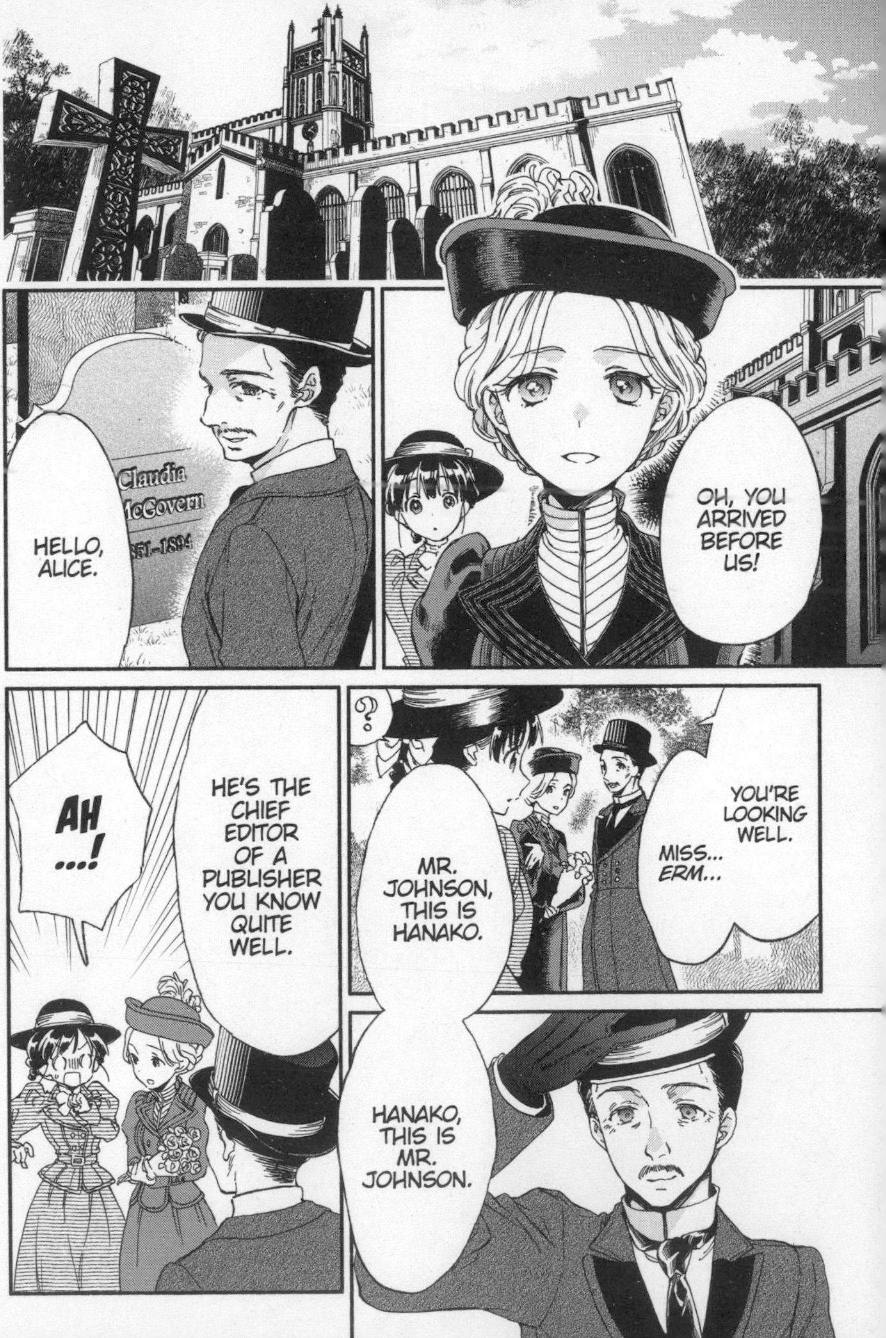
OH, YOU ARRIVED BEFORE US!
HELLO, ALICE.
YOU'RE LOOKING WELL.
MISS... ERM...
MR. JOHNSON, THIS IS HANAKO.
HANAKO, THIS IS MR. JOHNSON.
HE'S THE CHIEF EDITOR OF A PUBLISHER YOU KNOW QUITE WELL.
AH...!

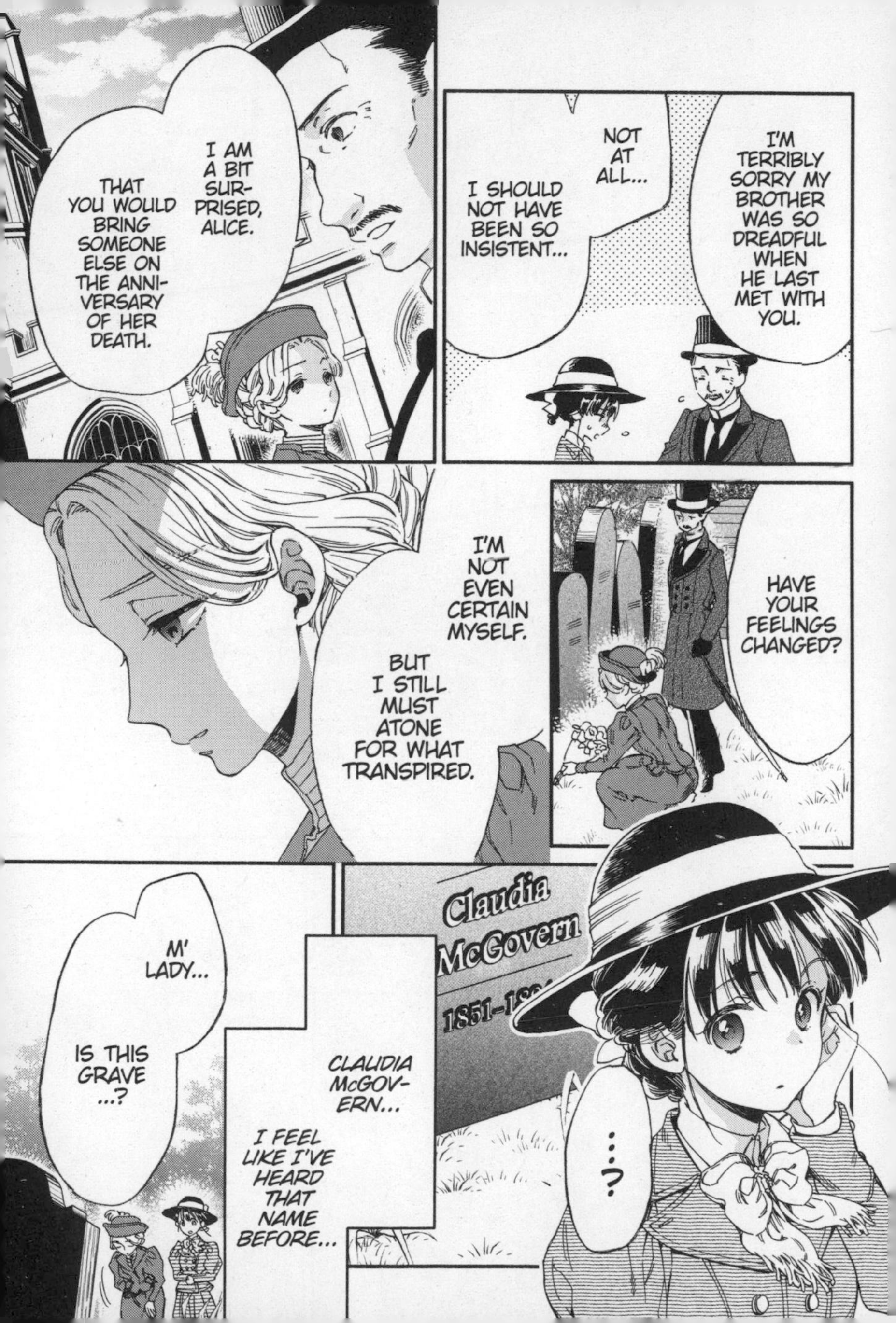
I'M TERRIBLY SORRY MY BROTHER WAS SO DREADFUL WHEN HE LAST MET WITH YOU.
NOT AT ALL...
I SHOULD NOT HAVE BEEN SO INSISTENT...
I AM A BIT SUR-PRISED, ALICE.
THAT YOU WOULD BRING SOMEONE ELSE ON THE ANNI-VERSARY OF HER DEATH.
HAVE YOUR FEELINGS CHANGED?
I'M NOT EVEN CERTAIN MYSELF.
BUT I STILL MUST ATONE FOR WHAT TRANSPIRED.
...?
Claudia McGovern
CLAUDIA McGOV-ERN...
I FEEL LIKE I'VE HEARD THAT NAME BEFORE...
M' LADY...
IS THIS GRAVE ...?

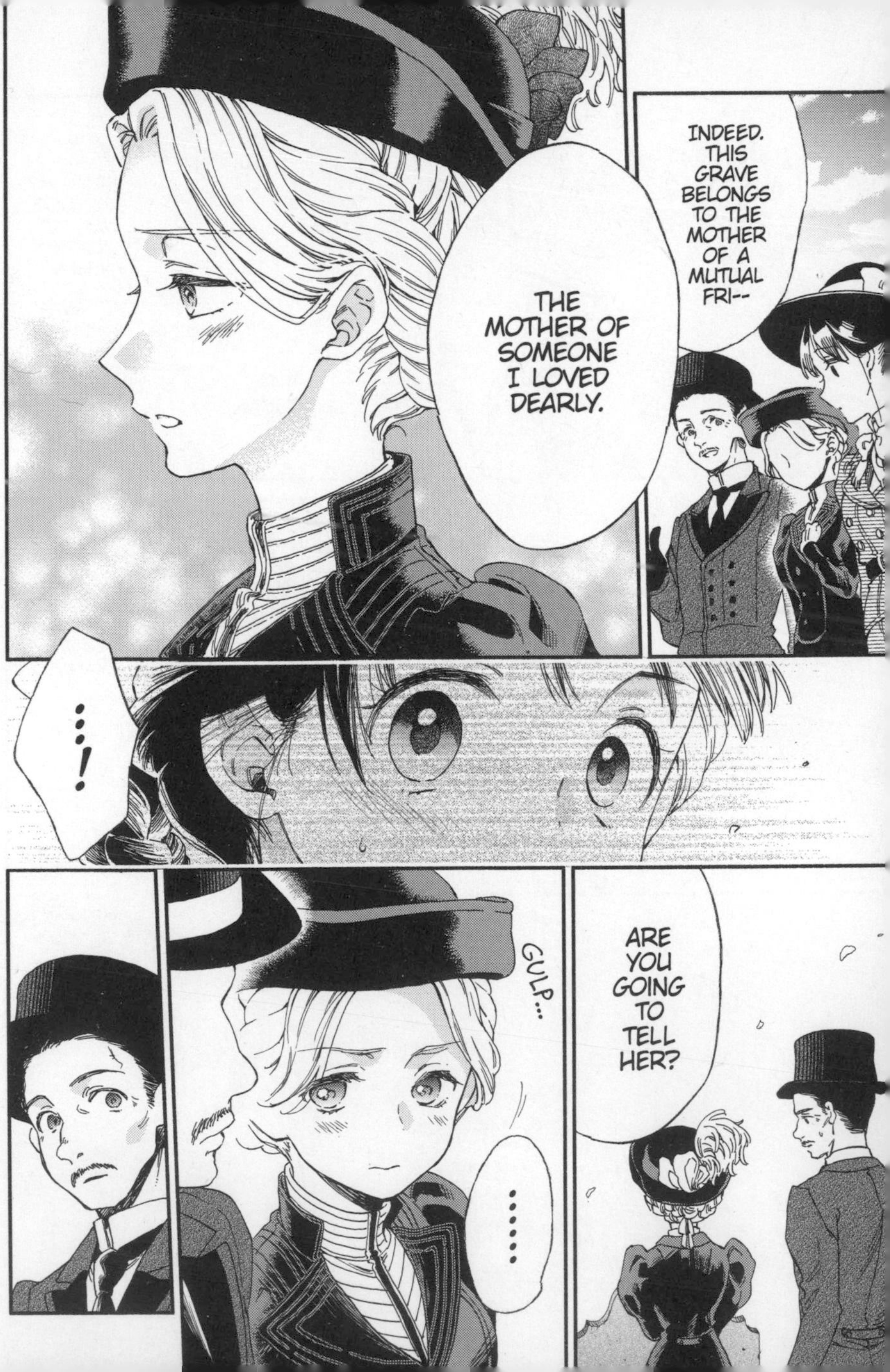
INDEED. THIS GRAVE BELONGS TO THE MOTHER OF A MUTUAL FRI--
THE MOTHER OF SOMEONE I LOVED DEARLY.
...!
ARE YOU GOING TO TELL HER?
GULP...
......

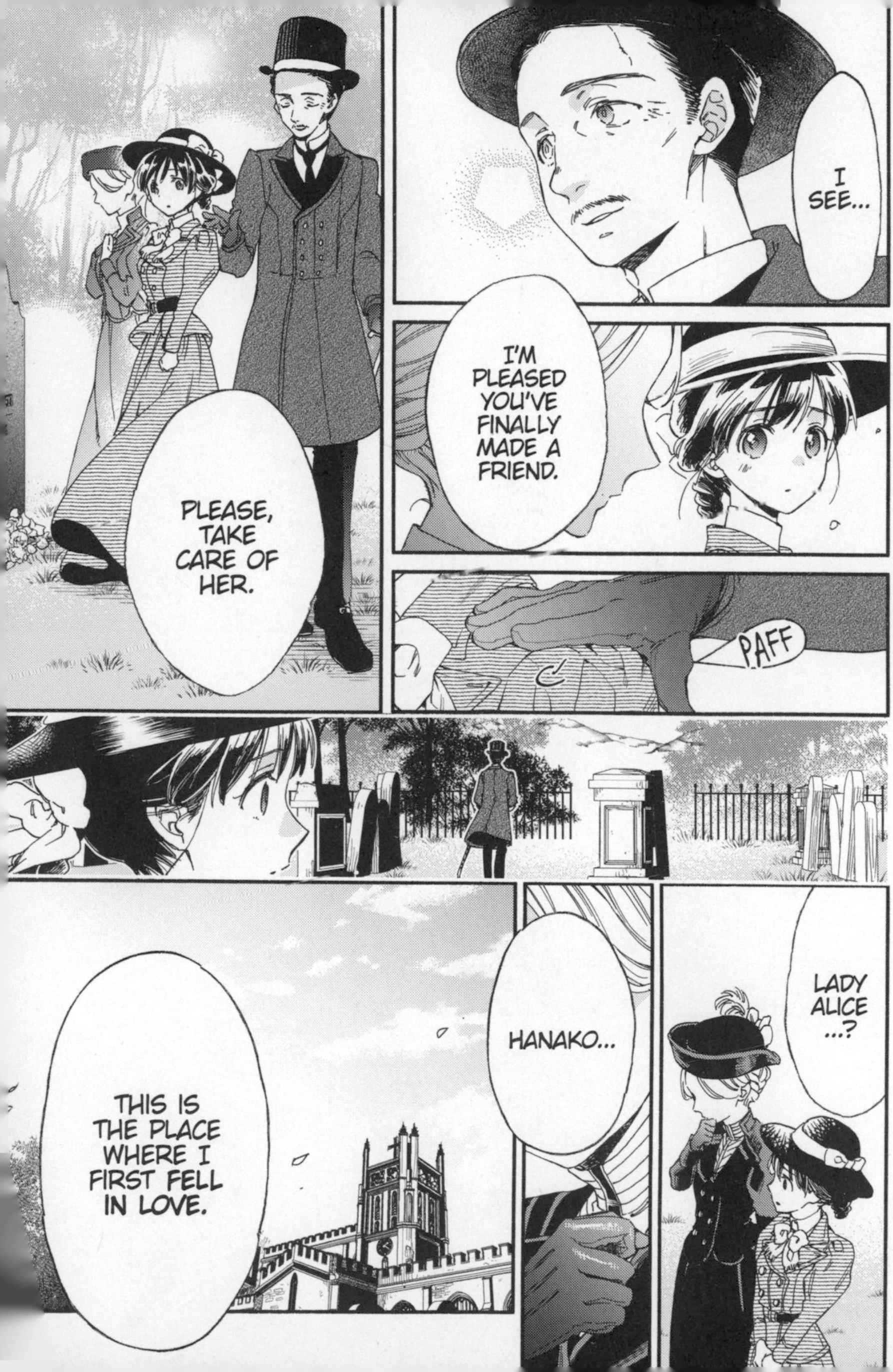
I SEE...
I'M PLEASED YOU'VE FINALLY MADE A FRIEND.
PAFF
PLEASE, TAKE CARE OF HER.
LADY ALICE ...?
HANAKO...
THIS IS THE PLACE WHERE I FIRST FELL IN LOVE.

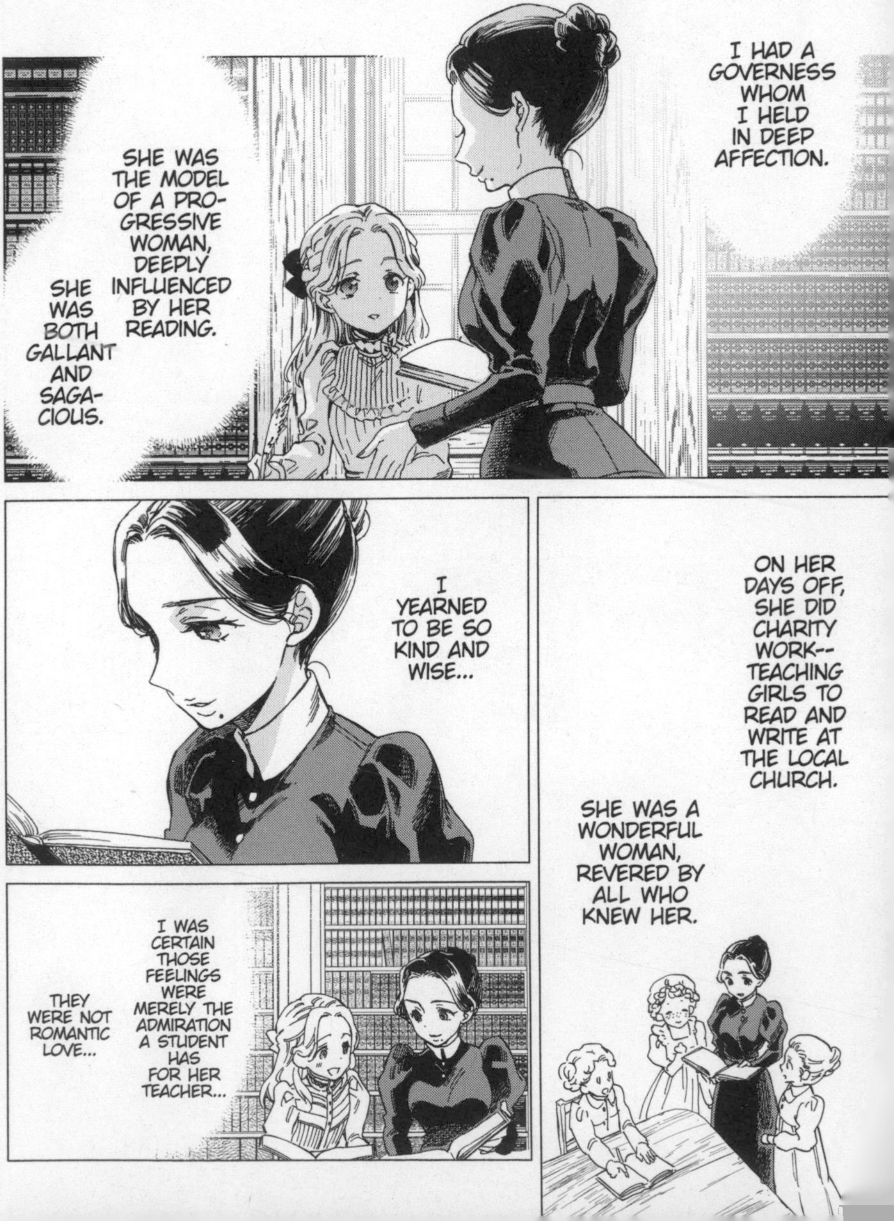
I HAD A GOVERNESS WHOM I HELD IN DEEP AFFECTION.
SHE WAS THE MODEL OF A PRO-GRESSIVE WOMAN, DEEPLY INFLUENCED BY HER READING.
SHE WAS BOTH GALLANT AND SAGA-CIOUS.
ON HER DAYS OFF, SHE DID CHARITY WORK--TEACHING GIRLS TO READ AND WRITE AT THE LOCAL CHURCH.
SHE WAS A WONDERFUL WOMAN, REVERED BY ALL WHO KNEW HER.
I YEARNED TO BE SO KIND AND WISE...
I WAS CERTAIN THOSE FEELINGS WERE MERELY THE ADMIRATION A STUDENT HAS FOR HER TEACHER...
THEY WERE NOT ROMANTIC LOVE...

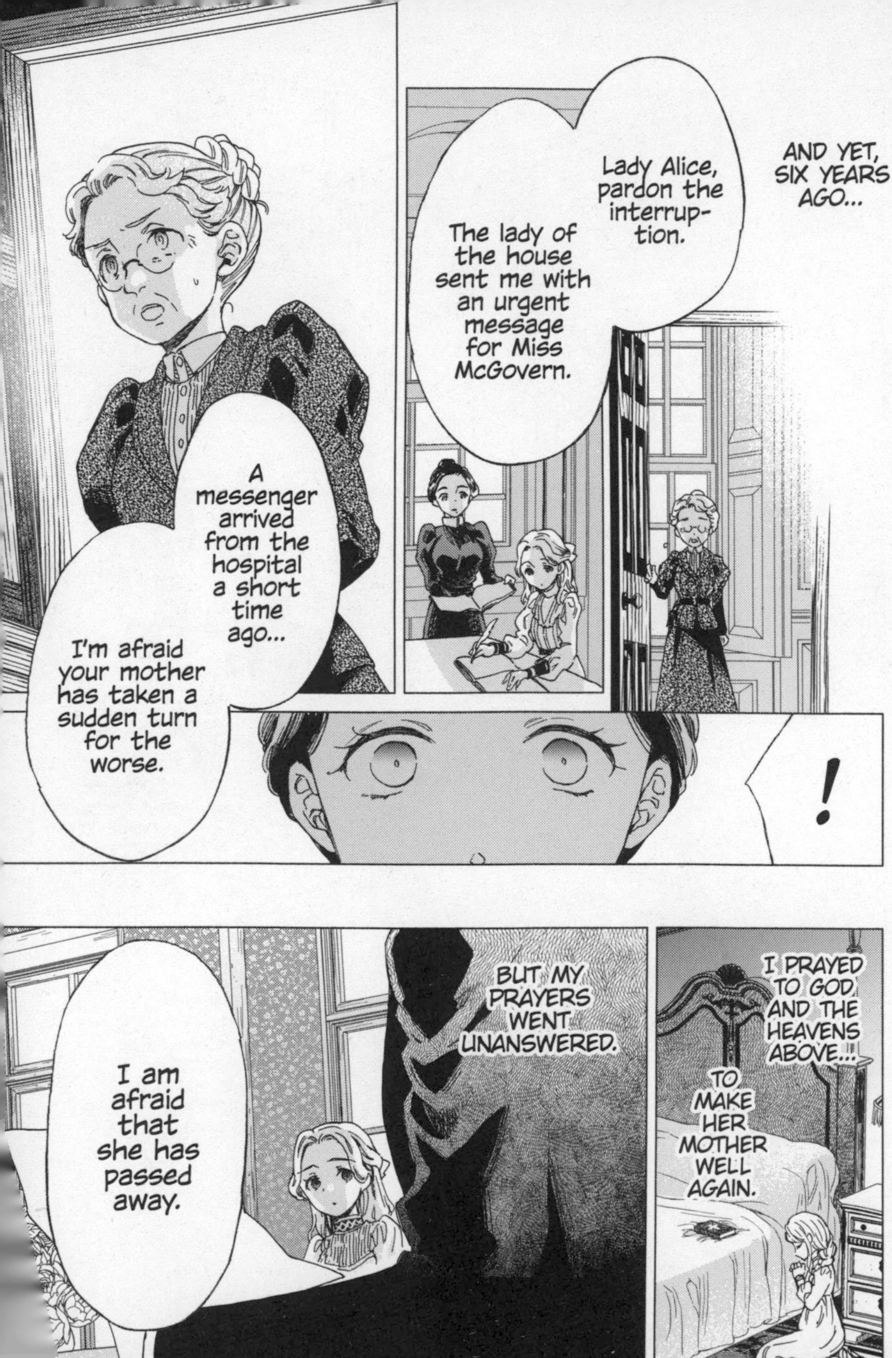
AND YET, SIX YEARS AGO...
Lady Alice, pardon the interruption.
The lady of the house sent me with an urgent message for Miss McGovern.
A messenger arrived from the hospital a short time ago...
I'm afraid your mother has taken a sudden turn for the worse.
!
I PRAYED TO GOD AND THE HEAVENS ABOVE...
TO MAKE HER MOTHER WELL AGAIN.
BUT MY PRAYERS WENT UNANSWERED.
I am afraid that she has passed away.

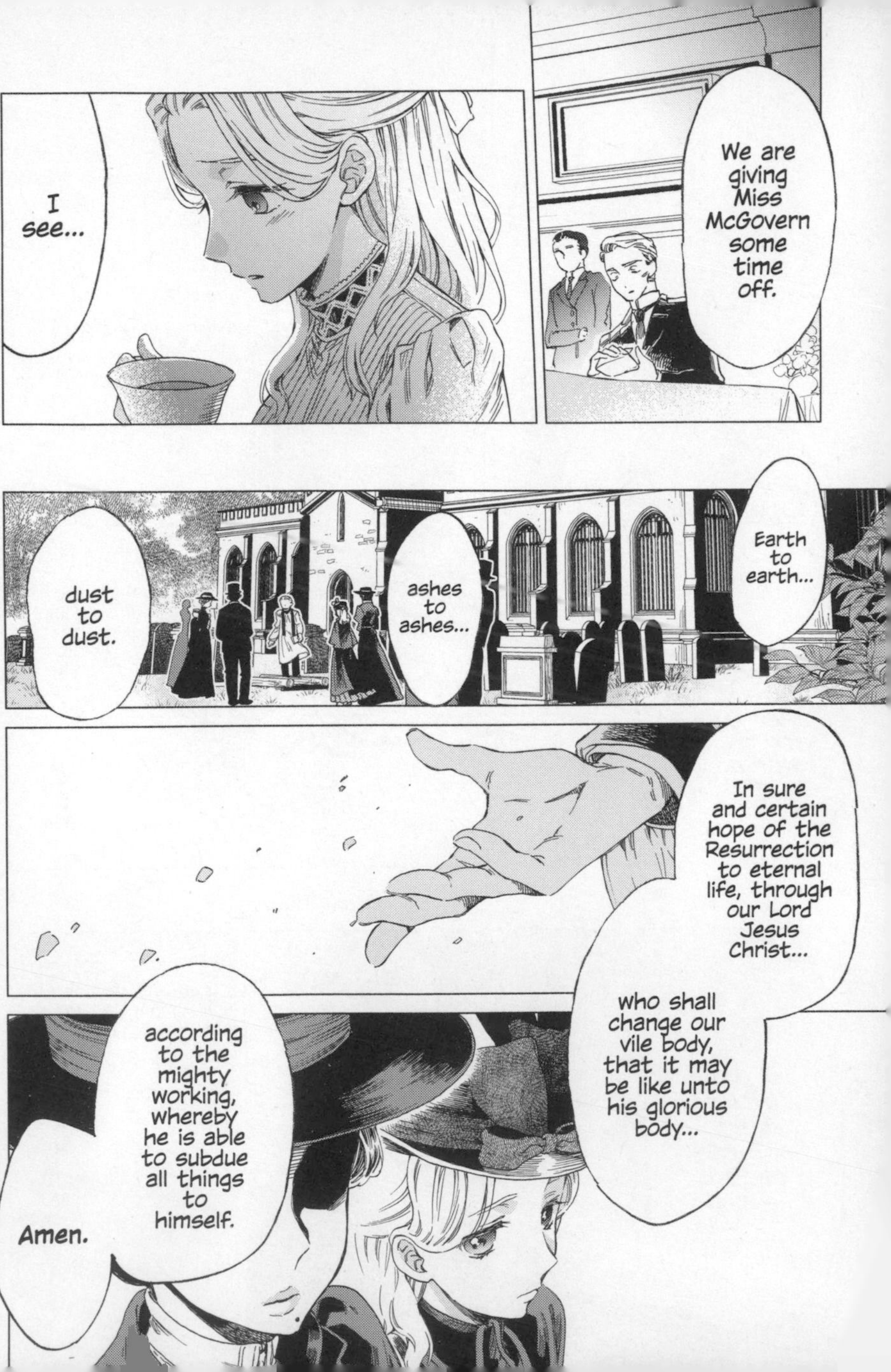
We are giving Miss McGovern some time off.
I see...
Earth to earth...
ashes to ashes...
dust to dust.
In sure and certain hope of the Resurrection to eternal life, through our Lord Jesus Christ...
who shall change our vile body, that it may be like unto his glorious body...
according to the mighty working, whereby he is able to subdue all things to himself.
Amen.

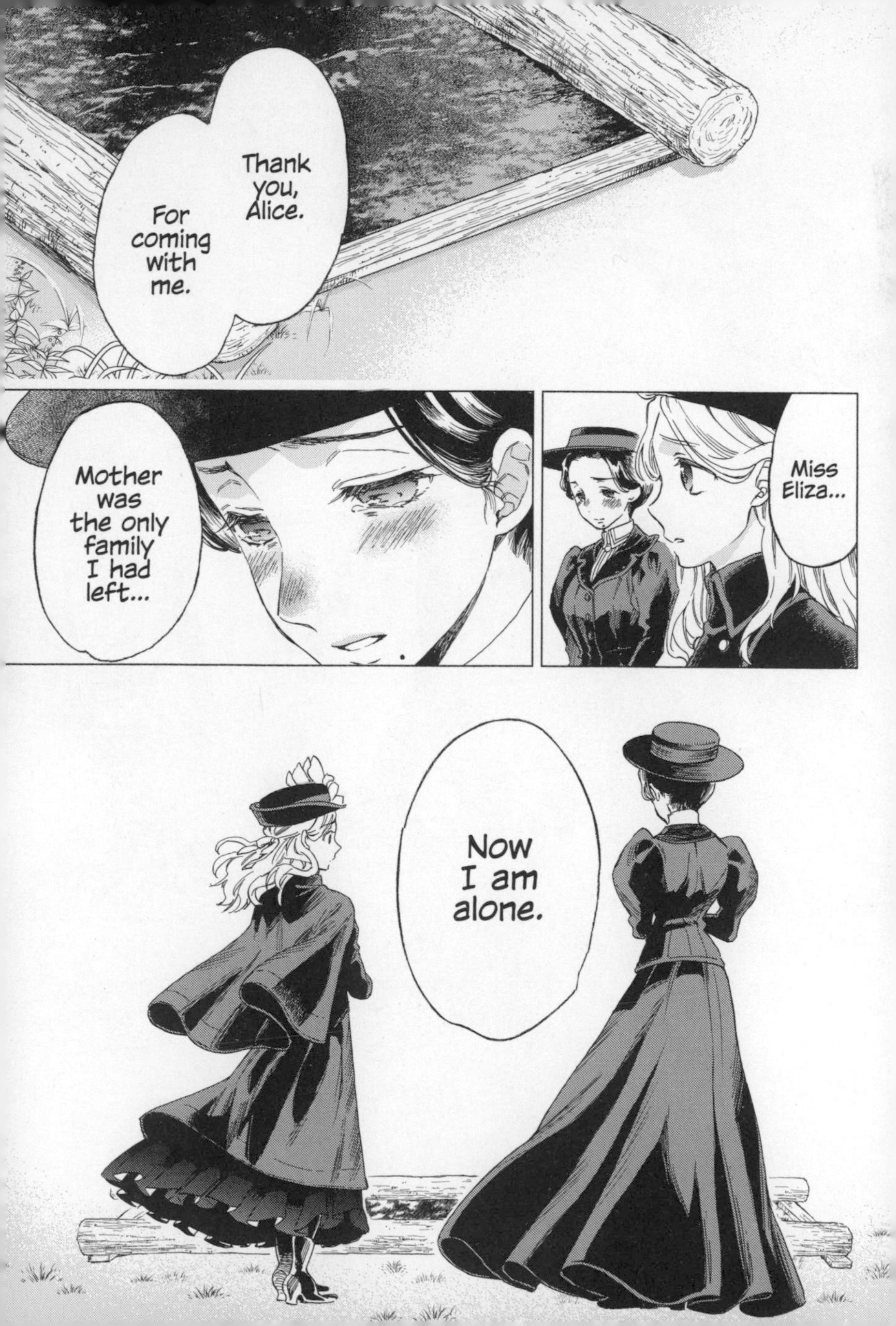
Thank you, Alice.
For coming with me.
Miss Eliza...
Mother was the only family I had left...
Now I am alone.

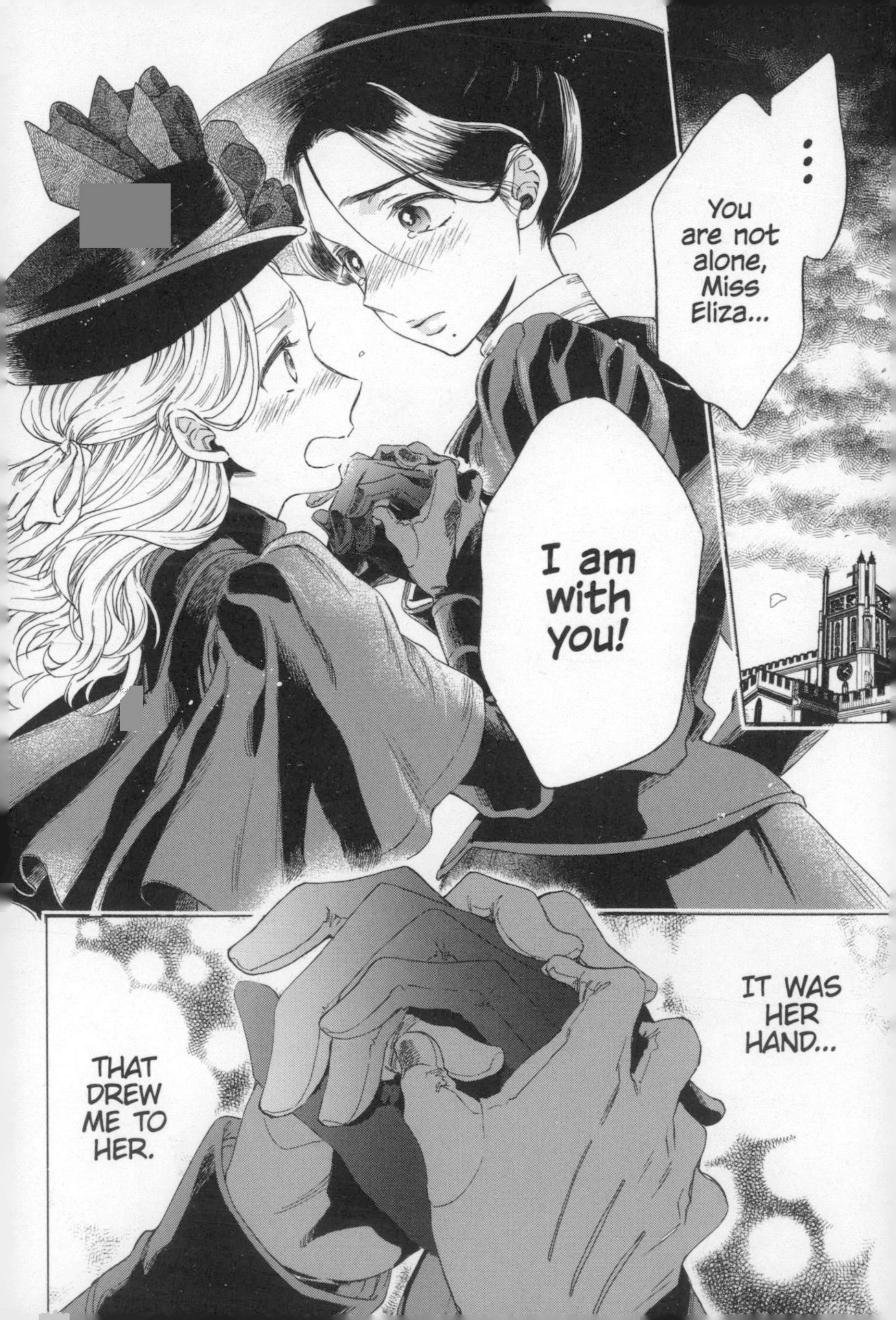
...
You are not alone, Miss Eliza...
I am with you!
IT WAS HER HAND...
THAT DREW ME TO HER.

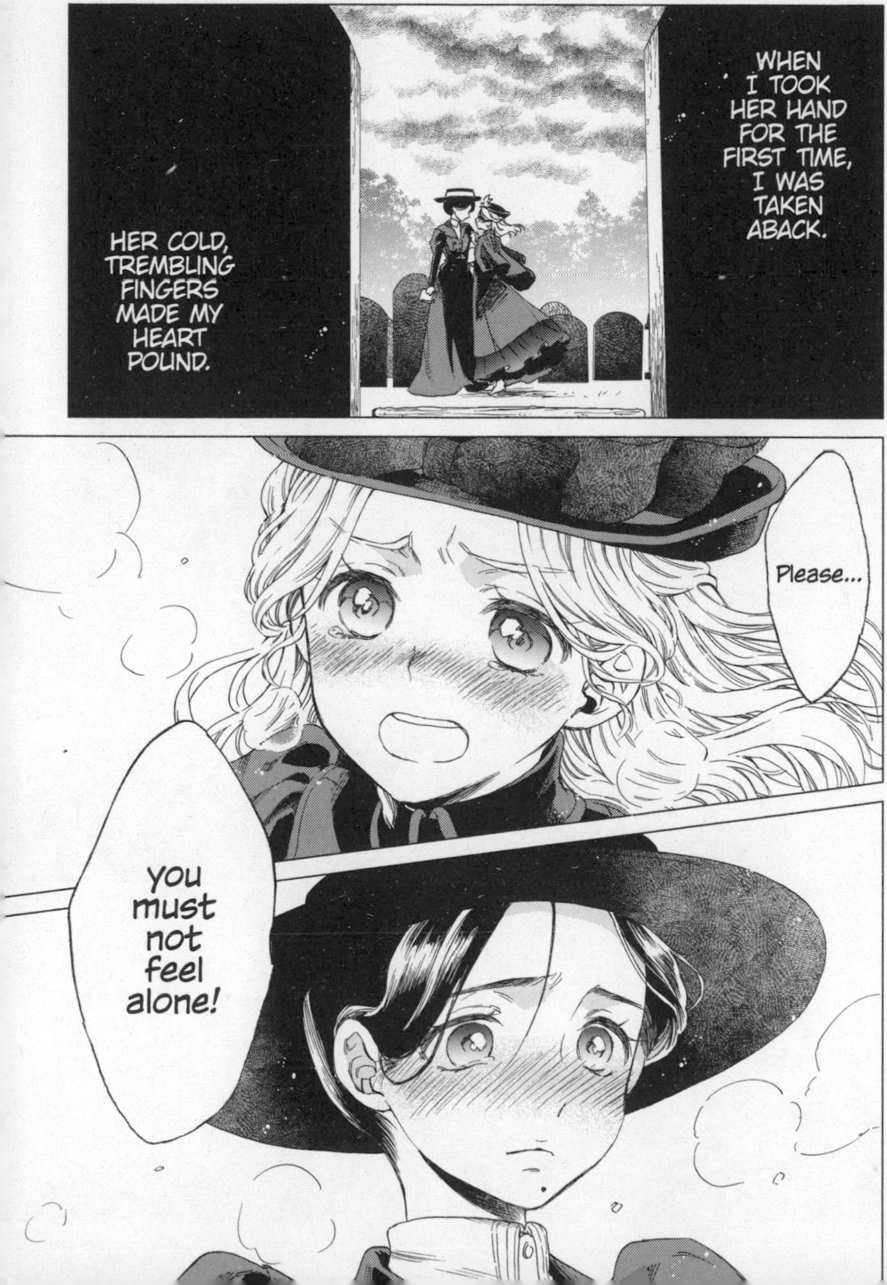
WHEN I TOOK HER HAND FOR THE FIRST TIME, I WAS TAKEN ABACK.
HER COLD, TREMBLING FINGERS MADE MY HEART POUND.
Please...
you must not feel alone!

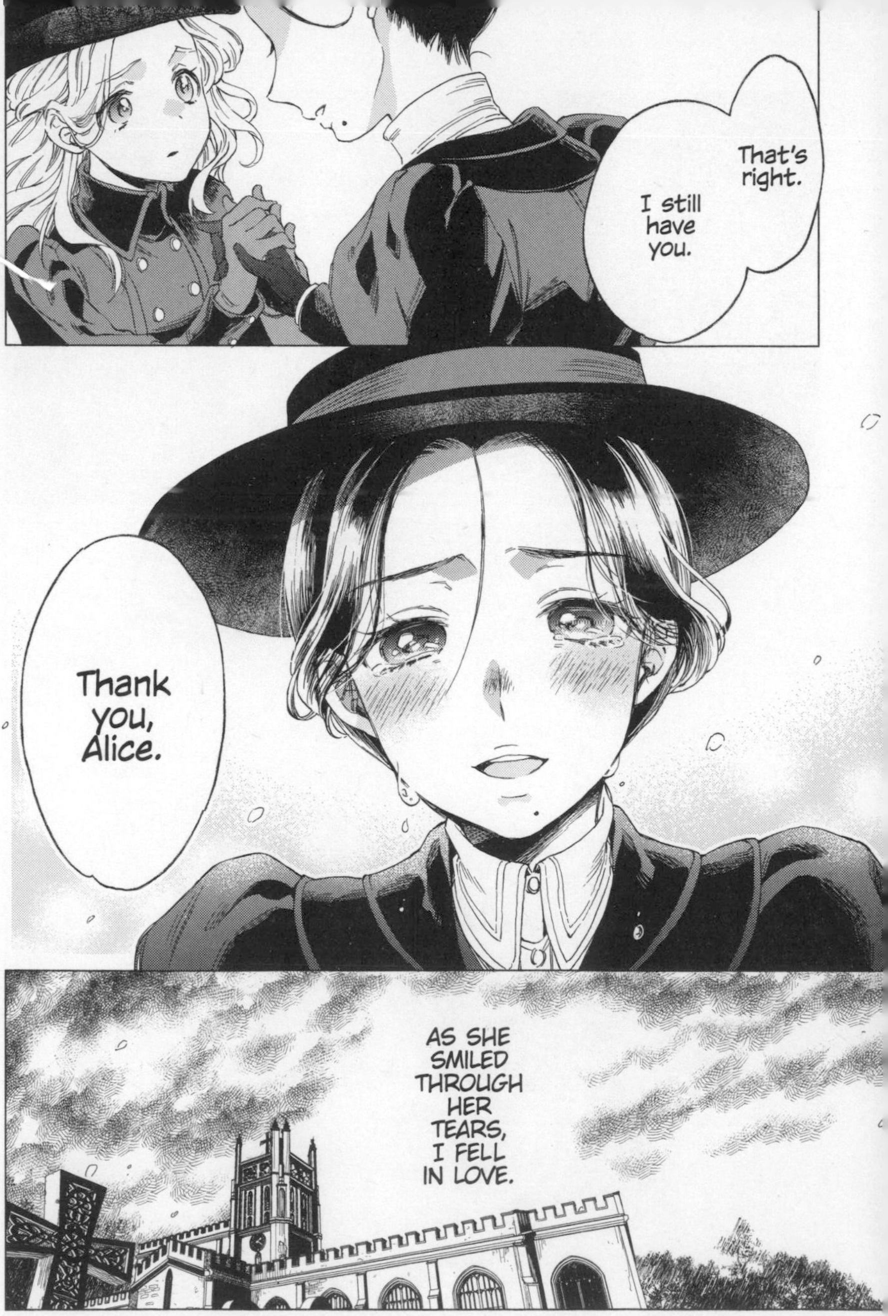
That's right.
I still have you.
Thank you, Alice.
AS SHE SMILED THROUGH HER TEARS, I FELL IN LOVE.

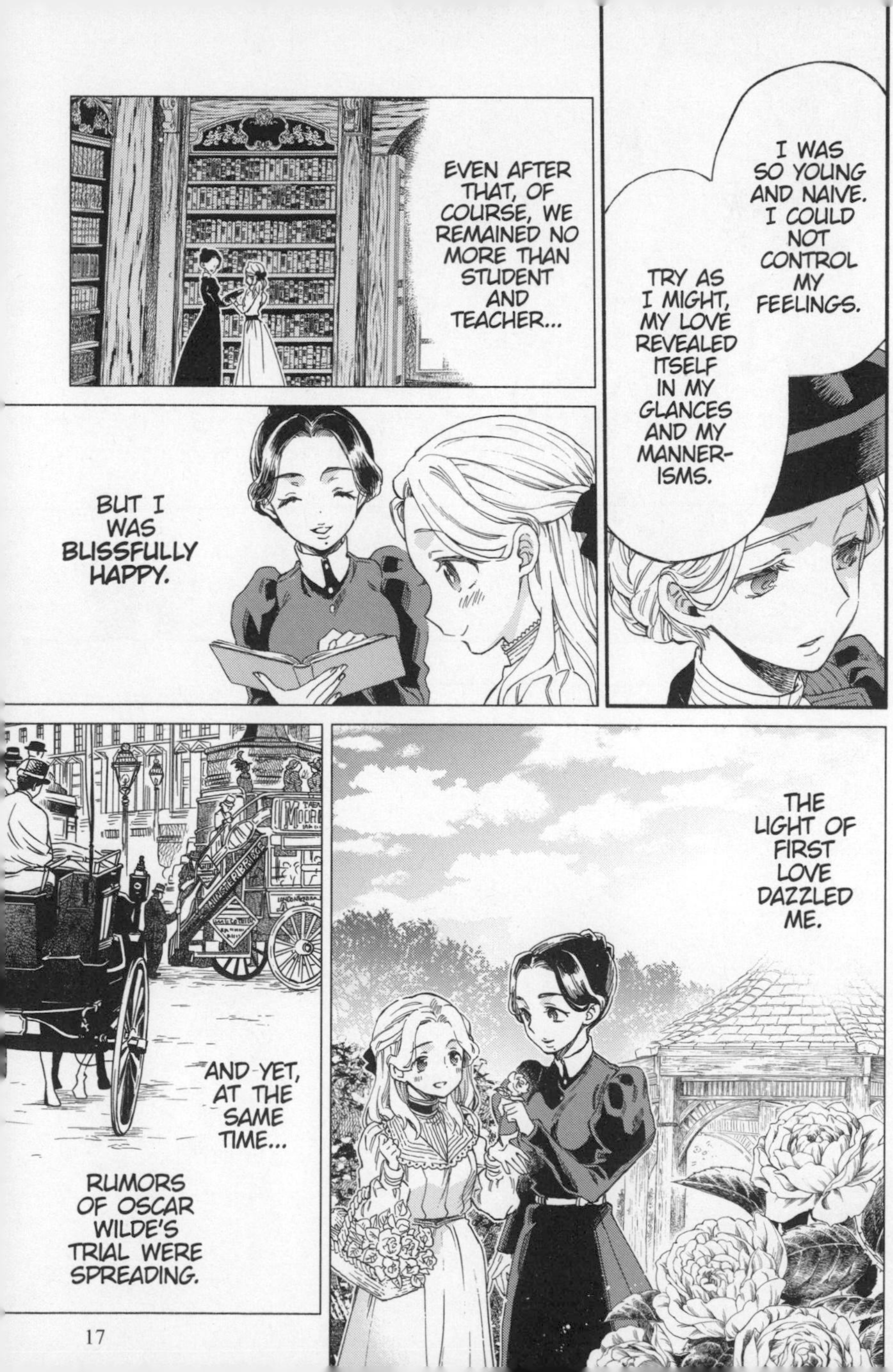
I WAS SO YOUNG AND NAIVE. I COULD NOT CONTROL MY FEELINGS.
TRY AS I MIGHT, MY LOVE REVEALED ITSELF IN MY GLANCES AND MY MANNER-ISMS.
EVEN AFTER THAT, OF COURSE, WE REMAINED NO MORE THAN STUDENT AND TEACHER...
BUT I WAS BLISSFULLY HAPPY.
THE LIGHT OF FIRST LOVE DAZZLED ME.
AND YET, AT THE SAME TIME...
RUMORS OF OSCAR WILDE'S TRIAL WERE SPREADING.

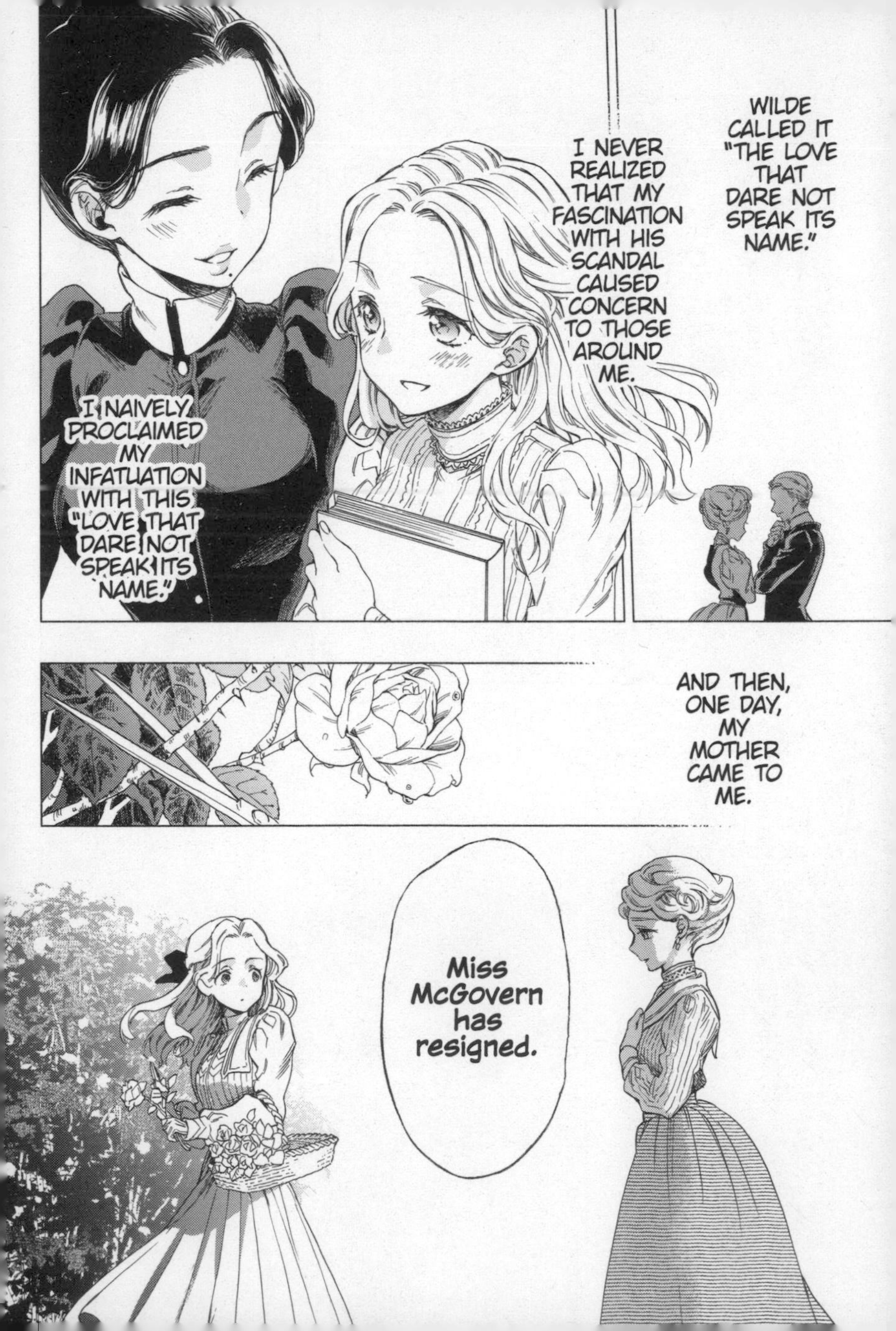
WILDE CALLED IT "THE LOVE THAT DARE NOT SPEAK ITS NAME."
I NEVER REALIZED THAT MY FASCINATION WITH HIS SCANDAL CAUSED CONCERN TO THOSE AROUND ME.
I NAIVELY PROCLAIMED MY INFATUATION WITH THIS "LOVE THAT DARE NOT SPEAK ITS NAME."
AND THEN, ONE DAY, MY MOTHER CAME TO ME.
Miss McGovern has resigned.

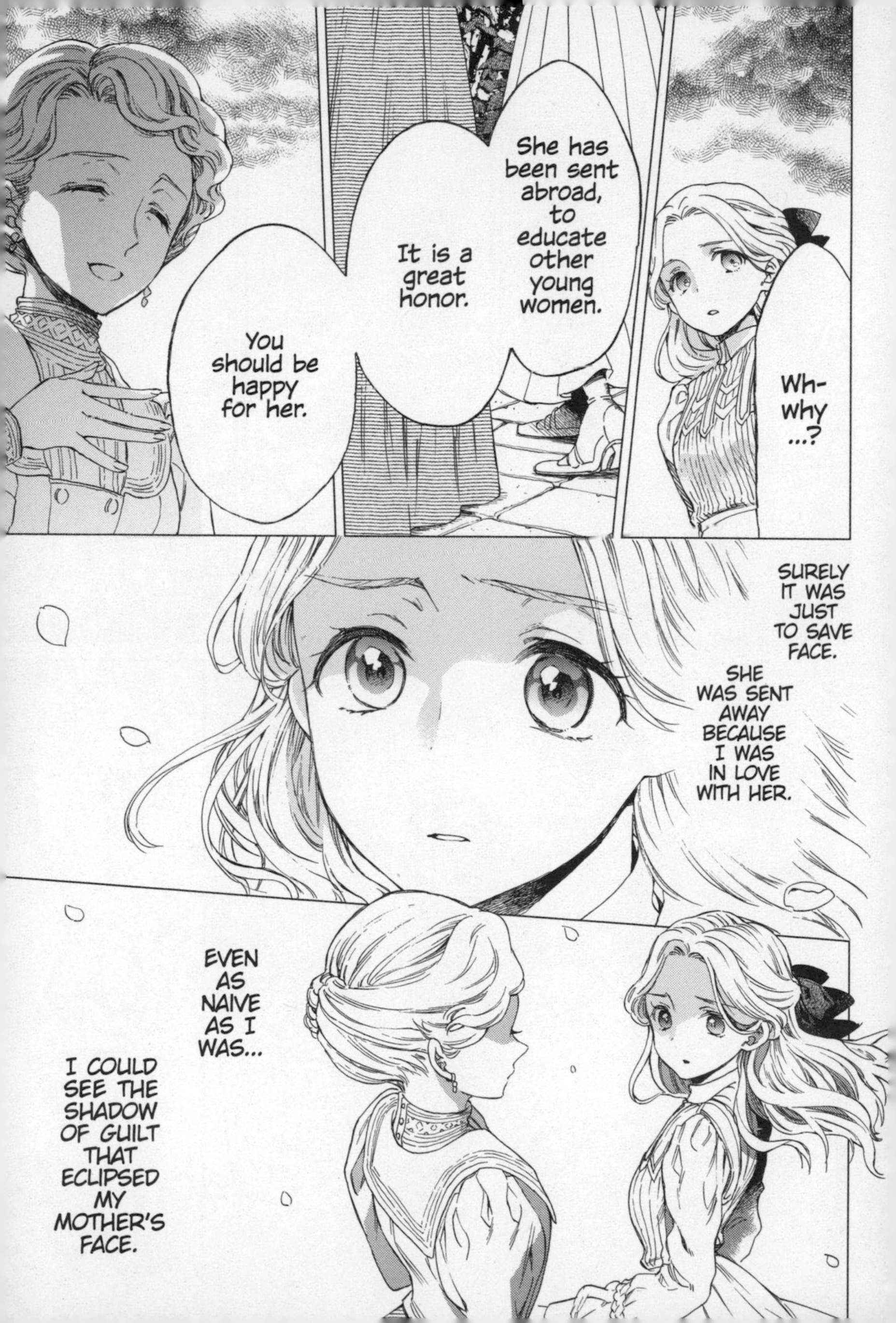

Wh-why ...?
She has been sent abroad, to educate other young women.
It is a great honor.
You should be happy for her.
SURELY IT WAS JUST TO SAVE FACE.
SHE WAS SENT AWAY BECAUSE I WAS IN LOVE WITH HER.
EVEN AS NAIVE AS I WAS...
I COULD SEE THE SHADOW OF GUILT THAT ECLIPSED MY MOTHER'S FACE.

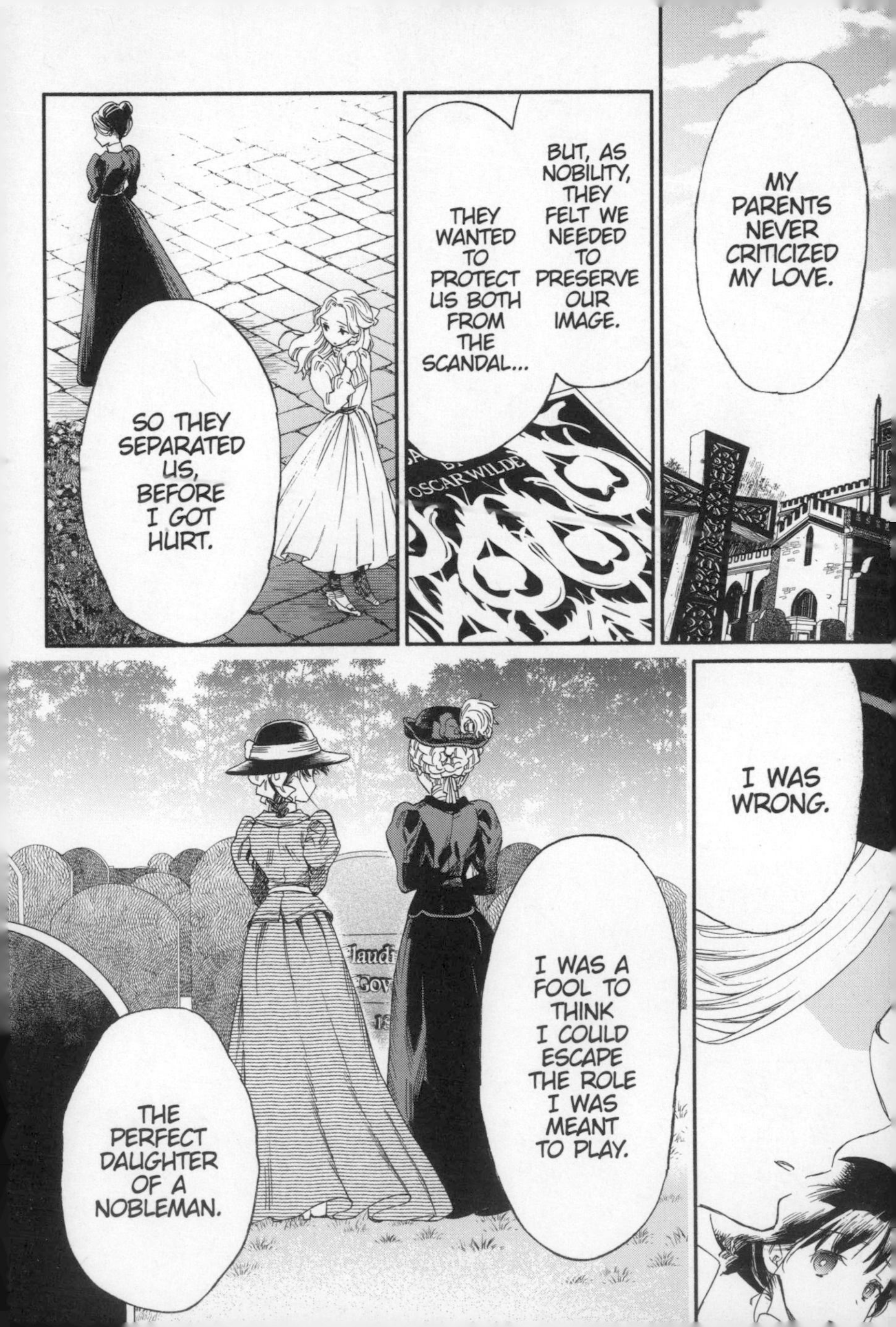
MY PARENTS NEVER CRITICIZED MY LOVE.
THEY WANTED TO PROTECT US BOTH FROM THE SCANDAL... BUT, AS NOBILITY, THEY FELT WE NEEDED TO PRESERVE OUR IMAGE.
OSCARWILDE
SO THEY SEPARATED US, BEFORE I GOT HURT.
I WAS WRONG.
I WAS A FOOL TO THINK I COULD ESCAPE THE ROLE I WAS MEANT TO PLAY.
THE PERFECT DAUGHTER OF A NOBLEMAN.

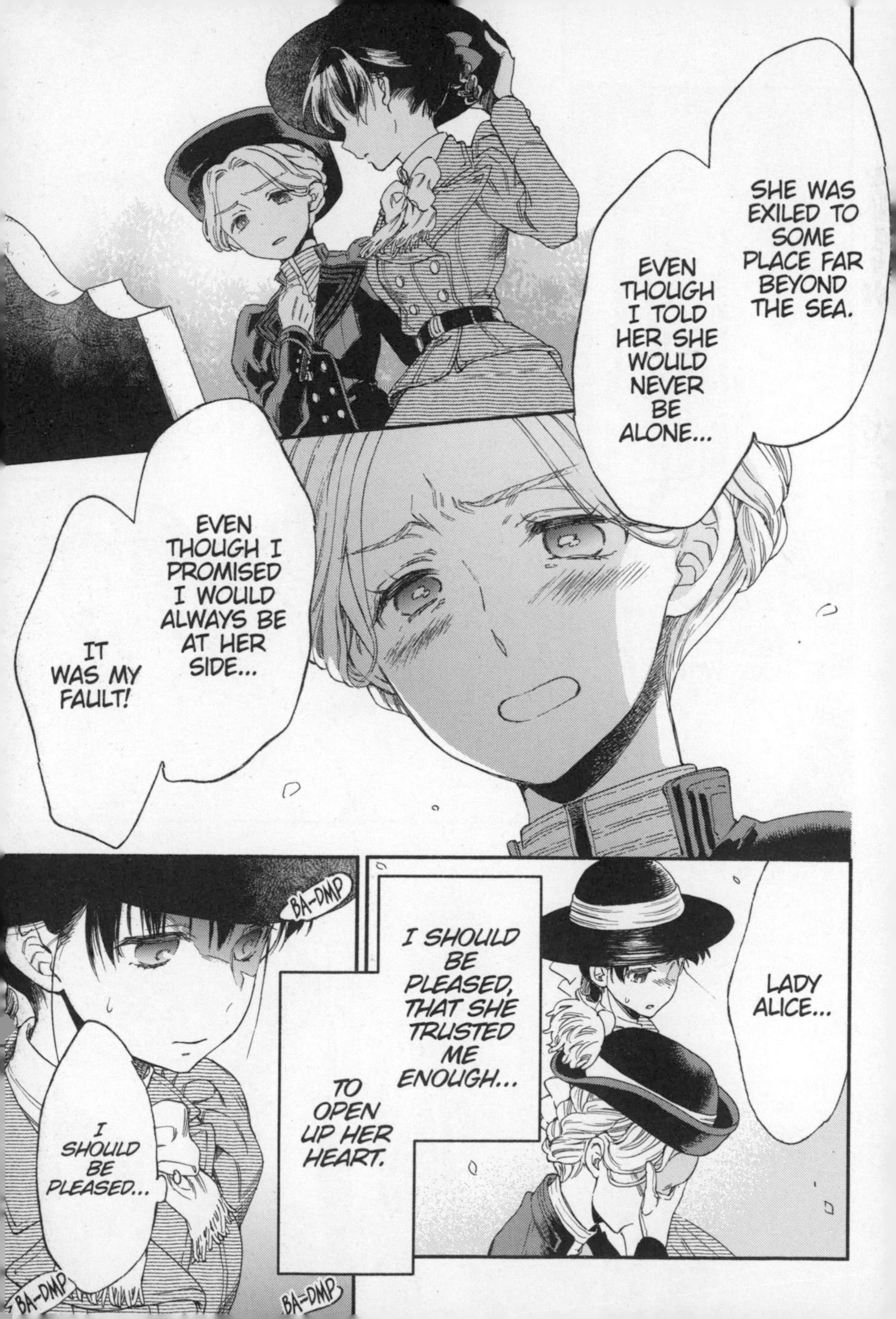
SHE WAS EXILED TO SOME PLACE FAR BEYOND THE SEA.
EVEN THOUGH I TOLD HER SHE WOULD NEVER BE ALONE...
EVEN THOUGH I PROMISED I WOULD ALWAYS BE AT HER SIDE...
IT WAS MY FAULT!
LADY ALICE...
BA-DMP
I SHOULD BE PLEASED, THAT SHE TRUSTED ME ENOUGH...
TO OPEN UP HER HEART.
I SHOULD BE PLEASED...
BA-DMP
BA-DMP

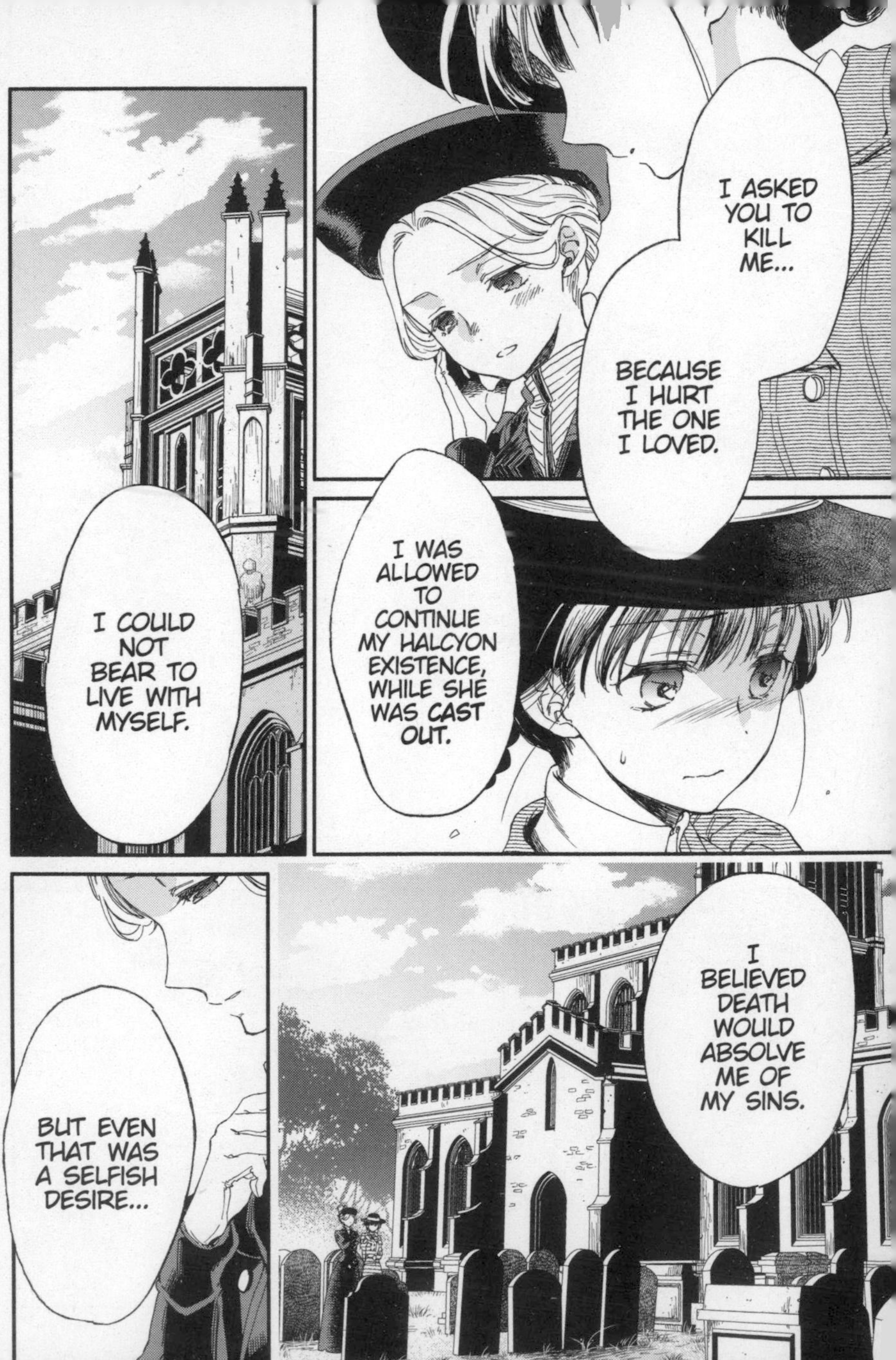
I ASKED YOU TO KILL ME...
BECAUSE I HURT THE ONE I LOVED.
I WAS ALLOWED TO CONTINUE MY HALCYON EXISTENCE, WHILE SHE WAS CAST OUT.
I COULD NOT BEAR TO LIVE WITH MYSELF.
I BELIEVED DEATH WOULD ABSOLVE ME OF MY SINS.
BUT EVEN THAT WAS A SELFISH DESIRE...

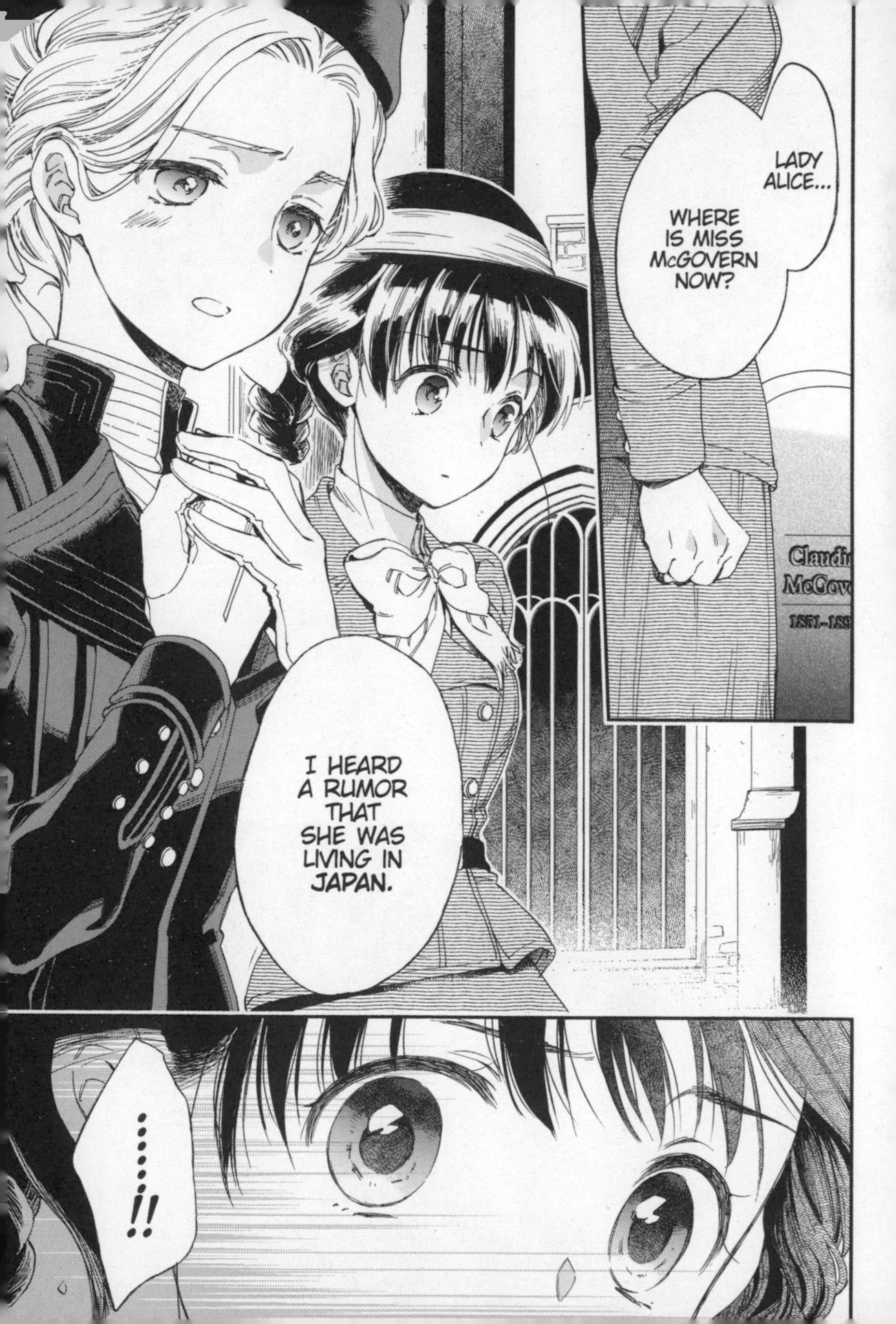
LADY ALICE... WHERE IS MISS McGOVERN NOW?
I HEARD A RUMOR THAT SHE WAS LIVING IN JAPAN.
......!!

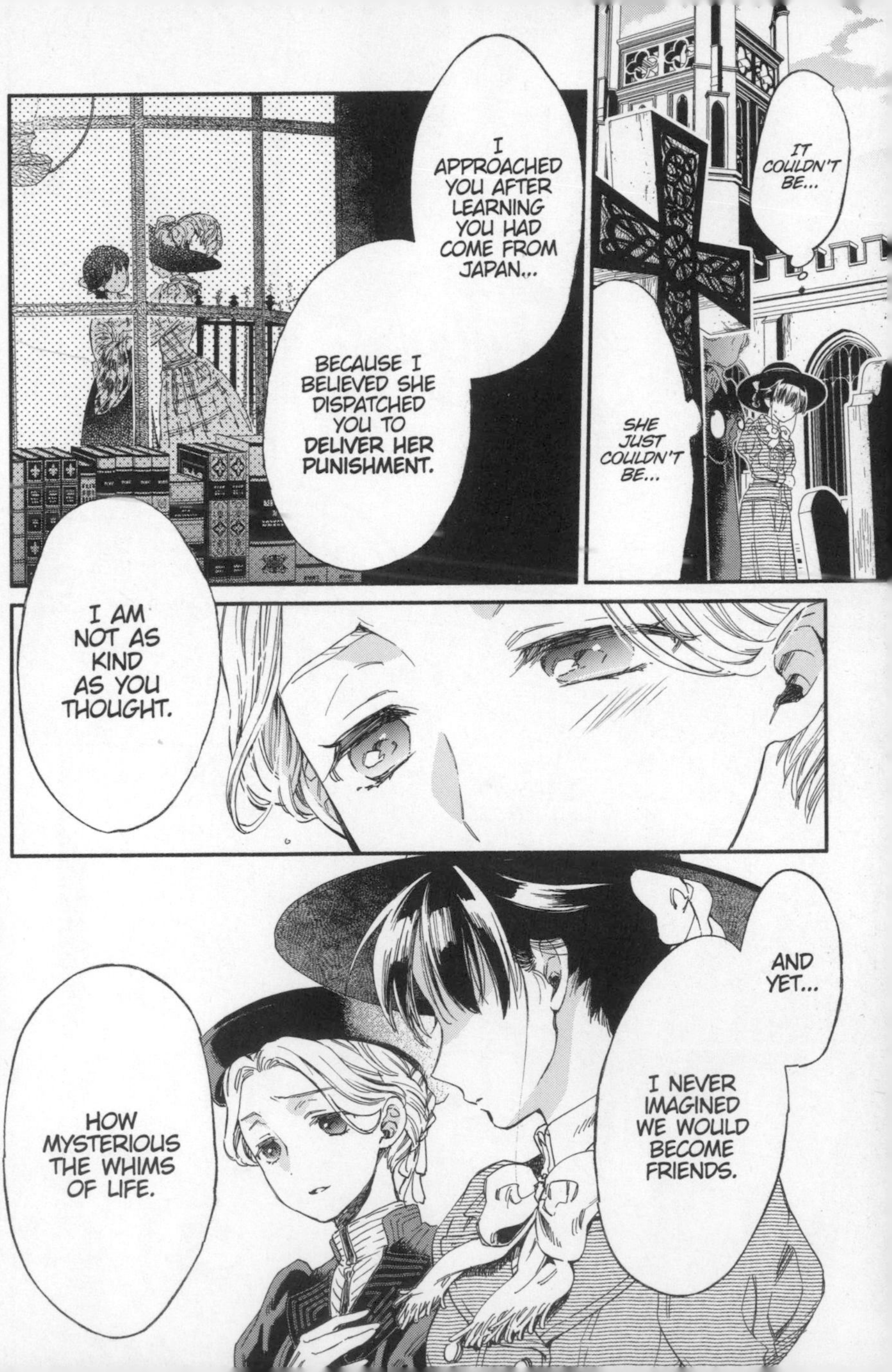
IT COULDN'T BE...
SHE JUST COULDN'T BE...
I APPROACHED YOU AFTER LEARNING YOU HAD COME FROM JAPAN...
BECAUSE I BELIEVED SHE DISPATCHED YOU TO DELIVER HER PUNISHMENT.
I AM NOT AS KIND AS YOU THOUGHT.
AND YET...
I NEVER IMAGINED WE WOULD BECOME FRIENDS.
HOW MYSTERIOUS THE WHIMS OF LIFE.

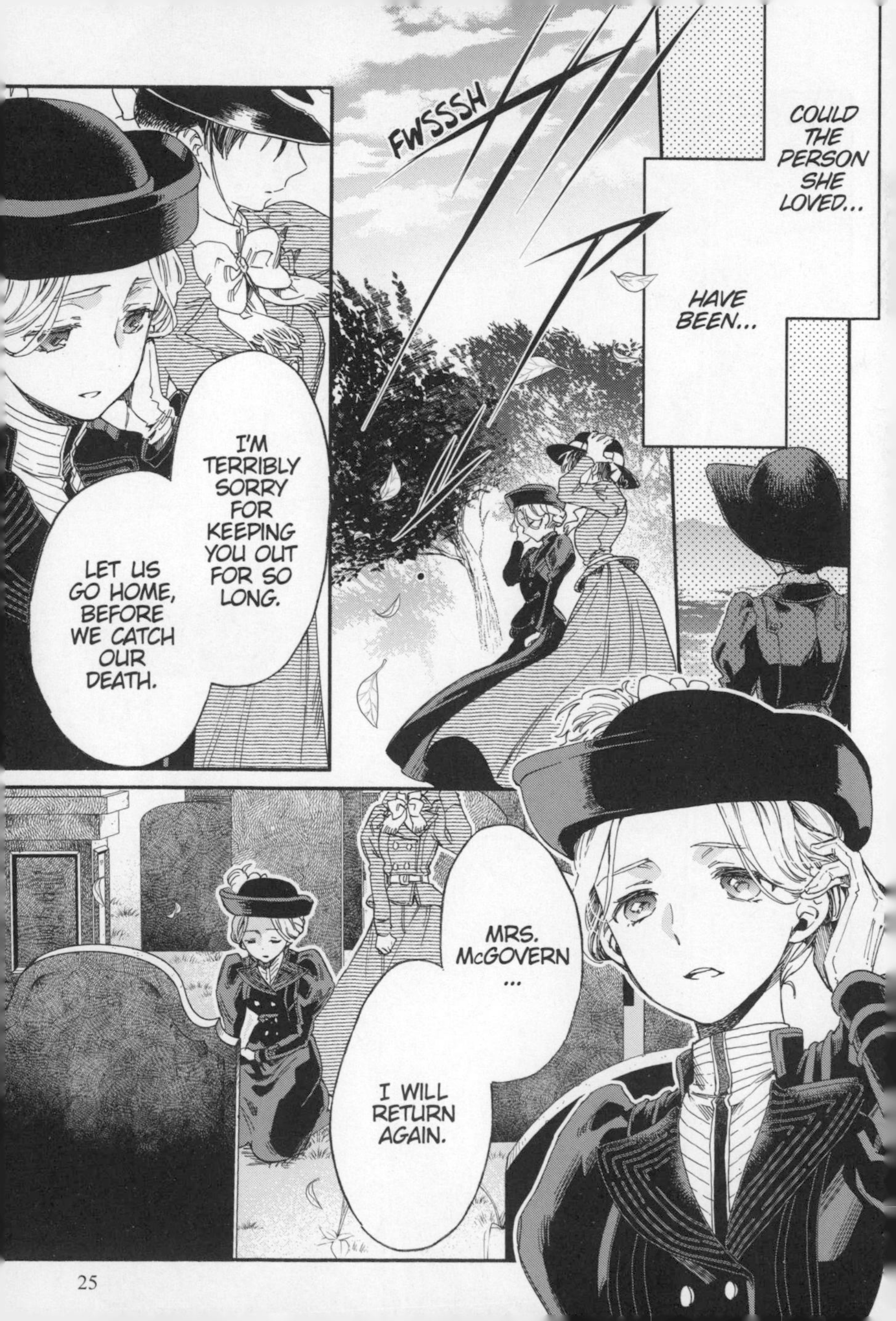
COULD THE PERSON SHE LOVED...
HAVE BEEN...
FWSSSH
I'M TERRIBLY SORRY FOR KEEPING YOU OUT FOR SO LONG.
LET US GO HOME, BEFORE WE CATCH OUR DEATH.
MRS. McGOVERN...
I WILL RETURN AGAIN.

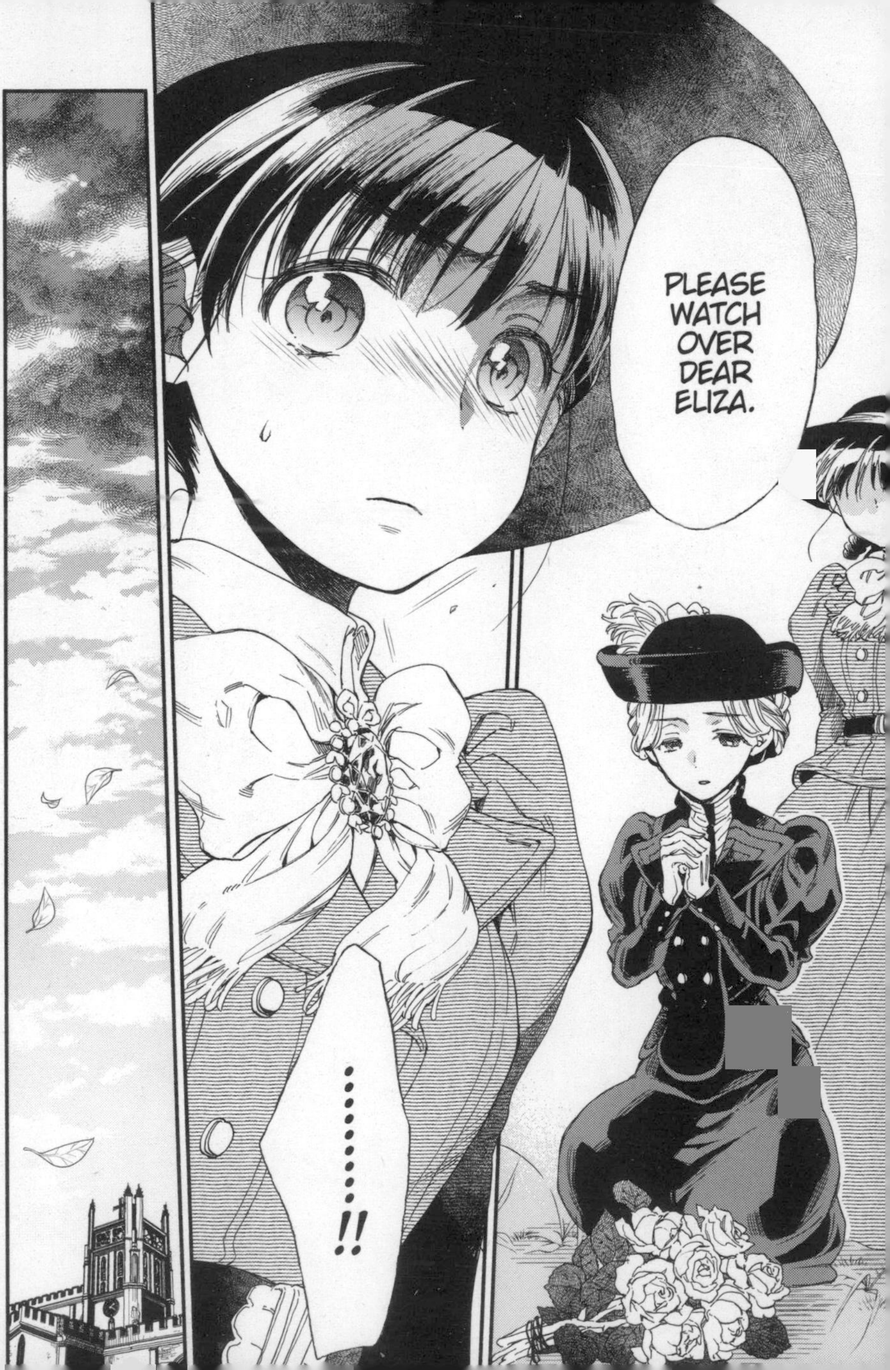
PLEASE WATCH OVER DEAR ELIZA.
......!!

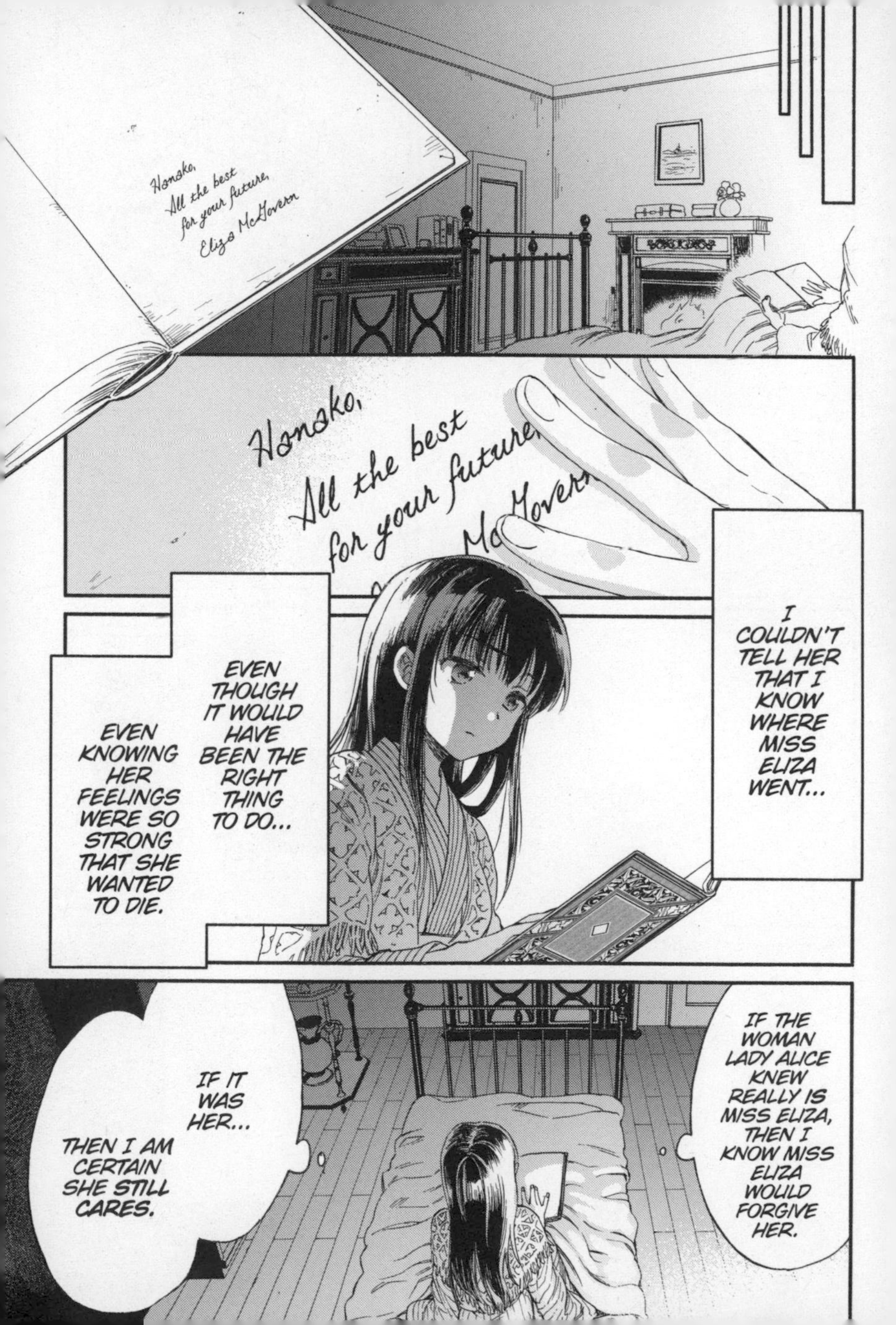
Hanako,
All the best
for your future,
Eliza McGovern
Hanako,
All the best
for your future,
I COULDN'T TELL HER THAT I KNOW WHERE MISS ELIZA WENT...
EVEN THOUGH IT WOULD HAVE BEEN THE RIGHT THING TO DO...
EVEN KNOWING HER FEELINGS WERE SO STRONG THAT SHE WANTED TO DIE.
IF THE WOMAN LADY ALICE KNEW REALLY IS MISS ELIZA, THEN I KNOW MISS ELIZA WOULD FORGIVE HER.
IF IT WAS HER...
THEN I AM CERTAIN SHE STILL CARES.

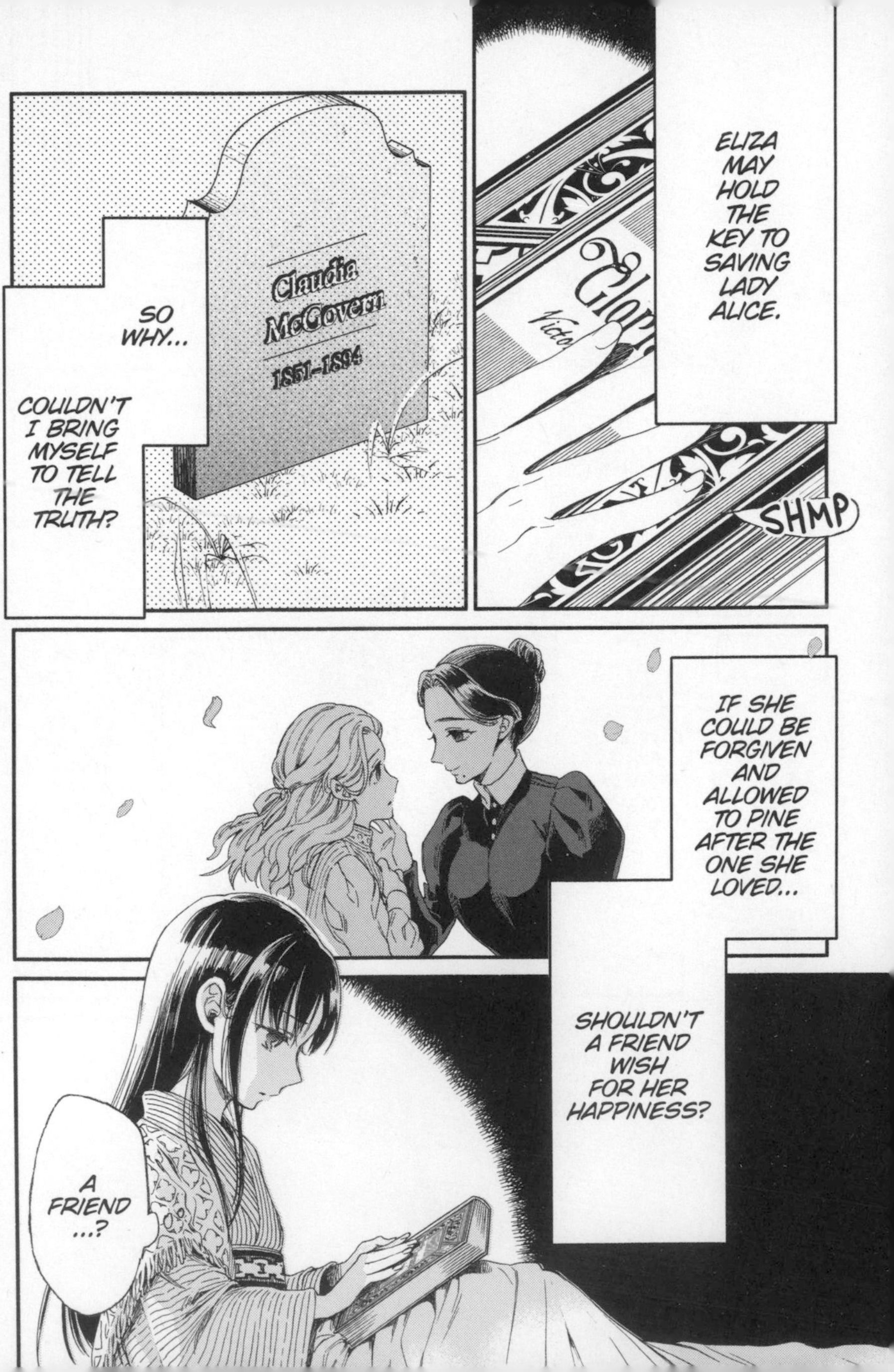
ELIZA MAY HOLD THE KEY TO SAVING LADY ALICE.
SHMP
Claudia McGovern
1851-1894
SO WHY...
COULDN'T I BRING MYSELF TO TELL THE TRUTH?
IF SHE COULD BE FORGIVEN AND ALLOWED TO PINE AFTER THE ONE SHE LOVED...
SHOULDN'T A FRIEND WISH FOR HER HAPPINESS?
A FRIEND ...?

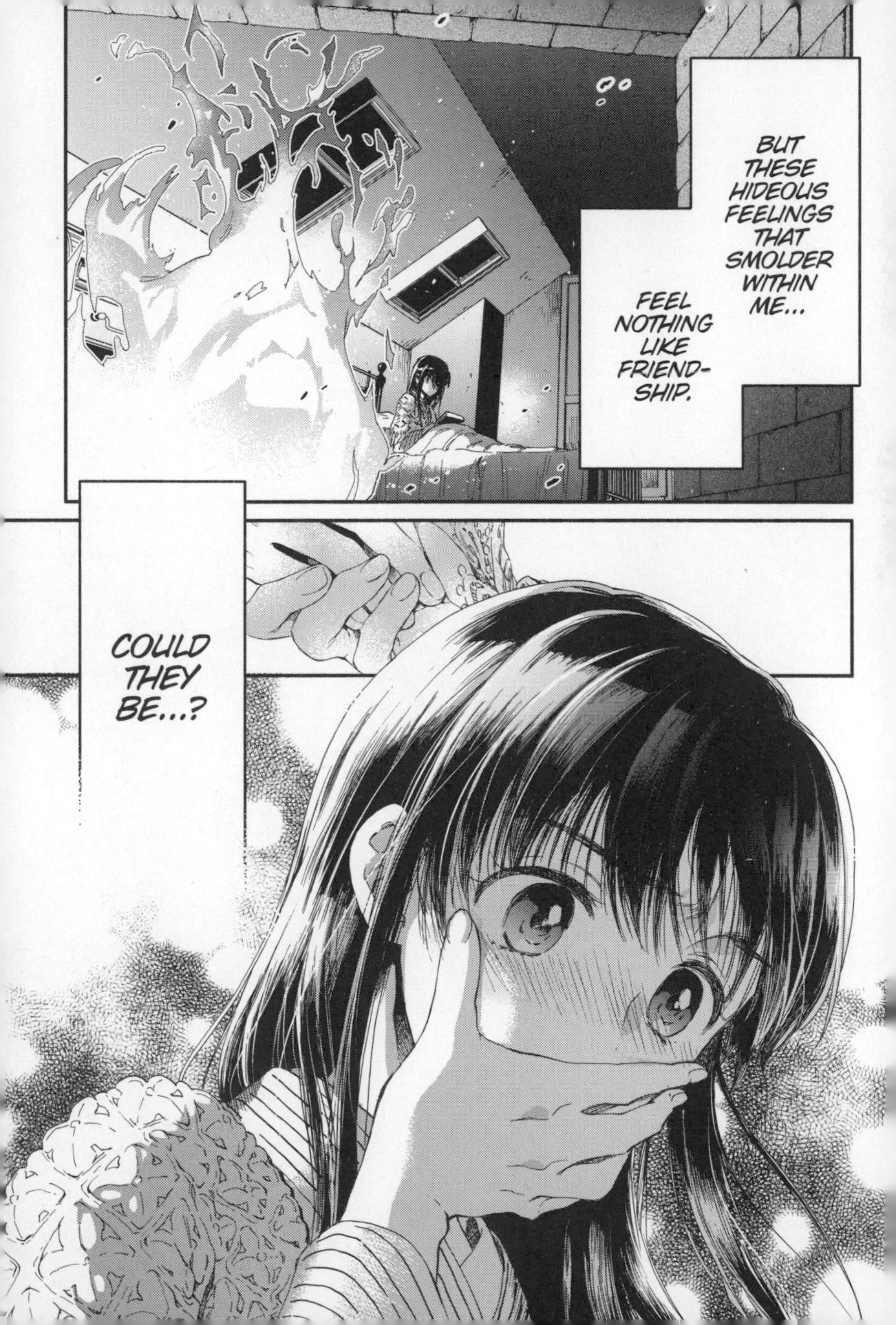
BUT THESE HIDEOUS FEELINGS THAT SMOLDER WITHIN ME...
FEEL NOTHING LIKE FRIEND-SHIP.
COULD THEY BE...?

Goodbye,
my Rose Garden

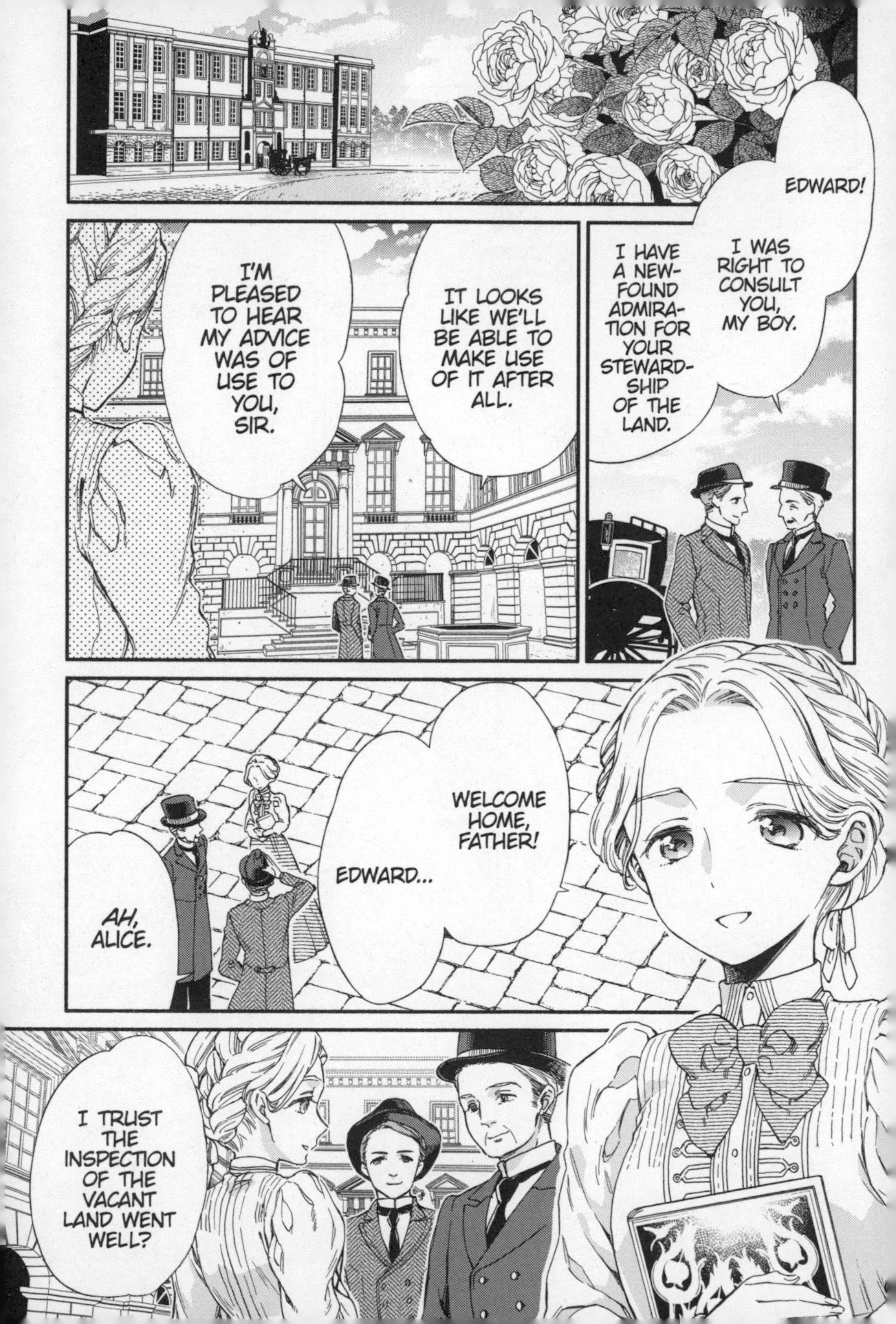
EDWARD!
I WAS RIGHT TO CONSULT YOU, MY BOY.
I HAVE A NEW-FOUND ADMIRATION FOR YOUR STEWARDSHIP OF THE LAND.
IT LOOKS LIKE WE'LL BE ABLE TO MAKE USE OF IT AFTER ALL.
I'M PLEASED TO HEAR MY ADVICE WAS OF USE TO YOU, SIR.
WELCOME HOME, FATHER!
EDWARD...
AH, ALICE.
I TRUST THE INSPECTION OF THE VACANT LAND WENT WELL?

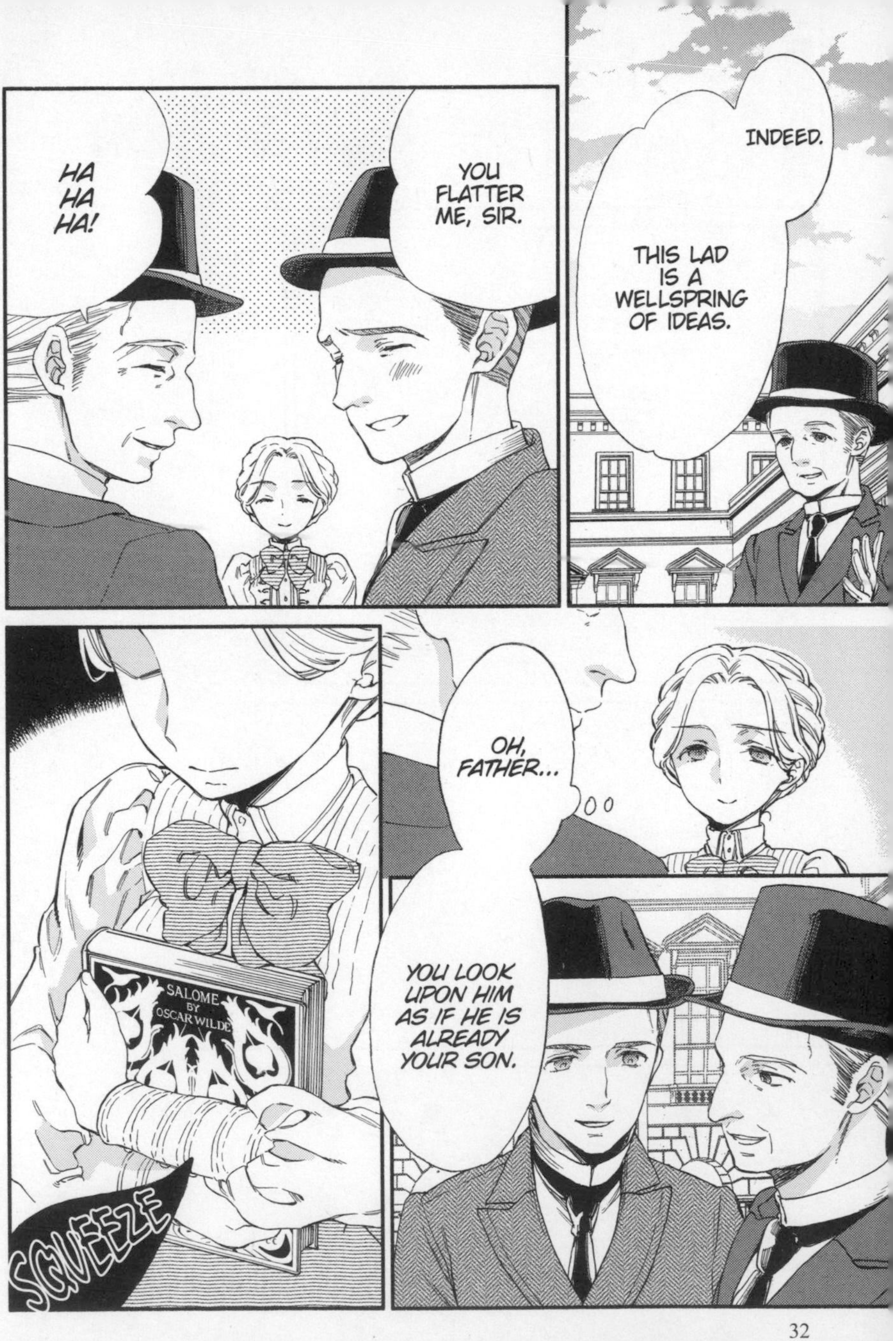
INDEED.
THIS LAD IS A WELLSPRING OF IDEAS.
YOU FLATTER ME, SIR.
HA HA HA!
OH, FATHER...
YOU LOOK UPON HIM AS IF HE IS ALREADY YOUR SON.
SALOME BY OSCAR WILDE
SQUEEZE

{ Chapter 7 }
The Shadow Eclipsing the Sun

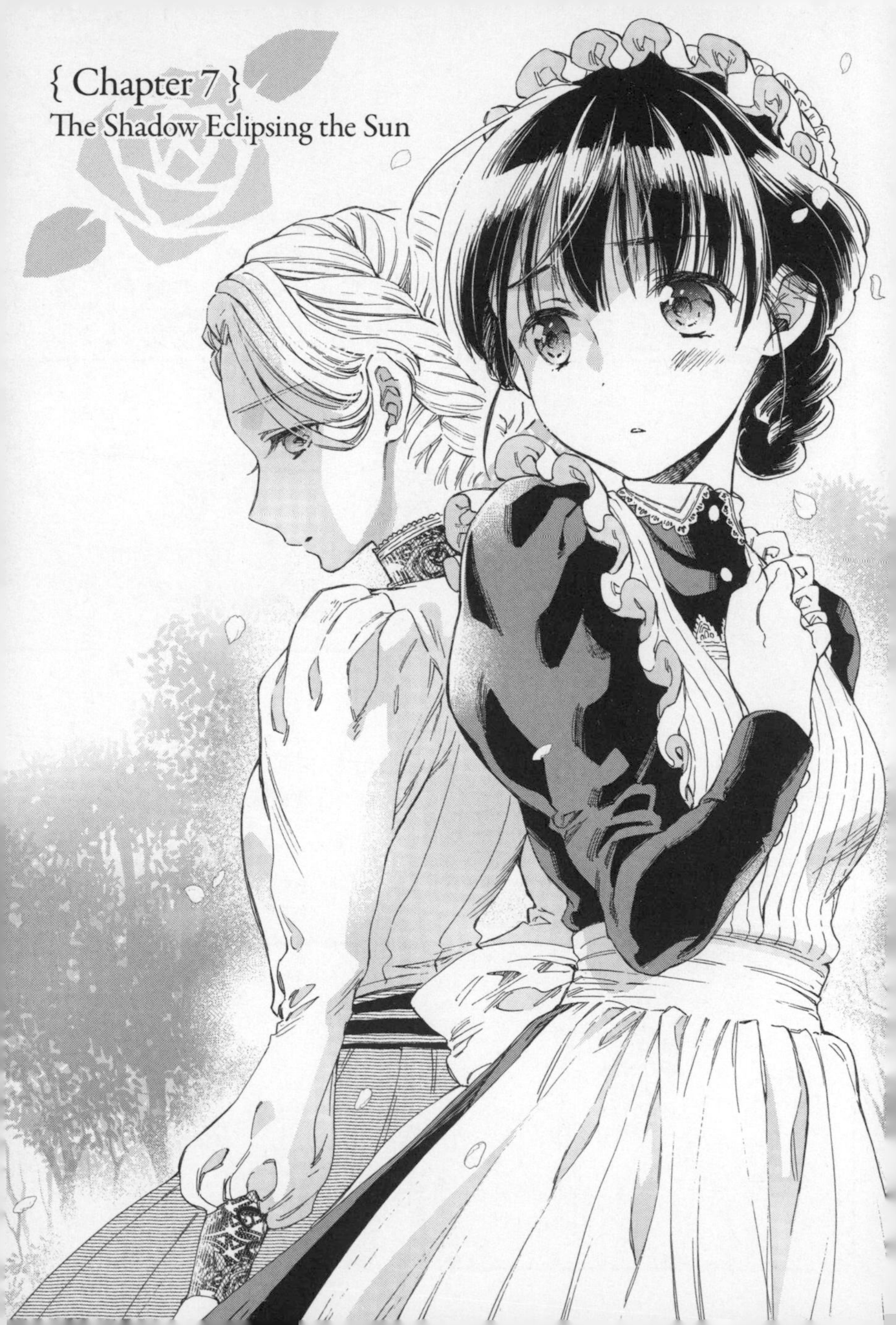

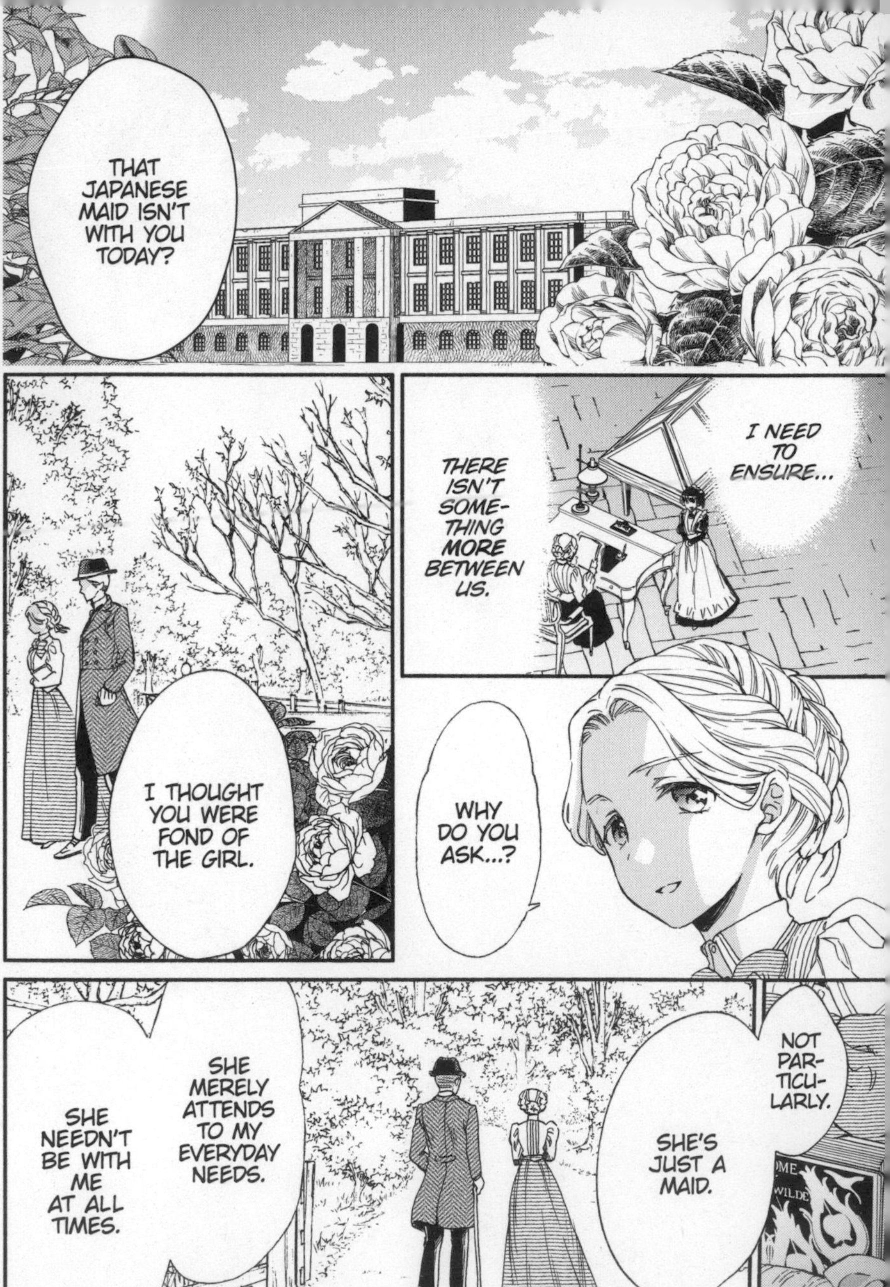
THAT JAPANESE MAID ISN'T WITH YOU TODAY?
I NEED TO ENSURE...
THERE ISN'T SOME-THING MORE BETWEEN US.
WHY DO YOU ASK...?
I THOUGHT YOU WERE FOND OF THE GIRL.
NOT PAR-TICU-LARLY.
SHE'S JUST A MAID.
SHE MERELY ATTENDS TO MY EVERYDAY NEEDS.
SHE NEEDN'T BE WITH ME AT ALL TIMES.

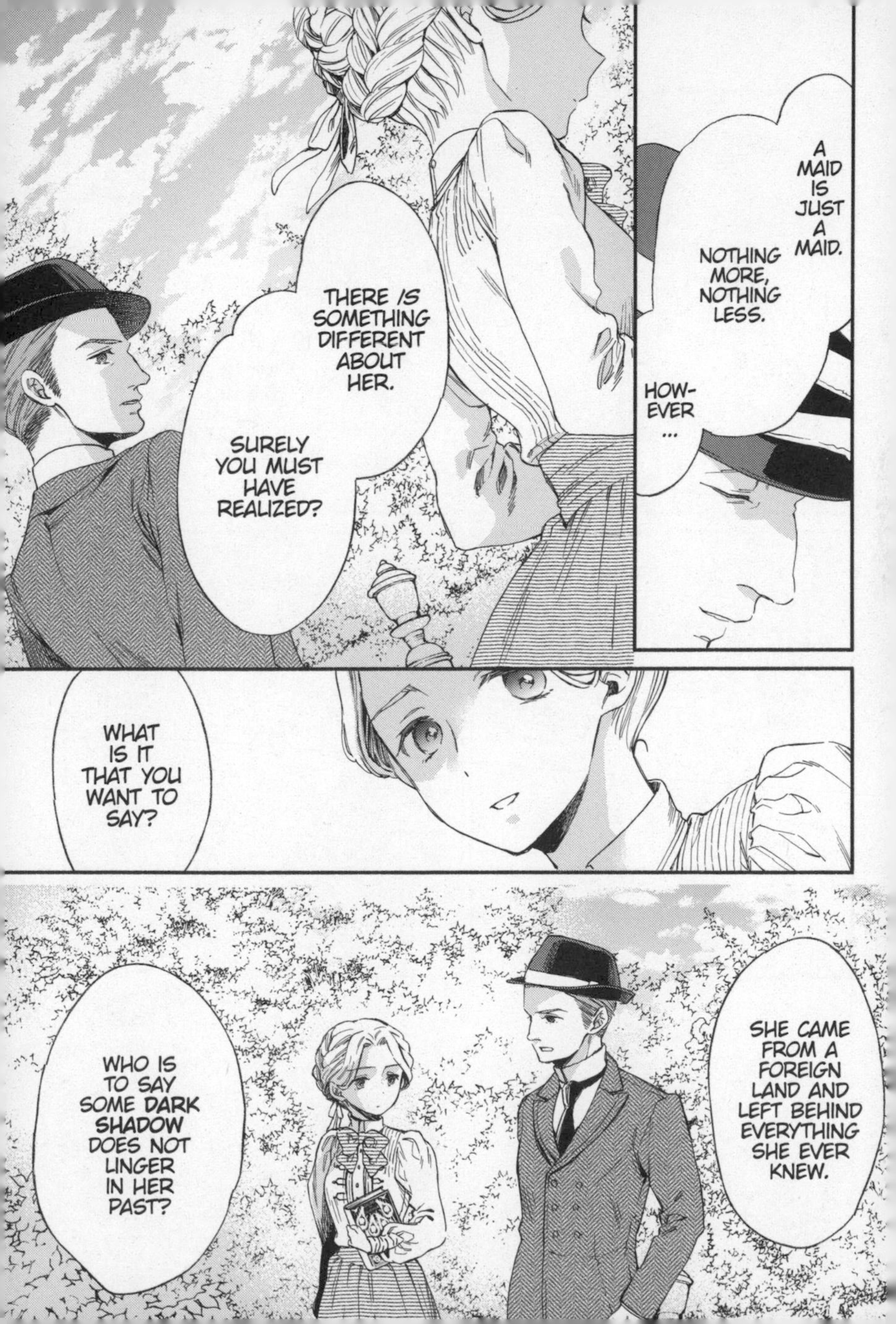
A MAID IS JUST A MAID.
NOTHING MORE, NOTHING LESS.
HOW-EVER ...
THERE IS SOMETHING DIFFERENT ABOUT HER.
SURELY YOU MUST HAVE REALIZED?
WHAT IS IT THAT YOU WANT TO SAY?
SHE CAME FROM A FOREIGN LAND AND LEFT BEHIND EVERYTHING SHE EVER KNEW.
WHO IS TO SAY SOME DARK SHADOW DOES NOT LINGER IN HER PAST?

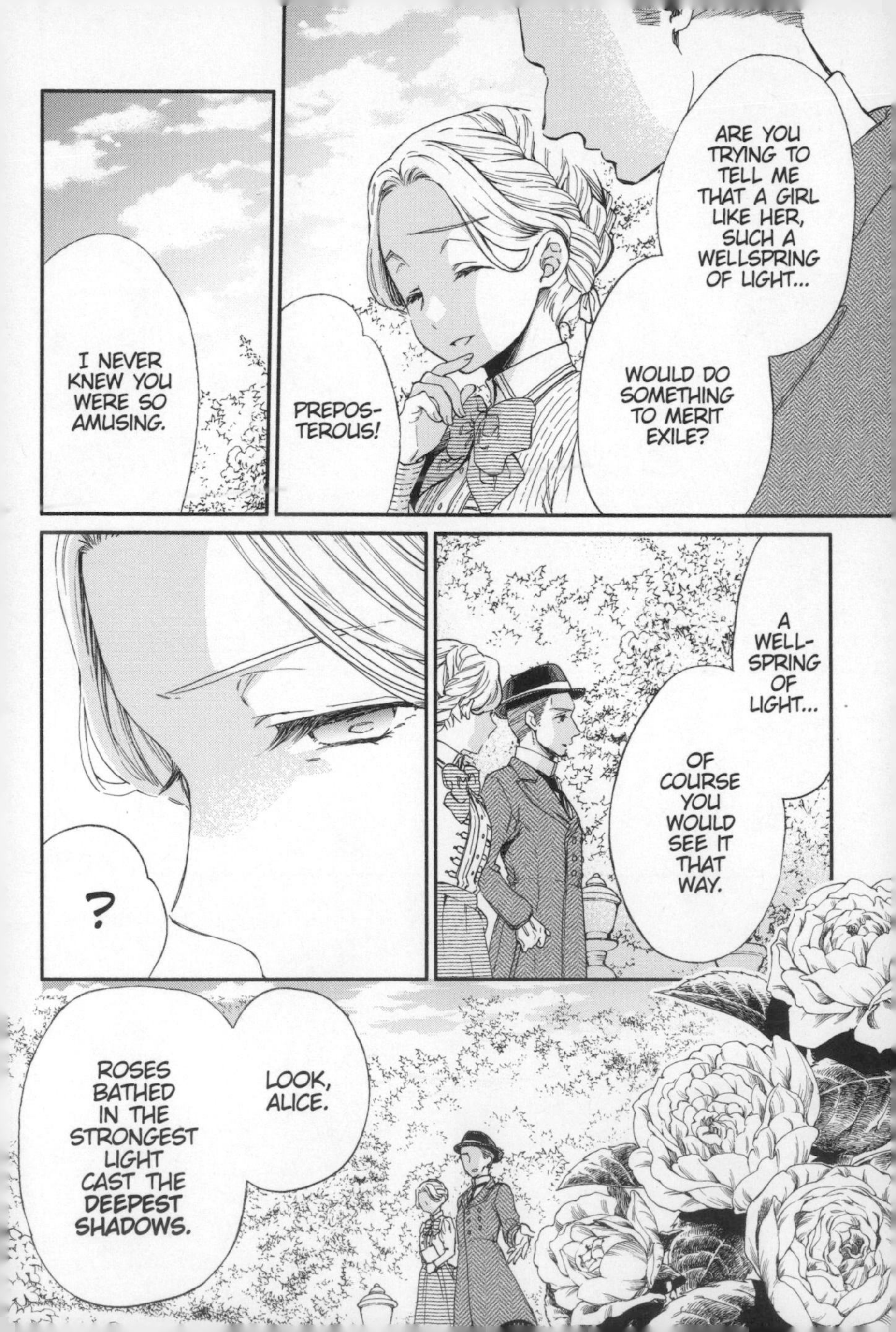
ARE YOU TRYING TO TELL ME THAT A GIRL LIKE HER, SUCH A WELLSPRING OF LIGHT...
WOULD DO SOMETHING TO MERIT EXILE?
PREPOS-TEROUS!
I NEVER KNEW YOU WERE SO AMUSING.
A WELL-SPRING OF LIGHT...
OF COURSE YOU WOULD SEE IT THAT WAY.
?
LOOK, ALICE.
ROSES BATHED IN THE STRONGEST LIGHT CAST THE DEEPEST SHADOWS.

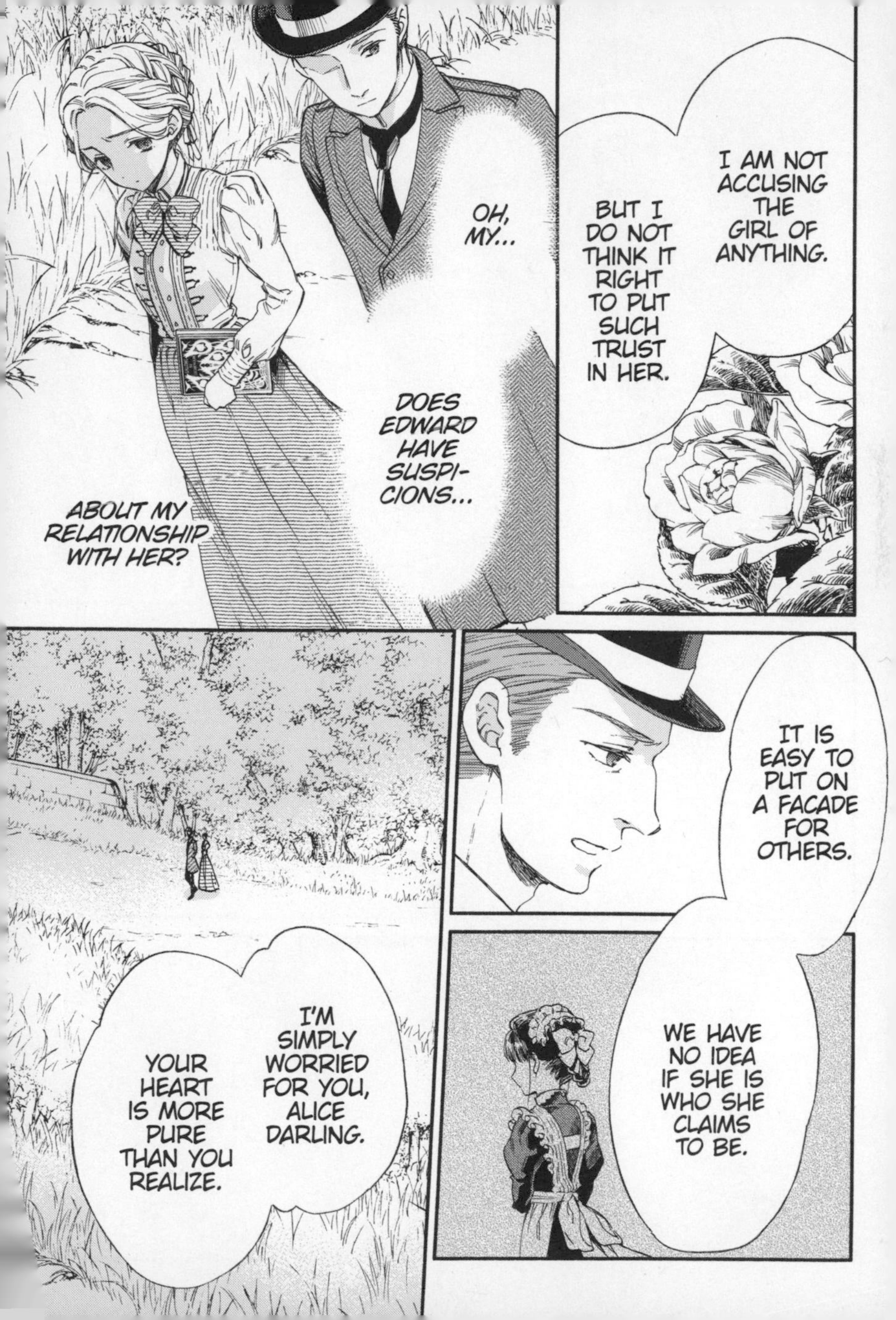
I AM NOT ACCUSING THE GIRL OF ANYTHING.
BUT I DO NOT THINK IT RIGHT TO PUT SUCH TRUST IN HER.
OH, MY...
DOES EDWARD HAVE SUSPICIONS...
ABOUT MY RELATIONSHIP WITH HER?
IT IS EASY TO PUT ON A FACADE FOR OTHERS.
WE HAVE NO IDEA IF SHE IS WHO SHE CLAIMS TO BE.
I'M SIMPLY WORRIED FOR YOU, ALICE DARLING.
YOUR HEART IS MORE PURE THAN YOU REALIZE.

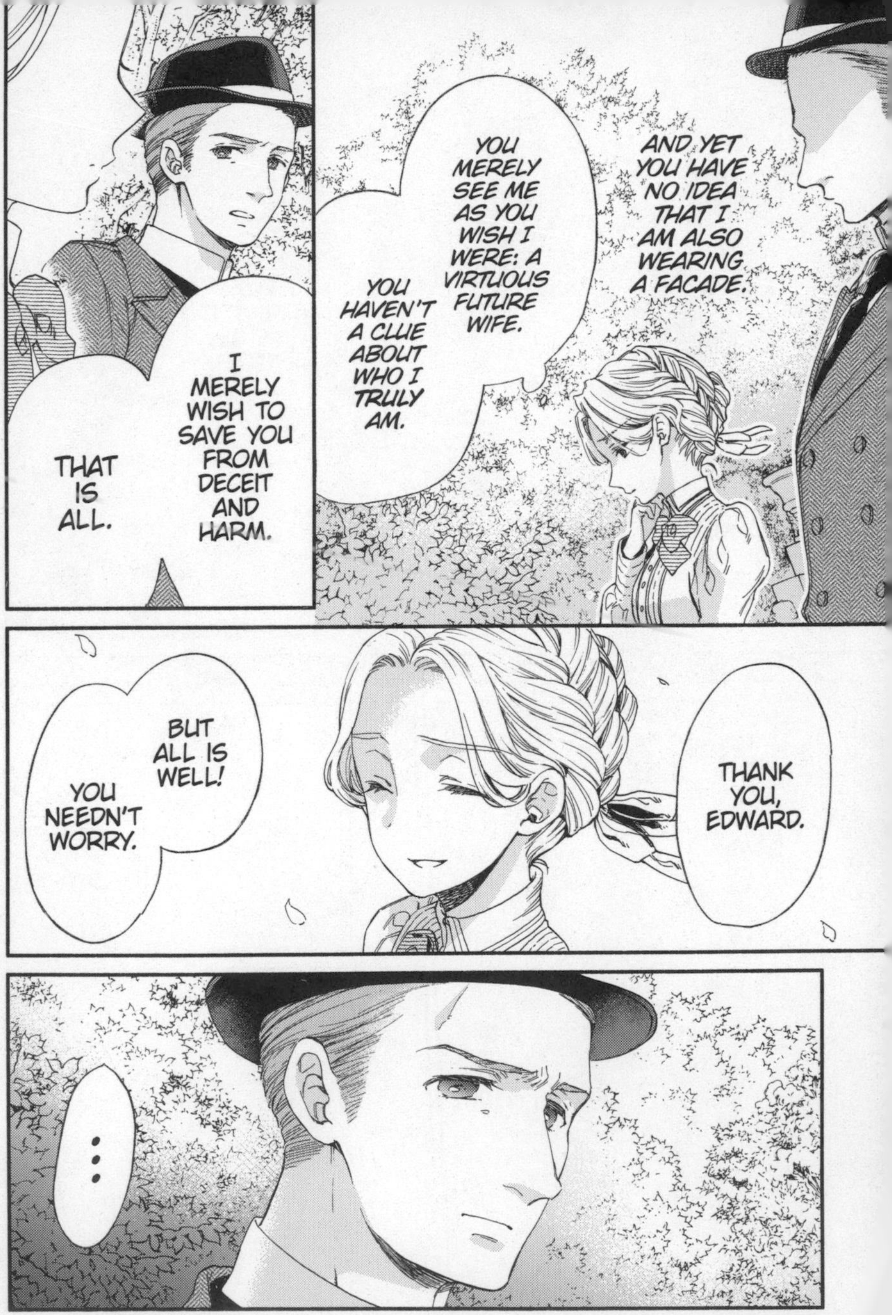
AND YET YOU HAVE NO IDEA THAT I AM ALSO WEARING A FACADE.
YOU MERELY SEE ME AS YOU WISH I WERE: A VIRTUOUS FUTURE WIFE.
YOU HAVEN'T A CLUE ABOUT WHO I TRULY AM.
I MERELY WISH TO SAVE YOU FROM DECEIT AND HARM.
THAT IS ALL.
THANK YOU, EDWARD.
BUT ALL IS WELL!
YOU NEEDN'T WORRY.
...

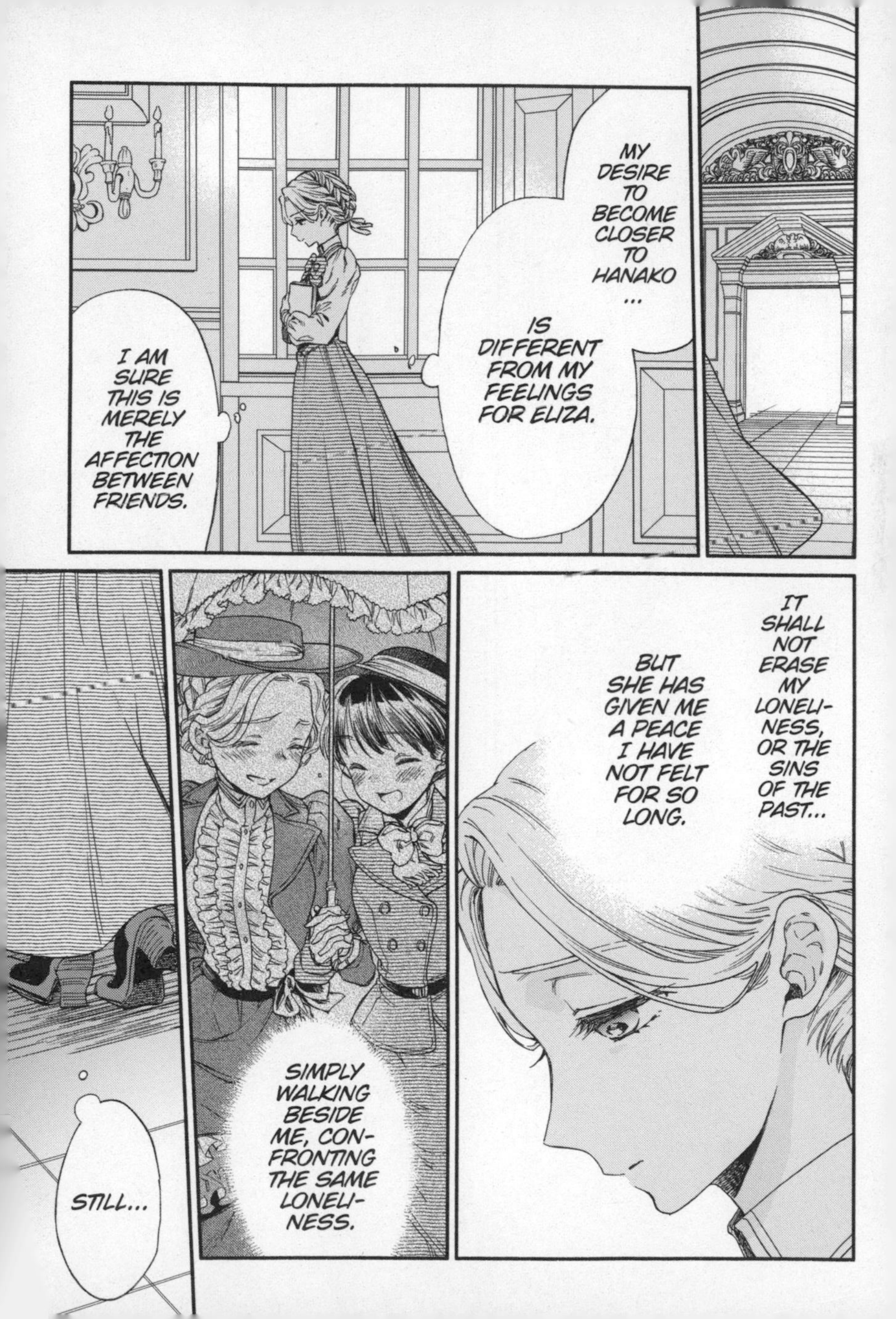
MY DESIRE TO BECOME CLOSER TO HANAKO ...
IS DIFFERENT FROM MY FEELINGS FOR ELIZA.
I AM SURE THIS IS MERELY THE AFFECTION BETWEEN FRIENDS.
IT SHALL NOT ERASE MY LONELI- NESS, OR THE SINS OF THE PAST...
BUT SHE HAS GIVEN ME A PEACE I HAVE NOT FELT FOR SO LONG.
SIMPLY WALKING BESIDE ME, CON- FRONTING THE SAME LONELI- NESS.
STILL...

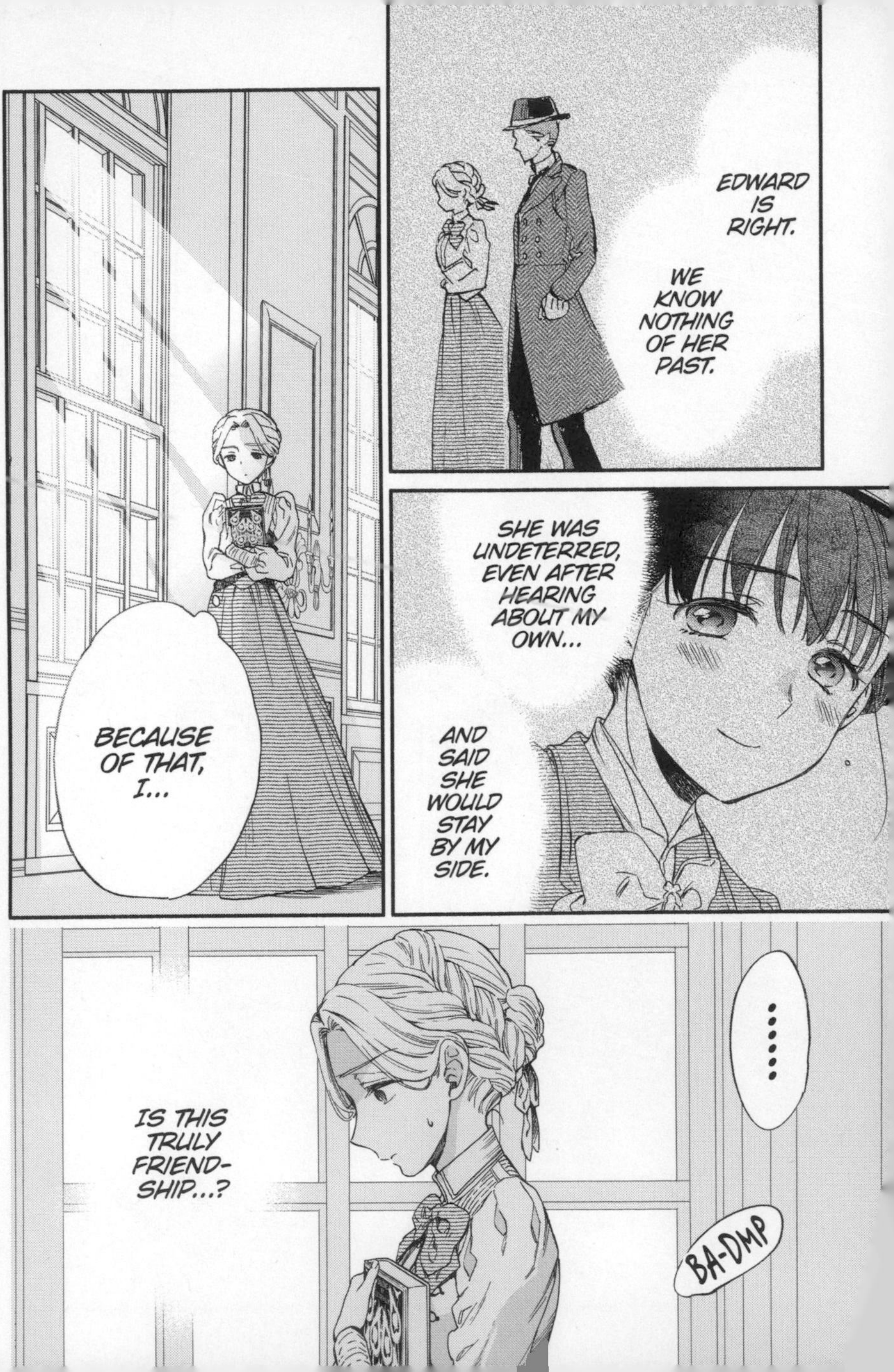
EDWARD IS RIGHT.
WE KNOW NOTHING OF HER PAST.
SHE WAS UNDETERRED, EVEN AFTER HEARING ABOUT MY OWN...
AND SAID SHE WOULD STAY BY MY SIDE.
BECAUSE OF THAT, I...
......
BA-DMP
IS THIS TRULY FRIEND-SHIP...?

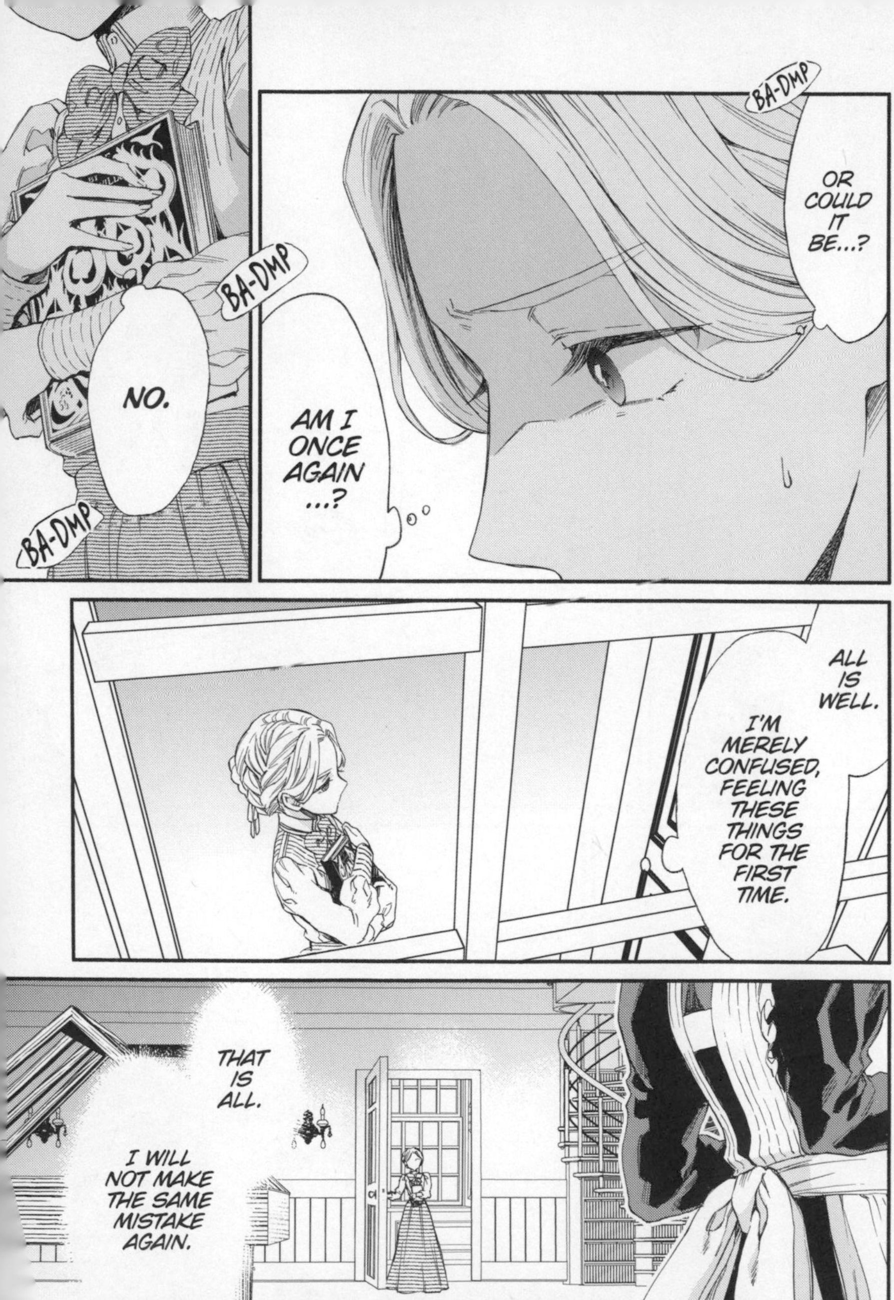
BA-DMP
OR COULD IT BE...?
AM I ONCE AGAIN ...?
BA-DMP
NO.
BA-DMP
ALL IS WELL.
I'M MERELY CONFUSED, FEELING THESE THINGS FOR THE FIRST TIME.
THAT IS ALL.
I WILL NOT MAKE THE SAME MISTAKE AGAIN.

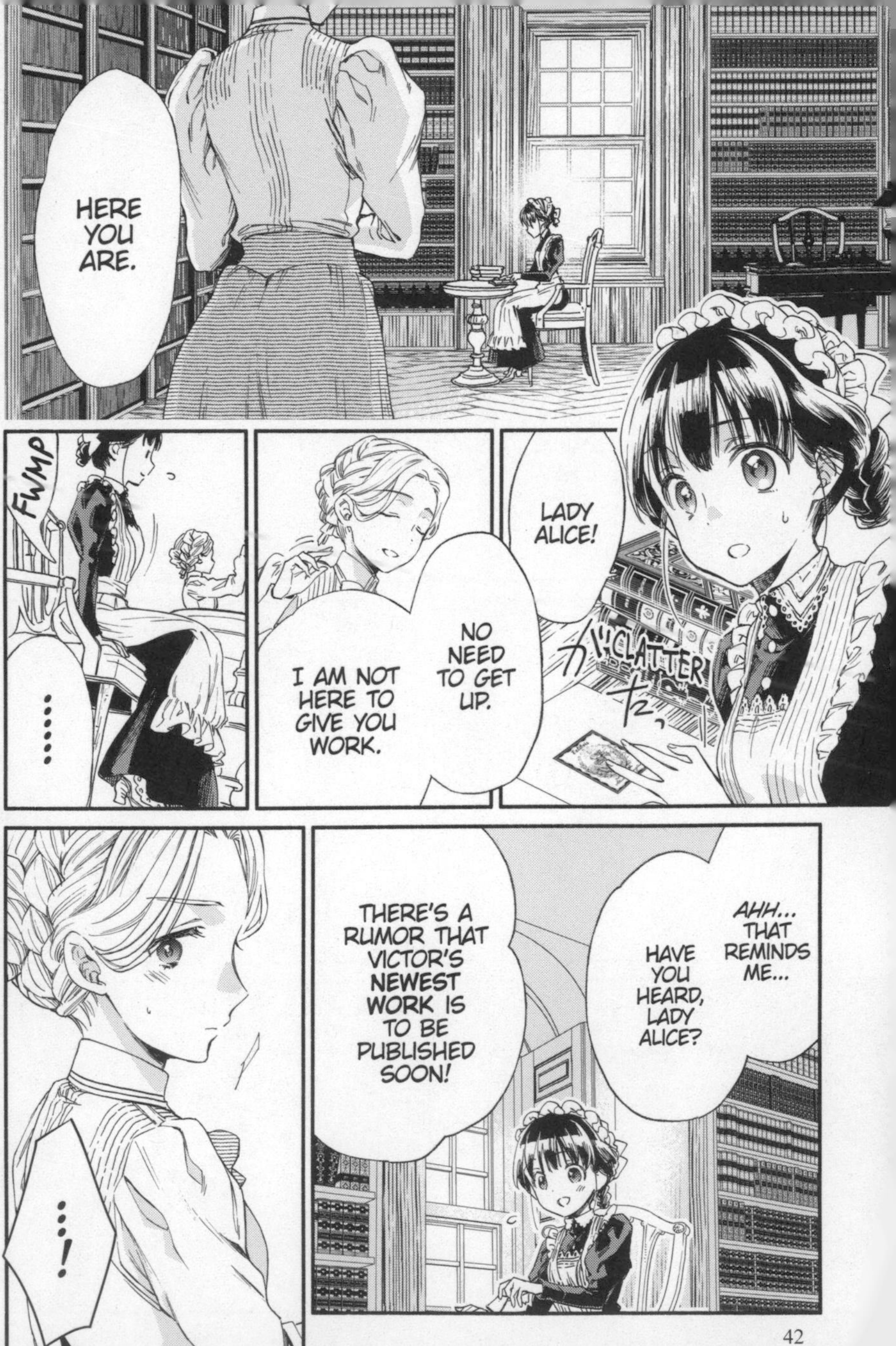
HERE YOU ARE.
LADY ALICE!
CLATTER
NO NEED TO GET UP.
I AM NOT HERE TO GIVE YOU WORK.
FWMP
......
AHH... THAT REMINDS ME...
HAVE YOU HEARD, LADY ALICE?
THERE'S A RUMOR THAT VICTOR'S NEWEST WORK IS TO BE PUBLISHED SOON!
...!

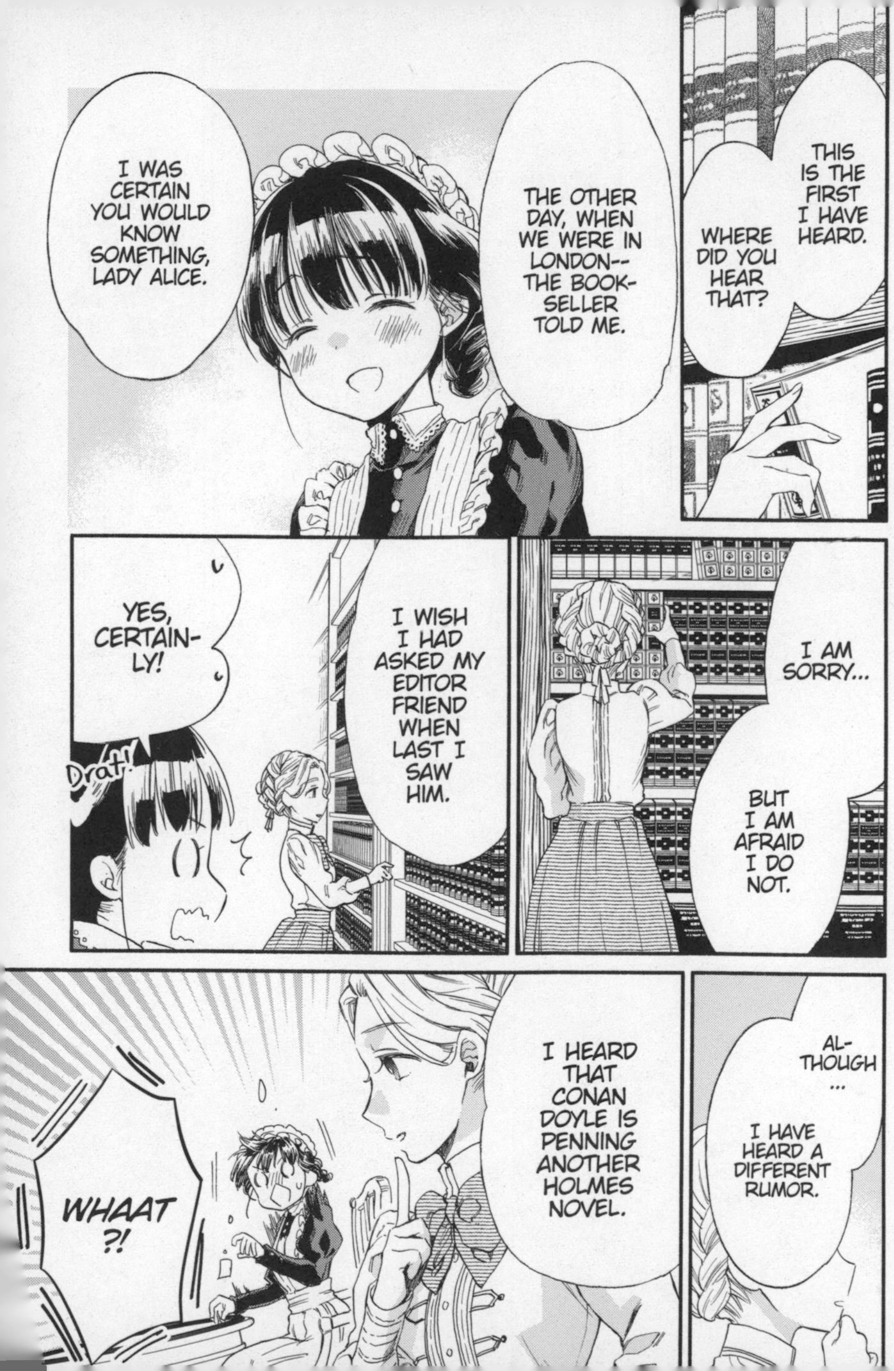
THIS IS THE FIRST I HAVE HEARD.
WHERE DID YOU HEAR THAT?
THE OTHER DAY, WHEN WE WERE IN LONDON-- THE BOOKSELLER TOLD ME.
I WAS CERTAIN YOU WOULD KNOW SOMETHING, LADY ALICE.
I AM SORRY...
BUT I AM AFRAID I DO NOT.
I WISH I HAD ASKED MY EDITOR FRIEND WHEN LAST I SAW HIM.
YES, CERTAIN-LY!
Drat!
AL-THOUGH...
I HAVE HEARD A DIFFERENT RUMOR.
I HEARD THAT CONAN DOYLE IS PENNING ANOTHER HOLMES NOVEL.
WHAAT?!

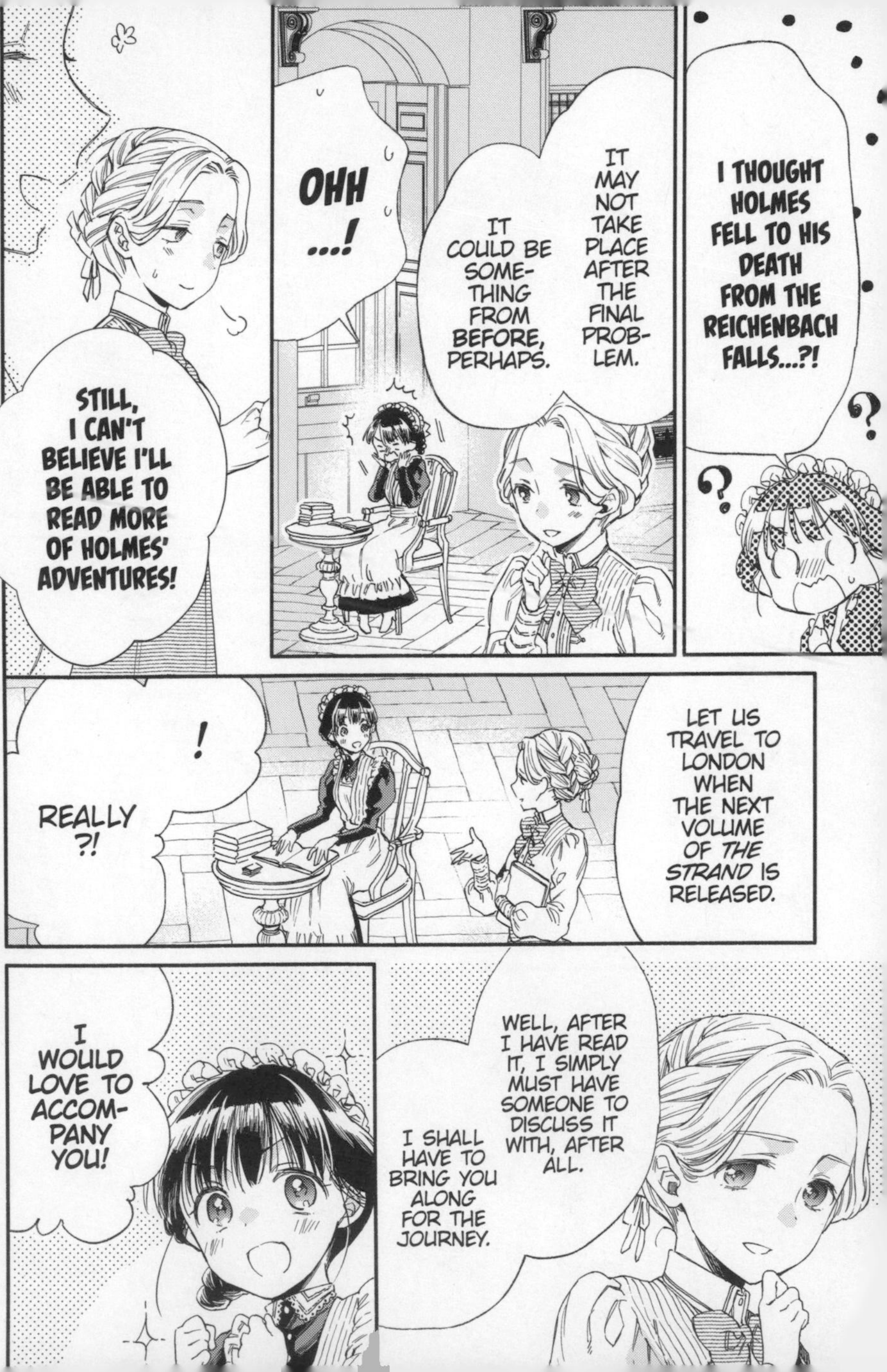
I THOUGHT HOLMES FELL TO HIS DEATH FROM THE REICHENBACH FALLS...?!
IT MAY NOT TAKE PLACE AFTER THE FINAL PROB-LEM.
IT COULD BE SOME-THING FROM BEFORE, PERHAPS.
OHH ...!
STILL, I CAN'T BELIEVE I'LL BE ABLE TO READ MORE OF HOLMES' ADVENTURES!
LET US TRAVEL TO LONDON WHEN THE NEXT VOLUME OF *THE STRAND* IS RELEASED.
!
REALLY ?!
WELL, AFTER I HAVE READ IT, I SIMPLY MUST HAVE SOMEONE TO DISCUSS IT WITH, AFTER ALL.
I SHALL HAVE TO BRING YOU ALONG FOR THE JOURNEY.
I WOULD LOVE TO ACCOM-PANY YOU!

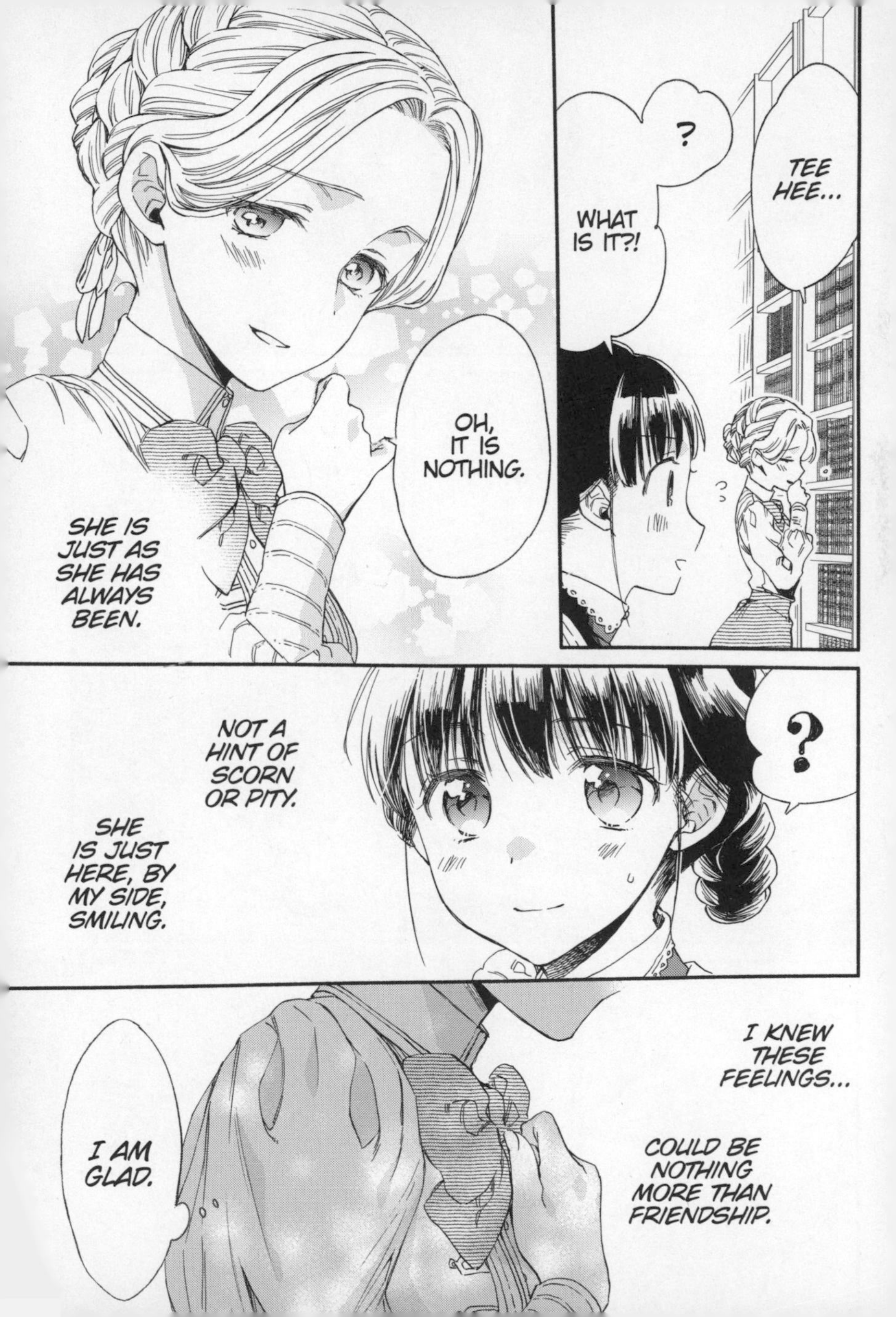
TEE HEE...
?
WHAT IS IT?!
OH, IT IS NOTHING.
SHE IS JUST AS SHE HAS ALWAYS BEEN.
?
NOT A HINT OF SCORN OR PITY.
SHE IS JUST HERE, BY MY SIDE, SMILING.
I KNEW THESE FEELINGS...
COULD BE NOTHING MORE THAN FRIENDSHIP.
I AM GLAD.

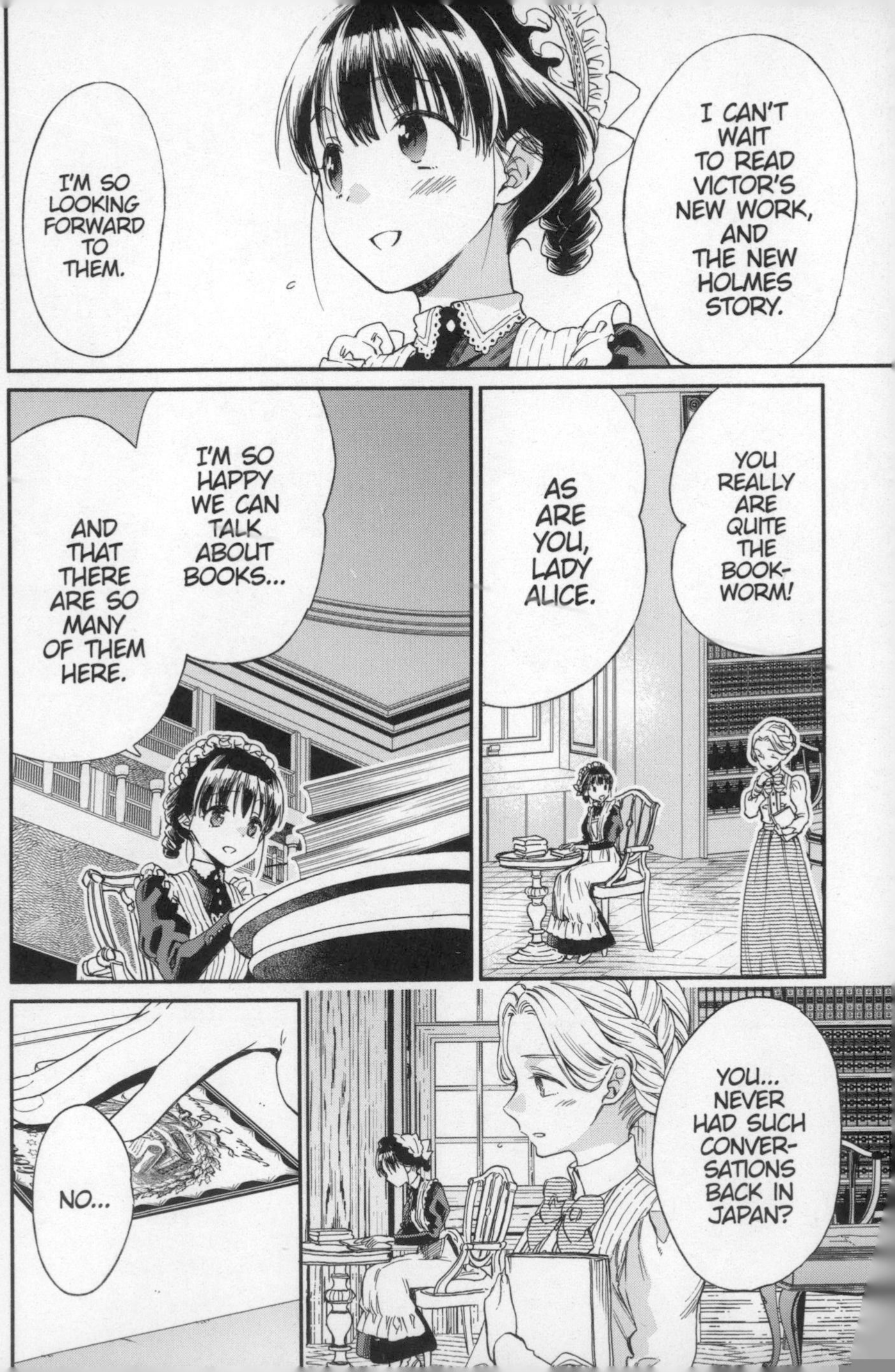
I CAN'T WAIT TO READ VICTOR'S NEW WORK, AND THE NEW HOLMES STORY.
I'M SO LOOKING FORWARD TO THEM.
YOU REALLY ARE QUITE THE BOOK-WORM!
AS ARE YOU, LADY ALICE.
I'M SO HAPPY WE CAN TALK ABOUT BOOKS...
AND THAT THERE ARE SO MANY OF THEM HERE.
YOU... NEVER HAD SUCH CONVER-SATIONS BACK IN JAPAN?
NO...

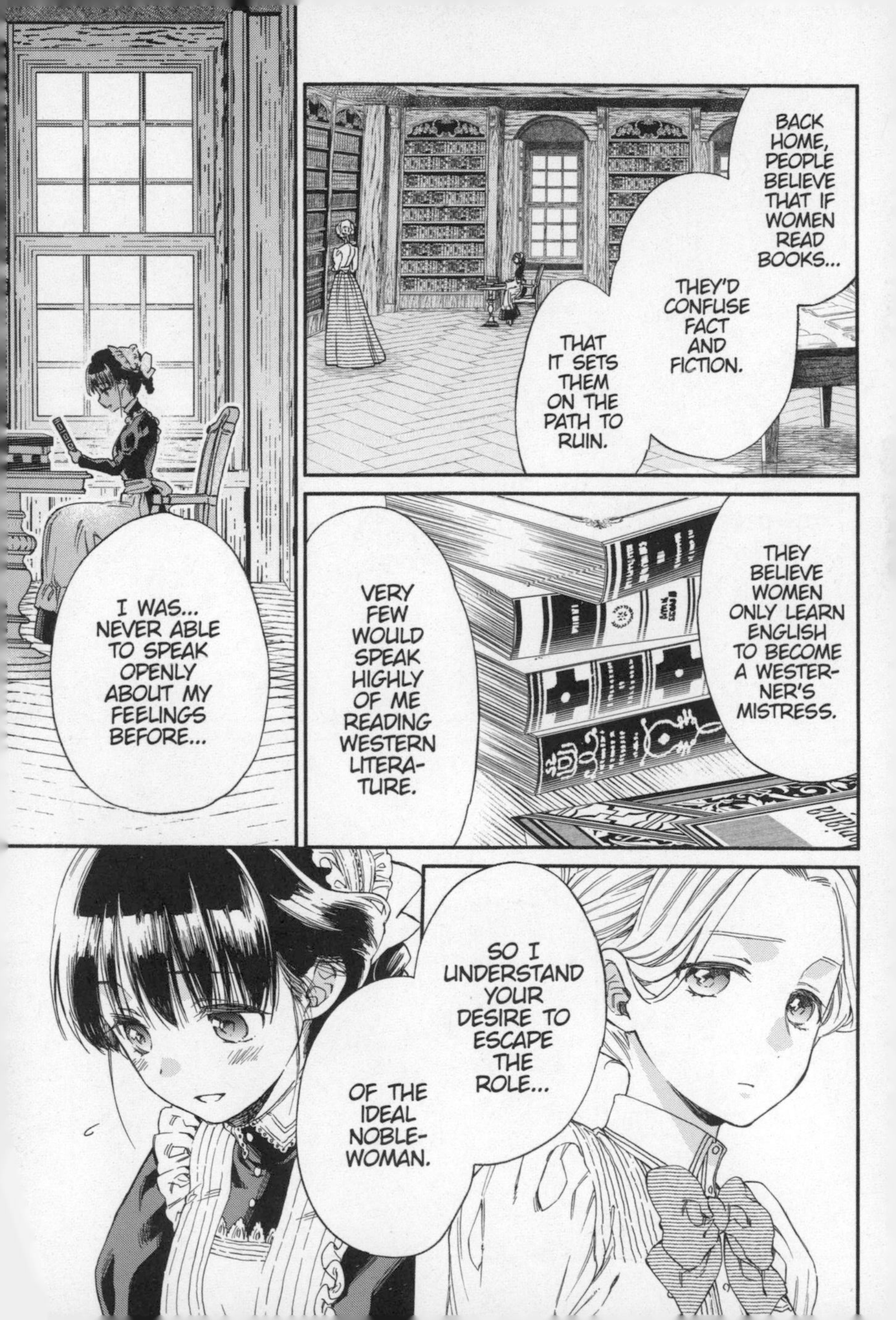
BACK HOME, PEOPLE BELIEVE THAT IF WOMEN READ BOOKS...
THEY'D CONFUSE FACT AND FICTION.
THAT IT SETS THEM ON THE PATH TO RUIN.
THEY BELIEVE WOMEN ONLY LEARN ENGLISH TO BECOME A WESTERNER'S MISTRESS.
VERY FEW WOULD SPEAK HIGHLY OF ME READING WESTERN LITERATURE.
I WAS... NEVER ABLE TO SPEAK OPENLY ABOUT MY FEELINGS BEFORE...
SO I UNDERSTAND YOUR DESIRE TO ESCAPE THE ROLE...
OF THE IDEAL NOBLEWOMAN.

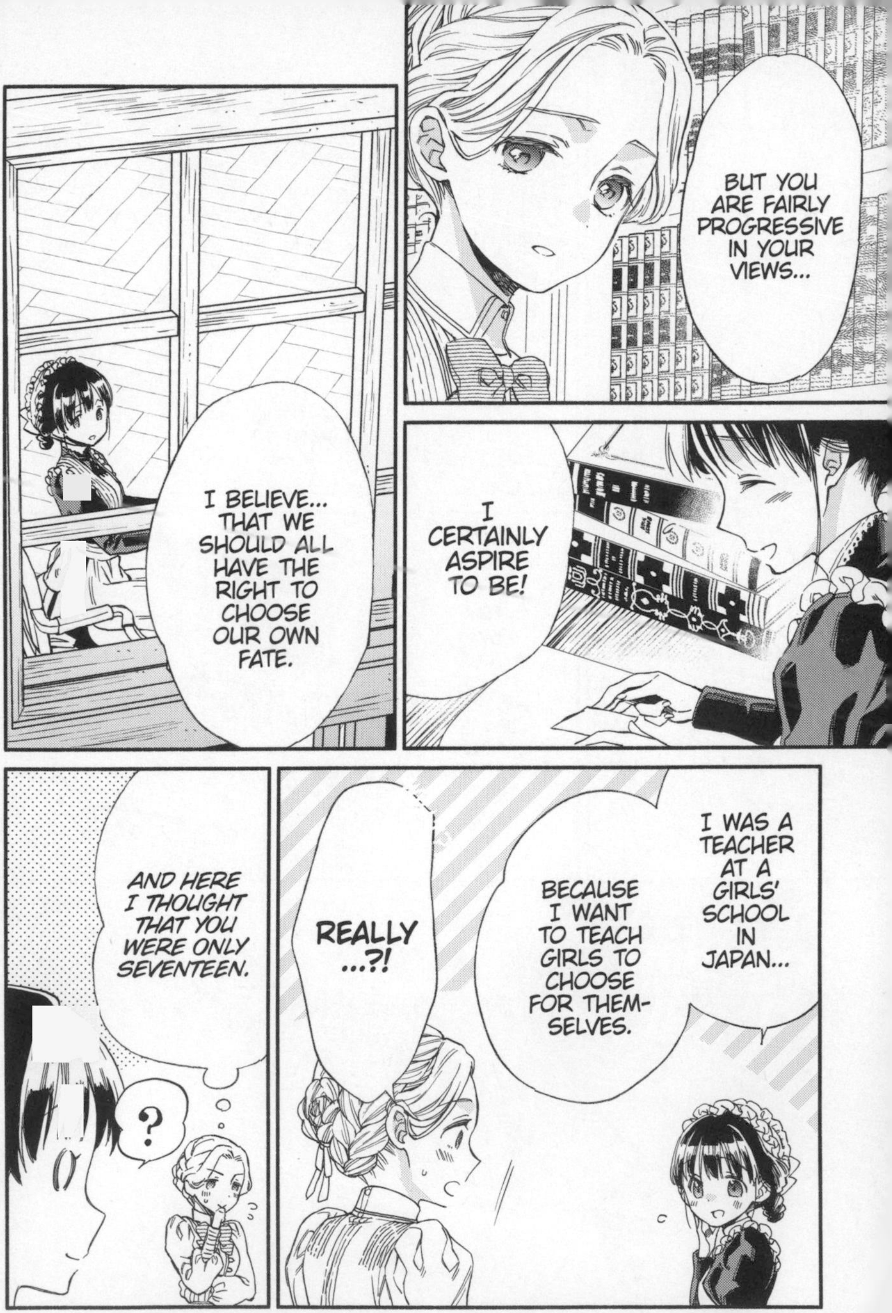
BUT YOU ARE FAIRLY PROGRESSIVE IN YOUR VIEWS...
I CERTAINLY ASPIRE TO BE!
I BELIEVE... THAT WE SHOULD ALL HAVE THE RIGHT TO CHOOSE OUR OWN FATE.
I WAS A TEACHER AT A GIRLS' SCHOOL IN JAPAN...
BECAUSE I WANT TO TEACH GIRLS TO CHOOSE FOR THEM-SELVES.
REALLY ...?!
AND HERE I THOUGHT THAT YOU WERE ONLY SEVENTEEN.
?

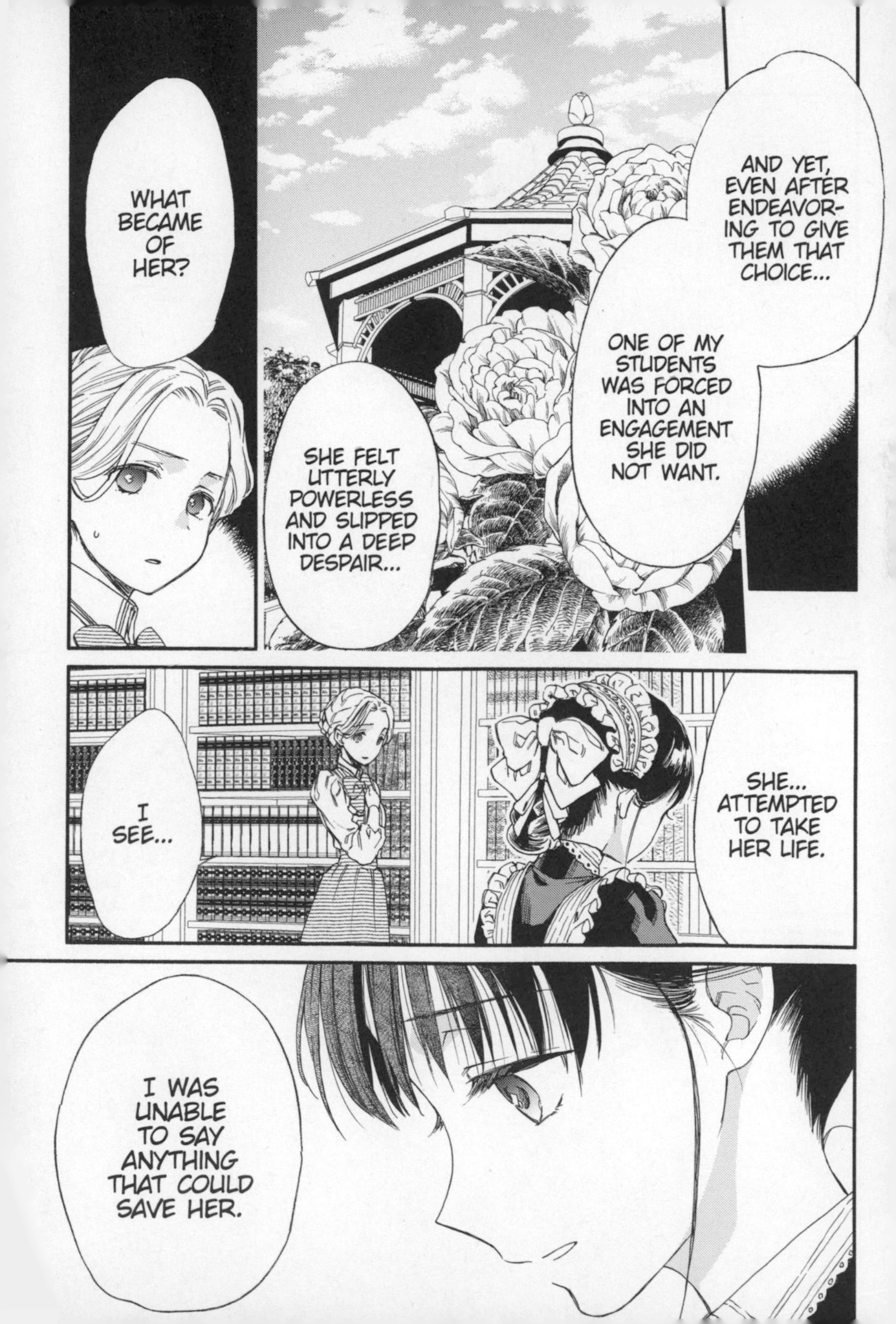
AND YET, EVEN AFTER ENDEAVOR-ING TO GIVE THEM THAT CHOICE...
ONE OF MY STUDENTS WAS FORCED INTO AN ENGAGEMENT SHE DID NOT WANT.
SHE FELT UTTERLY POWERLESS AND SLIPPED INTO A DEEP DESPAIR...
WHAT BECAME OF HER?
SHE... ATTEMPTED TO TAKE HER LIFE.
I SEE...
I WAS UNABLE TO SAY ANYTHING THAT COULD SAVE HER.

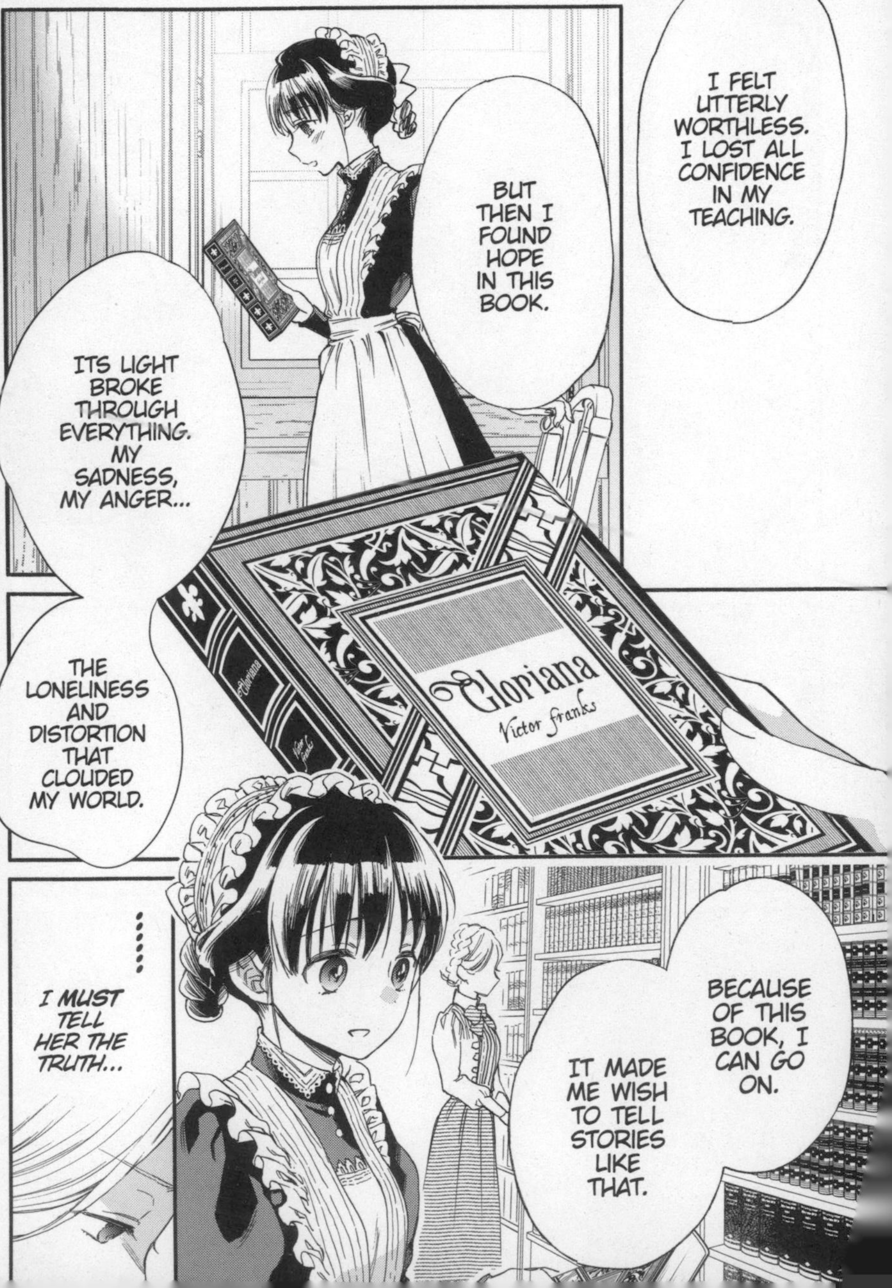
I FELT UTTERLY WORTHLESS. I LOST ALL CONFIDENCE IN MY TEACHING.
BUT THEN I FOUND HOPE IN THIS BOOK.
ITS LIGHT BROKE THROUGH EVERYTHING. MY SADNESS, MY ANGER...
Gloriana
Victor franks
THE LONELINESS AND DISTORTION THAT CLOUDED MY WORLD.
BECAUSE OF THIS BOOK, I CAN GO ON.
IT MADE ME WISH TO TELL STORIES LIKE THAT.
......
I MUST TELL HER THE TRUTH...

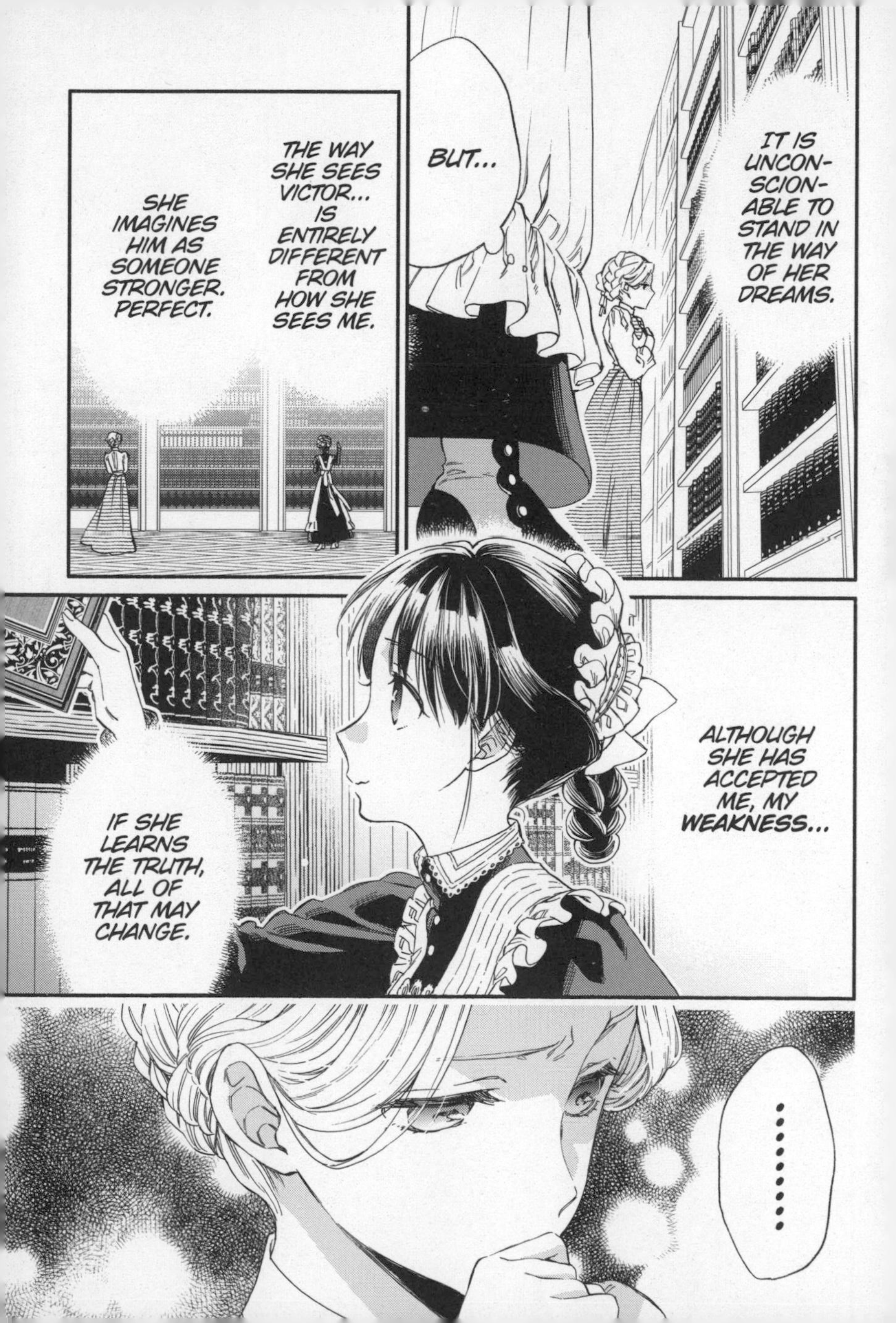

IT IS UNCON-SCION-ABLE TO STAND IN THE WAY OF HER DREAMS.
BUT...
THE WAY SHE SEES VICTOR... IS ENTIRELY DIFFERENT FROM HOW SHE SEES ME.
SHE IMAGINES HIM AS SOMEONE STRONGER. PERFECT.
ALTHOUGH SHE HAS ACCEPTED ME, MY WEAKNESS...
IF SHE LEARNS THE TRUTH, ALL OF THAT MAY CHANGE.
....

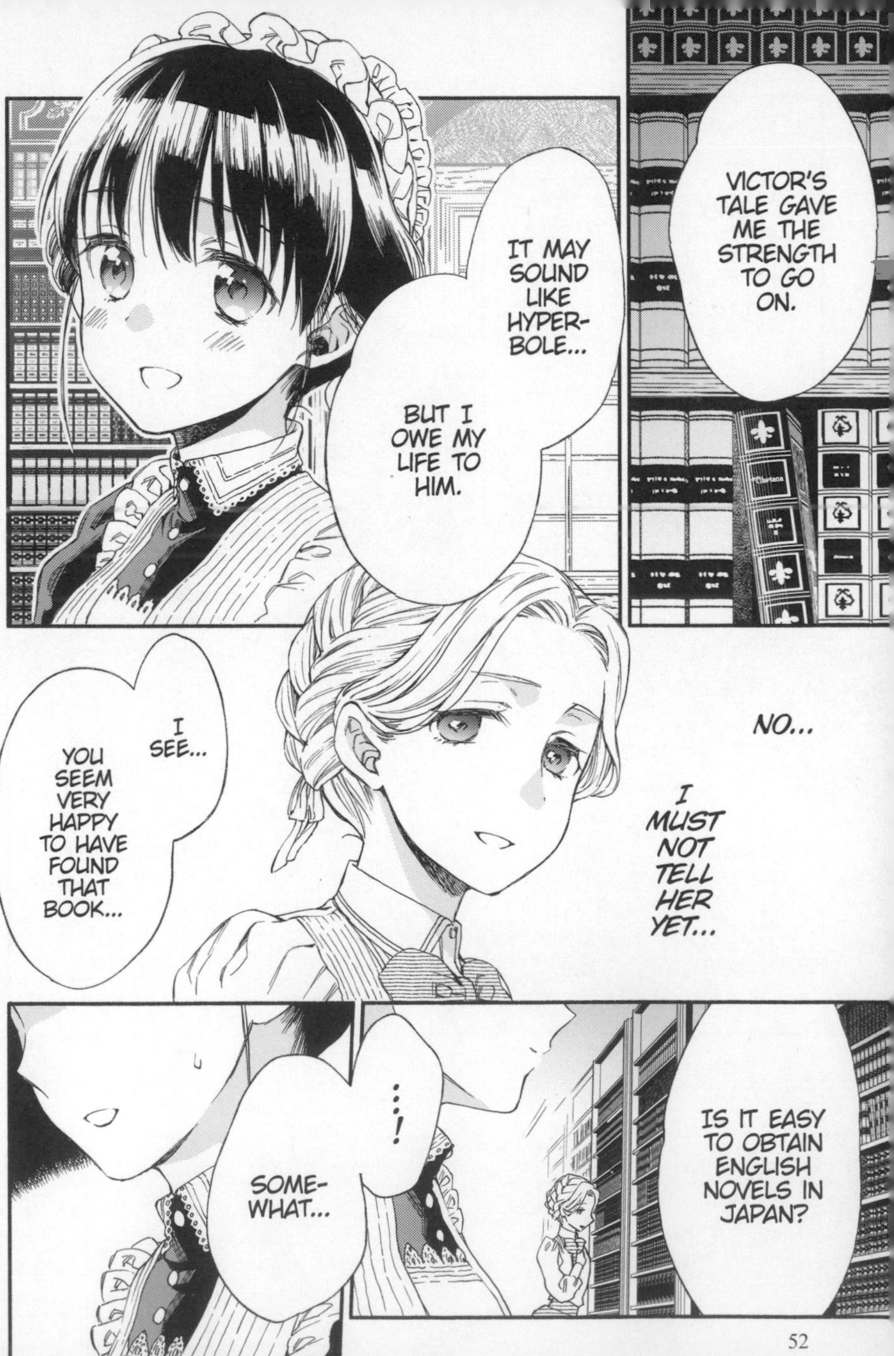
VICTOR'S TALE GAVE ME THE STRENGTH TO GO ON.
IT MAY SOUND LIKE HYPER-BOLE...
BUT I OWE MY LIFE TO HIM.
NO...
I MUST NOT TELL HER YET...
I SEE...
YOU SEEM VERY HAPPY TO HAVE FOUND THAT BOOK...
IS IT EASY TO OBTAIN ENGLISH NOVELS IN JAPAN?
...!
SOME-WHAT...

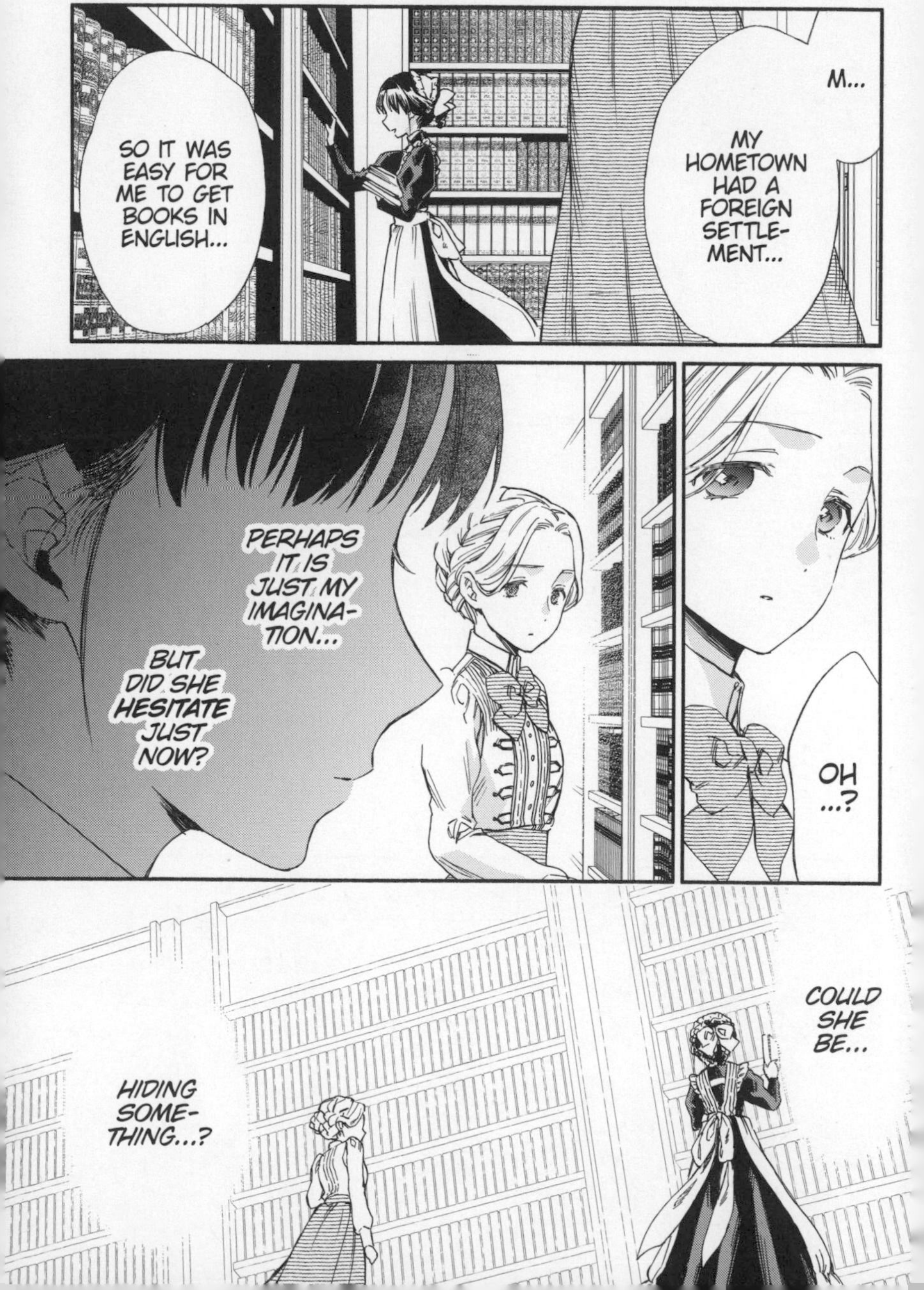
M...
MY HOMETOWN HAD A FOREIGN SETTLE-MENT...
SO IT WAS EASY FOR ME TO GET BOOKS IN ENGLISH...
OH ...?
PERHAPS IT IS JUST MY IMAGINA-TION...
BUT DID SHE HESITATE JUST NOW?
COULD SHE BE...
HIDING SOME-THING...?

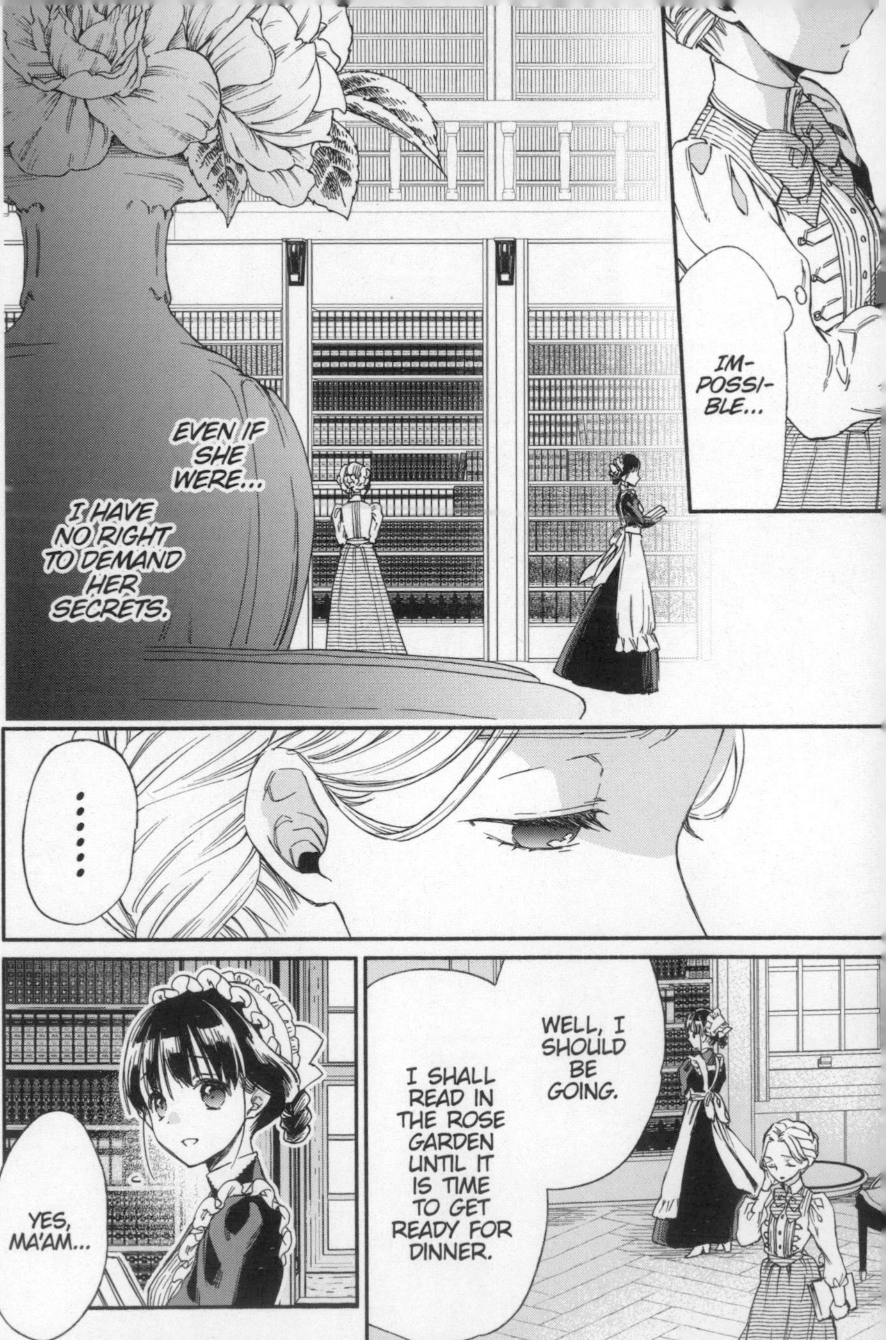
IM-POSSI-BLE...
EVEN IF SHE WERE...
I HAVE NO RIGHT TO DEMAND HER SECRETS.
......
WELL, I SHOULD BE GOING.
I SHALL READ IN THE ROSE GARDEN UNTIL IT IS TIME TO GET READY FOR DINNER.
YES, MA'AM...

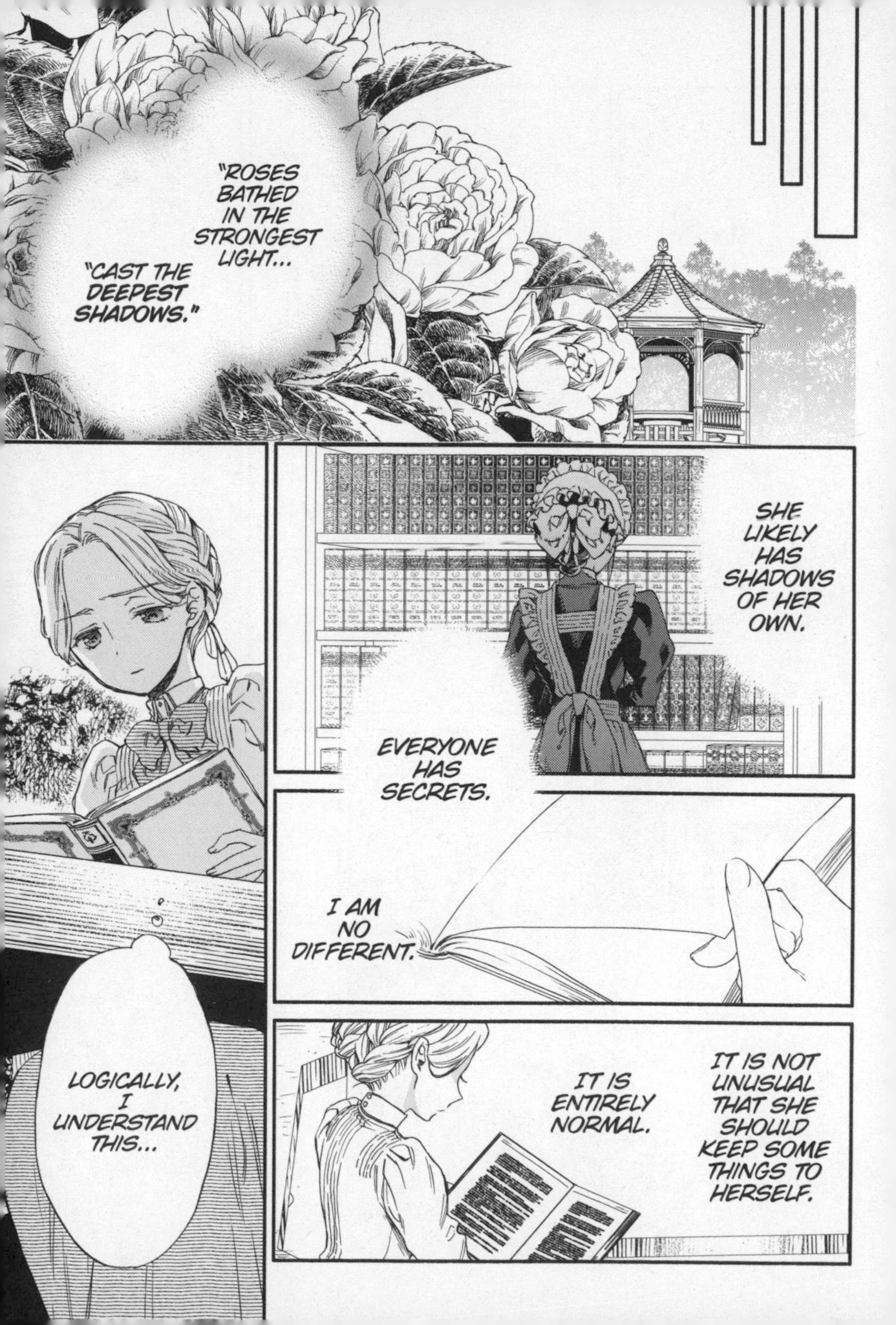
"ROSES BATHED IN THE STRONGEST LIGHT...
"CAST THE DEEPEST SHADOWS."
SHE LIKELY HAS SHADOWS OF HER OWN.
EVERYONE HAS SECRETS.
I AM NO DIFFERENT.
IT IS NOT UNUSUAL THAT SHE SHOULD KEEP SOME THINGS TO HERSELF.
IT IS ENTIRELY NORMAL.
LOGICALLY, I UNDERSTAND THIS...

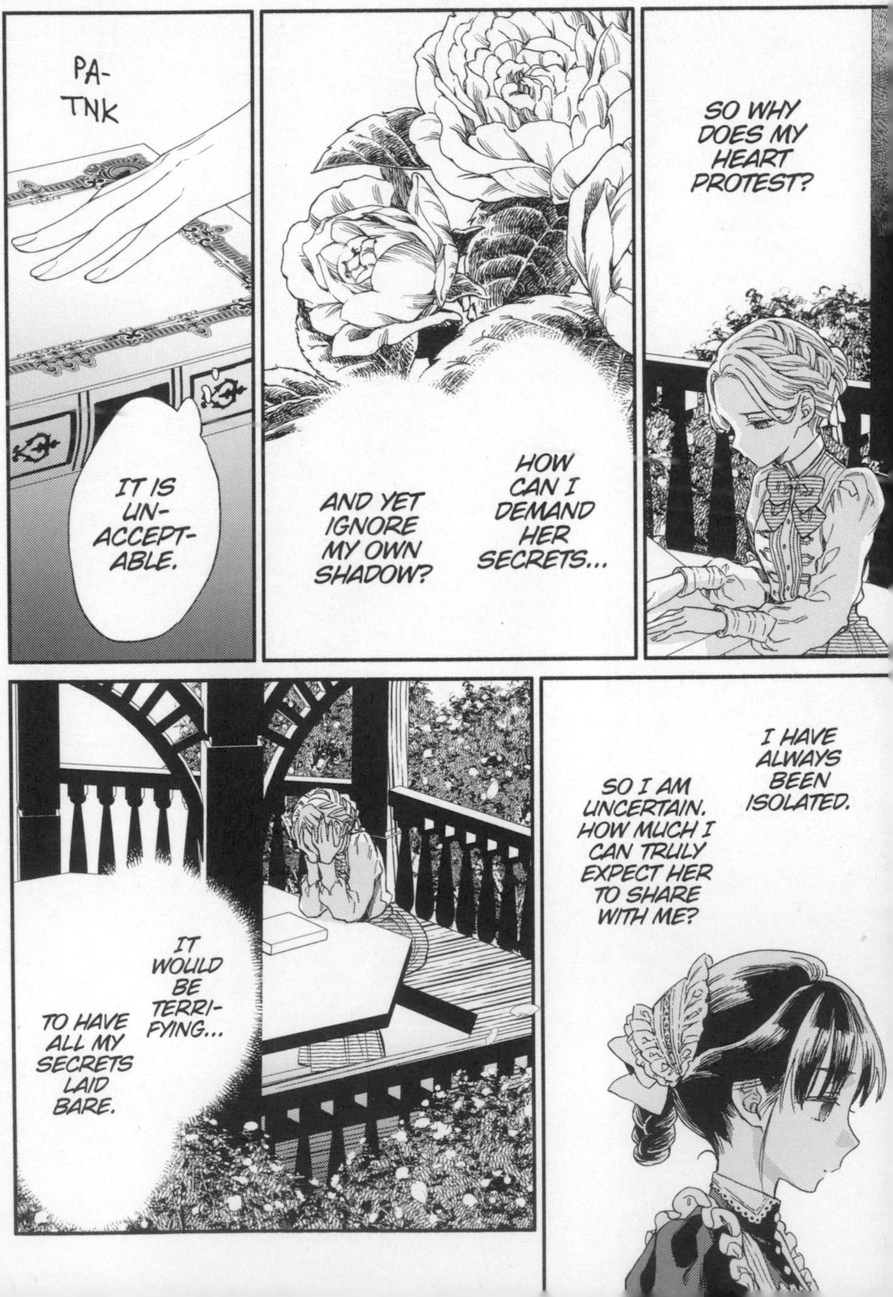
SO WHY DOES MY HEART PROTEST?
HOW CAN I DEMAND HER SECRETS...
AND YET IGNORE MY OWN SHADOW?
PA-TNK
IT IS UN-ACCEPT-ABLE.
I HAVE ALWAYS BEEN ISOLATED.
SO I AM UNCERTAIN. HOW MUCH I CAN TRULY EXPECT HER TO SHARE WITH ME?
IT WOULD BE TERRI-FYING...
TO HAVE ALL MY SECRETS LAID BARE.

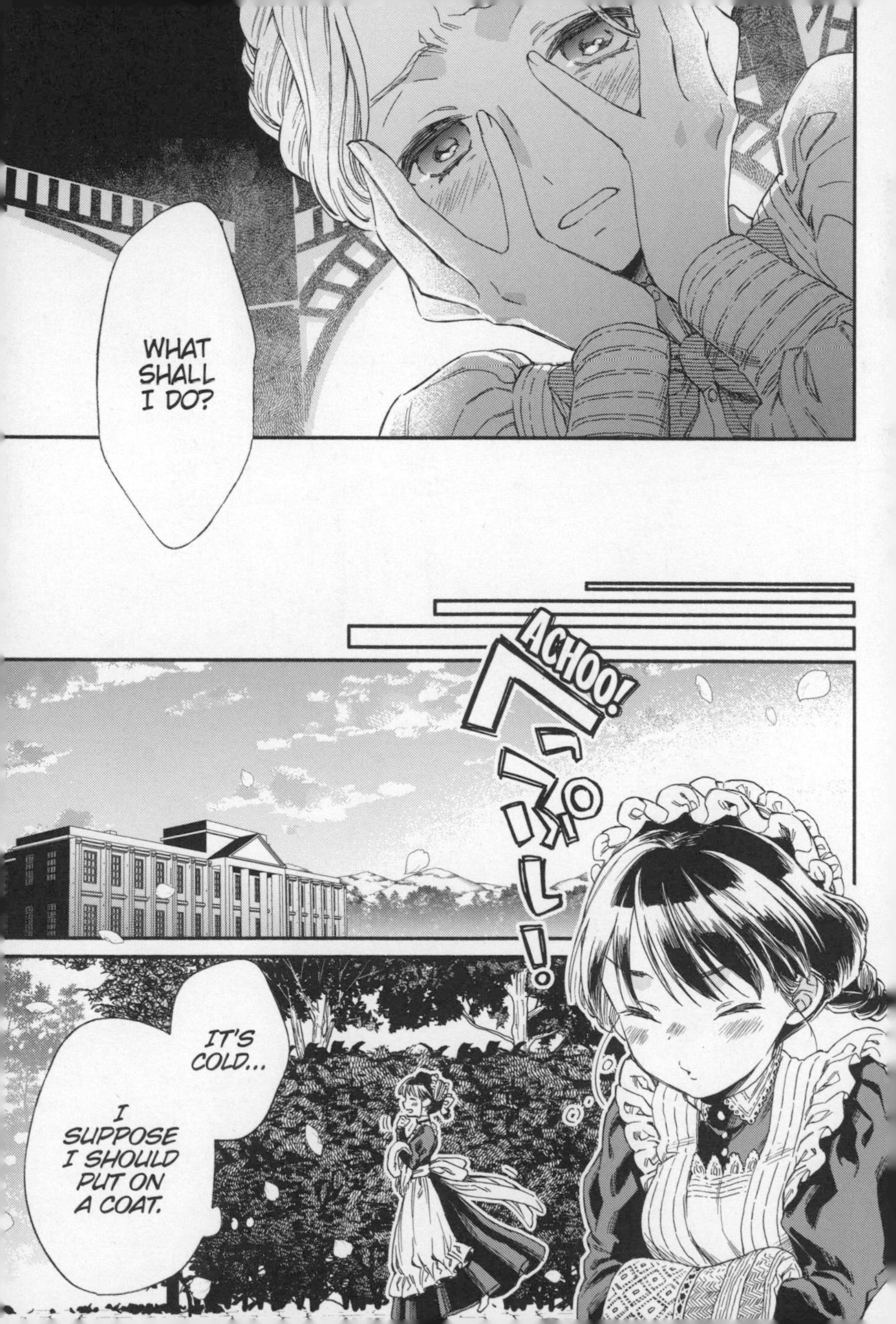
WHAT SHALL I DO?
ACHOO!
IT'S COLD...
I SUPPOSE I SHOULD PUT ON A COAT.

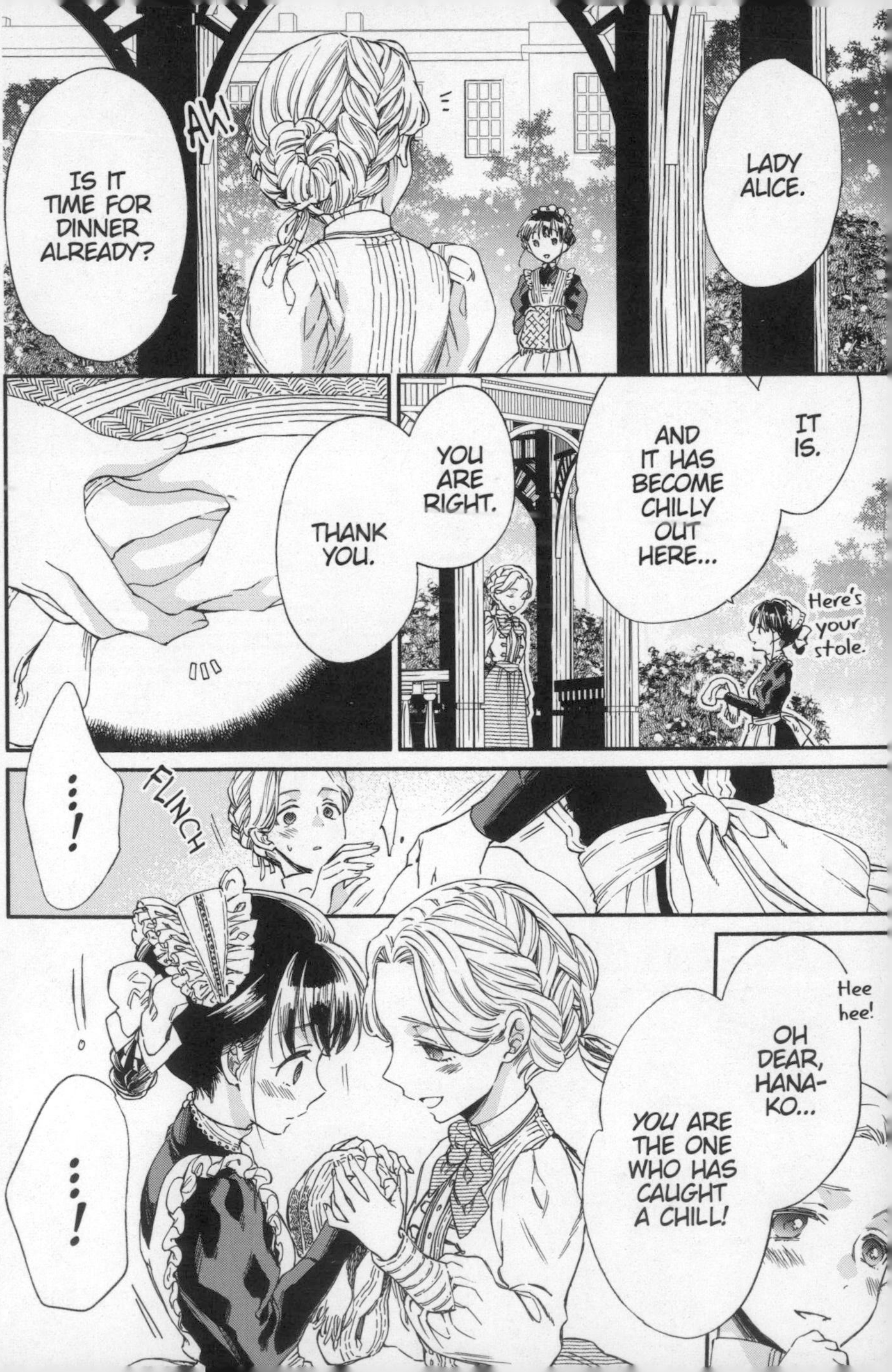
LADY ALICE.
AH!
IS IT TIME FOR DINNER ALREADY?
IT IS.
AND IT HAS BECOME CHILLY OUT HERE...
Here's your stole.
YOU ARE RIGHT.
THANK YOU.
FLINCH
...!
Hee hee!
OH DEAR, HANAKO...
YOU ARE THE ONE WHO HAS CAUGHT A CHILL!
...!

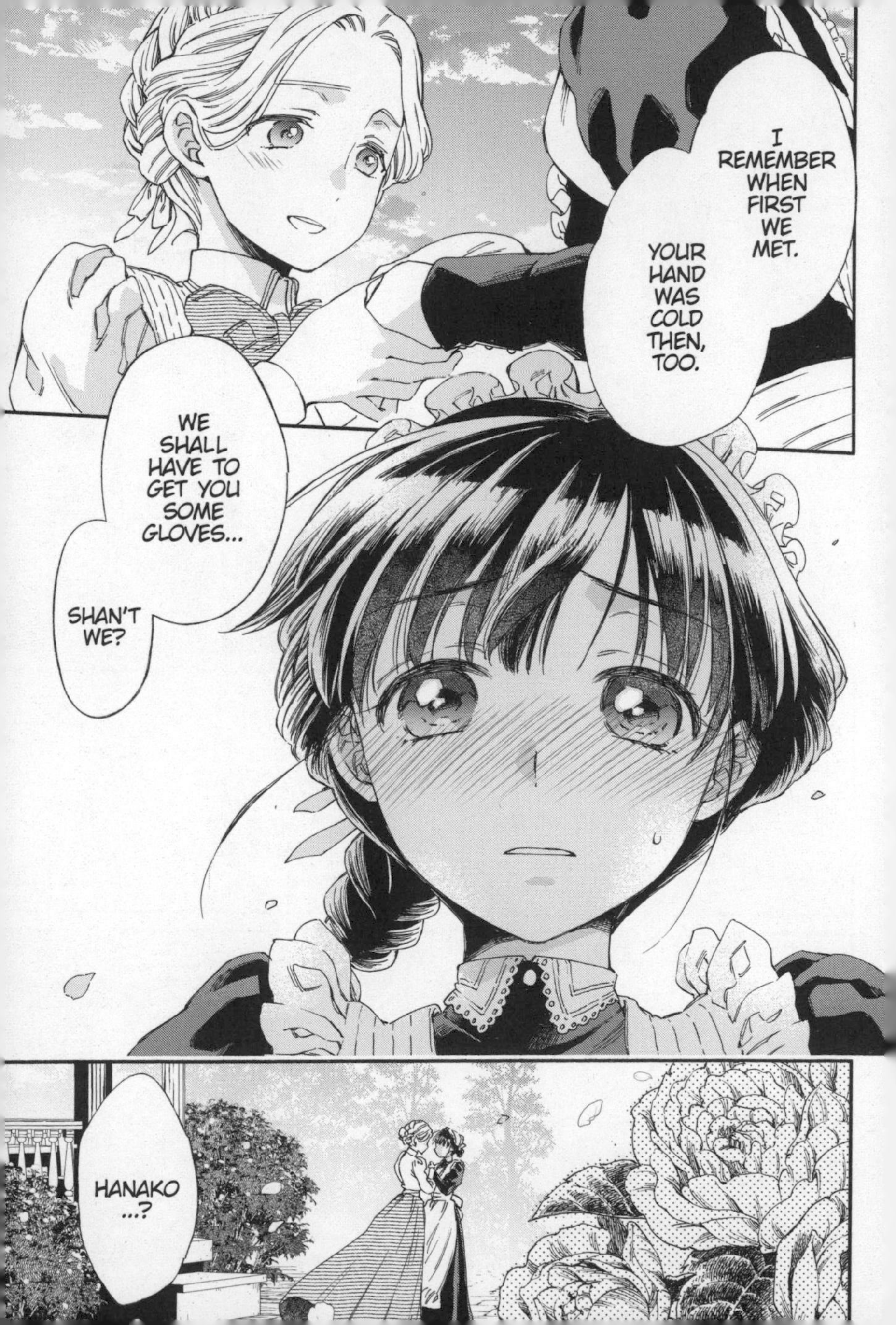
I REMEMBER WHEN FIRST WE MET.
YOUR HAND WAS COLD THEN, TOO.
WE SHALL HAVE TO GET YOU SOME GLOVES...
SHAN'T WE?
HANAKO ...?

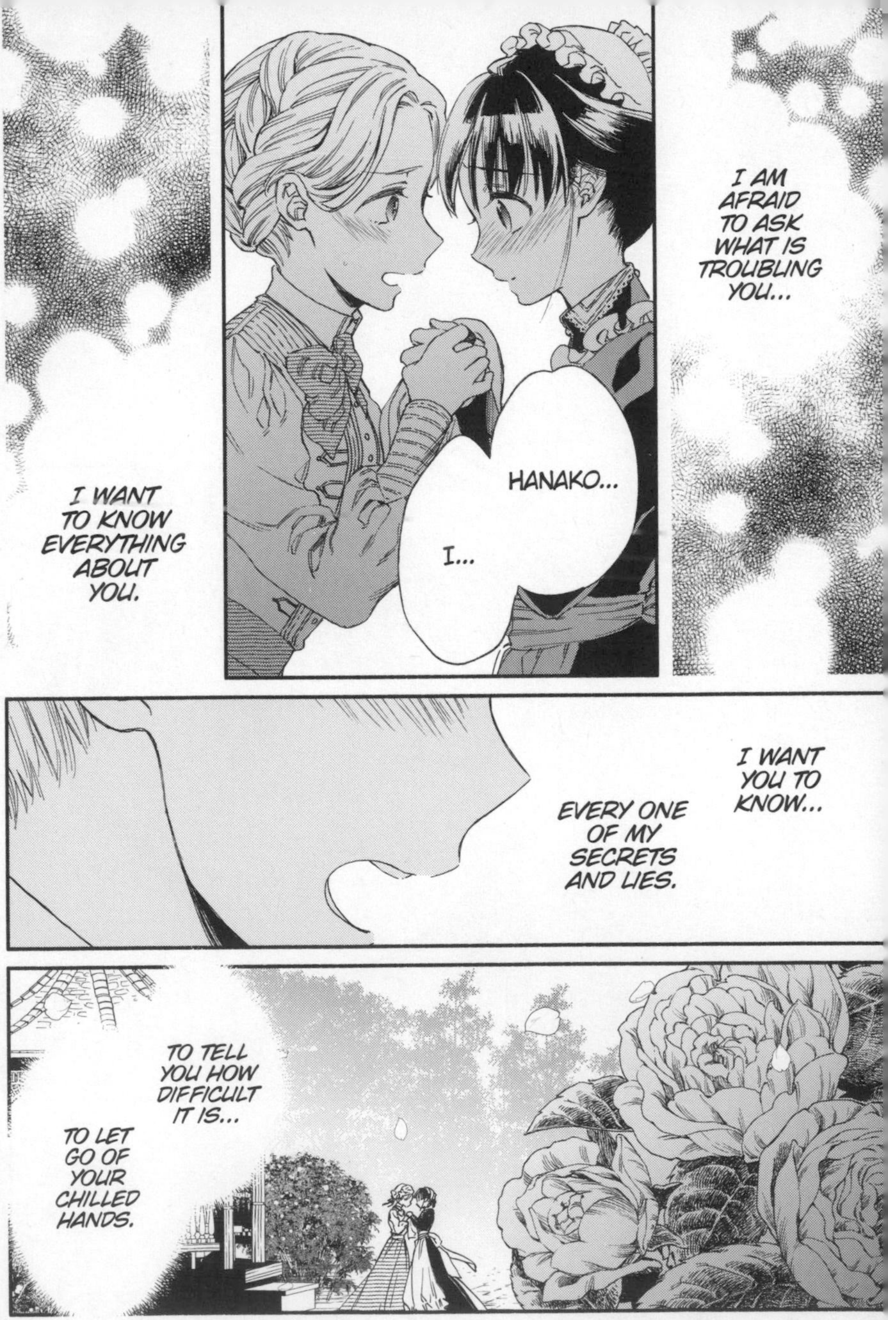

I AM AFRAID TO ASK WHAT IS TROUBLING YOU...
HANAKO...
I...
I WANT TO KNOW EVERYTHING ABOUT YOU.
I WANT YOU TO KNOW...
EVERY ONE OF MY SECRETS AND LIES.
TO TELL YOU HOW DIFFICULT IT IS...
TO LET GO OF YOUR CHILLED HANDS.

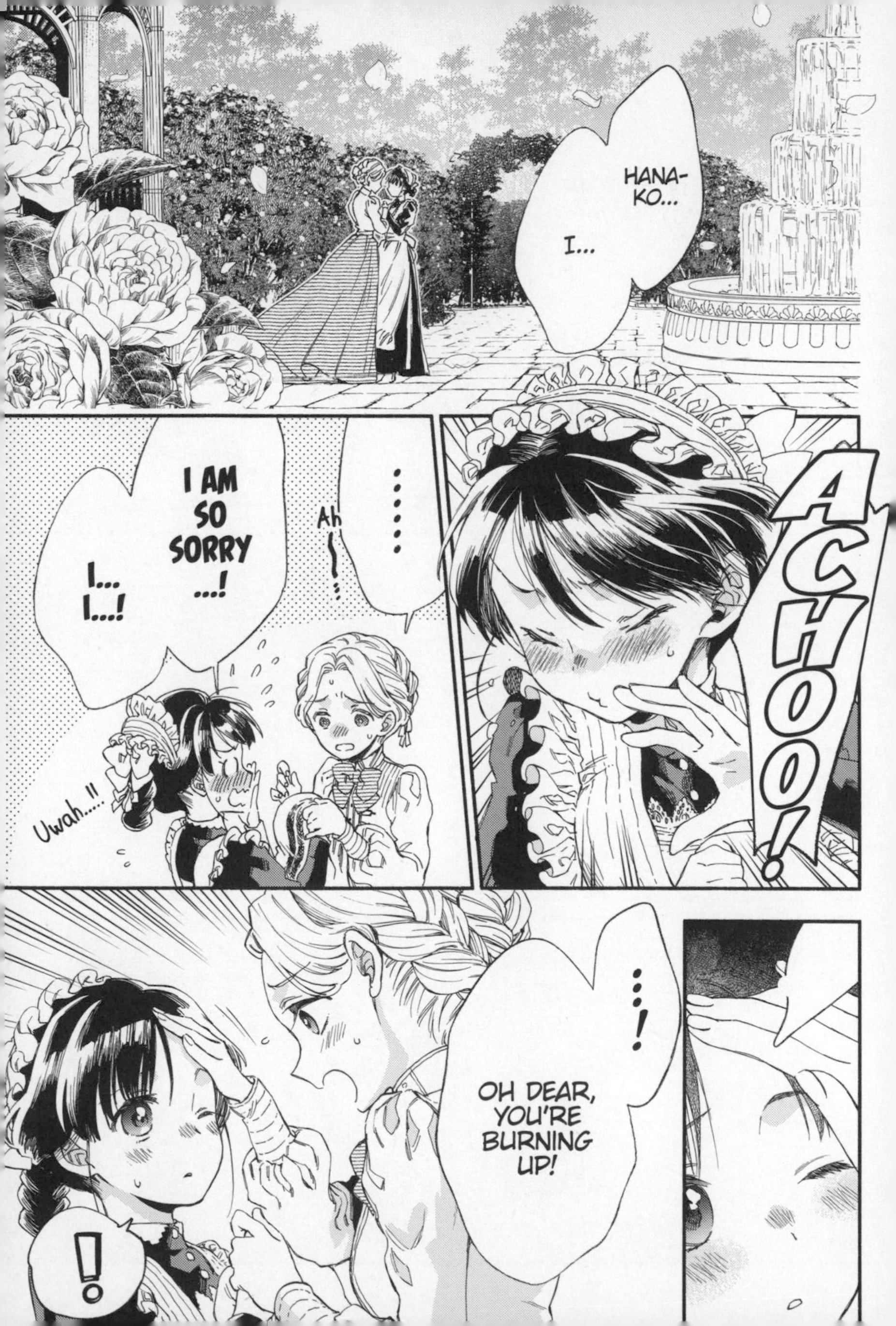
HANA-KO...
I...
ACHOO!
......
Ah~...
I AM SO SORRY...!
I... I...!
Uwah...!!
...!
OH DEAR, YOU'RE BURNING UP!
!

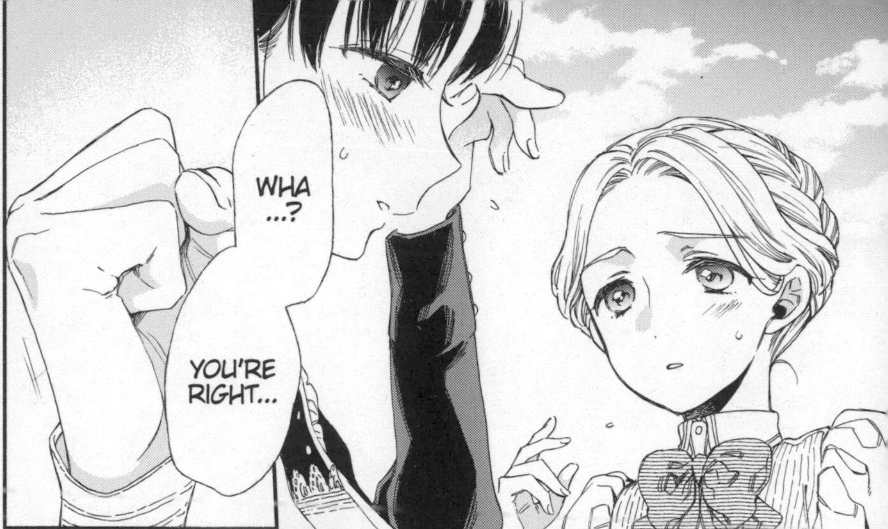
WHA ...?
YOU'RE RIGHT...
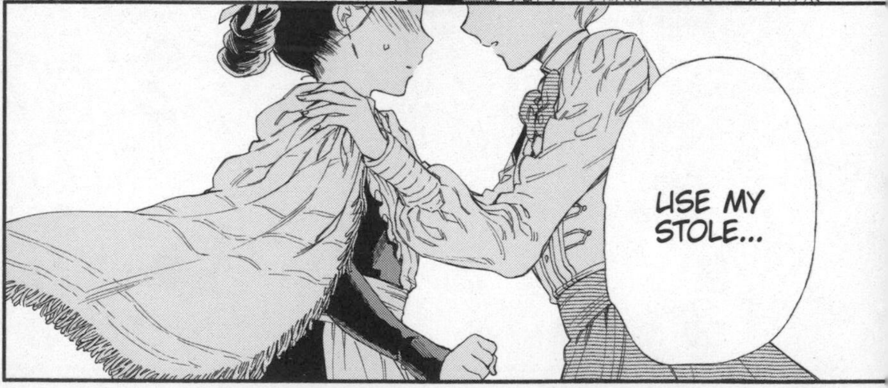
USE MY STOLE...
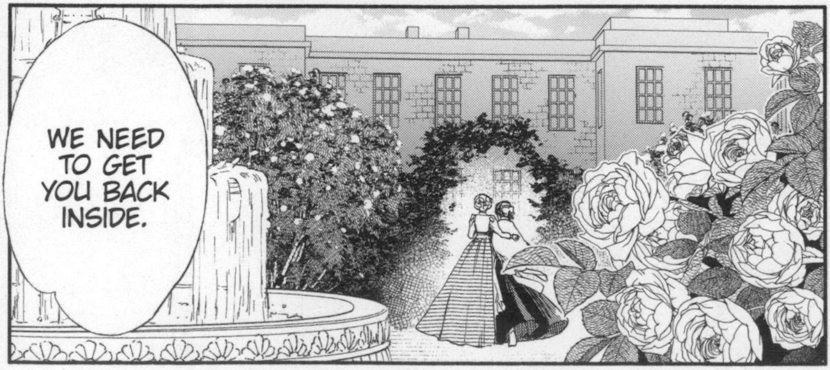
WE NEED TO GET YOU BACK INSIDE.

{ Chapter 8 }
The Flames of Cowardice Incinerate Your Heart

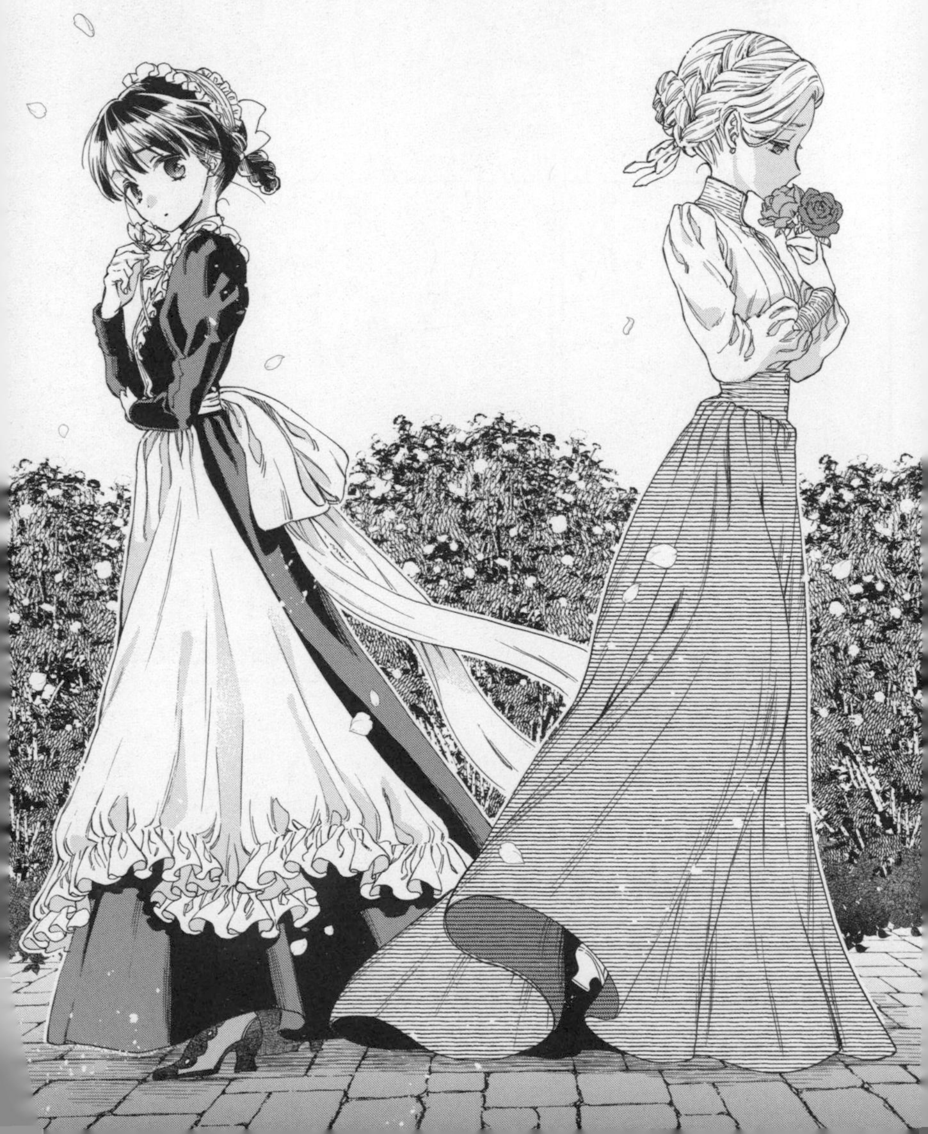

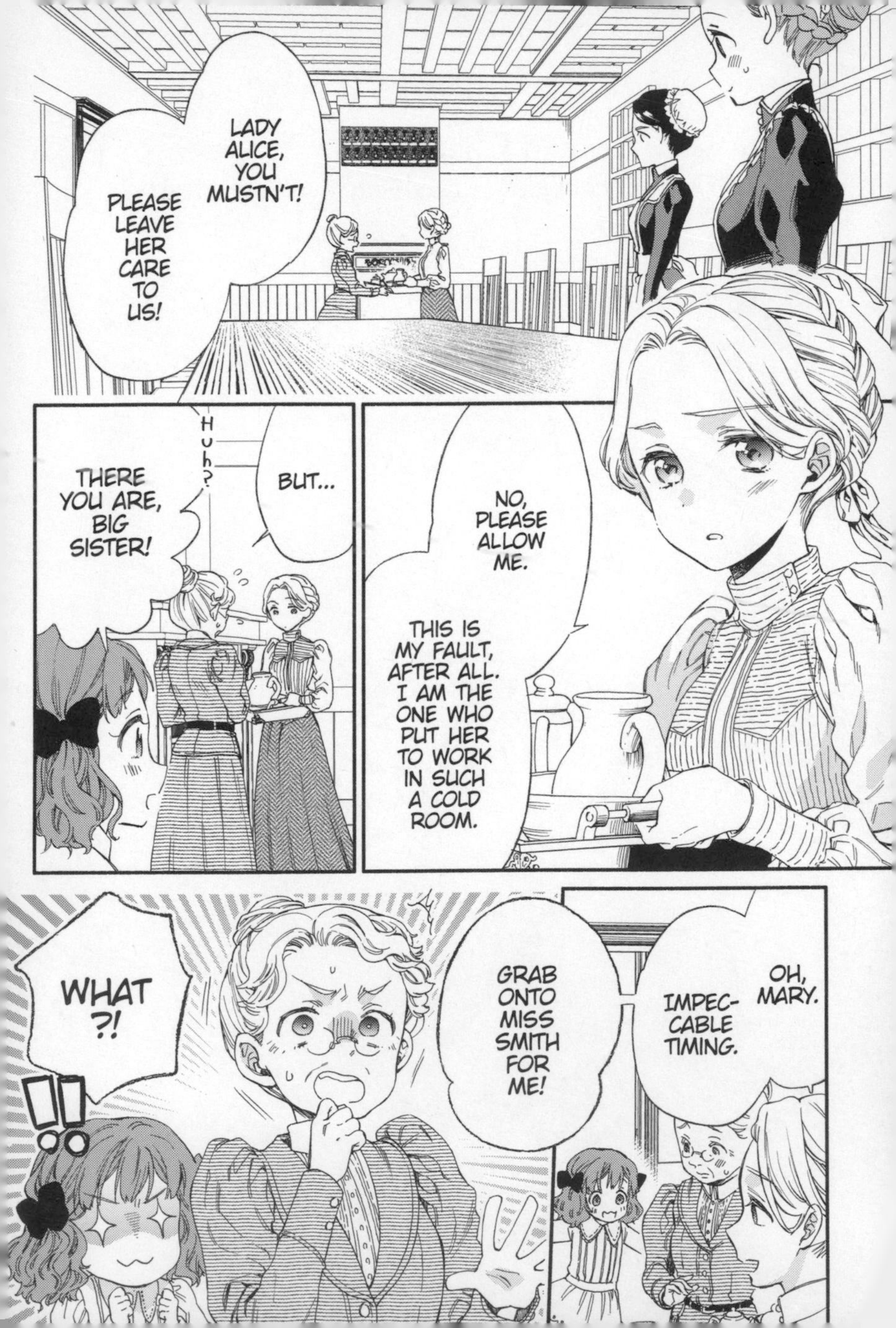
LADY ALICE, YOU MUSTN'T!
PLEASE LEAVE HER CARE TO US!
NO, PLEASE ALLOW ME.
THIS IS MY FAULT, AFTER ALL. I AM THE ONE WHO PUT HER TO WORK IN SUCH A COLD ROOM.
BUT...
Huh?
THERE YOU ARE, BIG SISTER!
OH, MARY.
IMPEC-CABLE TIMING.
GRAB ONTO MISS SMITH FOR ME!
WHAT?!
!!

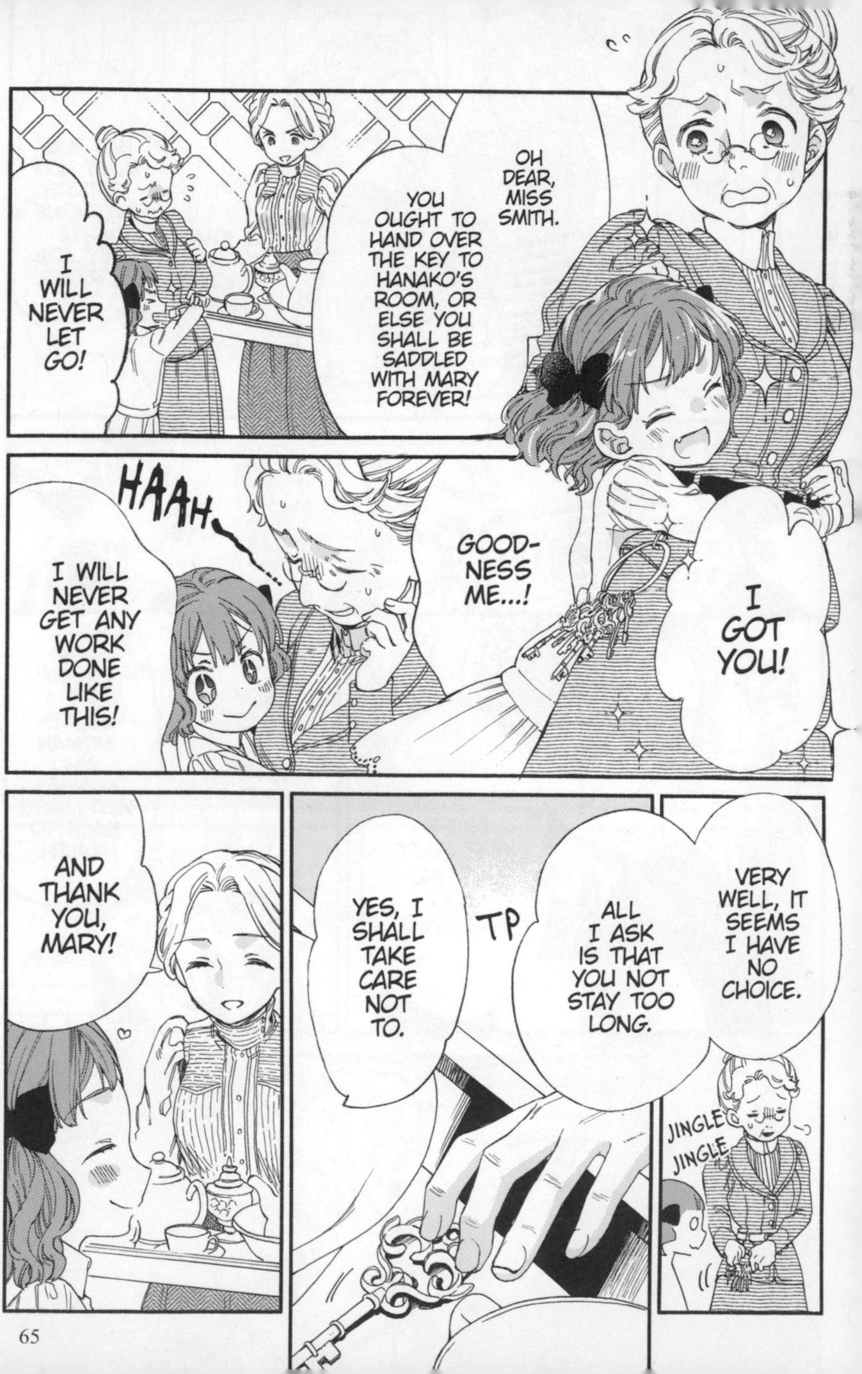
OH DEAR, MISS SMITH.
YOU OUGHT TO HAND OVER THE KEY TO HANAKO'S ROOM, OR ELSE YOU SHALL BE SADDLED WITH MARY FOREVER!
I WILL NEVER LET GO!
I GOT YOU!
GOODNESS ME...!
HAAAH
I WILL NEVER GET ANY WORK DONE LIKE THIS!
VERY WELL, IT SEEMS I HAVE NO CHOICE.
JINGLE
JINGLE
ALL I ASK IS THAT YOU NOT STAY TOO LONG.
TP
YES, I SHALL TAKE CARE NOT TO.
AND THANK YOU, MARY!

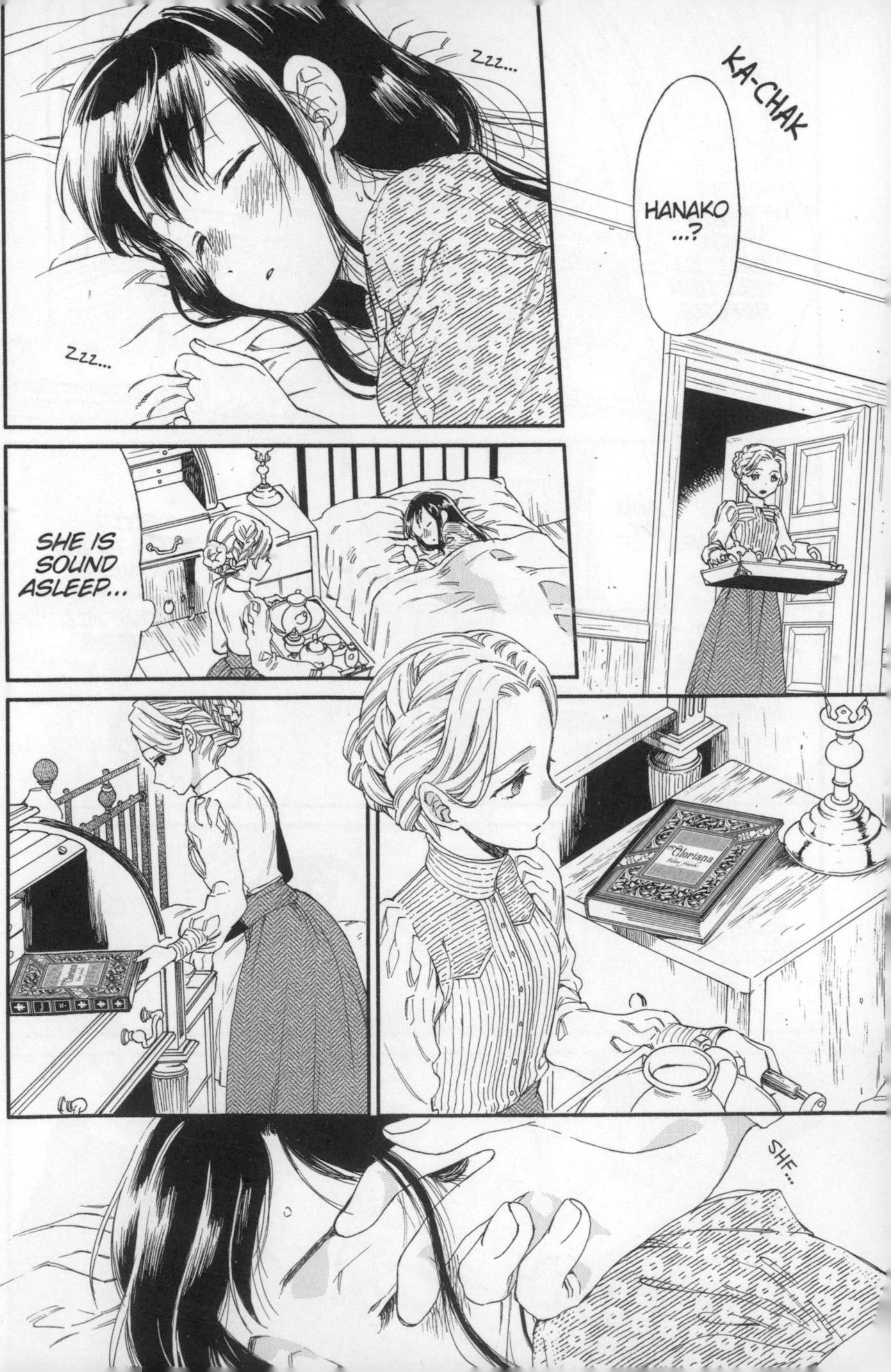
KA-CHAK
HANAKO ...?
Zzz...
Zzz...
SHE IS SOUND ASLEEP...
SHF...

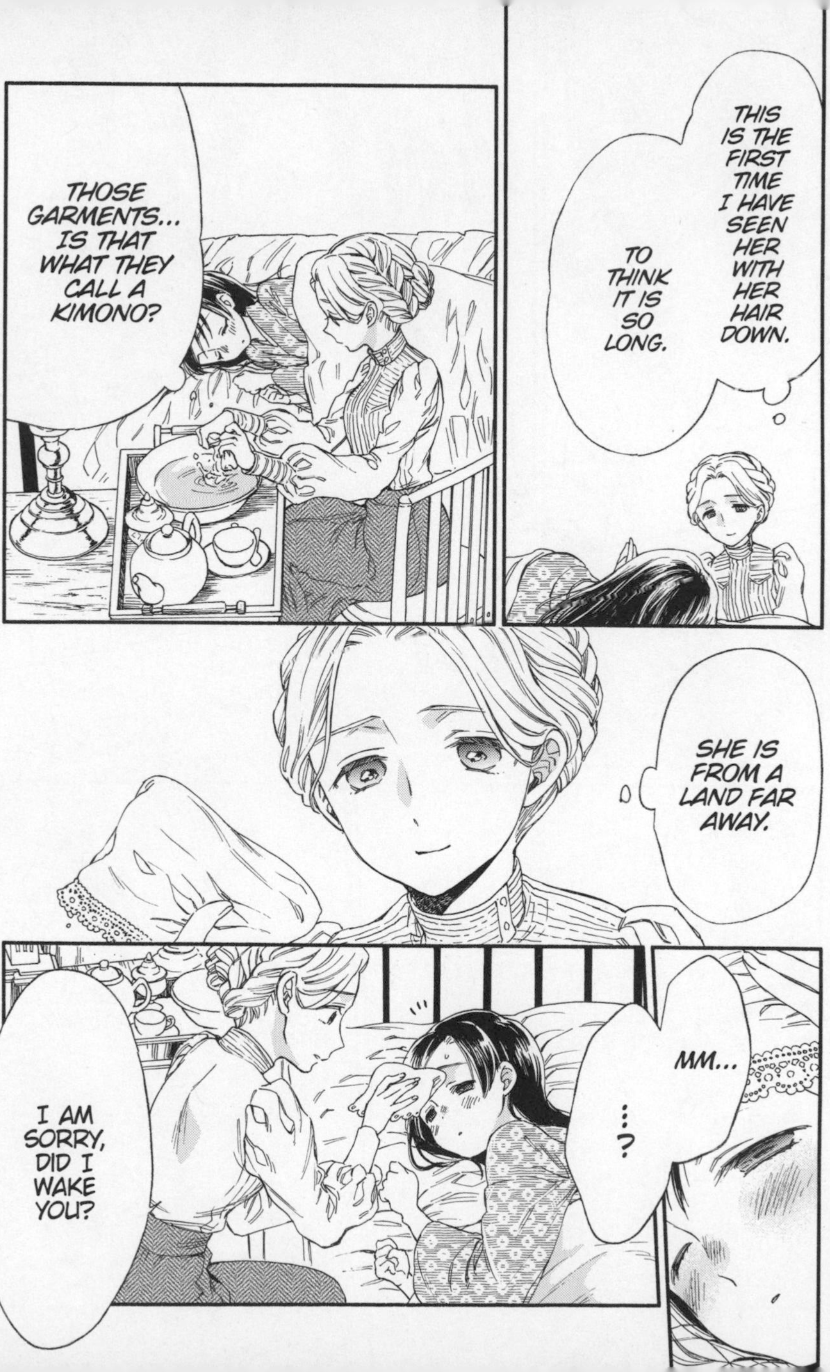
THIS IS THE FIRST TIME I HAVE SEEN HER WITH HER HAIR DOWN.
TO THINK IT IS SO LONG.
THOSE GARMENTS... IS THAT WHAT THEY CALL A KIMONO?
SHE IS FROM A LAND FAR AWAY.
MM...
...?
I AM SORRY, DID I WAKE YOU?

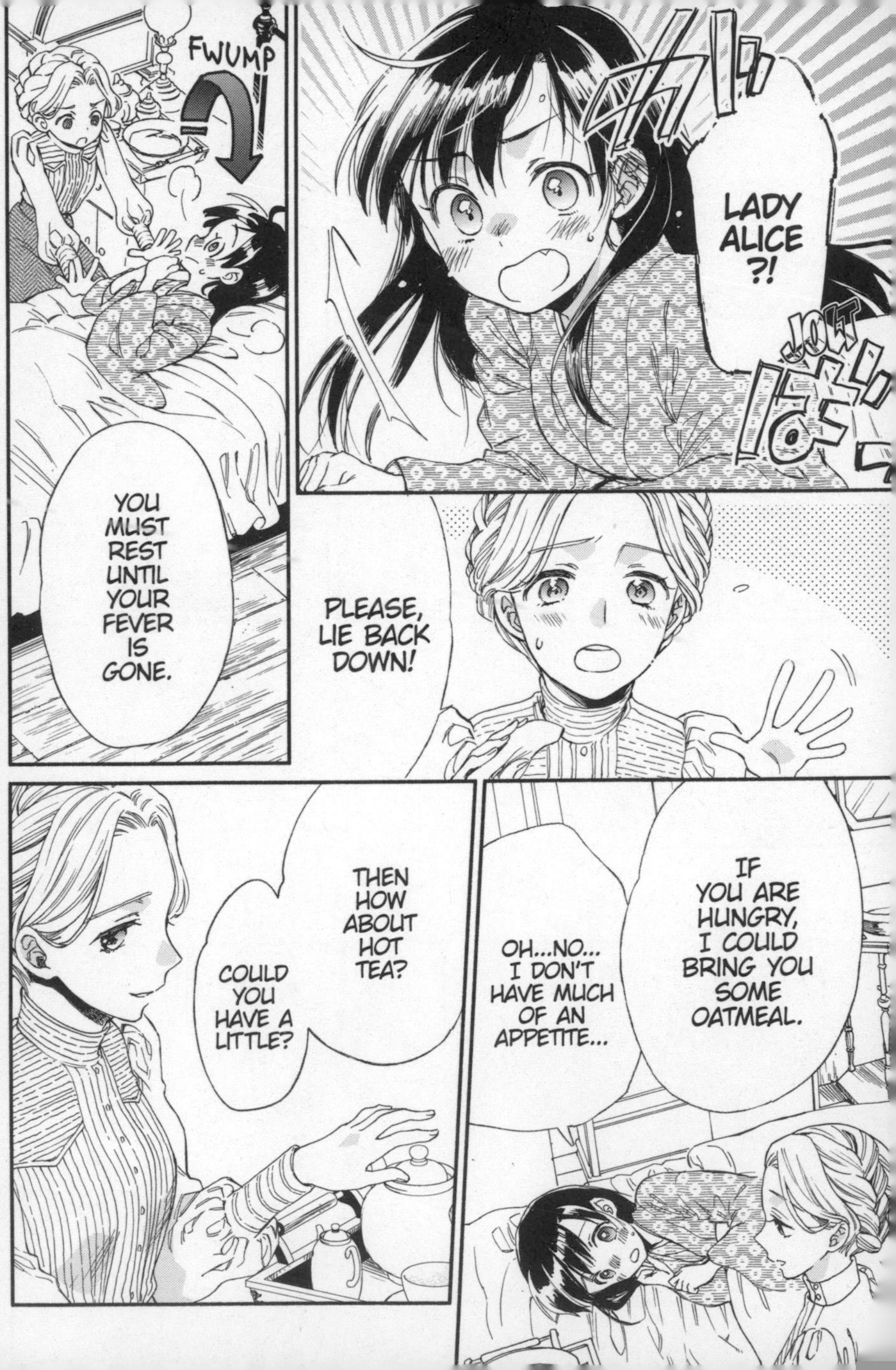
LADY ALICE ?!
JOLT
PLEASE, LIE BACK DOWN!
FWUMP
YOU MUST REST UNTIL YOUR FEVER IS GONE.
IF YOU ARE HUNGRY, I COULD BRING YOU SOME OATMEAL.
OH...NO... I DON'T HAVE MUCH OF AN APPETITE...
THEN HOW ABOUT HOT TEA?
COULD YOU HAVE A LITTLE?

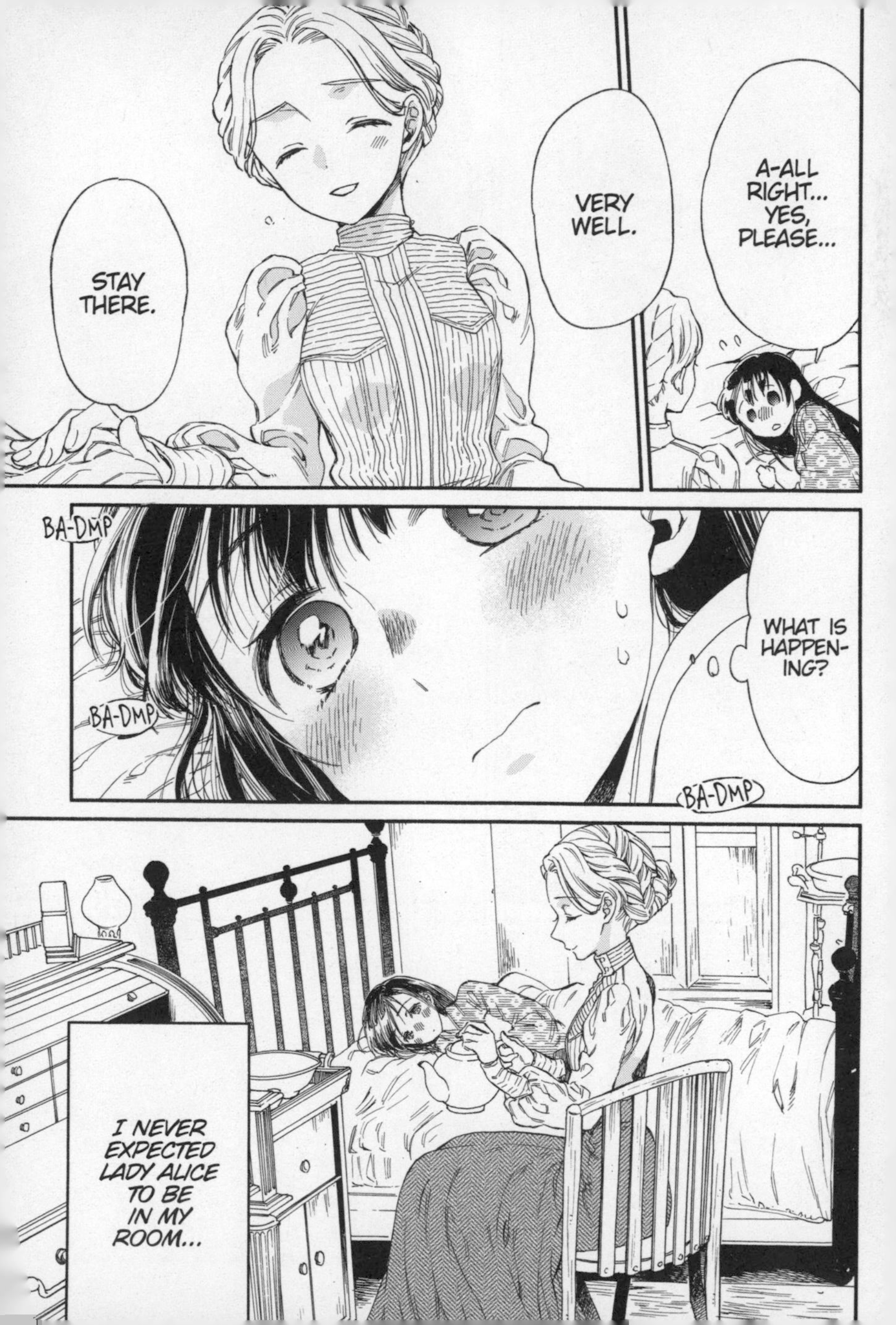
A-ALL RIGHT... YES, PLEASE...
VERY WELL.
STAY THERE.
WHAT IS HAPPENING?
BA-DMP
BA-DMP
BA-DMP
I NEVER EXPECTED LADY ALICE TO BE IN MY ROOM...

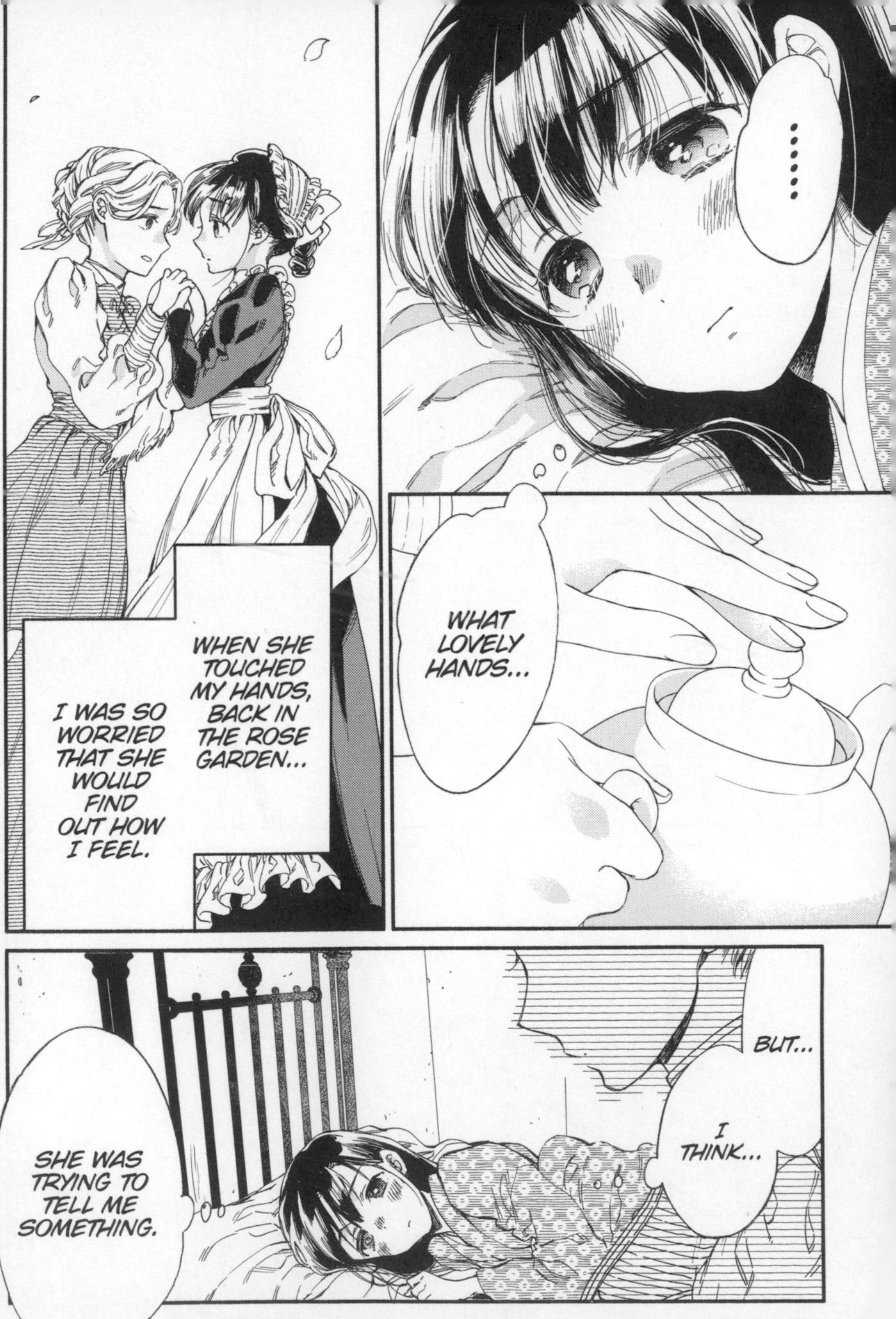
......
WHAT LOVELY HANDS...
WHEN SHE TOUCHED MY HANDS, BACK IN THE ROSE GARDEN...
I WAS SO WORRIED THAT SHE WOULD FIND OUT HOW I FEEL.
BUT...
I THINK...
SHE WAS TRYING TO TELL ME SOMETHING.

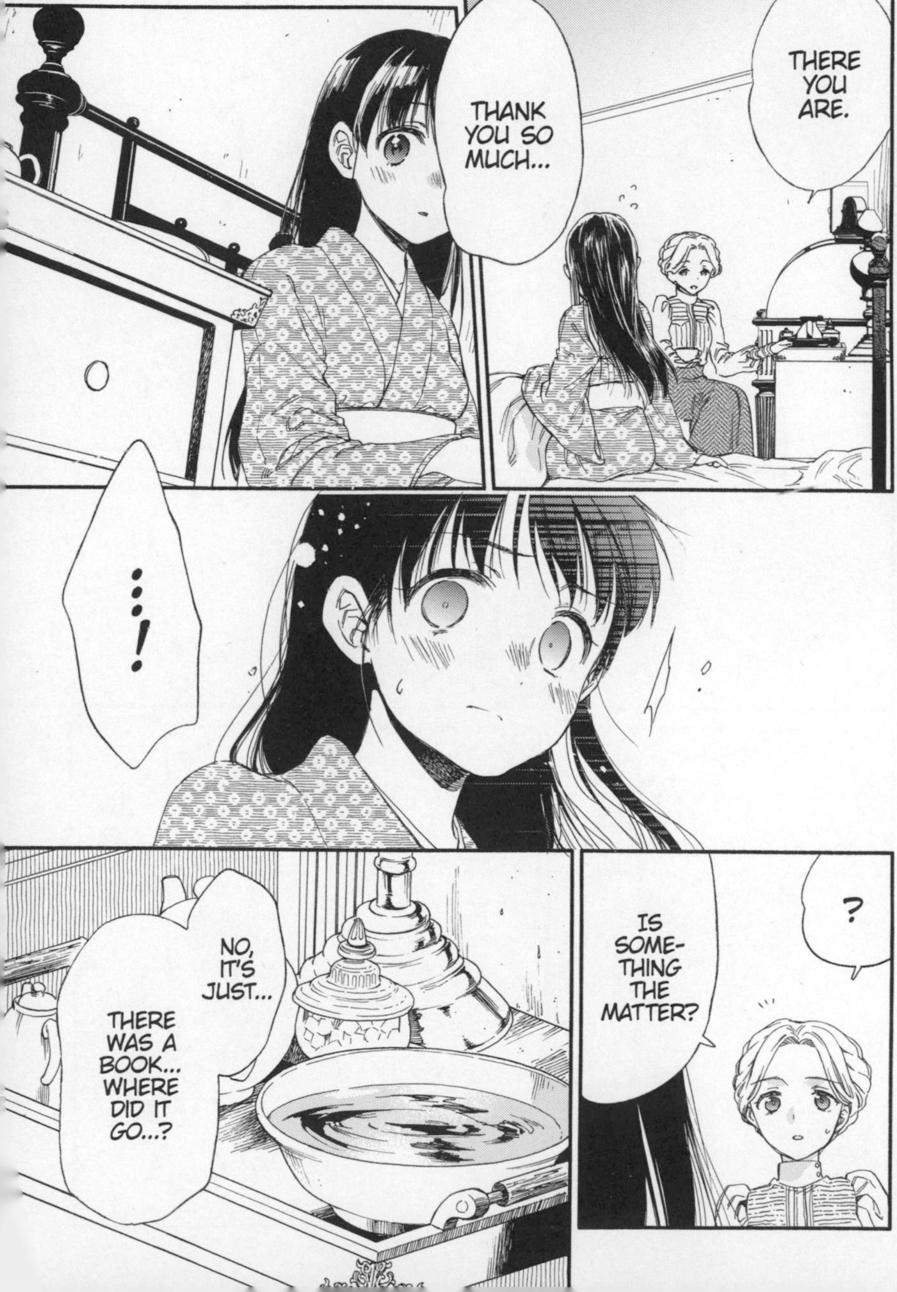
THERE YOU ARE.
THANK YOU SO MUCH...
...!
?
IS SOME-THING THE MATTER?
NO, IT'S JUST...
THERE WAS A BOOK... WHERE DID IT GO...?

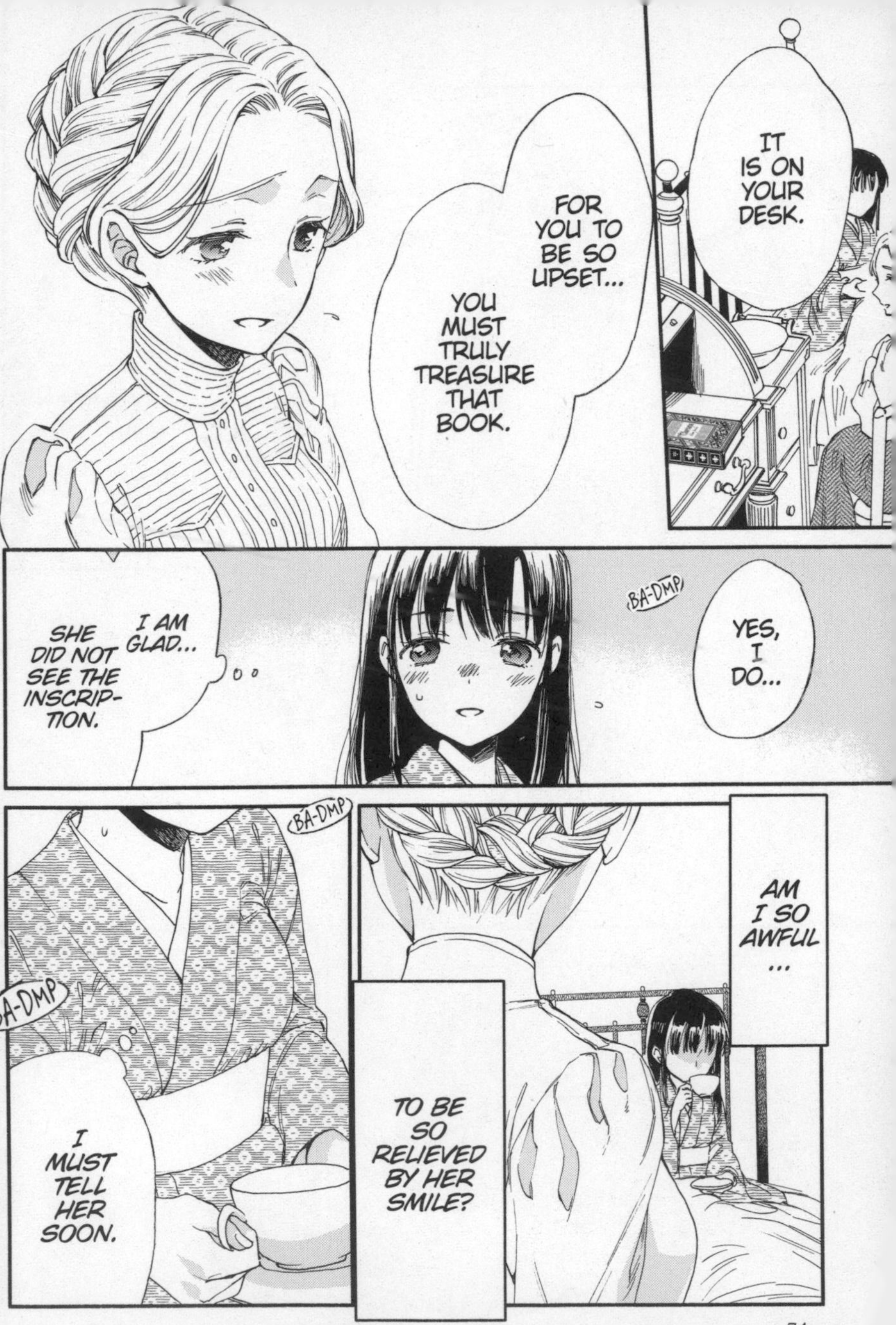
IT IS ON YOUR DESK.
FOR YOU TO BE SO UPSET...
YOU MUST TRULY TREASURE THAT BOOK.
BA-DMP
YES, I DO...
I AM GLAD...
SHE DID NOT SEE THE INSCRIPTION.
AM I SO AWFUL ...
TO BE SO RELIEVED BY HER SMILE?
BA-DMP
BA-DMP
I MUST TELL HER SOON.

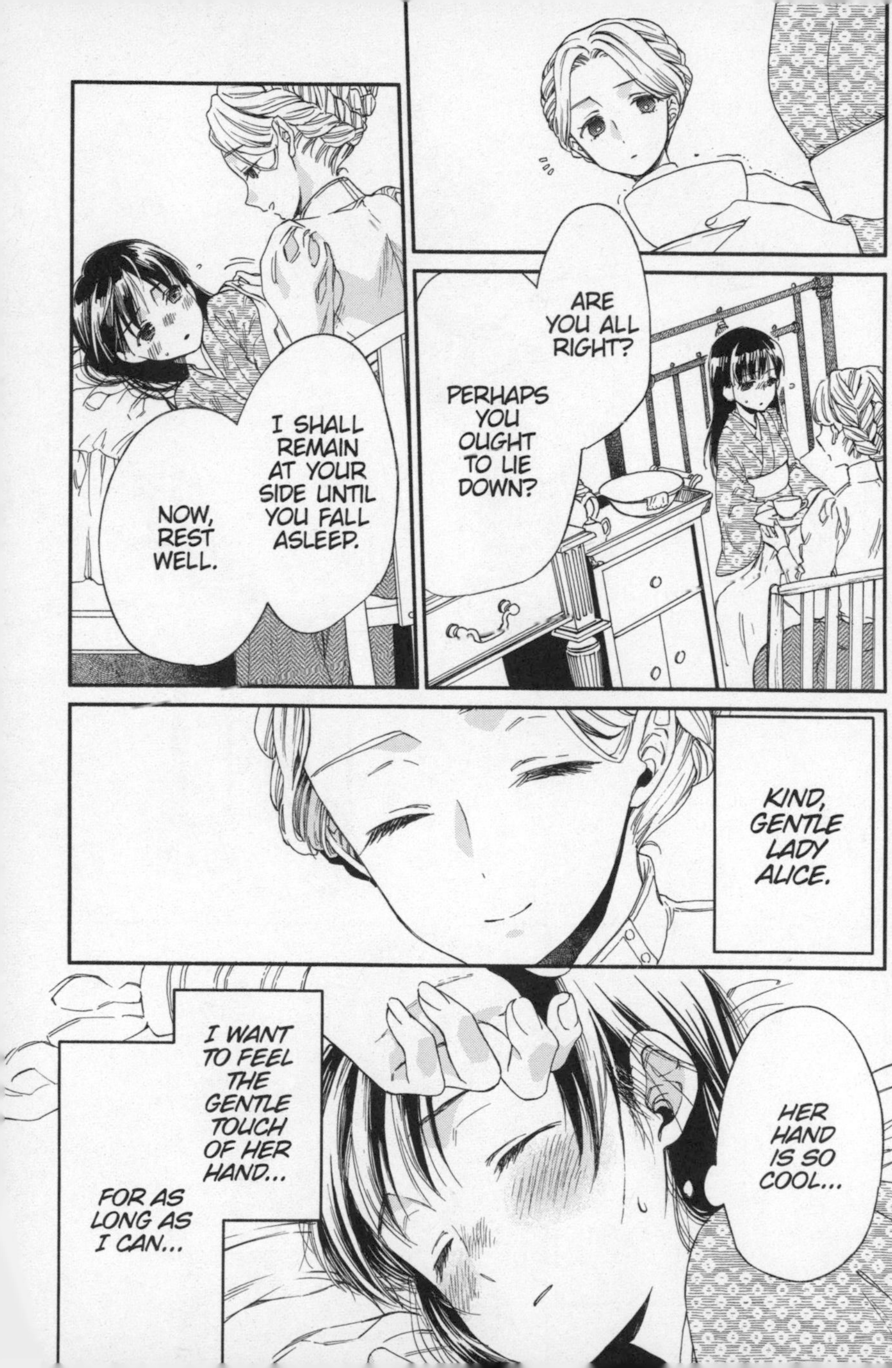
ARE YOU ALL RIGHT?
PERHAPS YOU OUGHT TO LIE DOWN?
I SHALL REMAIN AT YOUR SIDE UNTIL YOU FALL ASLEEP.
NOW, REST WELL.
KIND, GENTLE LADY ALICE.
HER HAND IS SO COOL...
I WANT TO FEEL THE GENTLE TOUCH OF HER HAND...
FOR AS LONG AS I CAN...

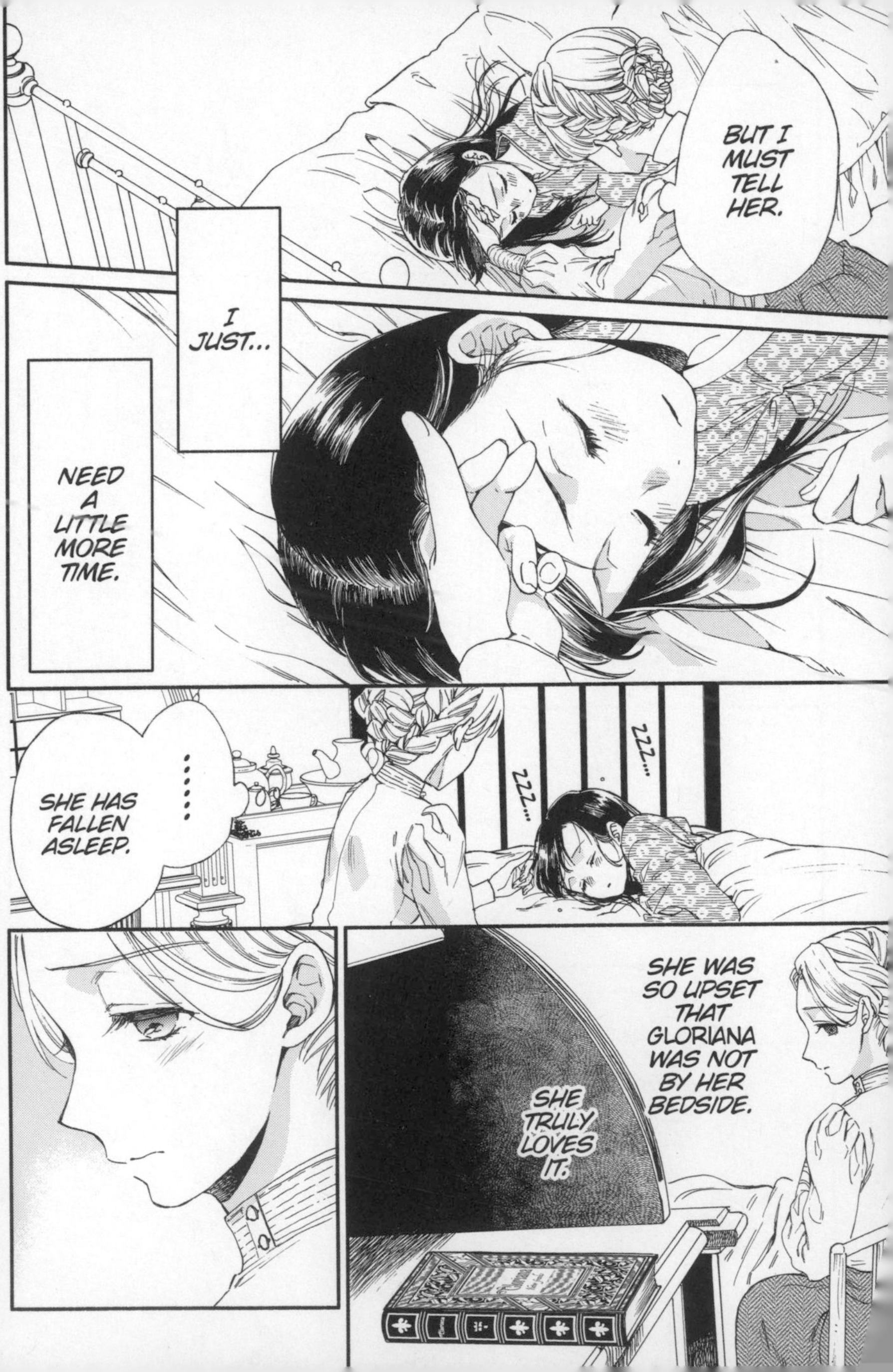
BUT I MUST TELL HER.
I JUST...
NEED A LITTLE MORE TIME.
ZZZ...
ZZZ...
......
SHE HAS FALLEN ASLEEP.
SHE WAS SO UPSET THAT GLORIANA WAS NOT BY HER BEDSIDE.
SHE TRULY LOVES IT.

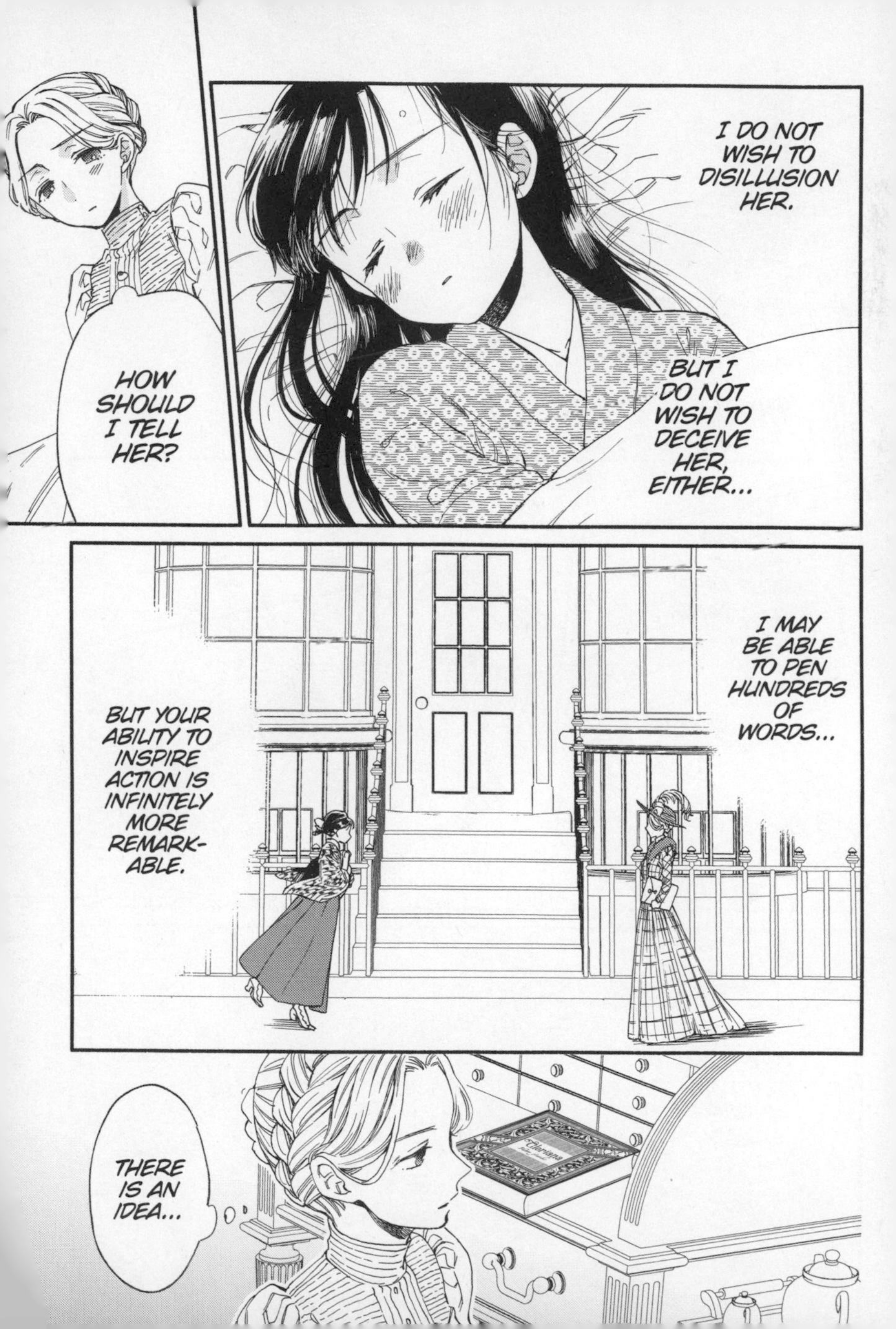
I DO NOT WISH TO DISILLUSION HER.
BUT I DO NOT WISH TO DECEIVE HER, EITHER...
HOW SHOULD I TELL HER?
I MAY BE ABLE TO PEN HUNDREDS OF WORDS...
BUT YOUR ABILITY TO INSPIRE ACTION IS INFINITELY MORE REMARK-ABLE.
THERE IS AN IDEA...

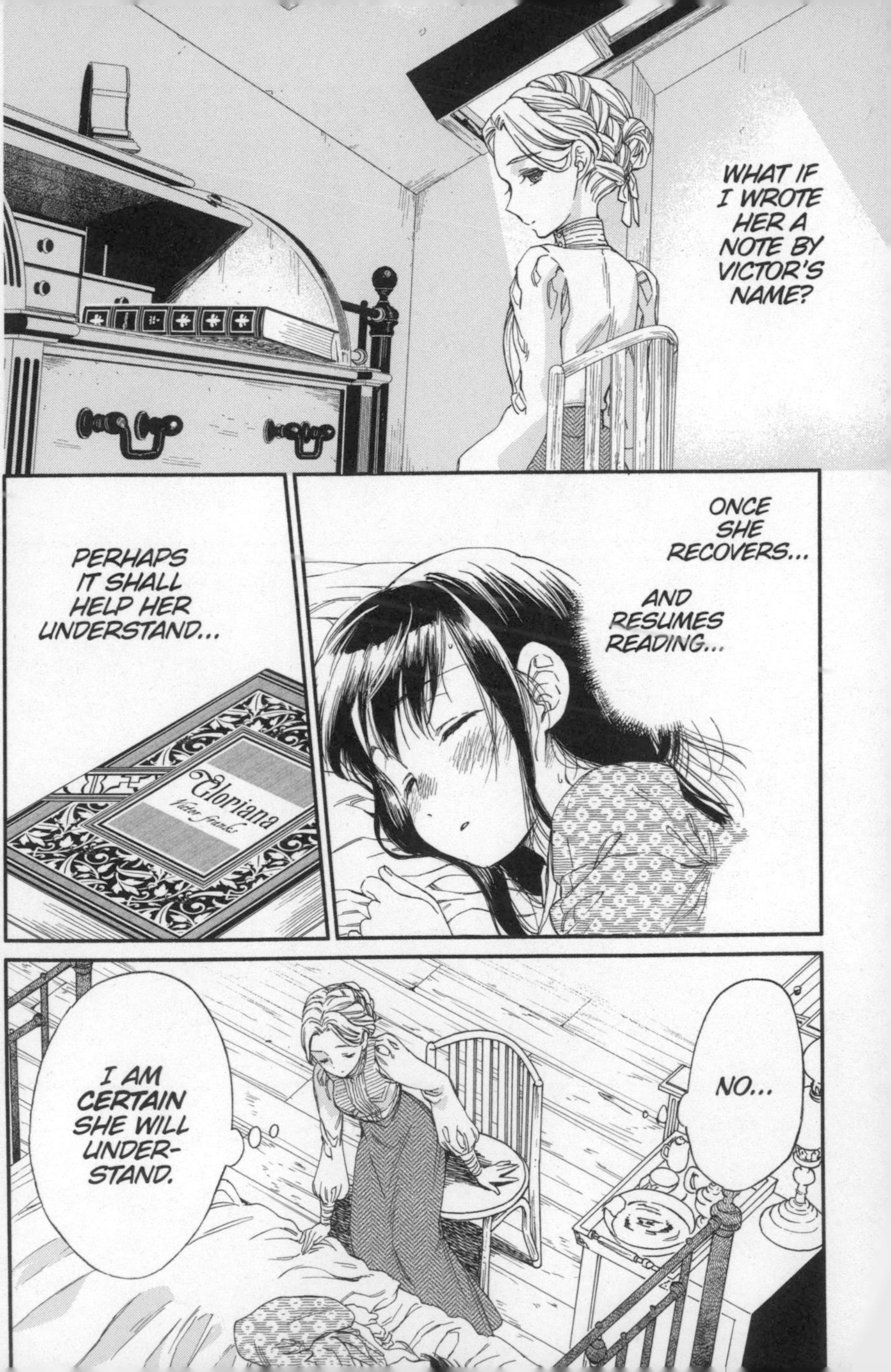

WHAT IF I WROTE HER A NOTE BY VICTOR'S NAME?
ONCE SHE RECOVERS...
AND RESUMES READING...
PERHAPS IT SHALL HELP HER UNDERSTAND...
Gloriana
Victor Franks
NO...
I AM CERTAIN SHE WILL UNDER-STAND.

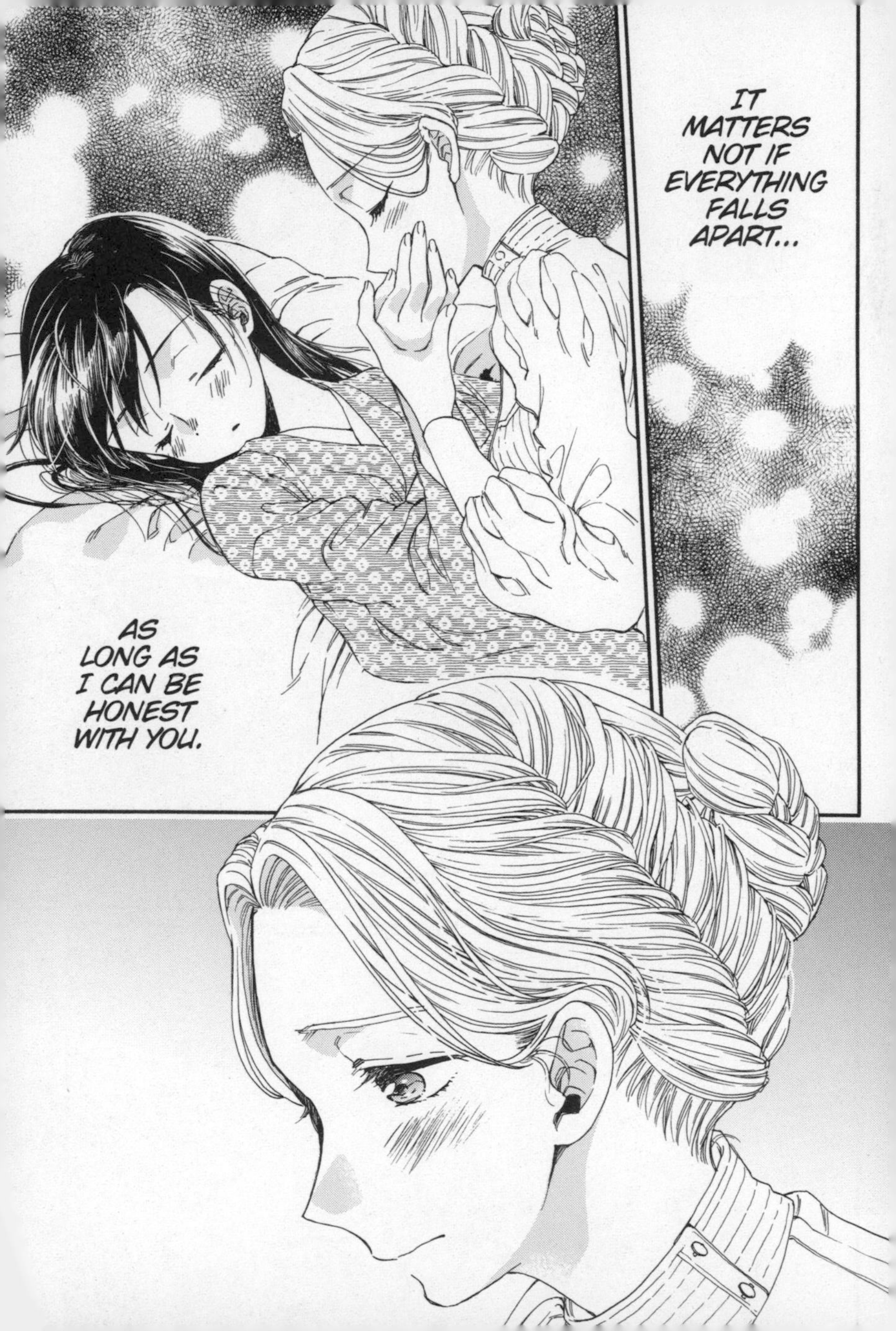
IT MATTERS NOT IF EVERYTHING FALLS APART...
AS LONG AS I CAN BE HONEST WITH YOU.

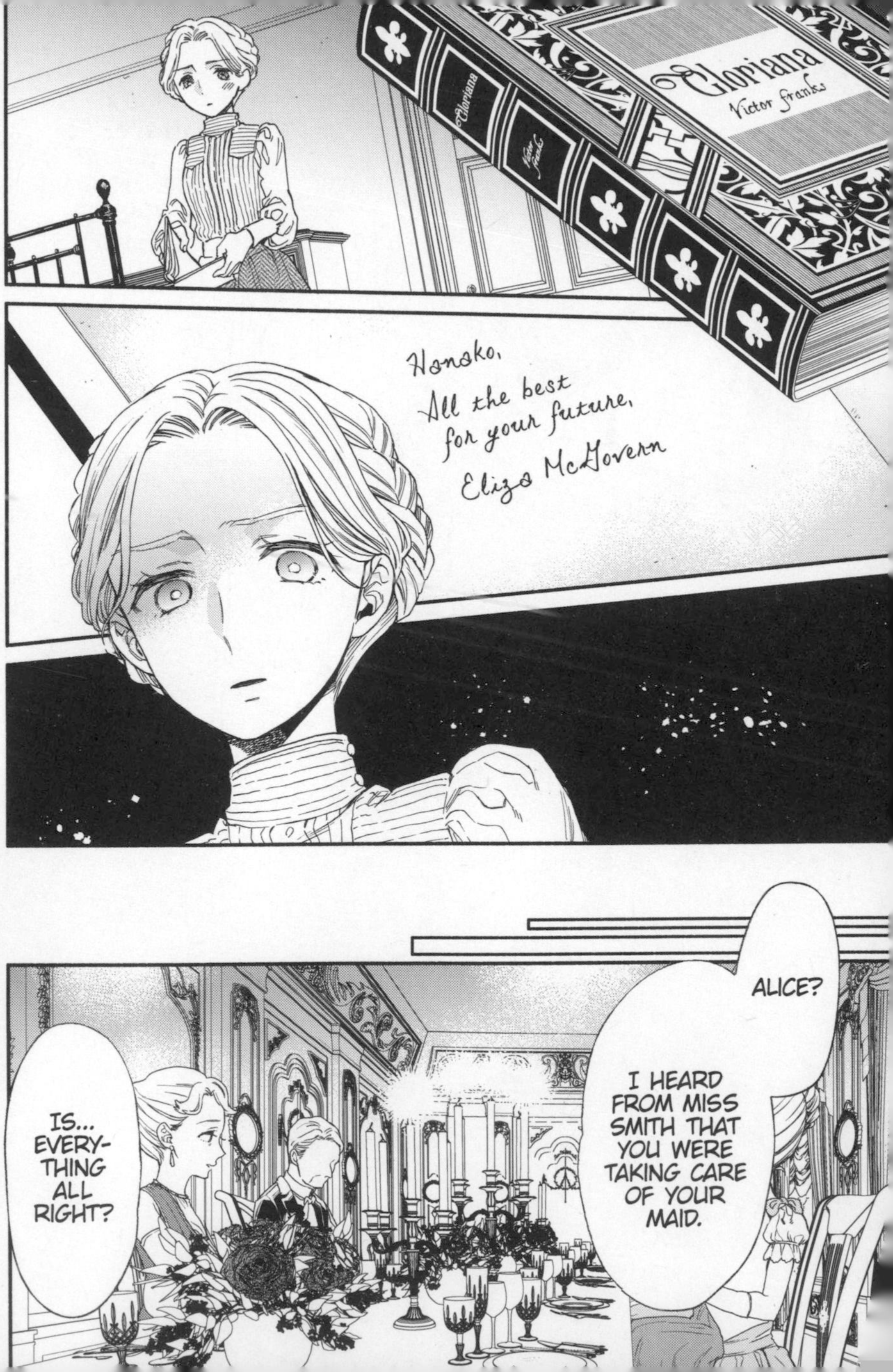
Gloriana
Victor franks
Hanako,
All the best
for your future,
Eliza McGovern
ALICE?
I HEARD FROM MISS SMITH THAT YOU WERE TAKING CARE OF YOUR MAID.
IS... EVERYTHING ALL RIGHT?

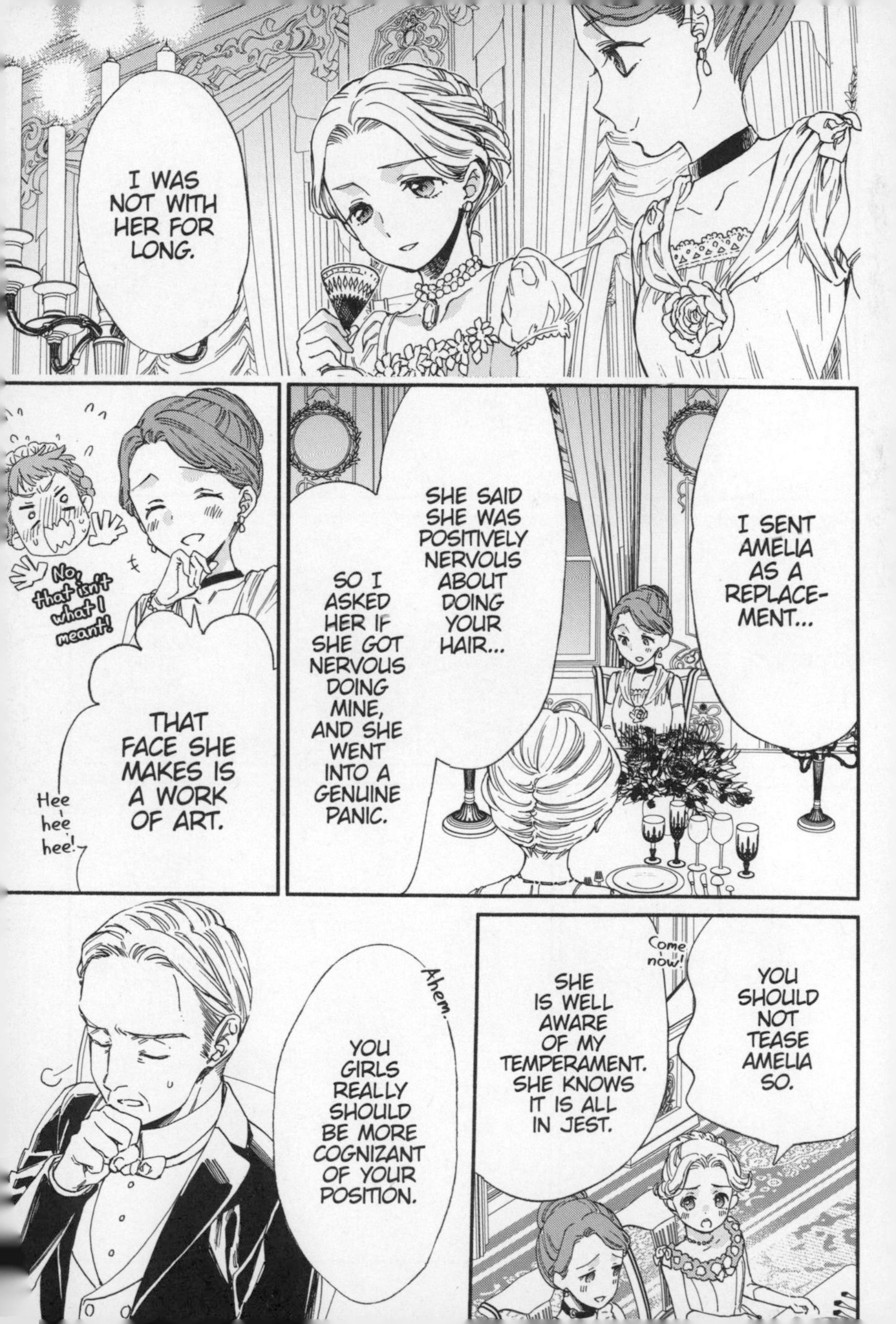
I WAS NOT WITH HER FOR LONG.
I SENT AMELIA AS A REPLACEMENT...
SHE SAID SHE WAS POSITIVELY NERVOUS ABOUT DOING YOUR HAIR...
SO I ASKED HER IF SHE GOT NERVOUS DOING MINE, AND SHE WENT INTO A GENUINE PANIC.
THAT FACE SHE MAKES IS A WORK OF ART.
Hee hee hee!
No, that isn't what I meant!
YOU SHOULD NOT TEASE AMELIA SO.
Come now!
SHE IS WELL AWARE OF MY TEMPERAMENT. SHE KNOWS IT IS ALL IN JEST.
Ahem.
YOU GIRLS REALLY SHOULD BE MORE COGNIZANT OF YOUR POSITION.

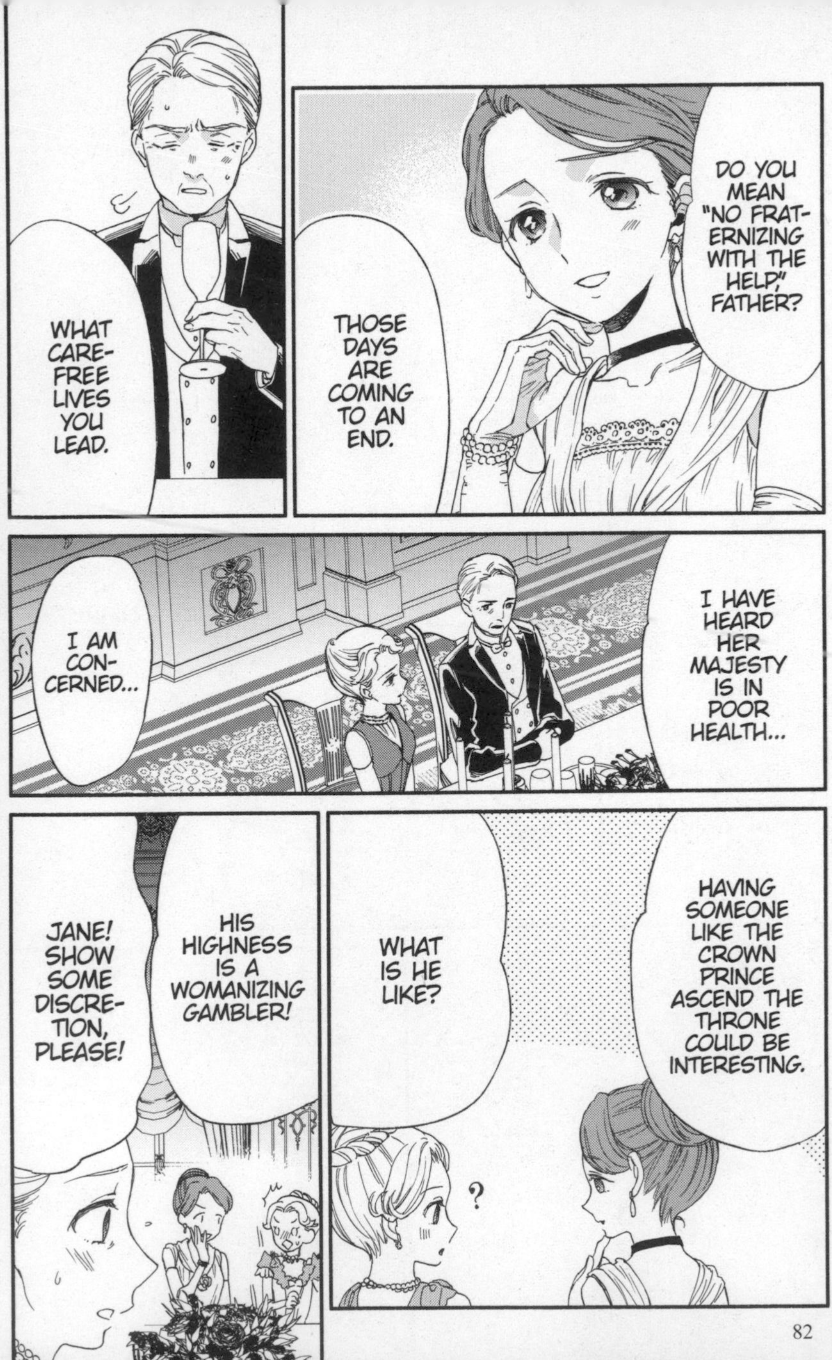
DO YOU MEAN "NO FRAT-ERNIZING WITH THE HELP," FATHER?
THOSE DAYS ARE COMING TO AN END.
WHAT CARE-FREE LIVES YOU LEAD.
I HAVE HEARD HER MAJESTY IS IN POOR HEALTH...
I AM CON-CERNED...
HAVING SOMEONE LIKE THE CROWN PRINCE ASCEND THE THRONE COULD BE INTERESTING.
WHAT IS HE LIKE?
?
HIS HIGHNESS IS A WOMANIZING GAMBLER!
JANE! SHOW SOME DISCRE-TION, PLEASE!

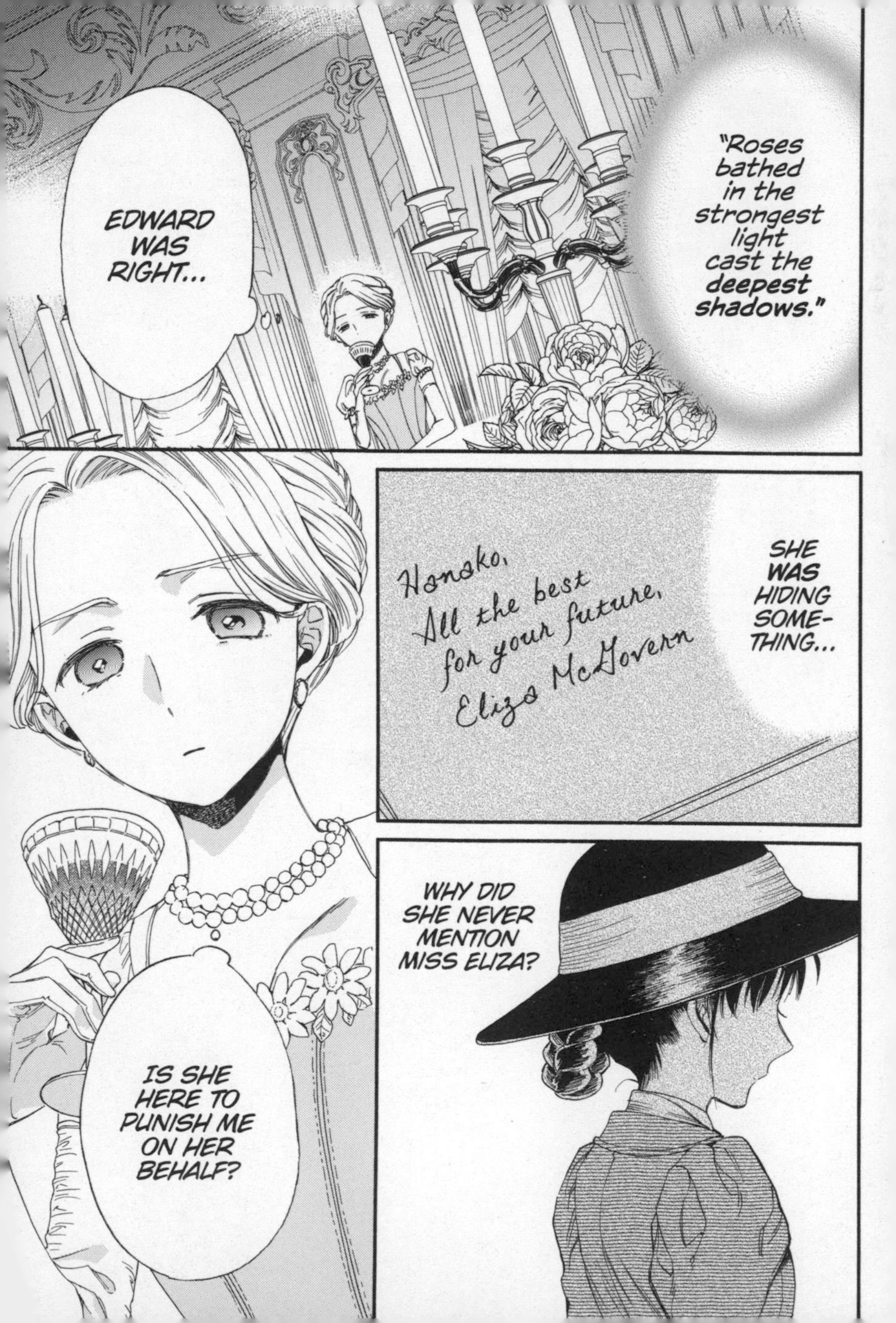
"Roses bathed in the strongest light cast the deepest shadows."
EDWARD WAS RIGHT...
SHE WAS HIDING SOME-THING...
Hanako,
All the best for your future,
Eliza McGovern
WHY DID SHE NEVER MENTION MISS ELIZA?
IS SHE HERE TO PUNISH ME ON HER BEHALF?

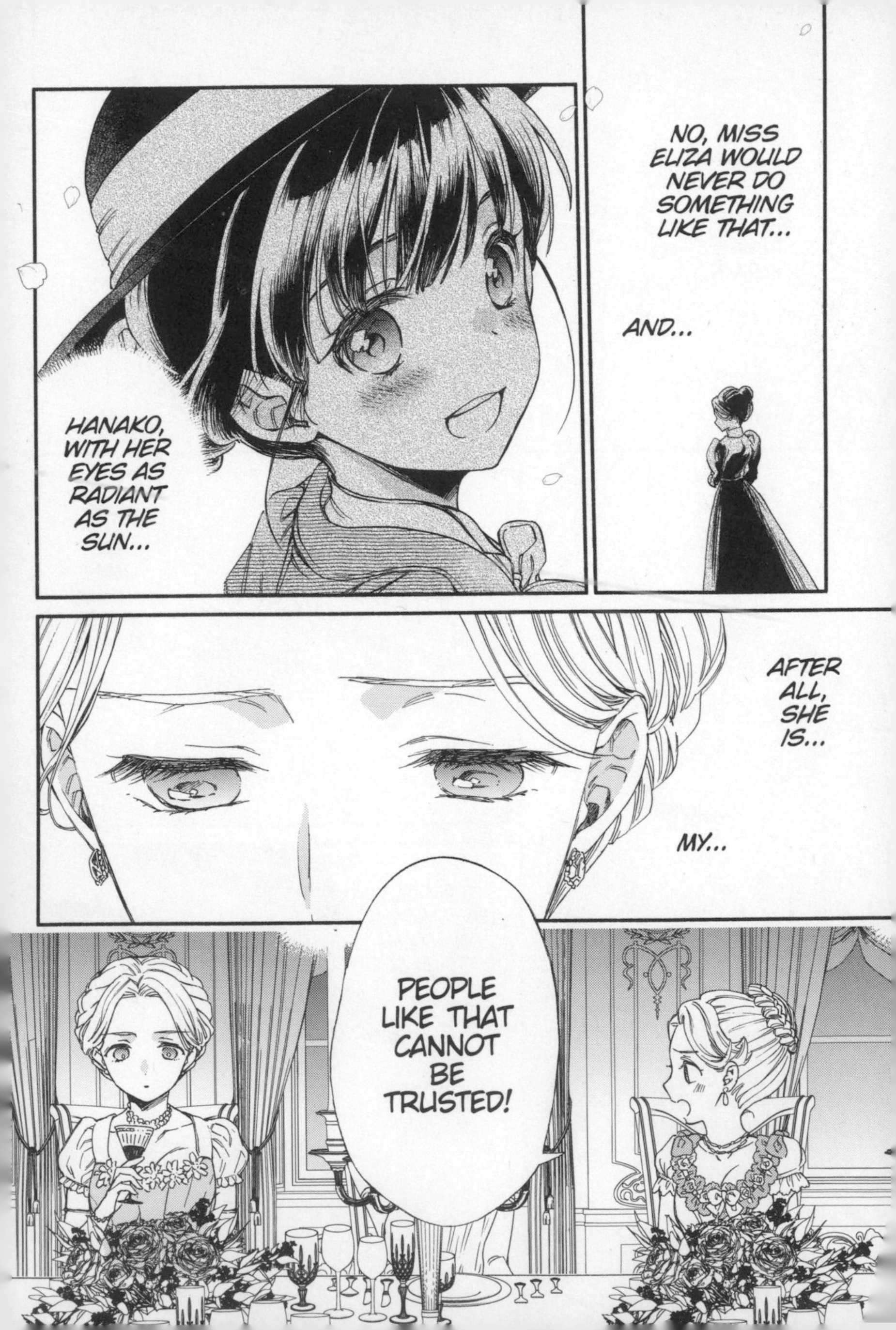
NO, MISS ELIZA WOULD NEVER DO SOMETHING LIKE THAT...
AND...
HANAKO, WITH HER EYES AS RADIANT AS THE SUN...
AFTER ALL, SHE IS...
MY...
PEOPLE LIKE THAT CANNOT BE TRUSTED!

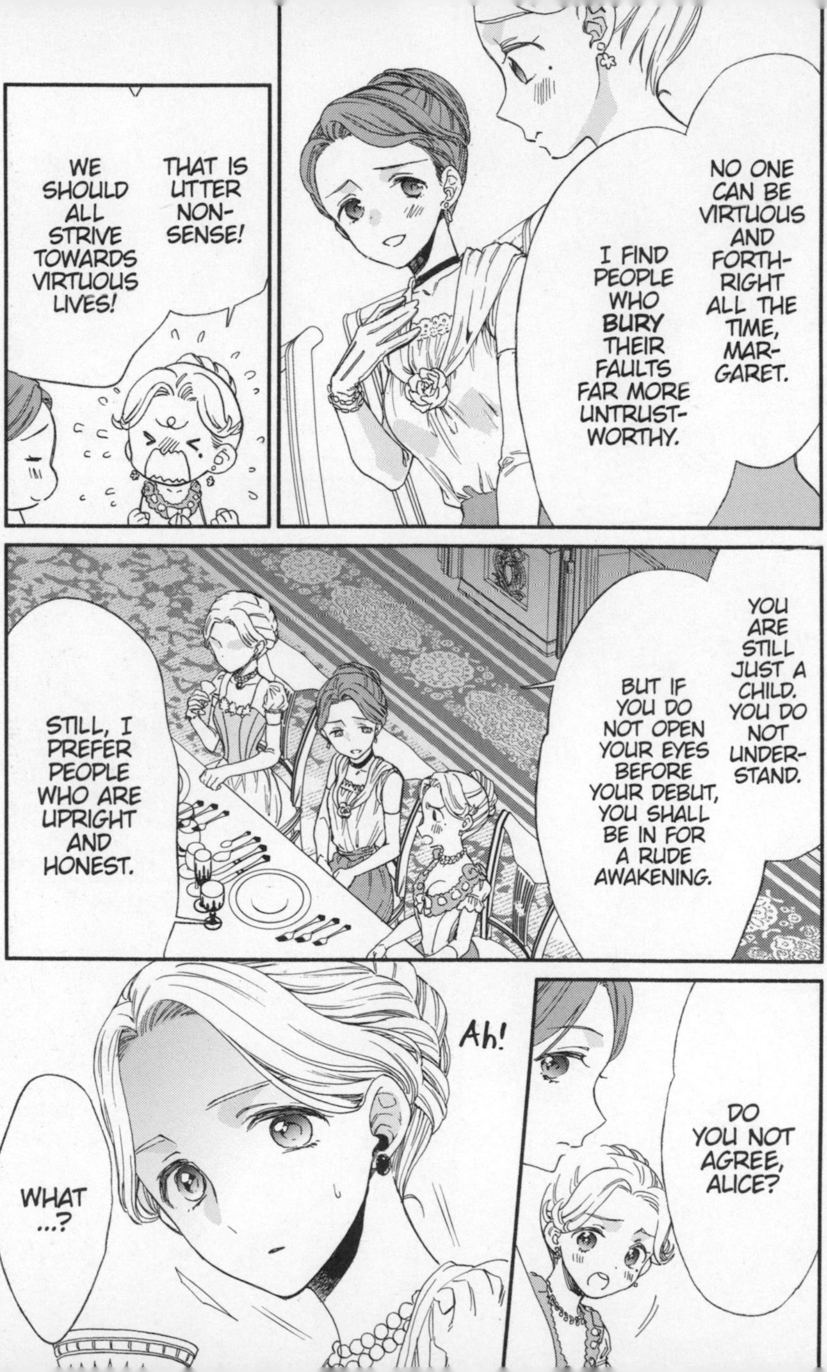
NO ONE CAN BE VIRTUOUS AND FORTH-RIGHT ALL THE TIME, MAR-GARET.
I FIND PEOPLE WHO BURY THEIR FAULTS FAR MORE UNTRUST-WORTHY.
THAT IS UTTER NON-SENSE!
WE SHOULD ALL STRIVE TOWARDS VIRTUOUS LIVES!
YOU ARE STILL JUST A CHILD. YOU DO NOT UNDER-STAND.
BUT IF YOU DO NOT OPEN YOUR EYES BEFORE YOUR DEBUT, YOU SHALL BE IN FOR A RUDE AWAKENING.
STILL, I PREFER PEOPLE WHO ARE UPRIGHT AND HONEST.
DO YOU NOT AGREE, ALICE?
Ah!
WHAT ...?

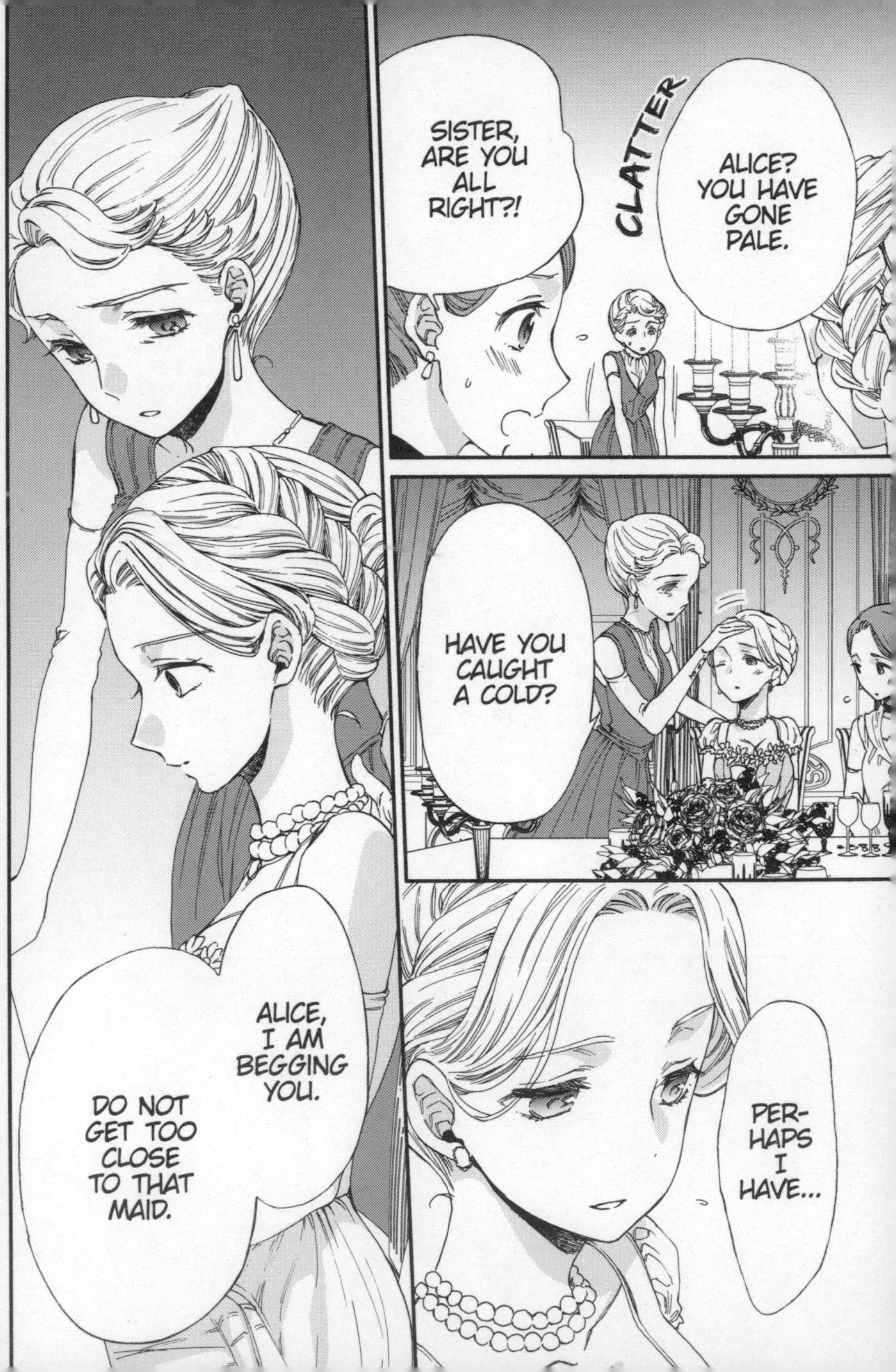
ALICE? YOU HAVE GONE PALE.
CLATTER
SISTER, ARE YOU ALL RIGHT?!
HAVE YOU CAUGHT A COLD?
PER-HAPS I HAVE...
ALICE, I AM BEGGING YOU.
DO NOT GET TOO CLOSE TO THAT MAID.

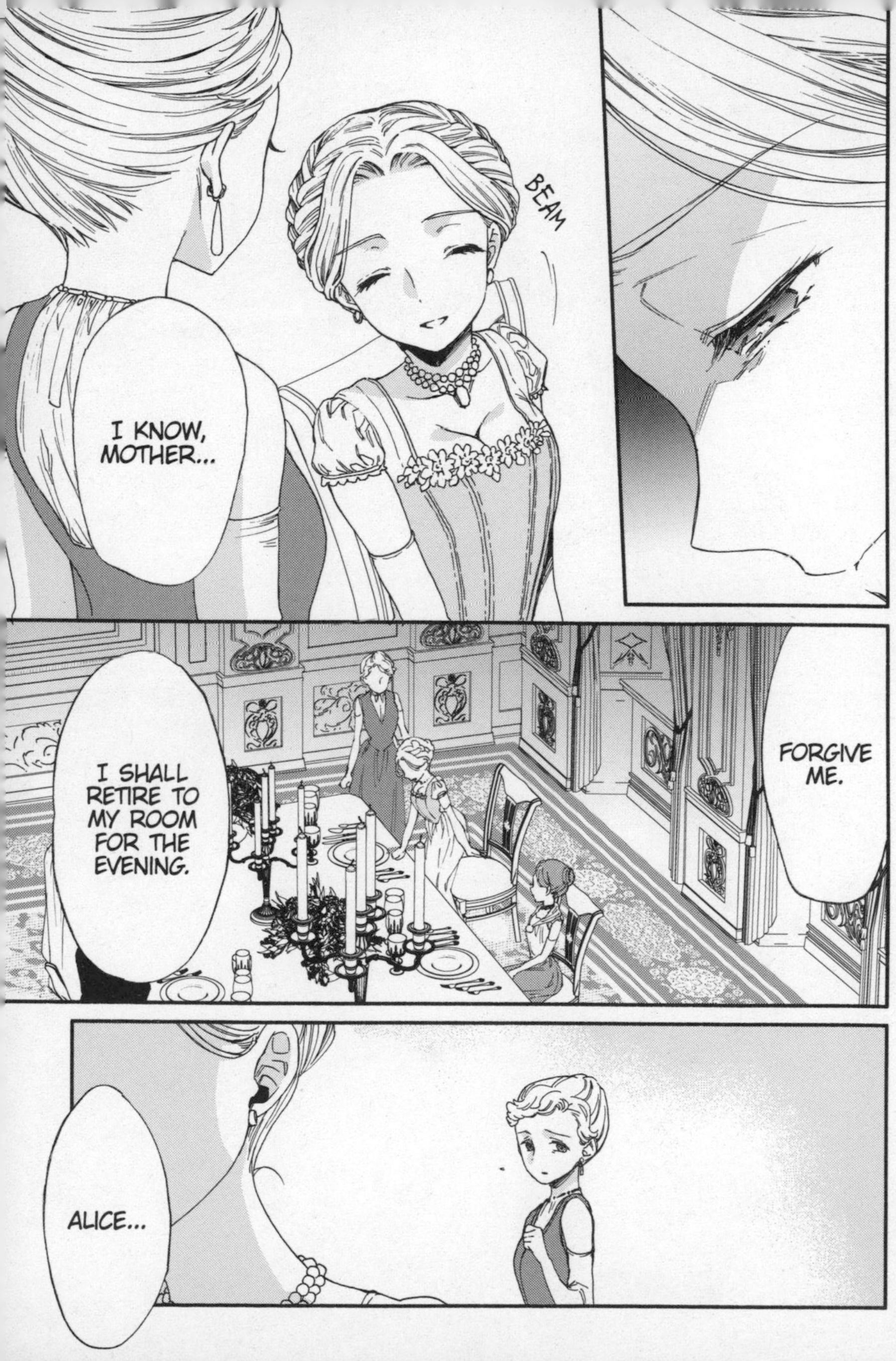
BEAM
I KNOW, MOTHER...
FORGIVE ME.
I SHALL RETIRE TO MY ROOM FOR THE EVENING.
ALICE...

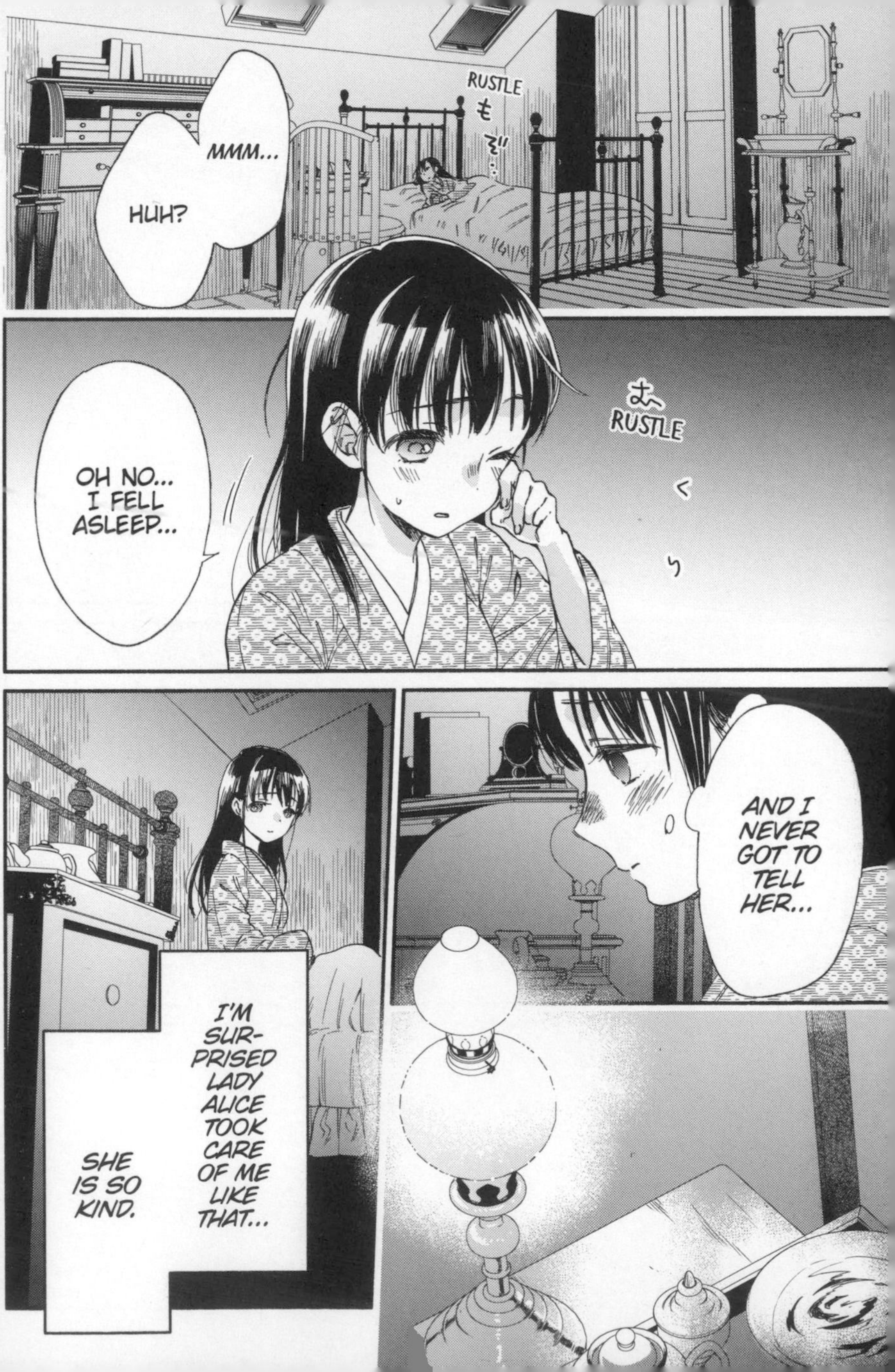

RUSTLE
MMM...
HUH?
RUSTLE
OH NO... I FELL ASLEEP...
AND I NEVER GOT TO TELL HER...
I'M SUR-PRISED LADY ALICE TOOK CARE OF ME LIKE THAT...
SHE IS SO KIND.

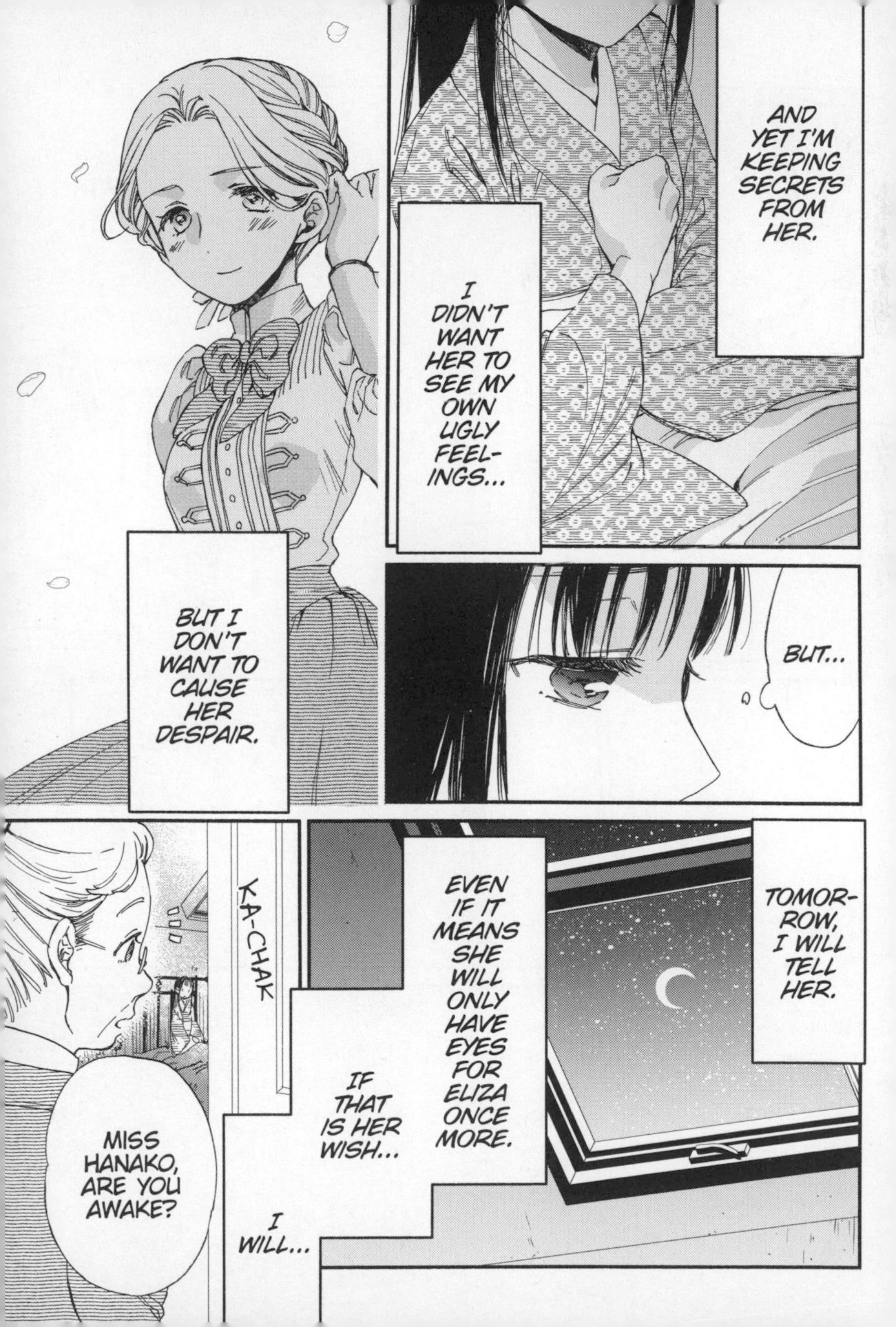
AND YET I'M KEEPING SECRETS FROM HER.
I DIDN'T WANT HER TO SEE MY OWN UGLY FEEL-INGS...
BUT...
BUT I DON'T WANT TO CAUSE HER DESPAIR.
TOMOR-ROW, I WILL TELL HER.
EVEN IF IT MEANS SHE WILL ONLY HAVE EYES FOR ELIZA ONCE MORE.
IF THAT IS HER WISH...
I WILL...
KA-CHAK
MISS HANAKO, ARE YOU AWAKE?

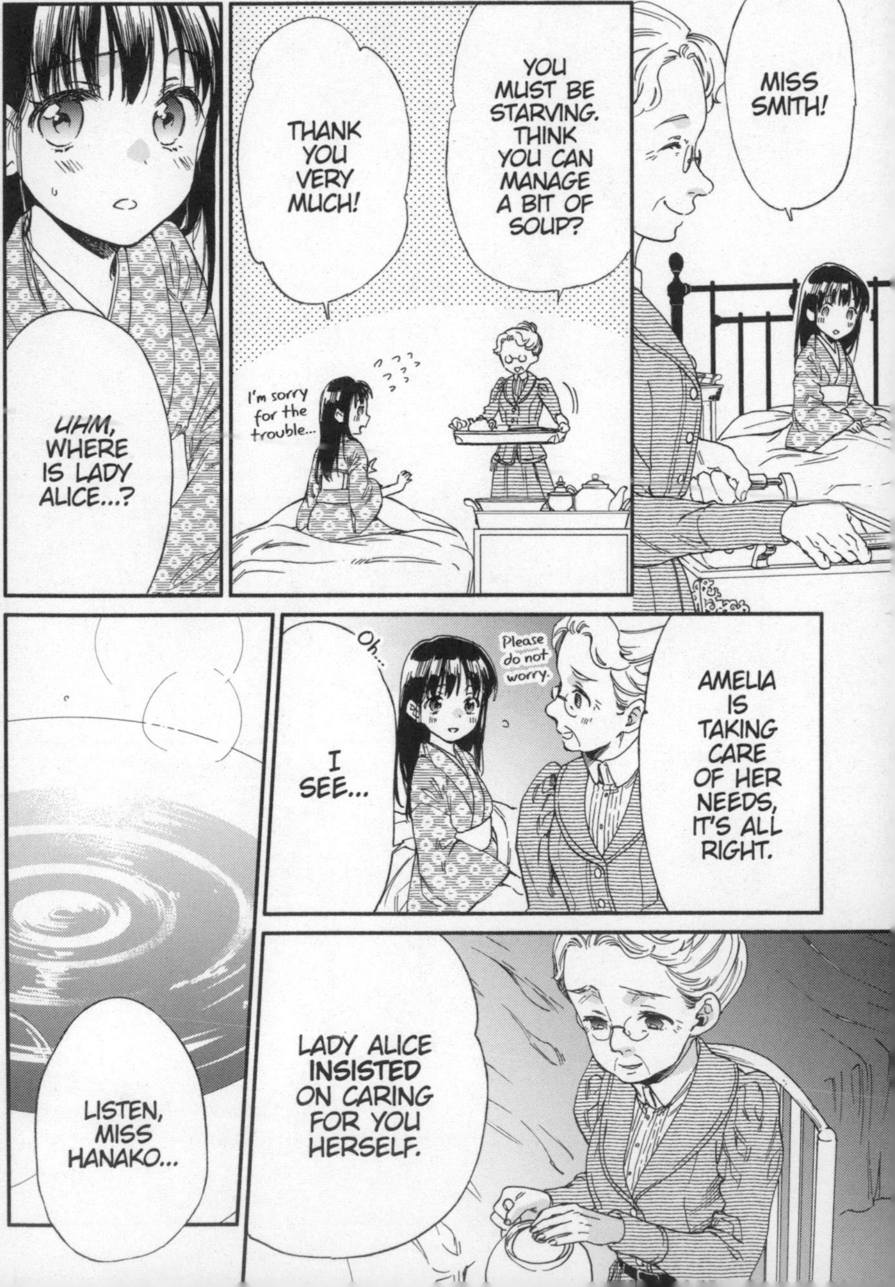
MISS SMITH!
YOU MUST BE STARVING. THINK YOU CAN MANAGE A BIT OF SOUP?
THANK YOU VERY MUCH!
I'm sorry for the trouble...
UHM, WHERE IS LADY ALICE...?
AMELIA IS TAKING CARE OF HER NEEDS, IT'S ALL RIGHT.
Please do not worry.
Oh...
I SEE...
LADY ALICE INSISTED ON CARING FOR YOU HERSELF.
LISTEN, MISS HANAKO...

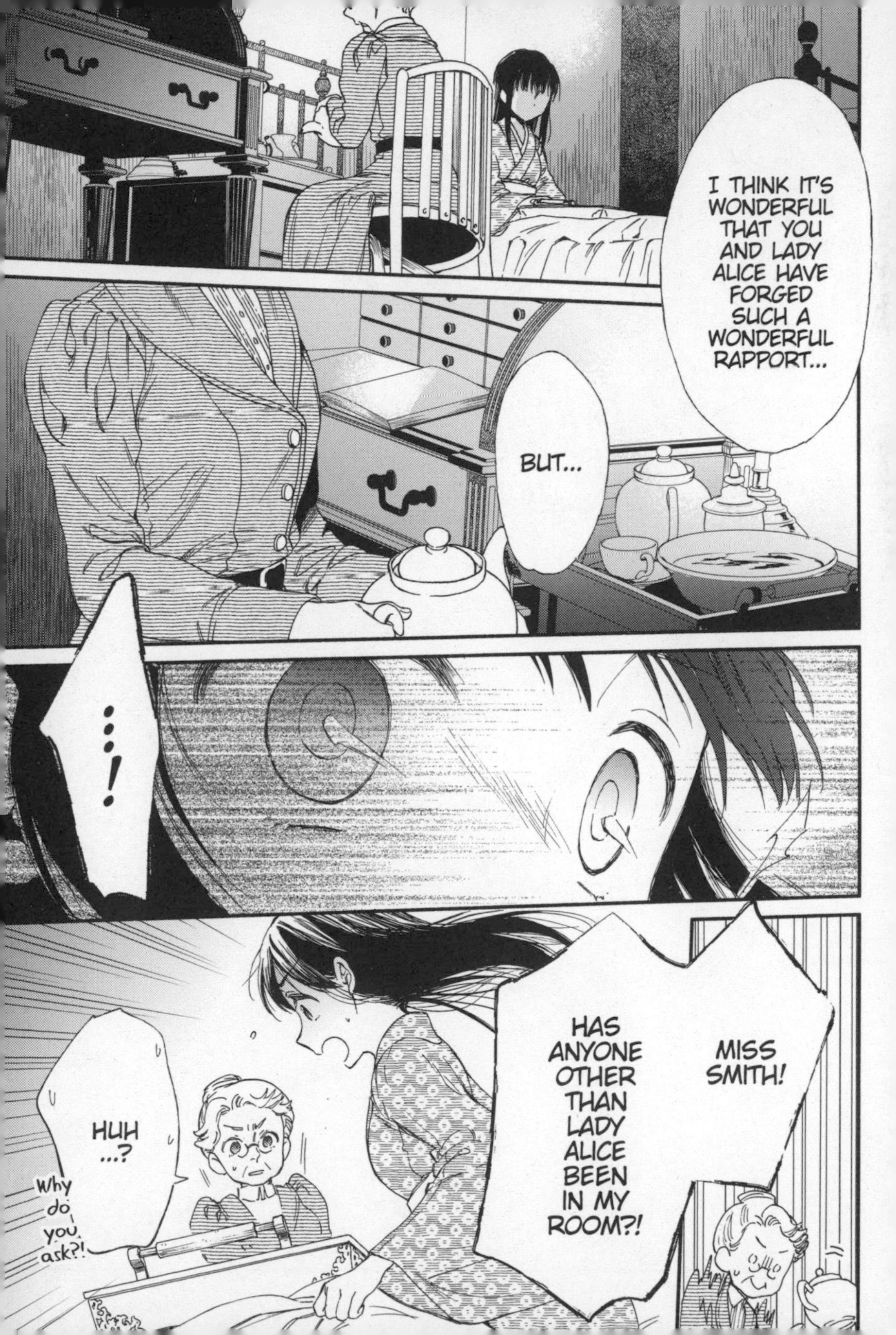
I THINK IT'S WONDERFUL THAT YOU AND LADY ALICE HAVE FORGED SUCH A WONDERFUL RAPPORT...
BUT...
...!
MISS SMITH!
HAS ANYONE OTHER THAN LADY ALICE BEEN IN MY ROOM?!
HUH ...?
Why do you ask?!

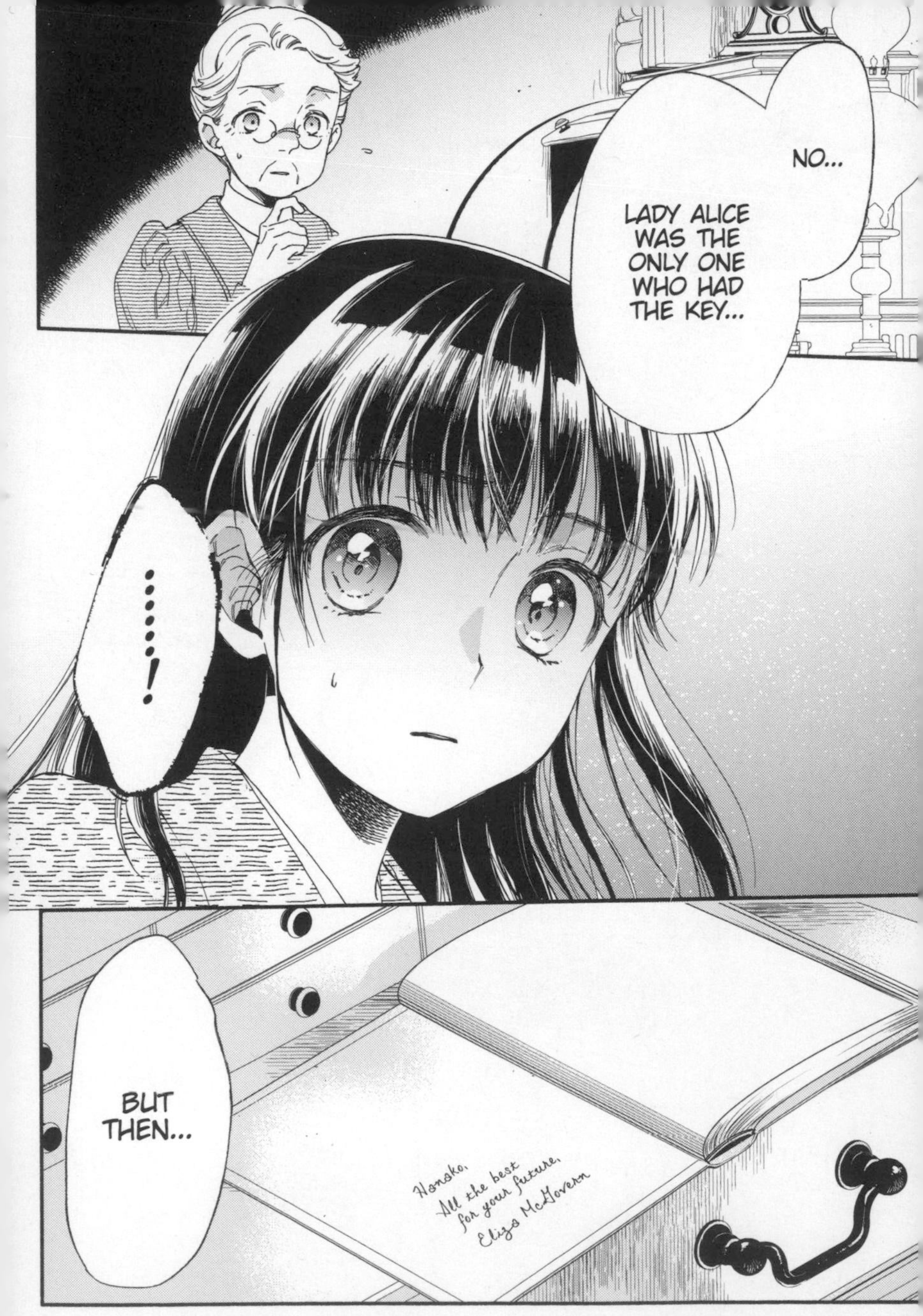
NO...
LADY ALICE WAS THE ONLY ONE WHO HAD THE KEY...
......!
BUT THEN...
Hanako,
All the best
for your future,
Eliza McGovern

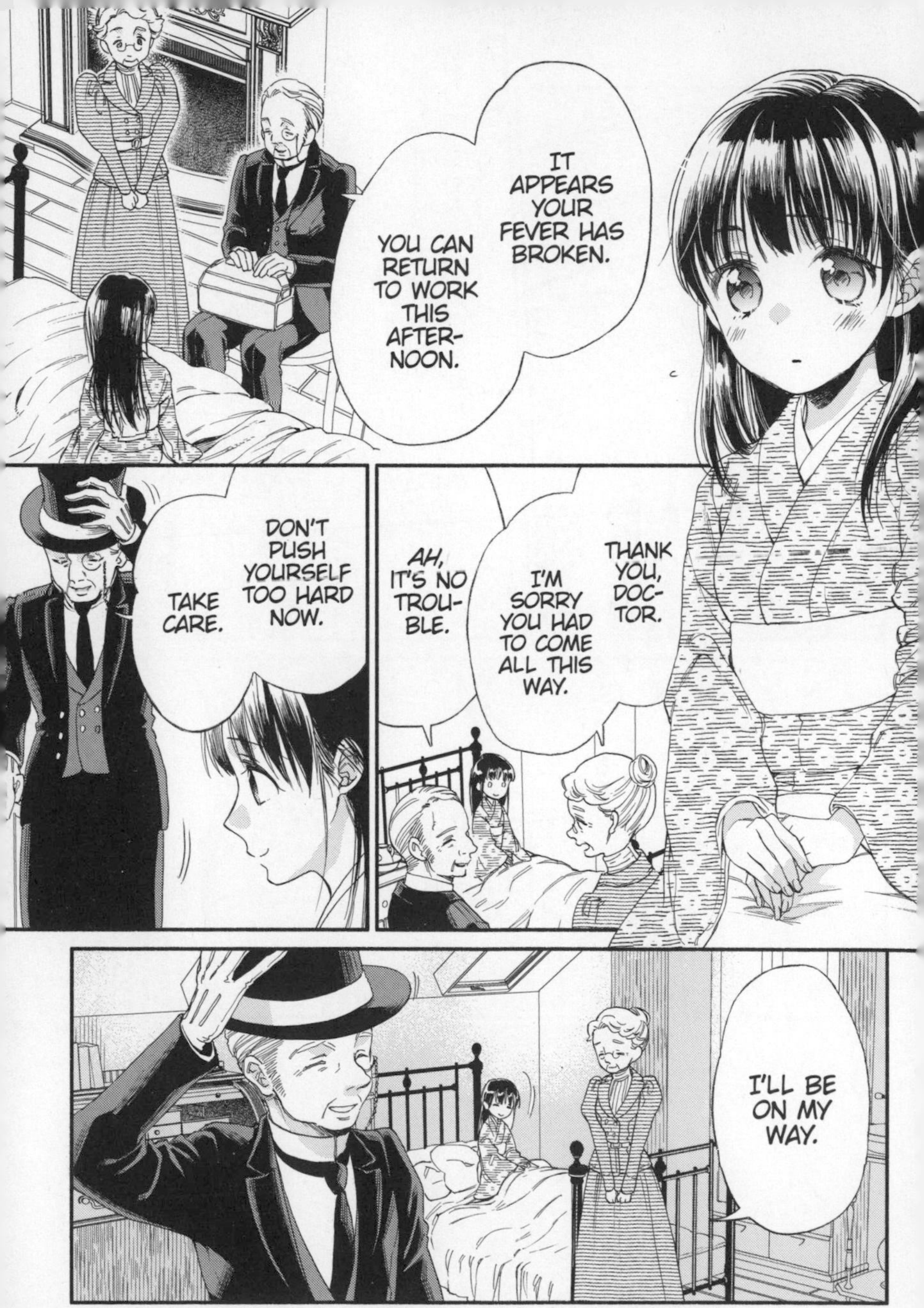
IT APPEARS YOUR FEVER HAS BROKEN.
YOU CAN RETURN TO WORK THIS AFTER-NOON.
THANK YOU, DOC-TOR.
I'M SORRY YOU HAD TO COME ALL THIS WAY.
AH, IT'S NO TROU-BLE.
DON'T PUSH YOURSELF TOO HARD NOW.
TAKE CARE.
I'LL BE ON MY WAY.

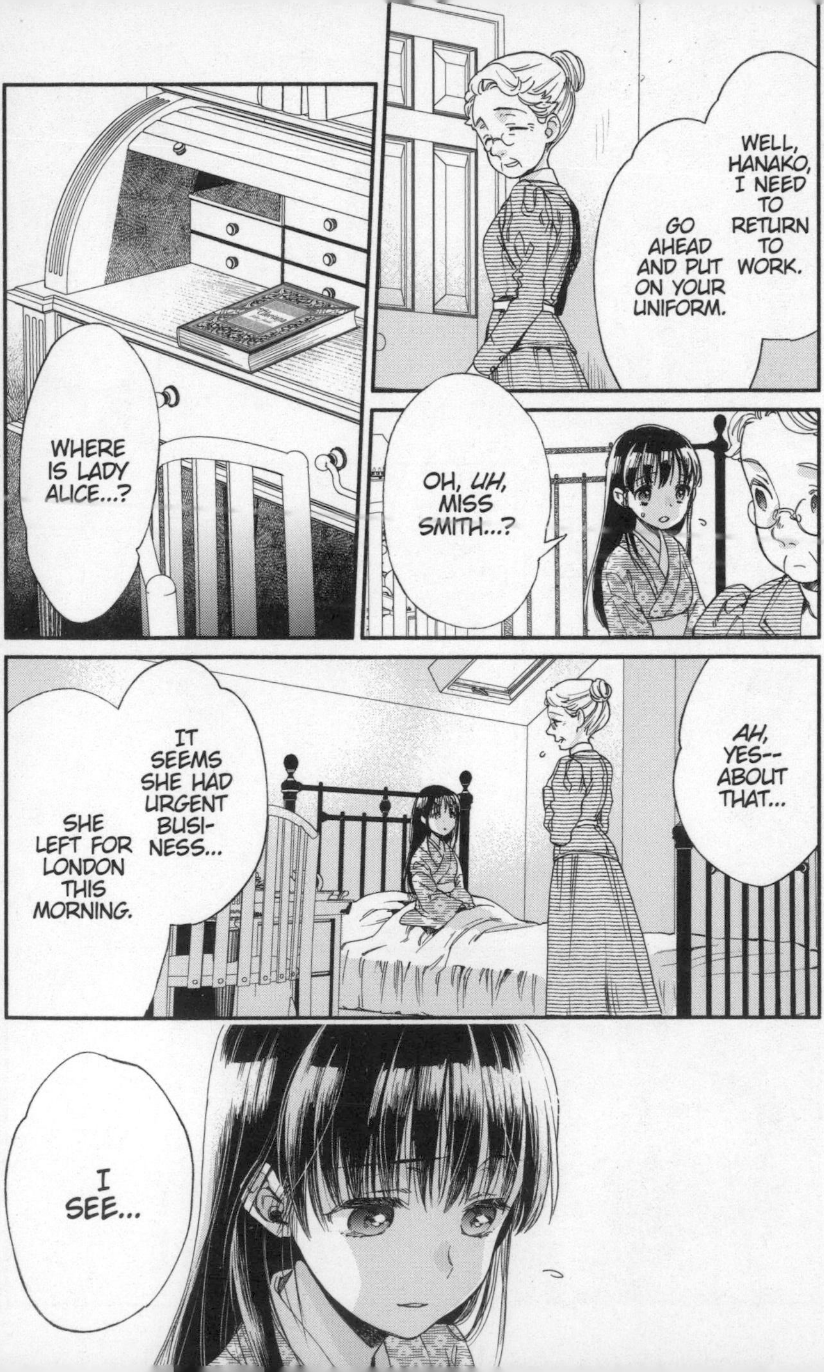
WELL, HANAKO, I NEED TO RETURN TO WORK.
GO AHEAD AND PUT ON YOUR UNIFORM.
OH, UH, MISS SMITH...?
WHERE IS LADY ALICE...?
AH, YES-- ABOUT THAT...
IT SEEMS SHE HAD URGENT BUSI- NESS...
SHE LEFT FOR LONDON THIS MORNING.
I SEE...

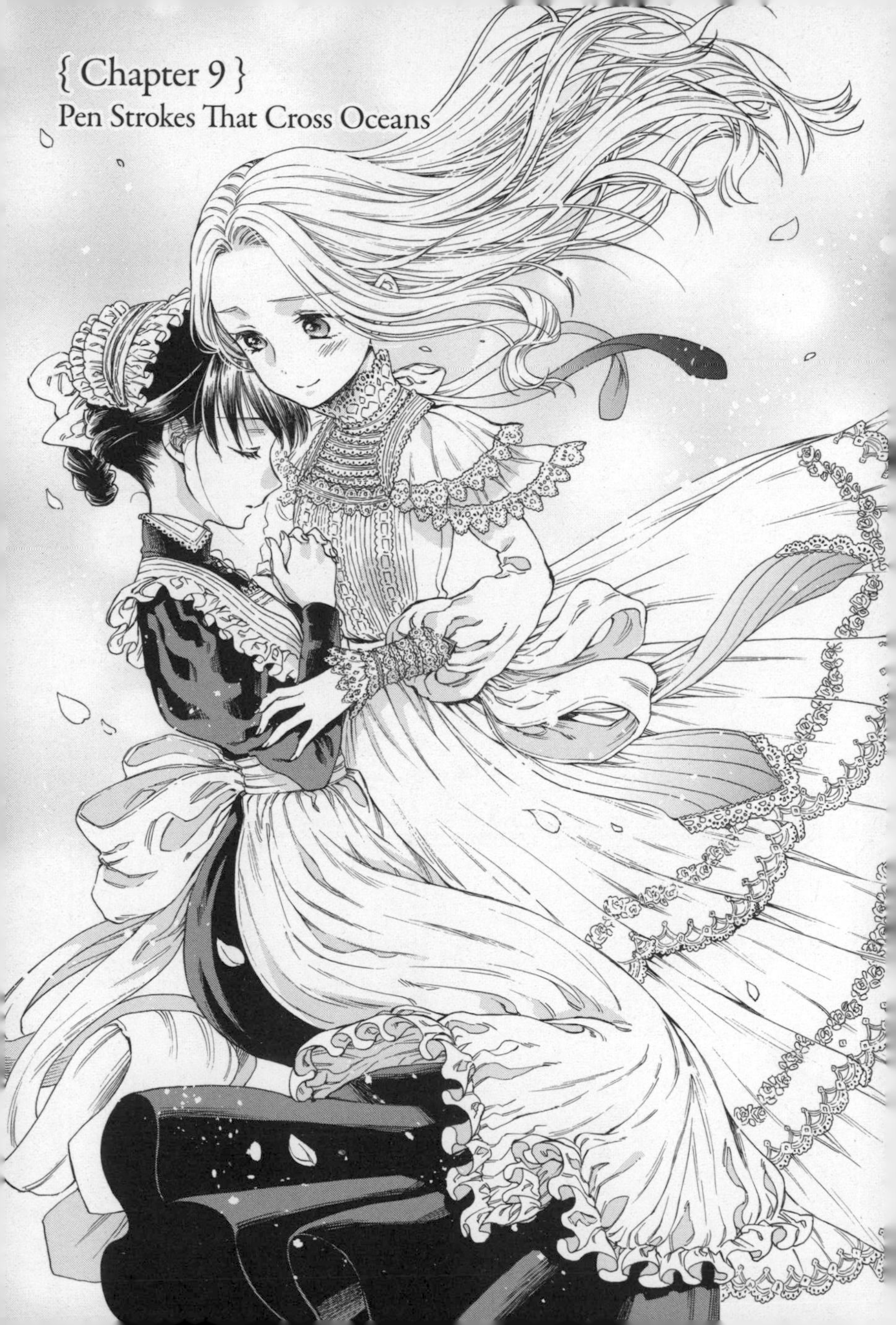
{ Chapter 9 }
Pen Strokes That Cross Oceans

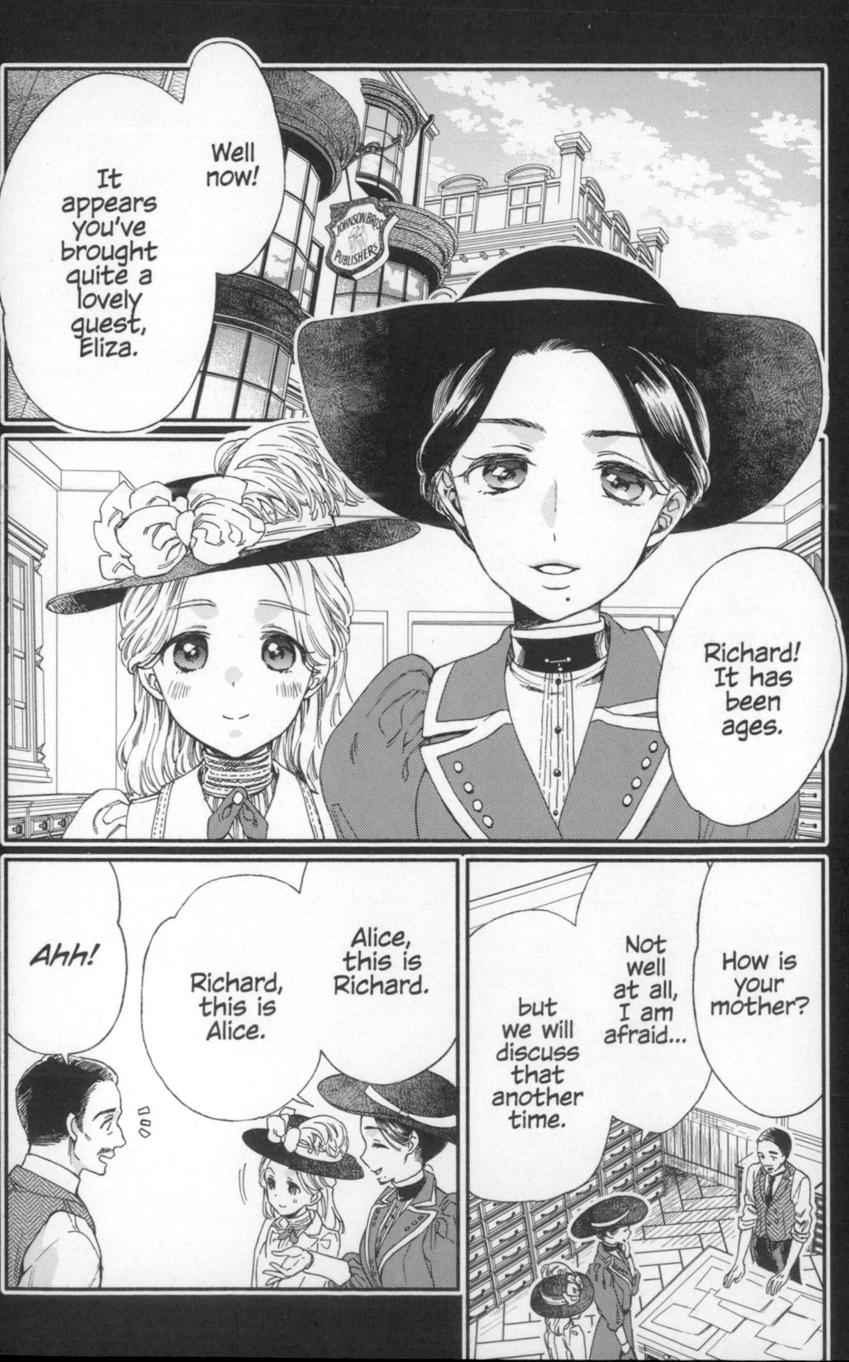
Well now!
It appears you've brought quite a lovely guest, Eliza.
JOHNSON BROS PUBLISHERS
Richard! It has been ages.
How is your mother?
Not well at all, I am afraid...
but we will discuss that another time.
Alice, this is Richard.
Richard, this is Alice.
Ahh!

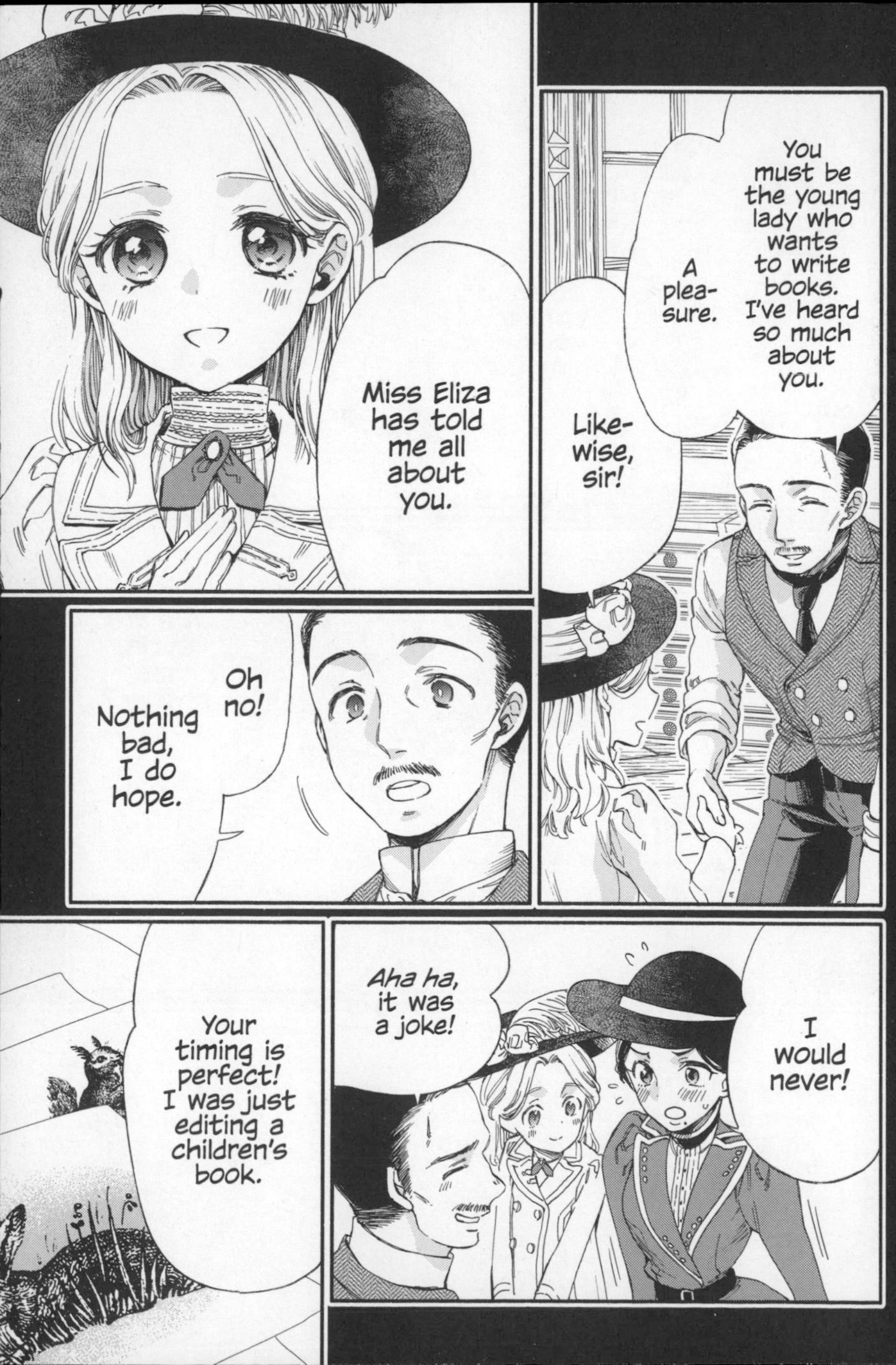
You must be the young lady who wants to write books. I've heard so much about you.
A pleasure.
Likewise, sir!
Miss Eliza has told me all about you.
Oh no!
Nothing bad, I do hope.
I would never!
Aha ha, it was a joke!
Your timing is perfect! I was just editing a children's book.

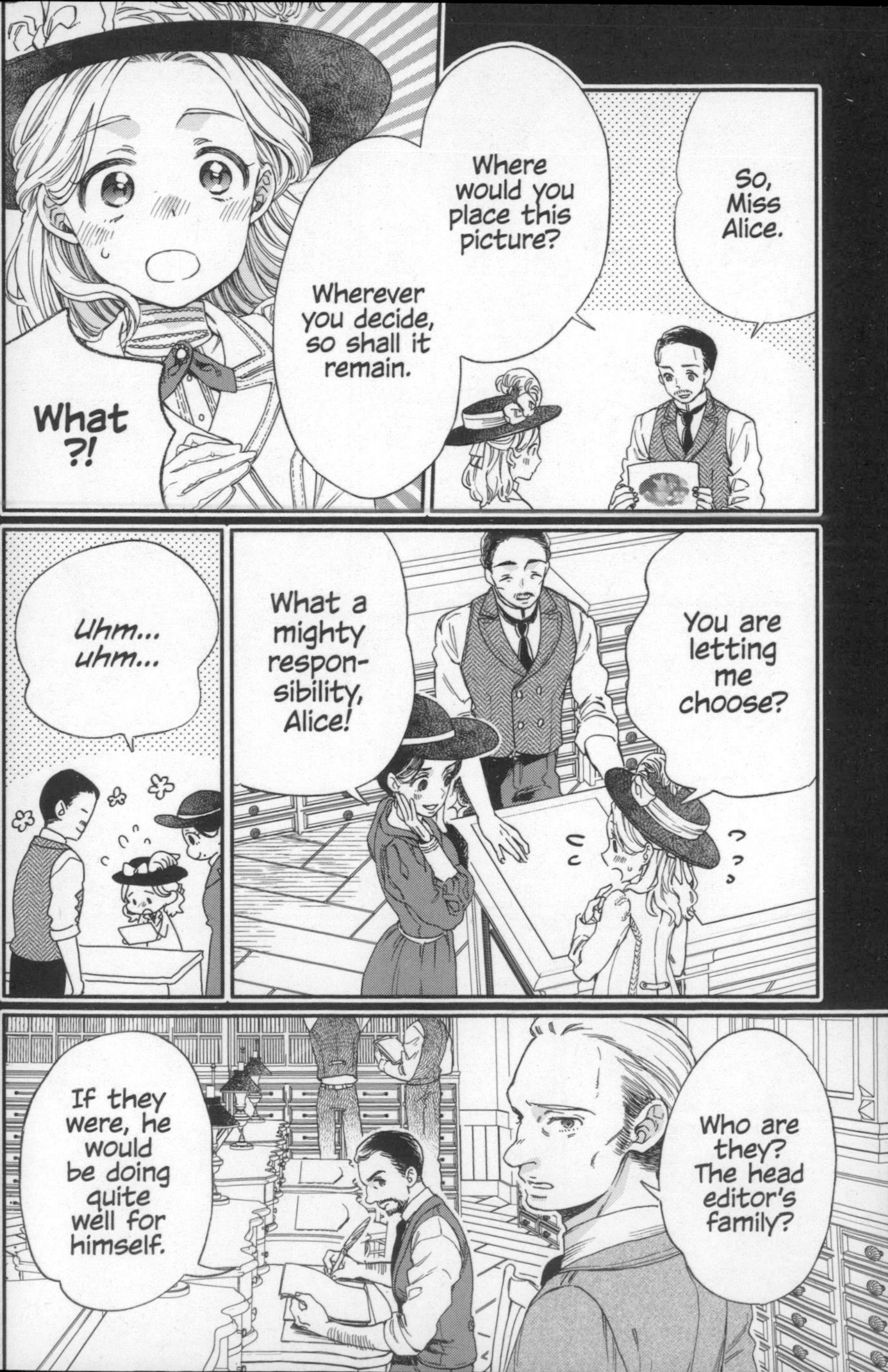

So, Miss Alice.
Where would you place this picture?
Wherever you decide, so shall it remain.
What ?!
You are letting me choose?
What a mighty respon-sibility, Alice!
Uhm... uhm...
Who are they? The head editor's family?
If they were, he would be doing quite well for himself.

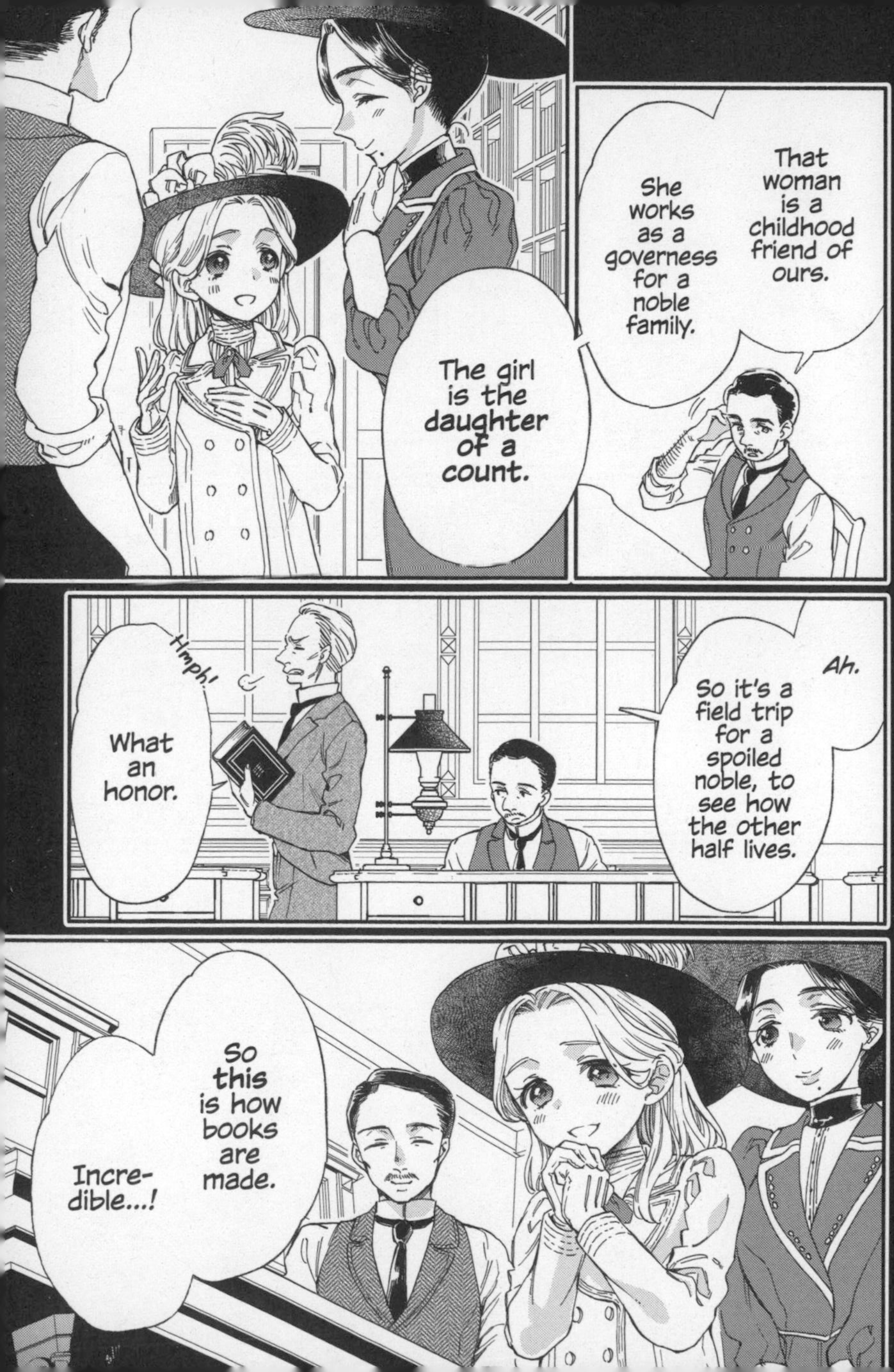
That woman is a childhood friend of ours.
She works as a governess for a noble family.
The girl is the daughter of a count.
Ah.
So it's a field trip for a spoiled noble, to see how the other half lives.
Hmph!
What an honor.
So this is how books are made.
Incredible...!

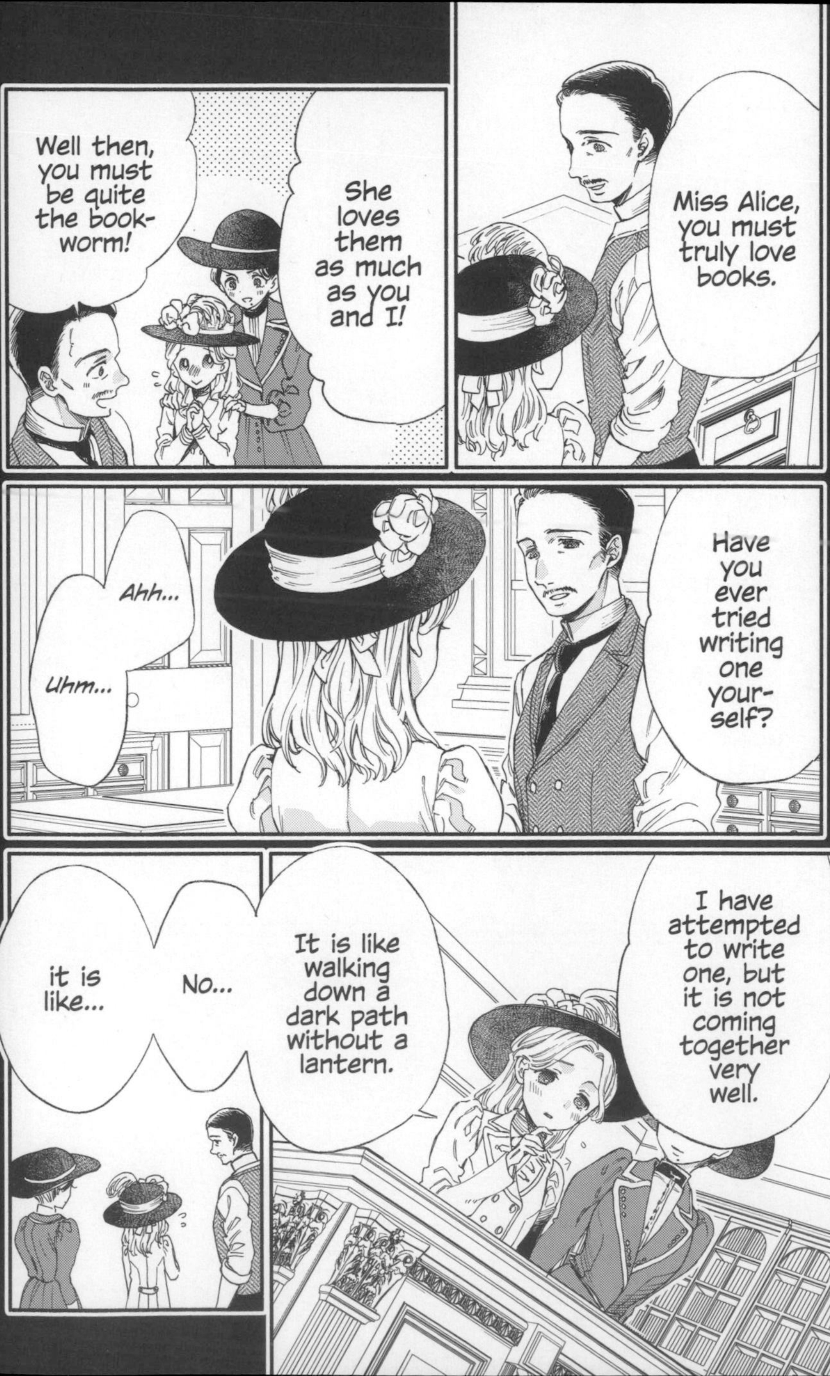

Miss Alice, you must truly love books.
She loves them as much as you and I!
Well then, you must be quite the book-worm!
Have you ever tried writing one your-self?
Ahh...
Uhm...
I have attempted to write one, but it is not coming together very well.
It is like walking down a dark path without a lantern.
No...
it is like...

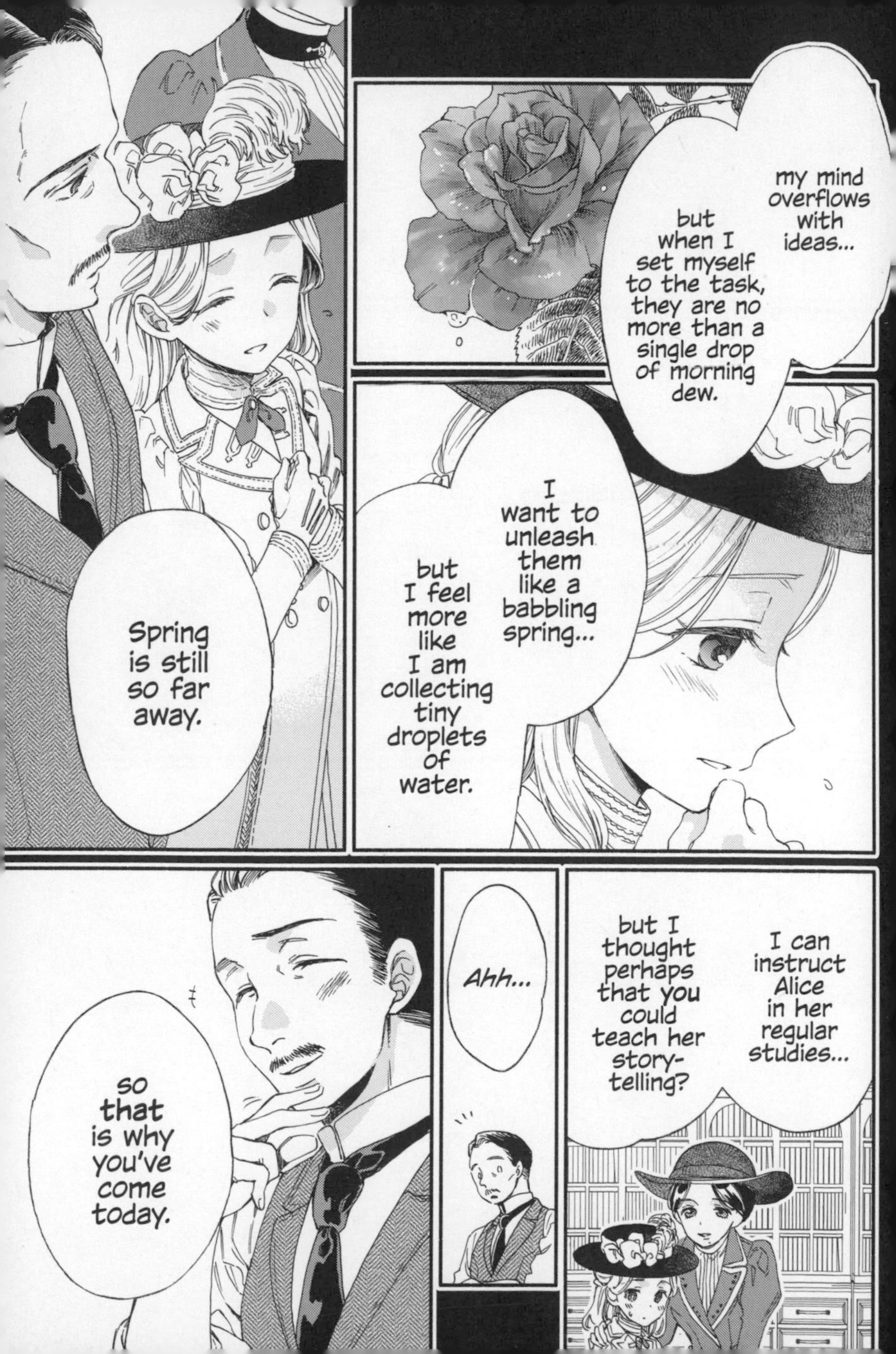
my mind overflows with ideas...
but when I set myself to the task, they are no more than a single drop of morning dew.
I want to unleash them like a babbling spring...
but I feel more like I am collecting tiny droplets of water.
Spring is still so far away.
I can instruct Alice in her regular studies...
but I thought perhaps that you could teach her story-telling?
Ahh...
so that is why you've come today.

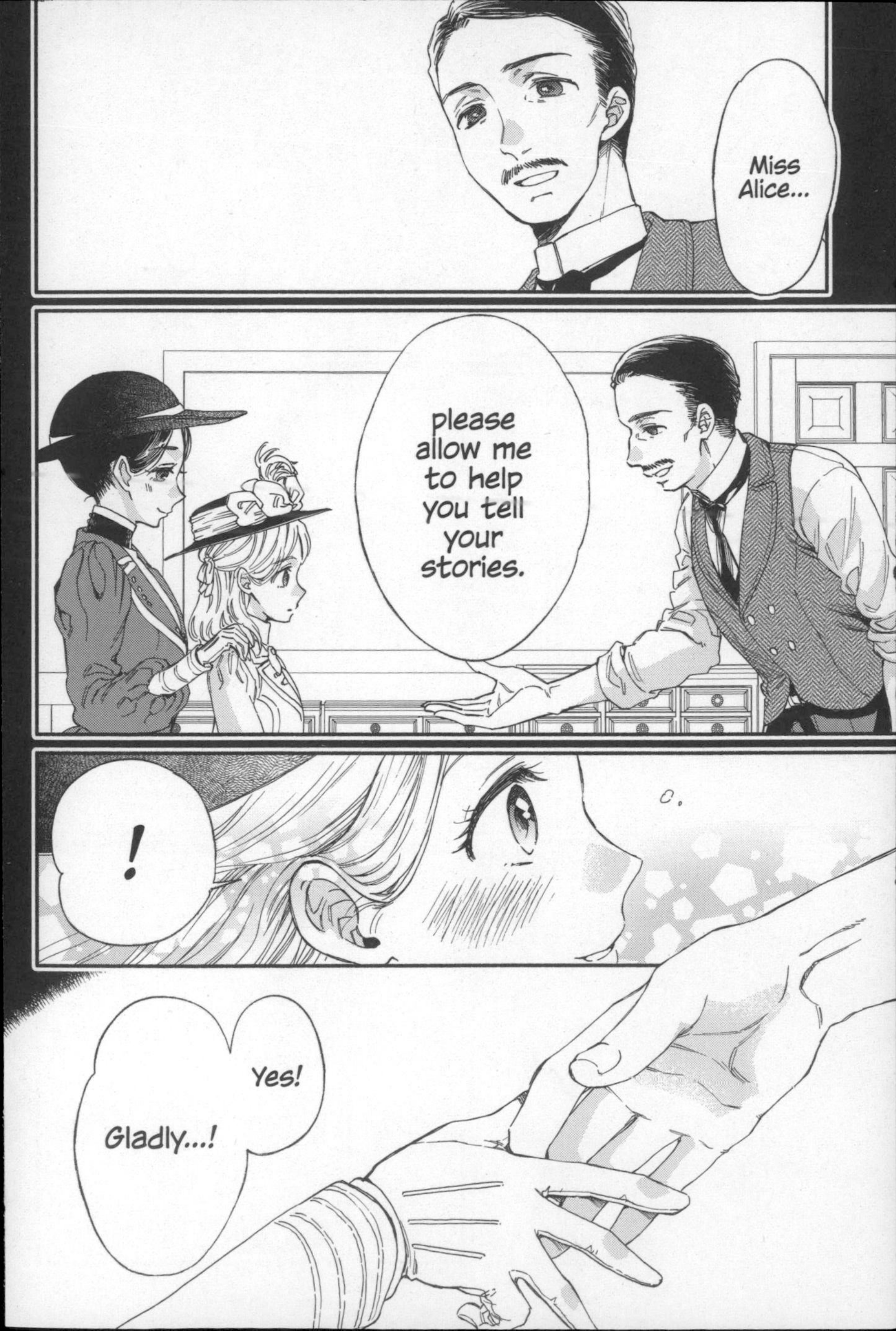
Miss Alice...
please allow me to help you tell your stories.
!
Yes!
Gladly...!

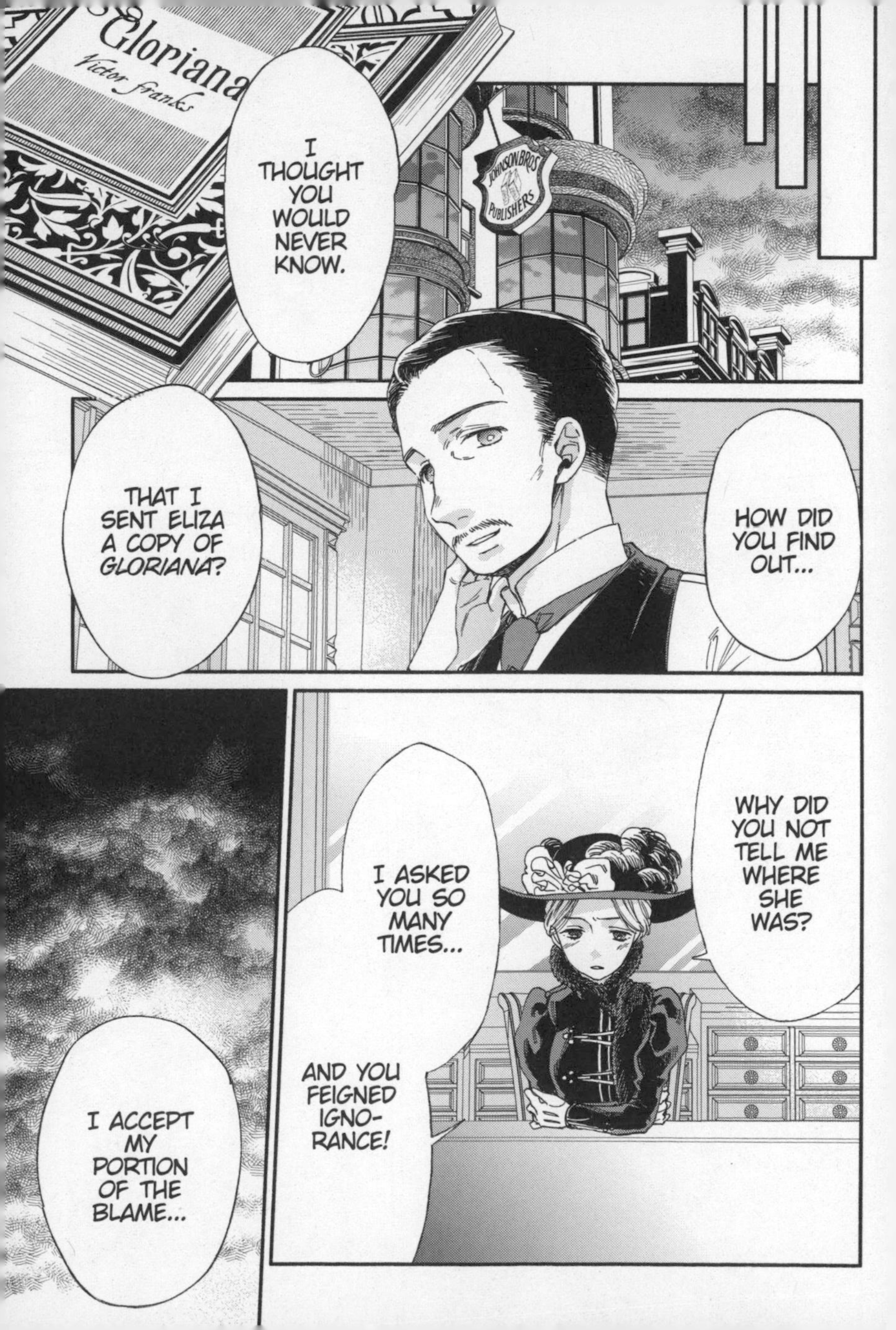
JOHNSON BROS PUBLISHERS
I THOUGHT YOU WOULD NEVER KNOW.
Gloriana
Victor franks
HOW DID YOU FIND OUT...
THAT I SENT ELIZA A COPY OF GLORIANA?
WHY DID YOU NOT TELL ME WHERE SHE WAS?
I ASKED YOU SO MANY TIMES...
AND YOU FEIGNED IGNO-RANCE!
I ACCEPT MY PORTION OF THE BLAME...

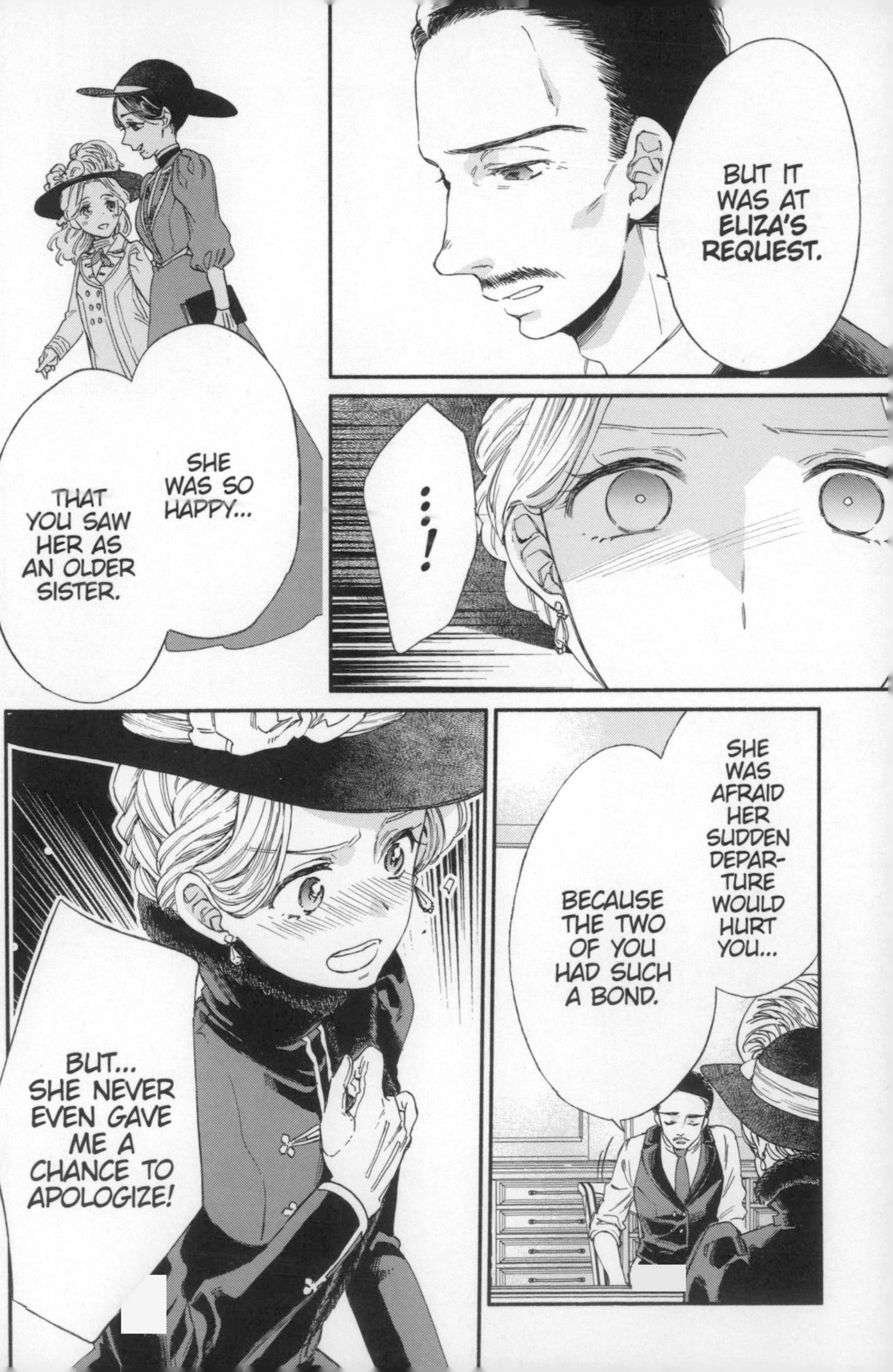
BUT IT WAS AT ELIZA'S REQUEST.
...!
SHE WAS SO HAPPY...
THAT YOU SAW HER AS AN OLDER SISTER.
SHE WAS AFRAID HER SUDDEN DEPARTURE WOULD HURT YOU...
BECAUSE THE TWO OF YOU HAD SUCH A BOND.
BUT... SHE NEVER EVEN GAVE ME A CHANCE TO APOLOGIZE!

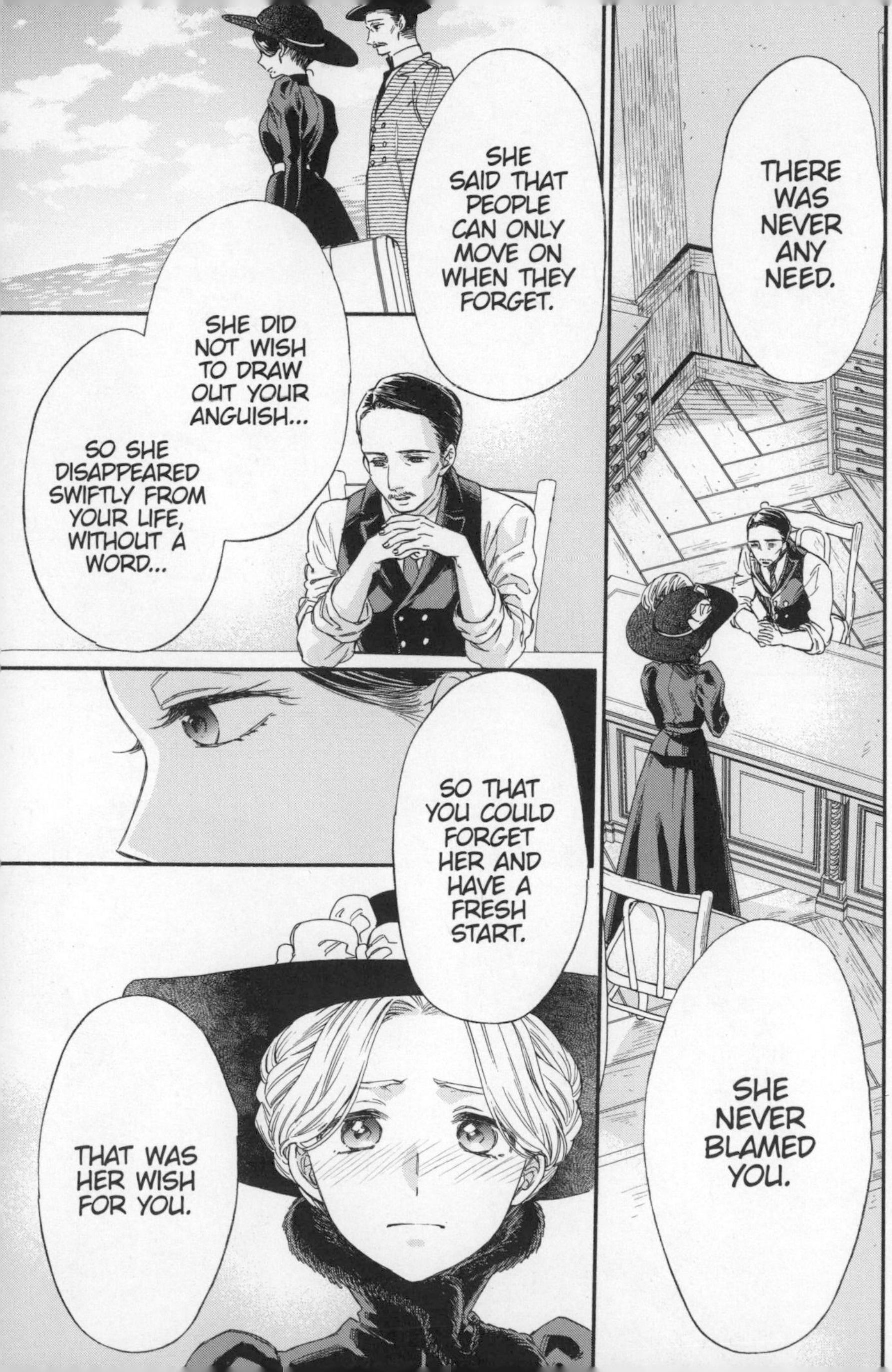
THERE WAS NEVER ANY NEED.
SHE NEVER BLAMED YOU.
SHE SAID THAT PEOPLE CAN ONLY MOVE ON WHEN THEY FORGET.
SHE DID NOT WISH TO DRAW OUT YOUR ANGUISH...
SO SHE DISAPPEARED SWIFTLY FROM YOUR LIFE, WITHOUT A WORD...
SO THAT YOU COULD FORGET HER AND HAVE A FRESH START.
THAT WAS HER WISH FOR YOU.

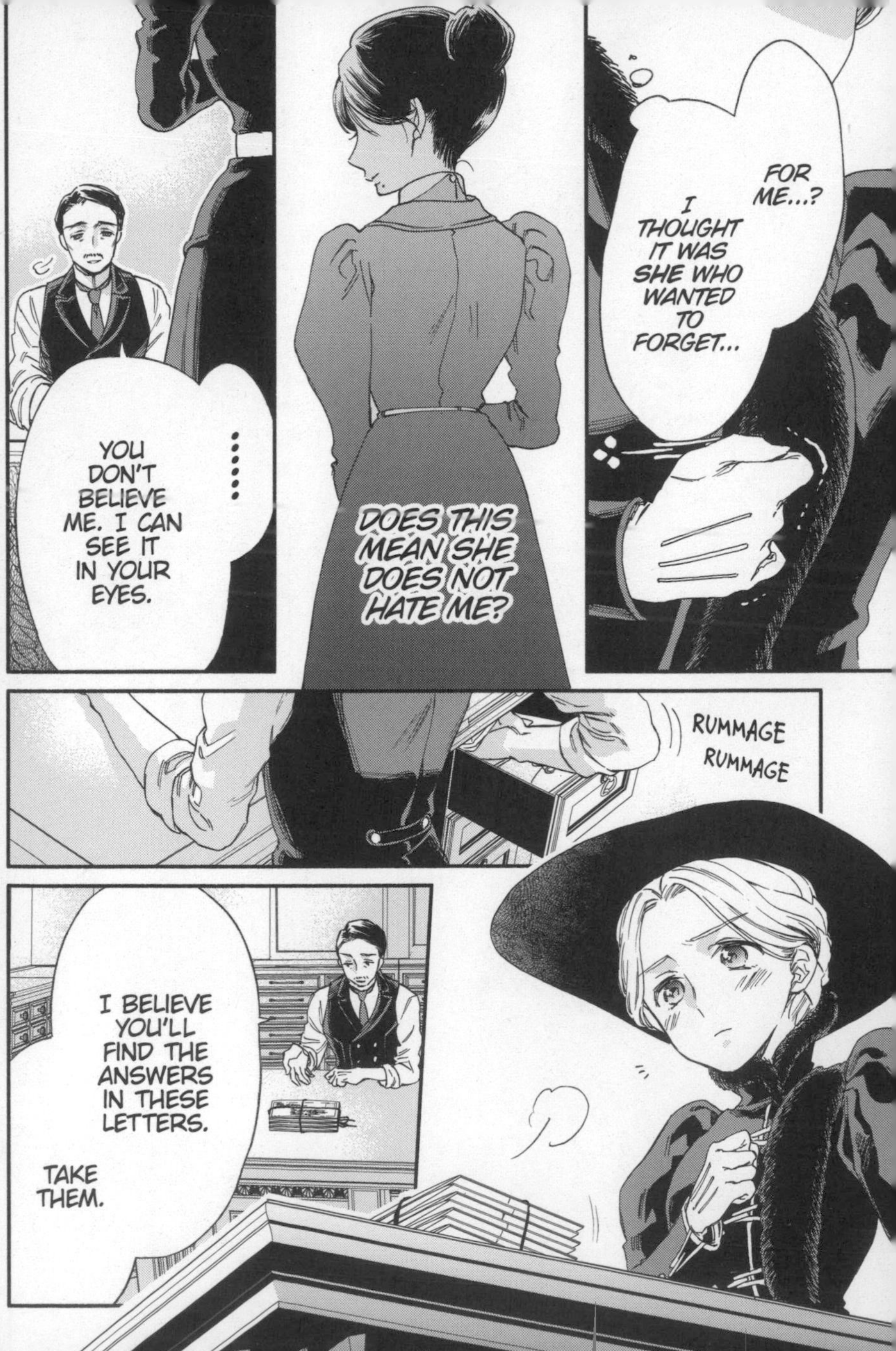
FOR ME...?
I THOUGHT IT WAS SHE WHO WANTED TO FORGET...
DOES THIS MEAN SHE DOES NOT HATE ME?
......
YOU DON'T BELIEVE ME. I CAN SEE IT IN YOUR EYES.
RUMMAGE RUMMAGE
I BELIEVE YOU'LL FIND THE ANSWERS IN THESE LETTERS.
TAKE THEM.

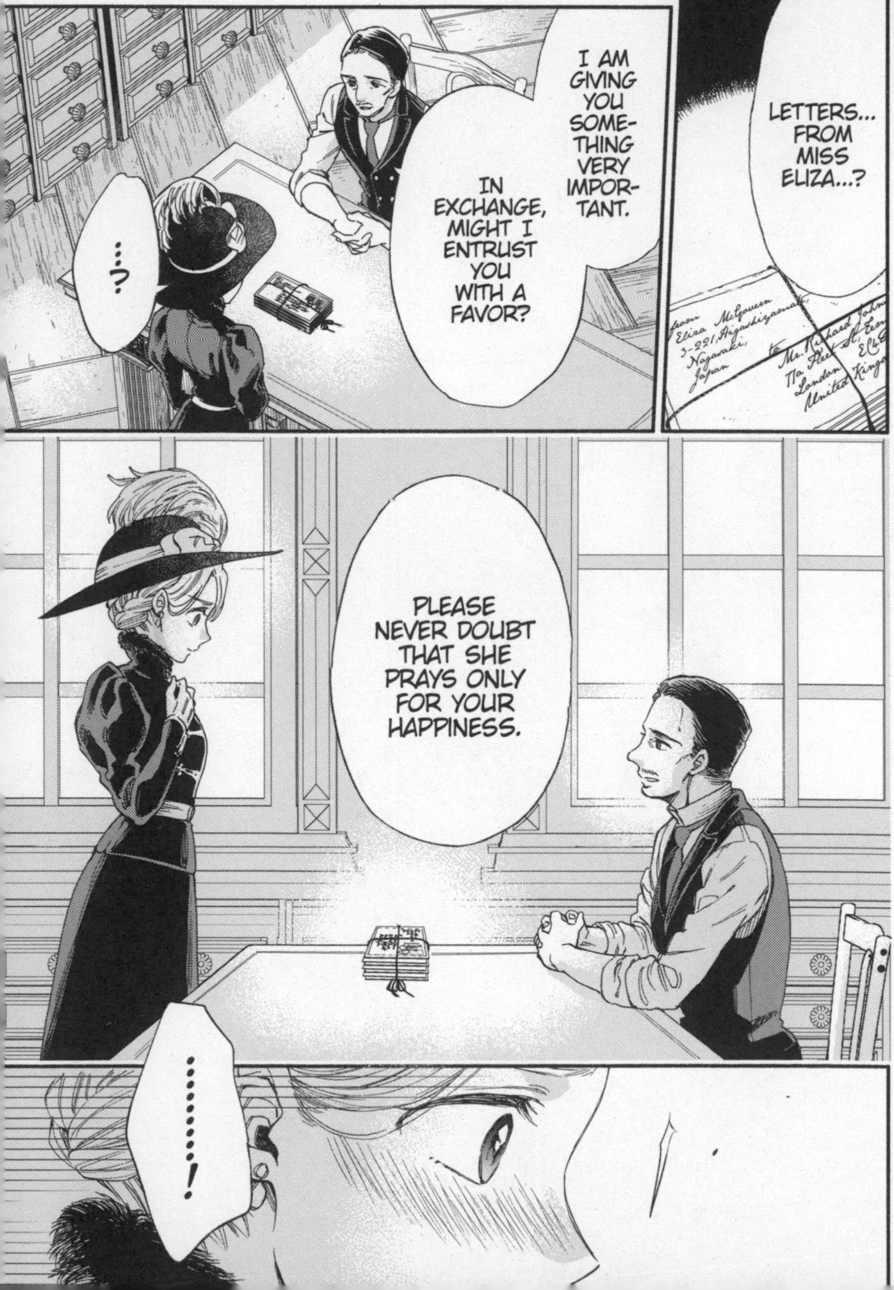
LETTERS... FROM MISS ELIZA...?
I AM GIVING YOU SOMETHING VERY IMPORTANT.
IN EXCHANGE, MIGHT I ENTRUST YOU WITH A FAVOR?
っ...
PLEASE NEVER DOUBT THAT SHE PRAYS ONLY FOR YOUR HAPPINESS.
.......!

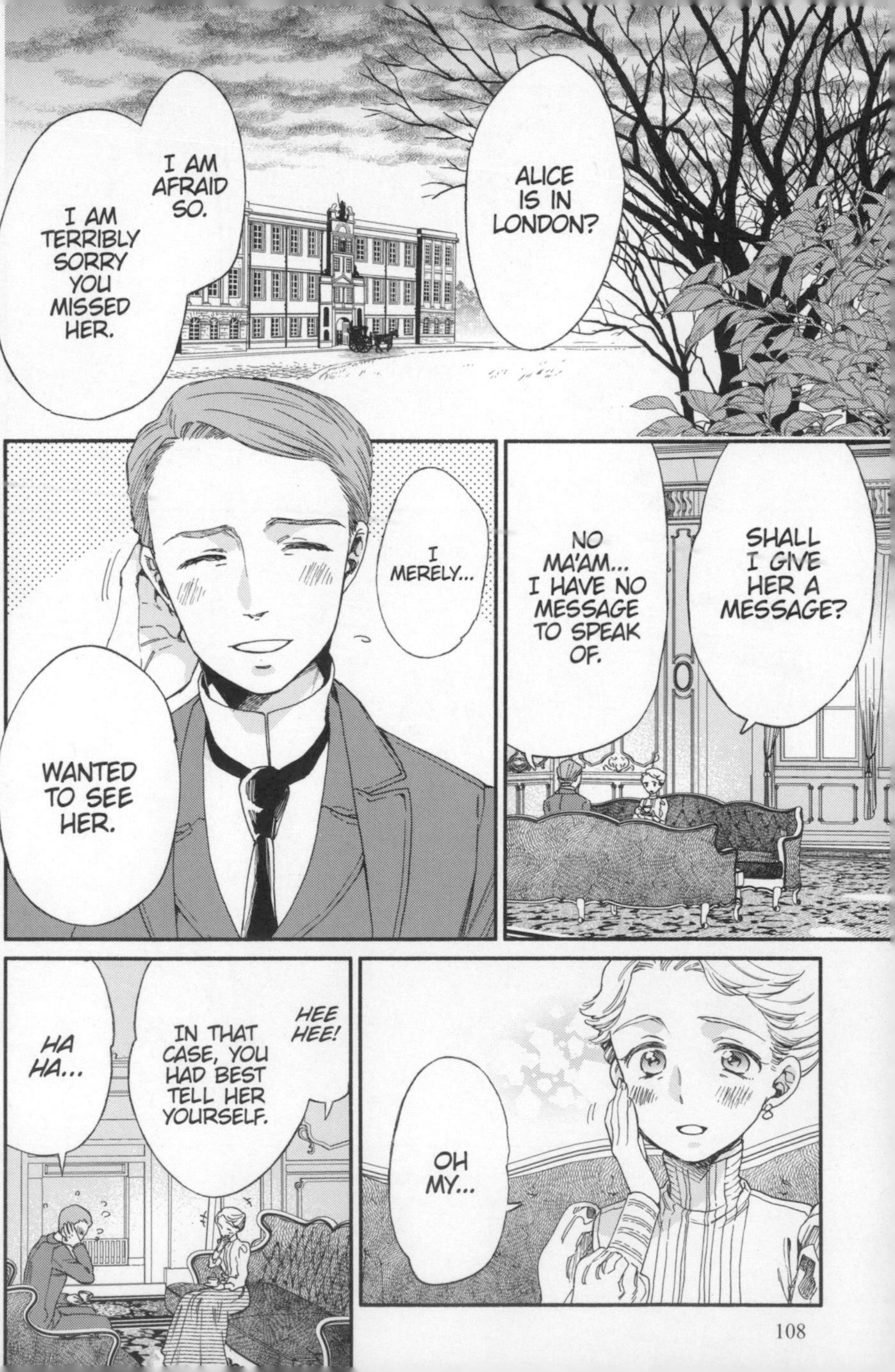
ALICE IS IN LONDON?
I AM AFRAID SO.
I AM TERRIBLY SORRY YOU MISSED HER.
SHALL I GIVE HER A MESSAGE?
NO MA'AM... I HAVE NO MESSAGE TO SPEAK OF.
I MERELY...
WANTED TO SEE HER.
OH MY...
HEE HEE!
IN THAT CASE, YOU HAD BEST TELL HER YOURSELF.
HA HA...

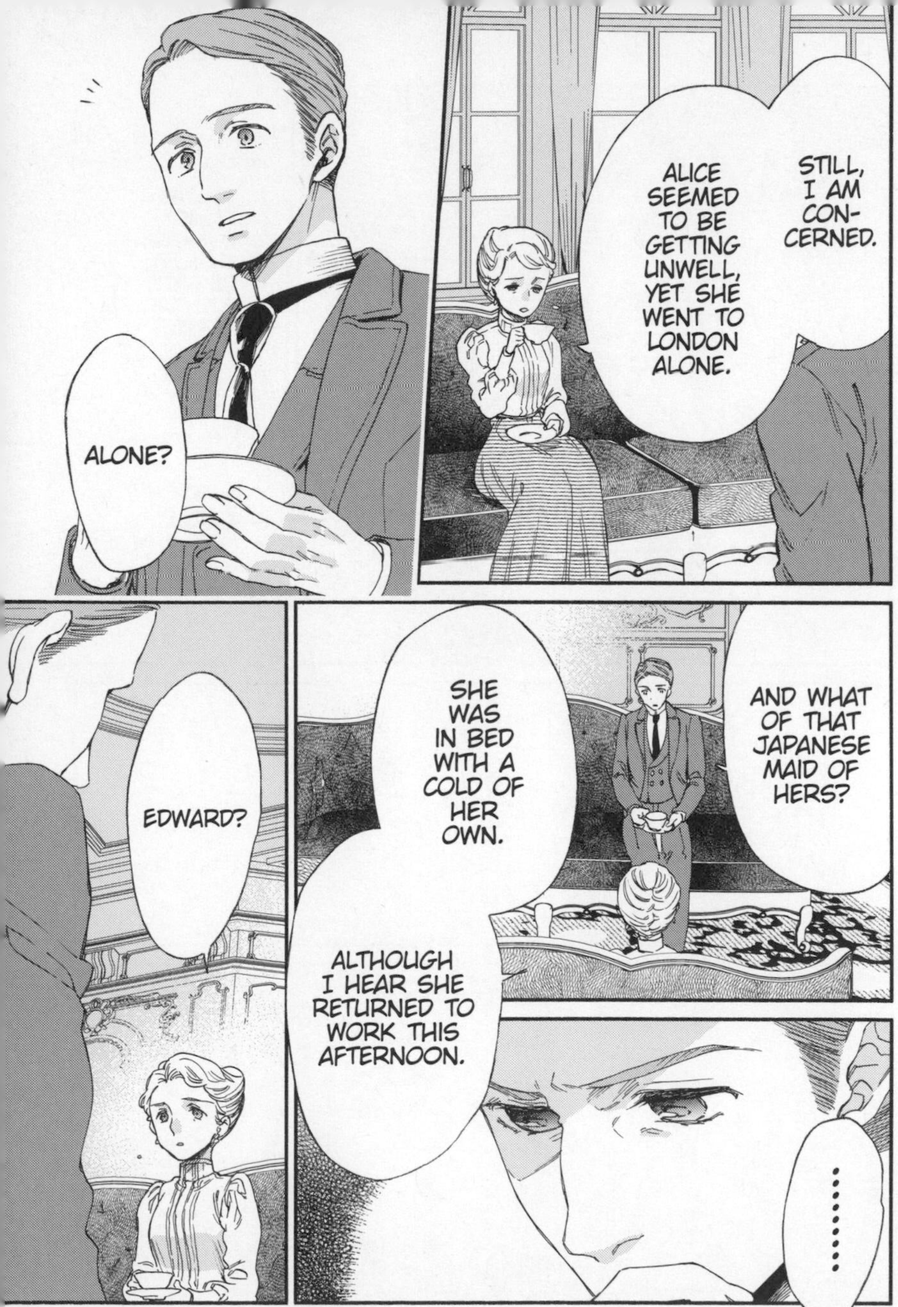
STILL, I AM CON-CERNED.
ALICE SEEMED TO BE GETTING UNWELL, YET SHE WENT TO LONDON ALONE.
ALONE?
AND WHAT OF THAT JAPANESE MAID OF HERS?
SHE WAS IN BED WITH A COLD OF HER OWN.
ALTHOUGH I HEAR SHE RETURNED TO WORK THIS AFTERNOON.
......
EDWARD?

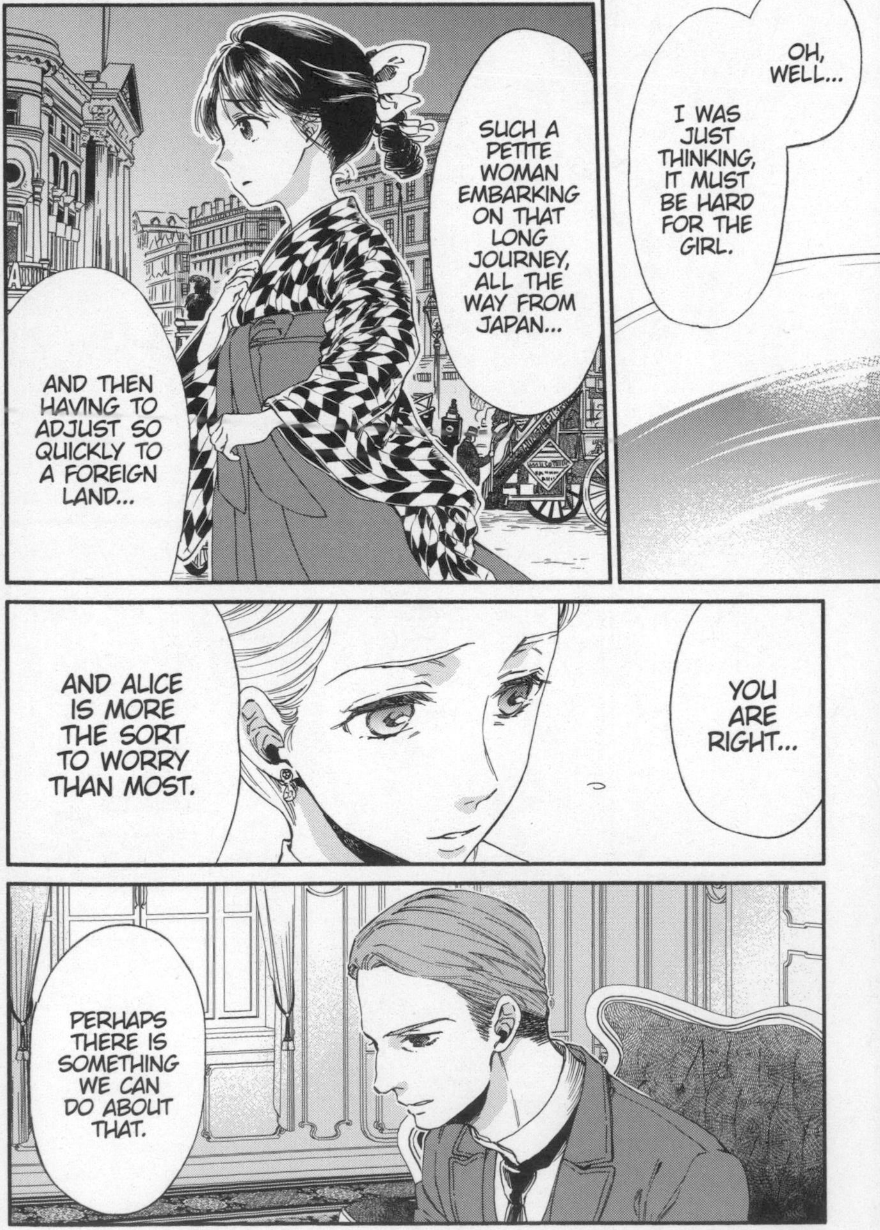
OH, WELL...
I WAS JUST THINKING, IT MUST BE HARD FOR THE GIRL.
SUCH A PETITE WOMAN EMBARKING ON THAT LONG JOURNEY, ALL THE WAY FROM JAPAN...
AND THEN HAVING TO ADJUST SO QUICKLY TO A FOREIGN LAND...
YOU ARE RIGHT...
AND ALICE IS MORE THE SORT TO WORRY THAN MOST.
PERHAPS THERE IS SOMETHING WE CAN DO ABOUT THAT.

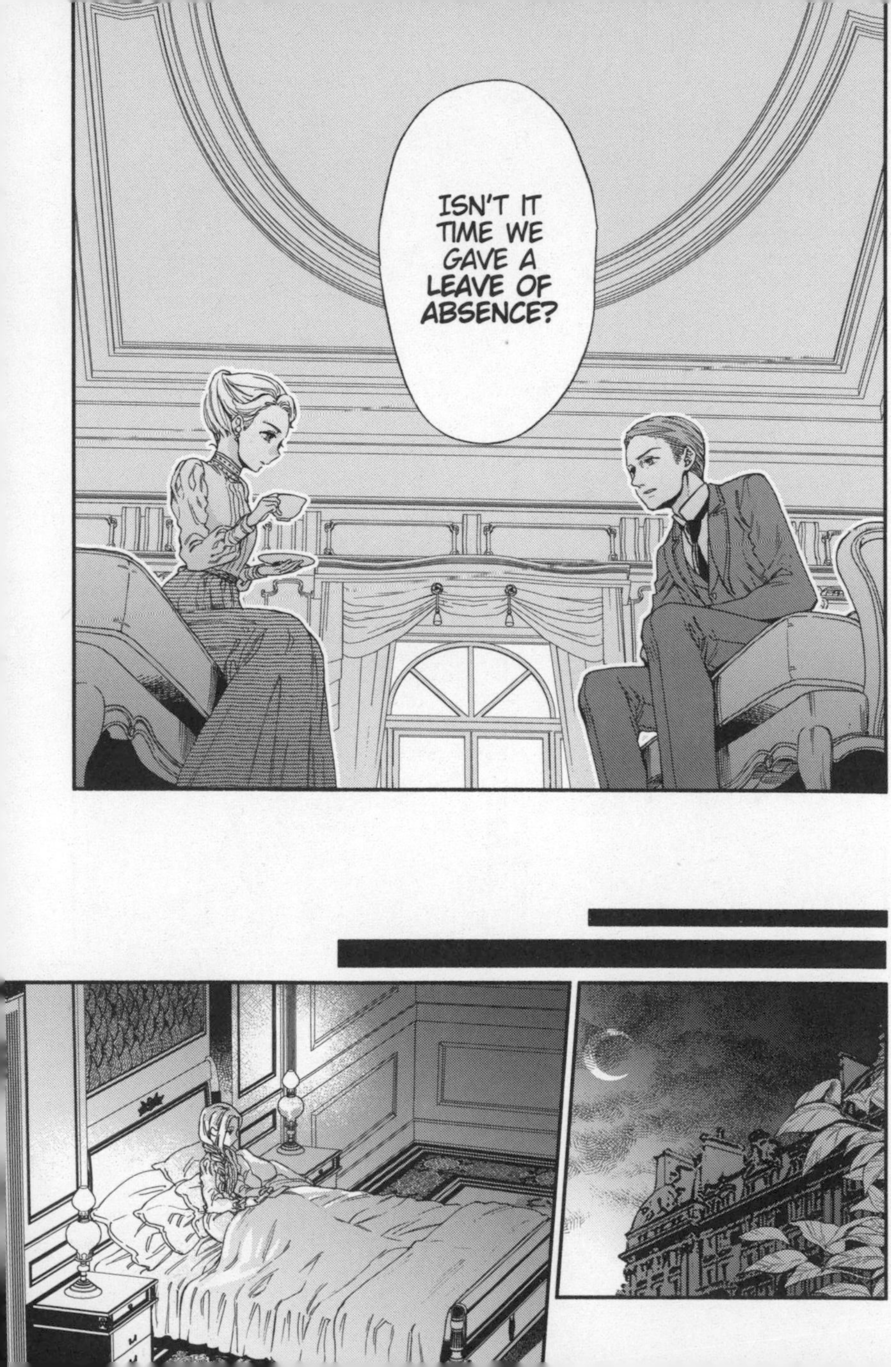
ISN'T IT TIME WE GAVE A LEAVE OF ABSENCE?

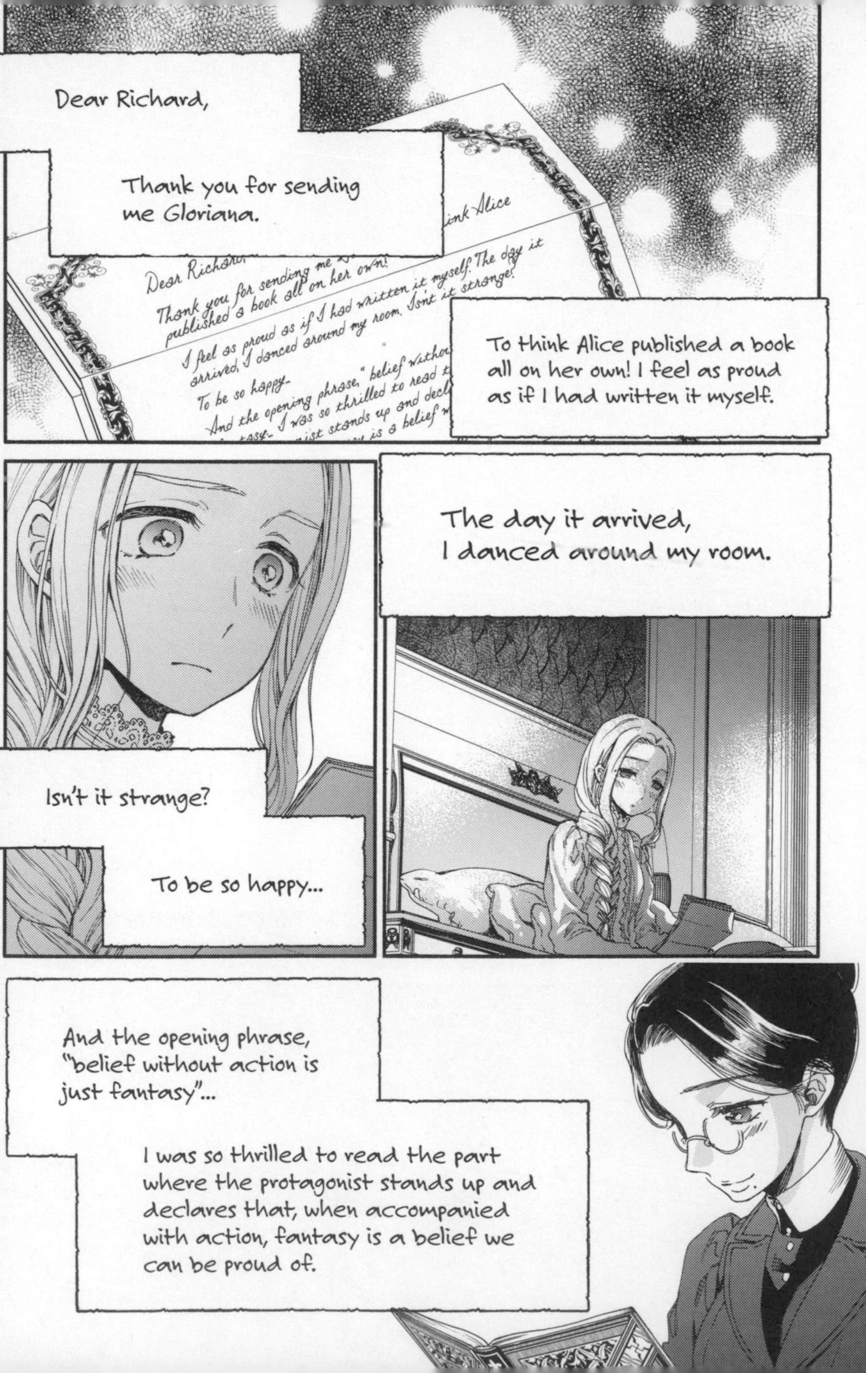

Dear Richard,
Thank you for sending me Gloriana.
To think Alice published a book all on her own! I feel as proud as if I had written it myself.
The day it arrived, I danced around my room.
Isn't it strange?
To be so happy...
And the opening phrase, "belief without action is just fantasy"...
I was so thrilled to read the part where the protagonist stands up and declares that, when accompanied with action, fantasy is a belief we can be proud of.

Through this book, I now understand what an intelligent woman Alice has become.

I was so proud and happy! I felt I couldn't sleep.

Dear Richard,
Thank you for sending me *Gloriana*. To think Alice published a book all on her own!

I feel as proud as if I had written it myself. The day it arrived, I danced around my room. Isn't it strange to be so happy...

And the opening phrase "belief without action is just fantasy"— I was so thrilled to read the part where the protagonist stands up and declares that, when accompanied with action, fantasy is a belief one can be proud of.

Through this book, I now understand what an intelligent woman Alice has become. I was so proud and happy!

I felt I couldn't sleep.

PLIP

MISS ELIZA...

EVEN NOW, MISS ELIZA IS STILL...

WATCHING OVER ME WITH THOSE GENTLE EYES.

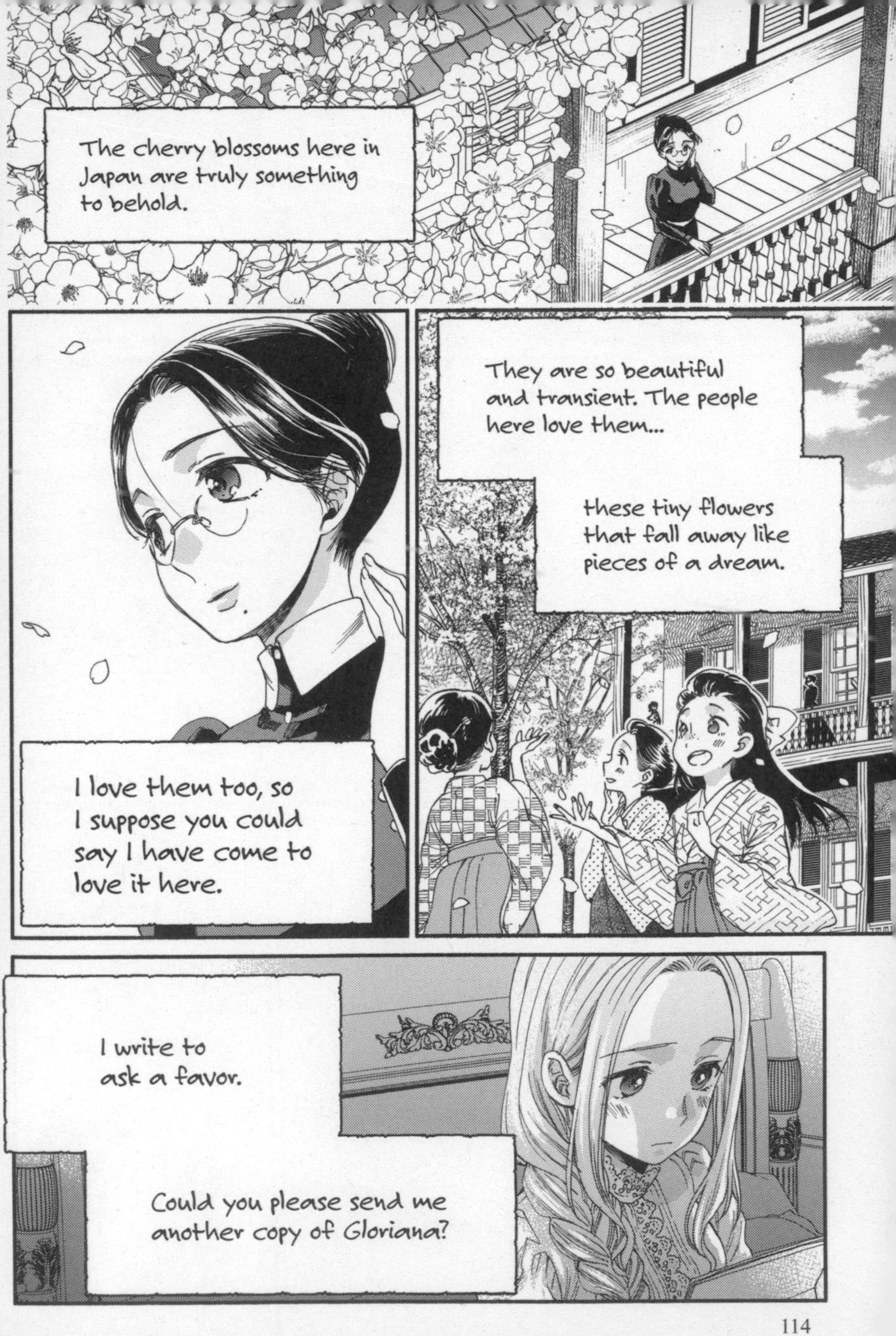
The cherry blossoms here in Japan are truly something to behold.
They are so beautiful and transient. The people here love them...
these tiny flowers that fall away like pieces of a dream.
I love them too, so I suppose you could say I have come to love it here.
I write to ask a favor.
Could you please send me another copy of Gloriana?

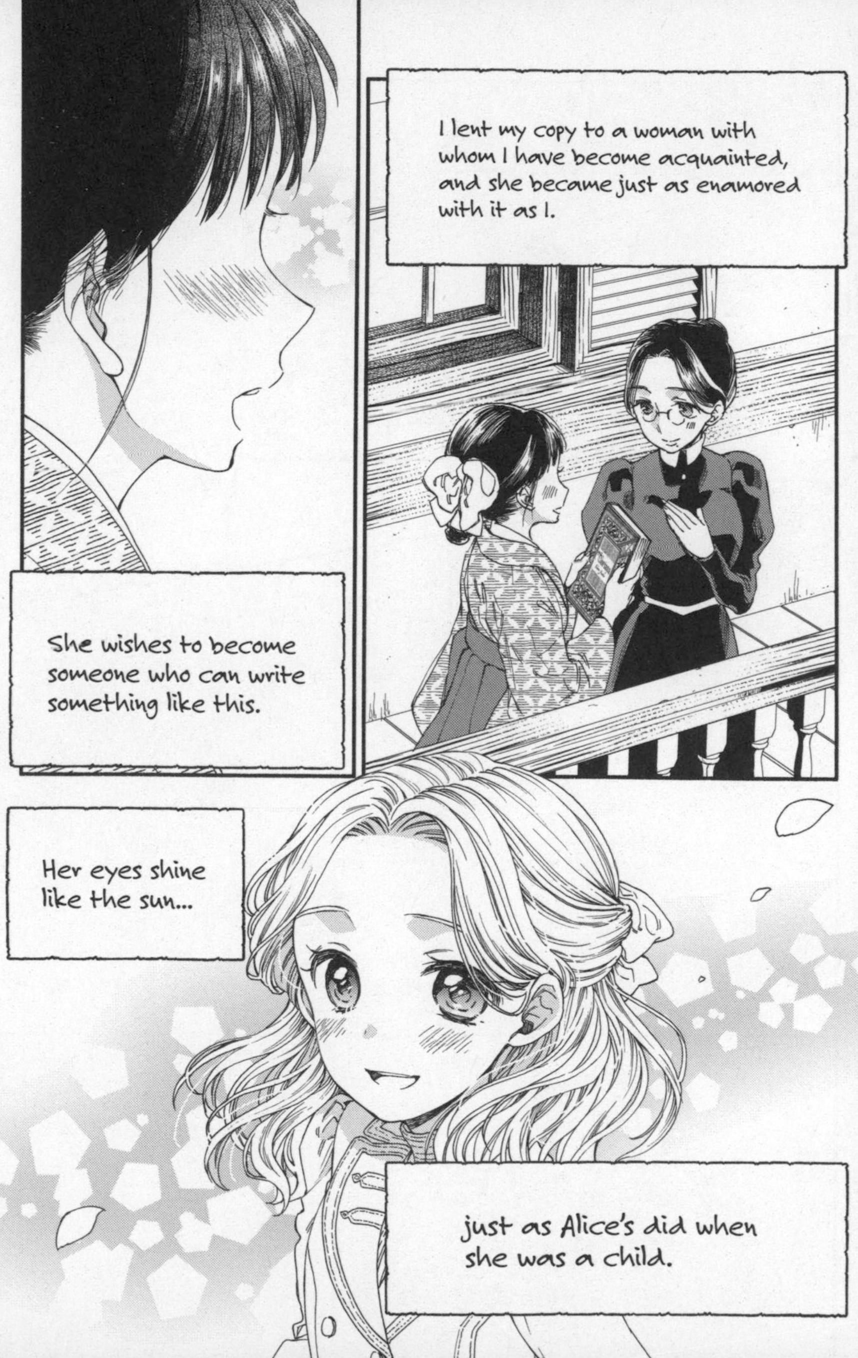
I lent my copy to a woman with whom I have become acquainted, and she became just as enamored with it as I.
She wishes to become someone who can write something like this.
Her eyes shine like the sun...
just as Alice's did when she was a child.

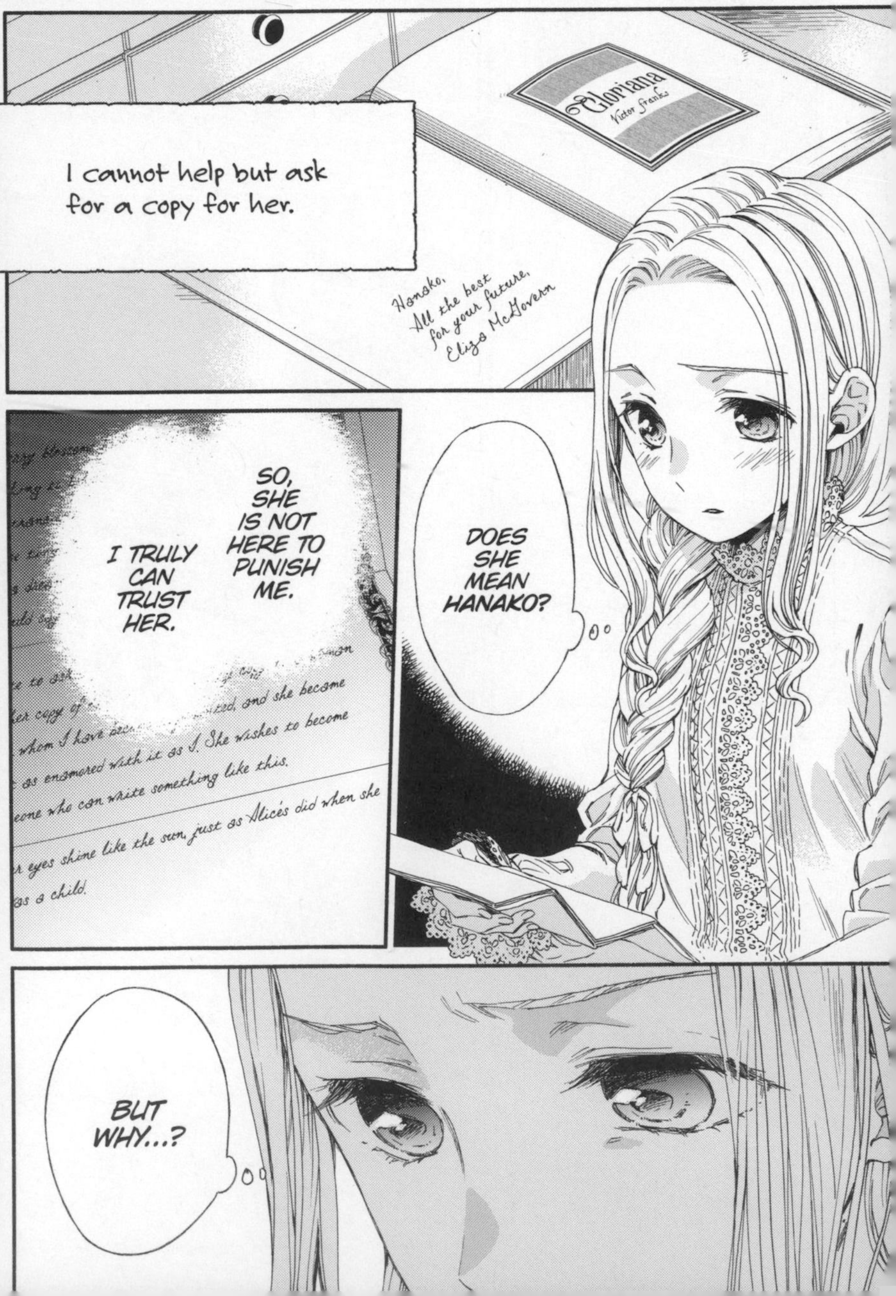
I cannot help but ask for a copy for her.
Gloriana
Victor Franks
Hanako,
All the best
for your future,
Eliza McGovern
DOES SHE MEAN HANAKO?
SO, SHE IS NOT HERE TO PUNISH ME.
I TRULY CAN TRUST HER.
as enamored with it as I. She wishes to become
one who can write something like this.
eyes shine like the sun, just as Alice's did when she
as a child.
BUT WHY...?

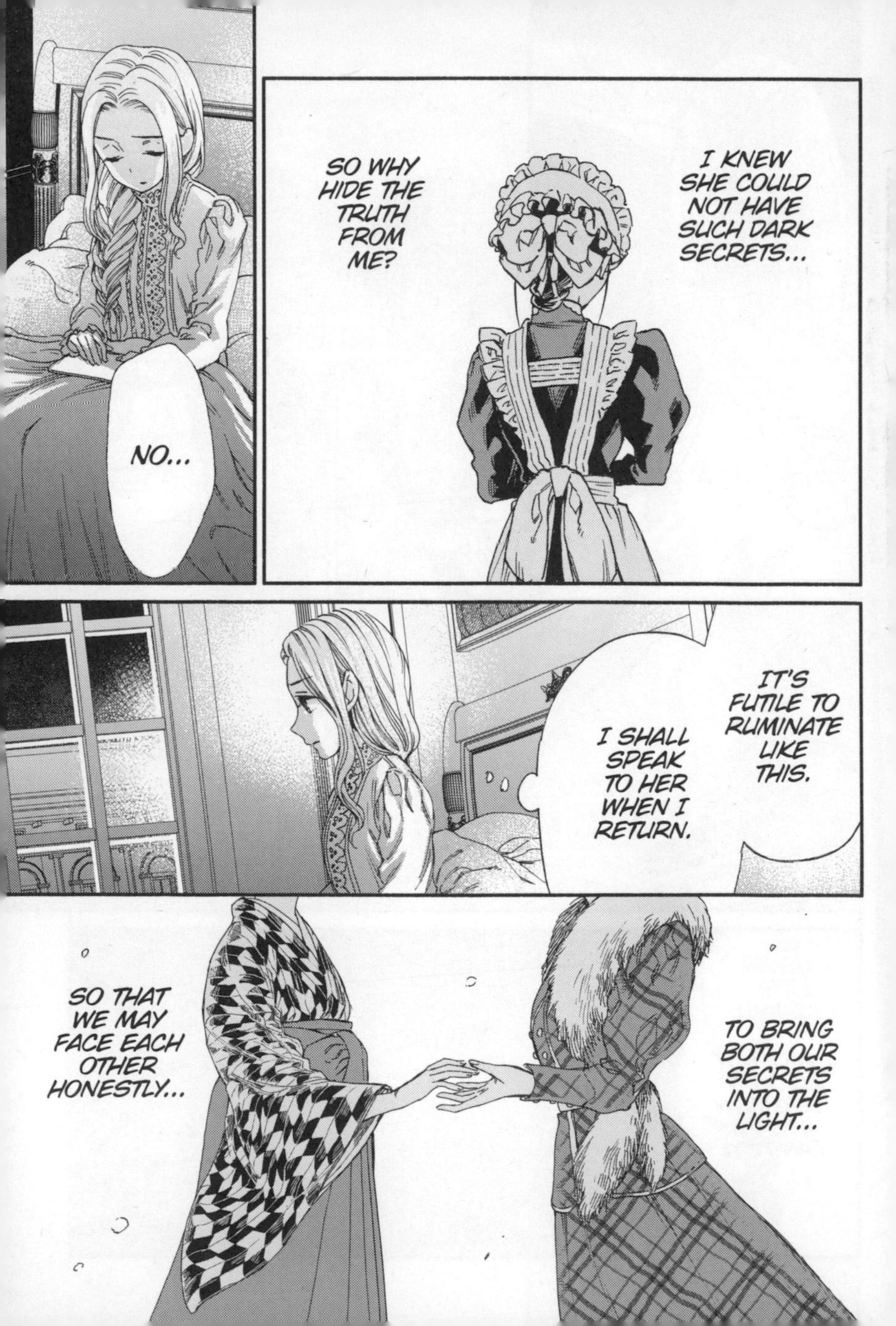
I KNEW SHE COULD NOT HAVE SUCH DARK SECRETS...
SO WHY HIDE THE TRUTH FROM ME?
NO...
IT'S FUTILE TO RUMINATE LIKE THIS.
I SHALL SPEAK TO HER WHEN I RETURN.
TO BRING BOTH OUR SECRETS INTO THE LIGHT...
SO THAT WE MAY FACE EACH OTHER HONESTLY...

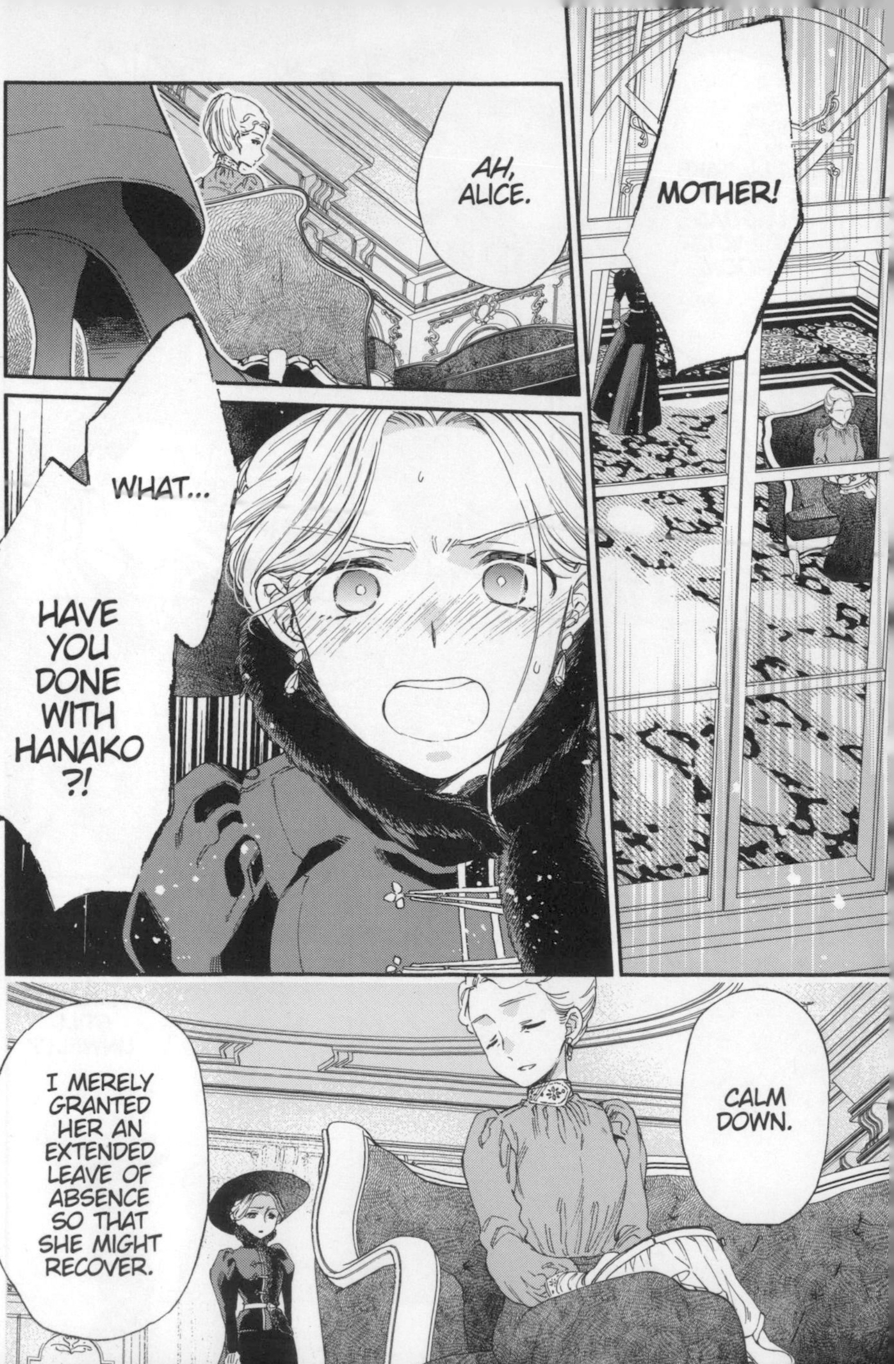
MOTHER!
AH, ALICE.
WHAT...
HAVE YOU DONE WITH HANAKO?!
CALM DOWN.
I MERELY GRANTED HER AN EXTENDED LEAVE OF ABSENCE SO THAT SHE MIGHT RECOVER.

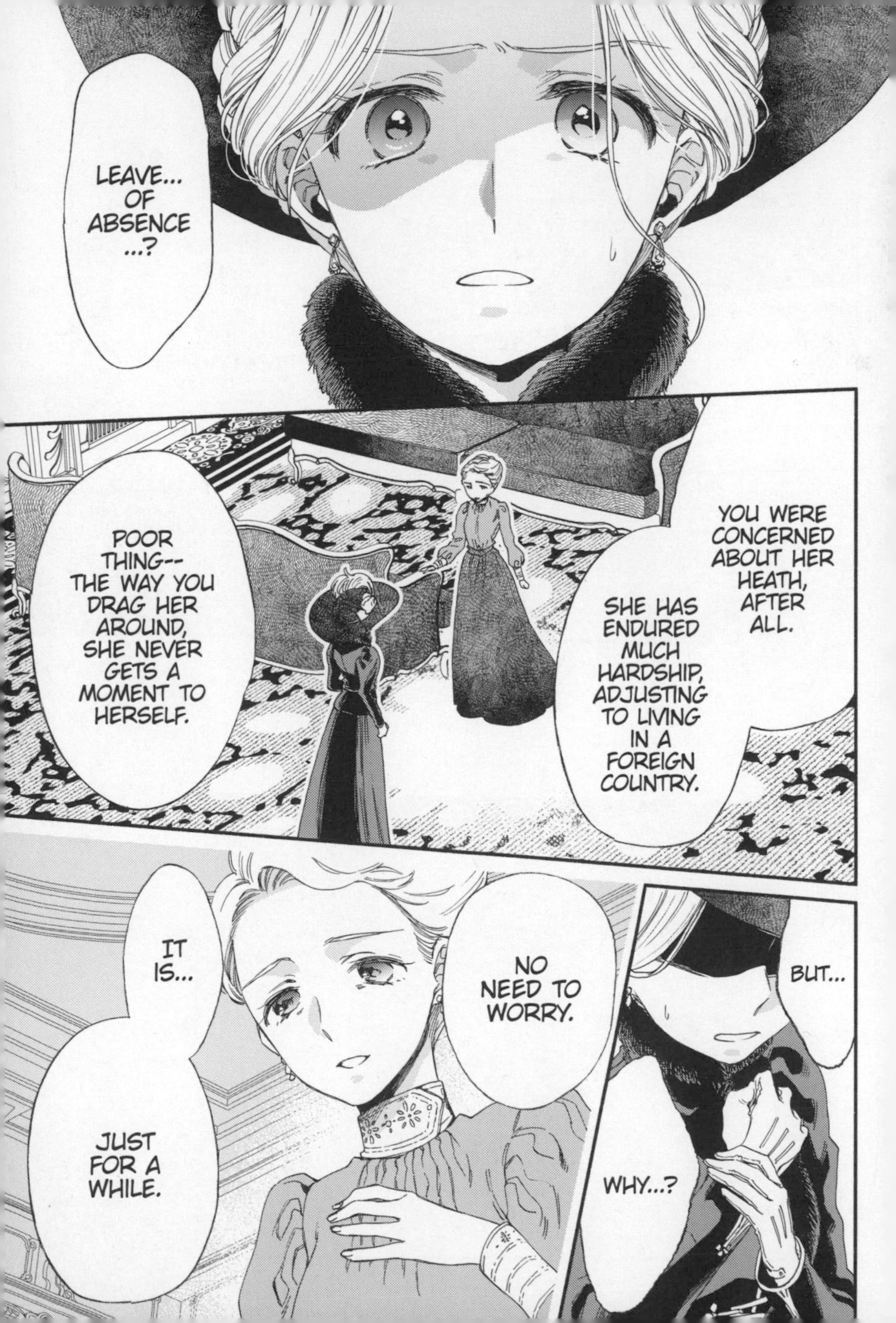
LEAVE... OF ABSENCE ...?
YOU WERE CONCERNED ABOUT HER HEATH, AFTER ALL.
SHE HAS ENDURED MUCH HARDSHIP, ADJUSTING TO LIVING IN A FOREIGN COUNTRY.
POOR THING-- THE WAY YOU DRAG HER AROUND, SHE NEVER GETS A MOMENT TO HERSELF.
BUT...
WHY...?
NO NEED TO WORRY.
IT IS...
JUST FOR A WHILE.

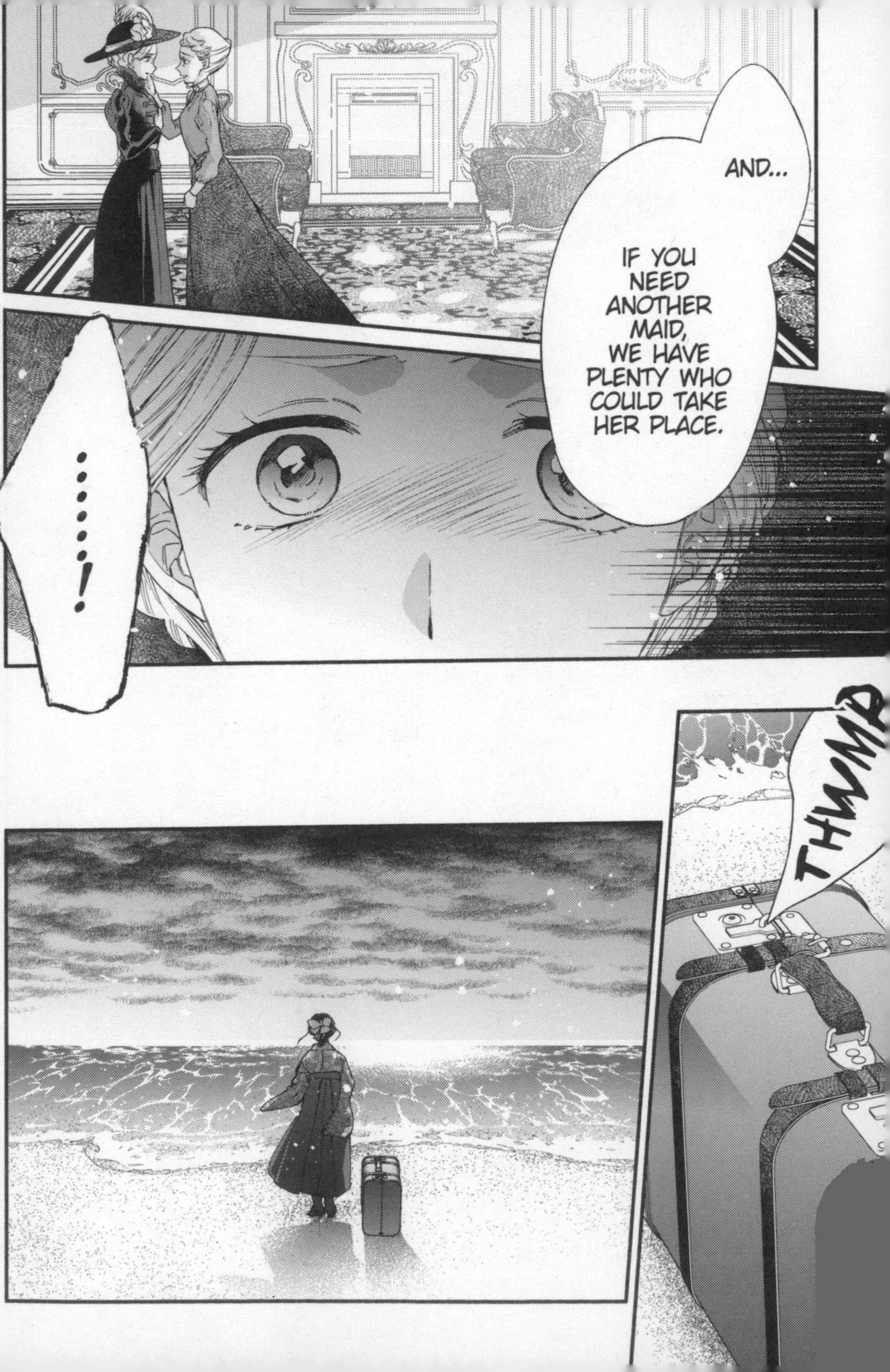
AND...
IF YOU NEED ANOTHER MAID, WE HAVE PLENTY WHO COULD TAKE HER PLACE.
......!
THUMP

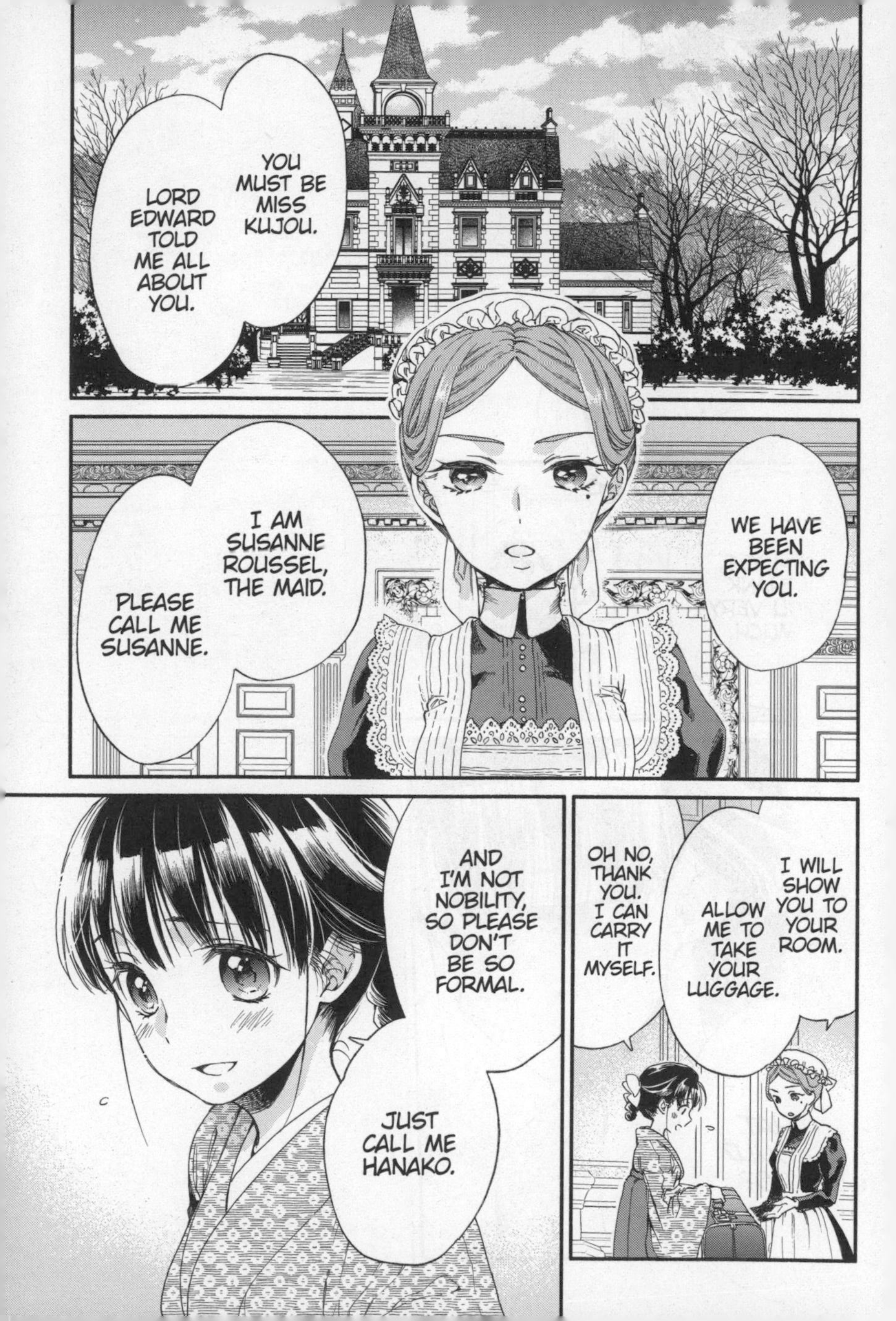
YOU MUST BE MISS KUJOU.
LORD EDWARD TOLD ME ALL ABOUT YOU.
WE HAVE BEEN EXPECTING YOU.
I AM SUSANNE ROUSSEL, THE MAID.
PLEASE CALL ME SUSANNE.
I WILL SHOW YOU TO YOUR ROOM.
ALLOW ME TO TAKE YOUR LUGGAGE.
OH NO, THANK YOU. I CAN CARRY IT MYSELF.
AND I'M NOT NOBILITY, SO PLEASE DON'T BE SO FORMAL.
JUST CALL ME HANAKO.

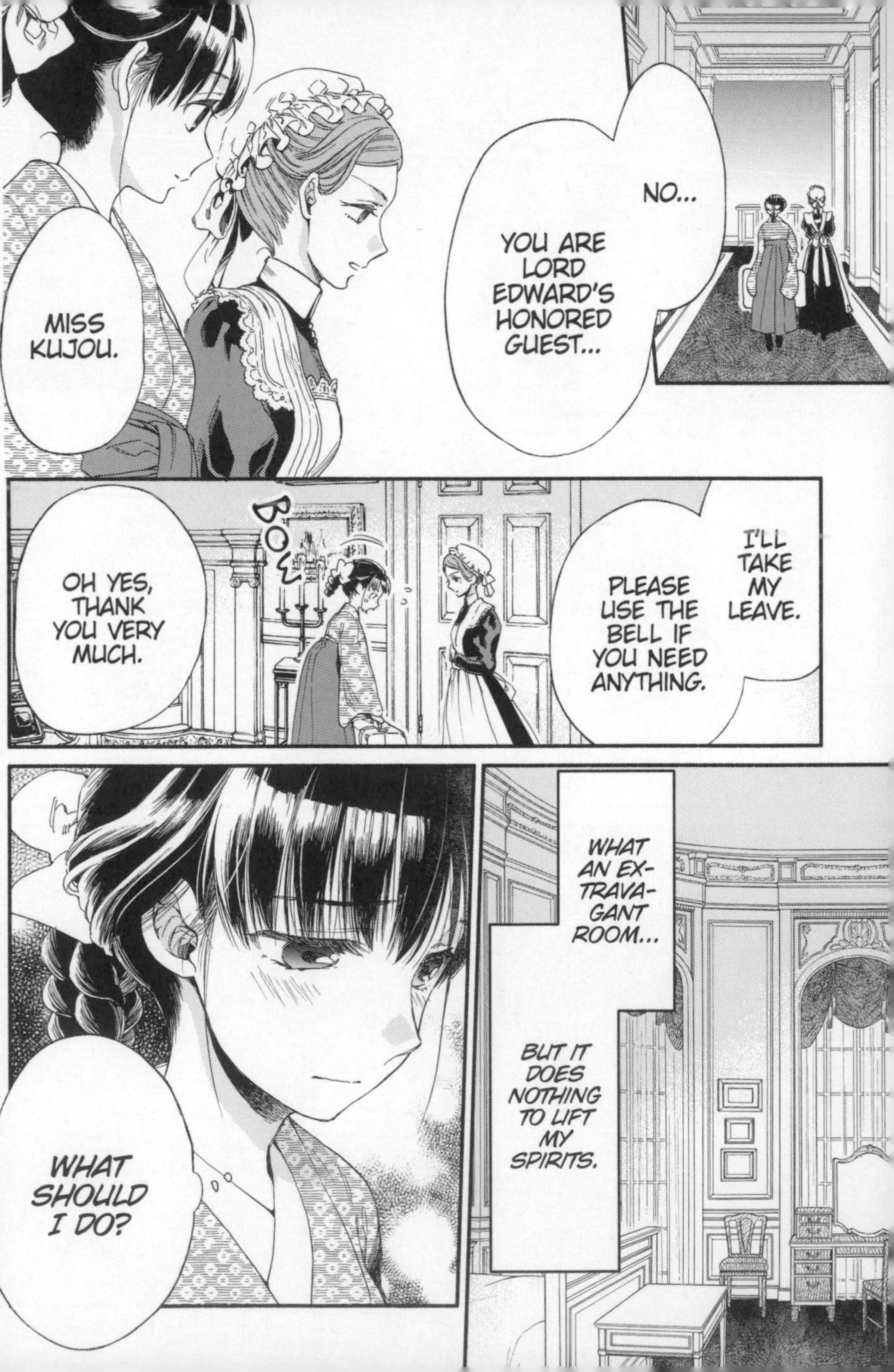
NO...
YOU ARE LORD EDWARD'S HONORED GUEST...
MISS KUJOU.
I'LL TAKE MY LEAVE.
PLEASE USE THE BELL IF YOU NEED ANYTHING.
BOW
OH YES, THANK YOU VERY MUCH.
WHAT AN EXTRAVAGANT ROOM...
BUT IT DOES NOTHING TO LIFT MY SPIRITS.
WHAT SHOULD I DO?

{ Chapter 10 }
The Sea Breeze Draws the Sun's Radiance

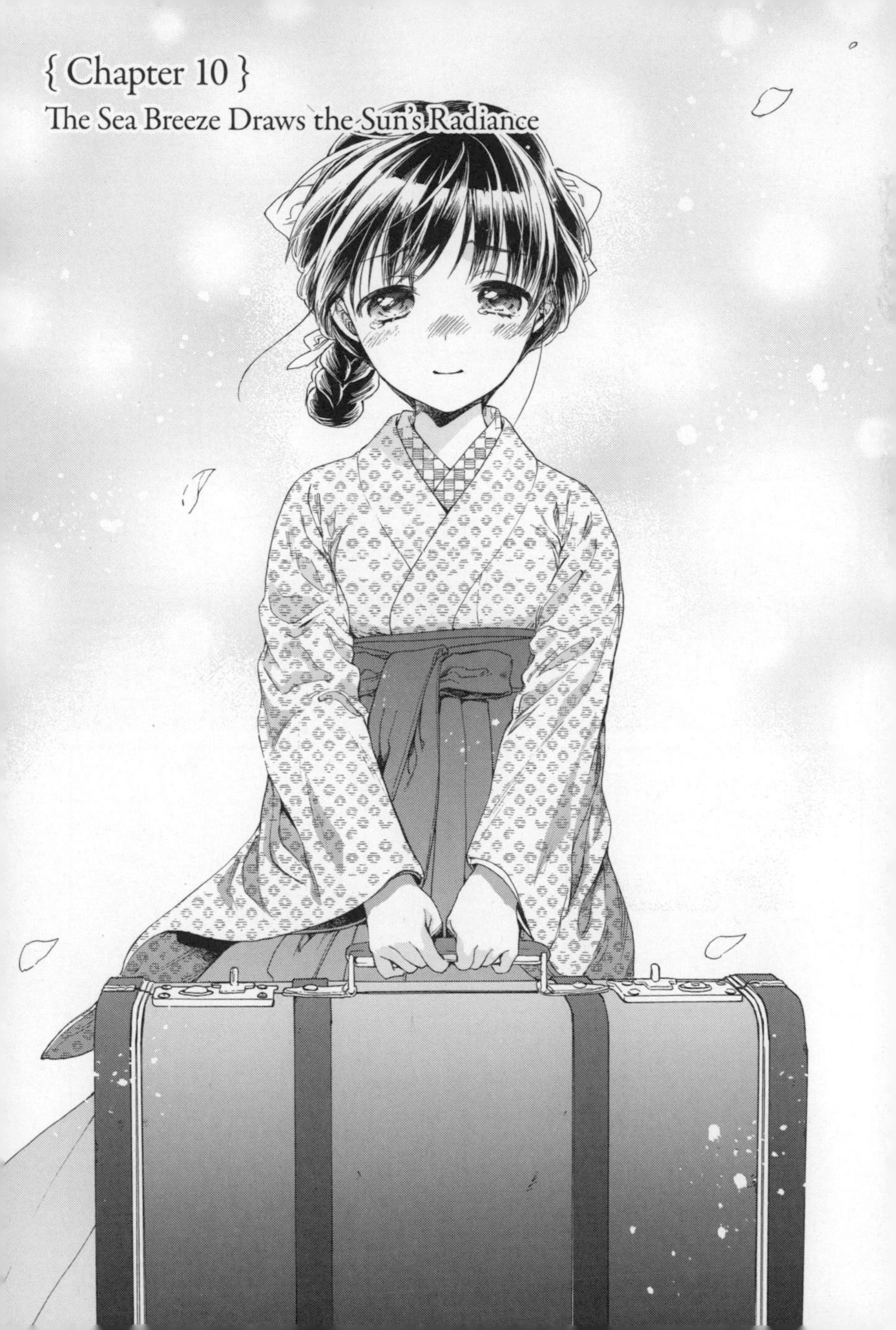

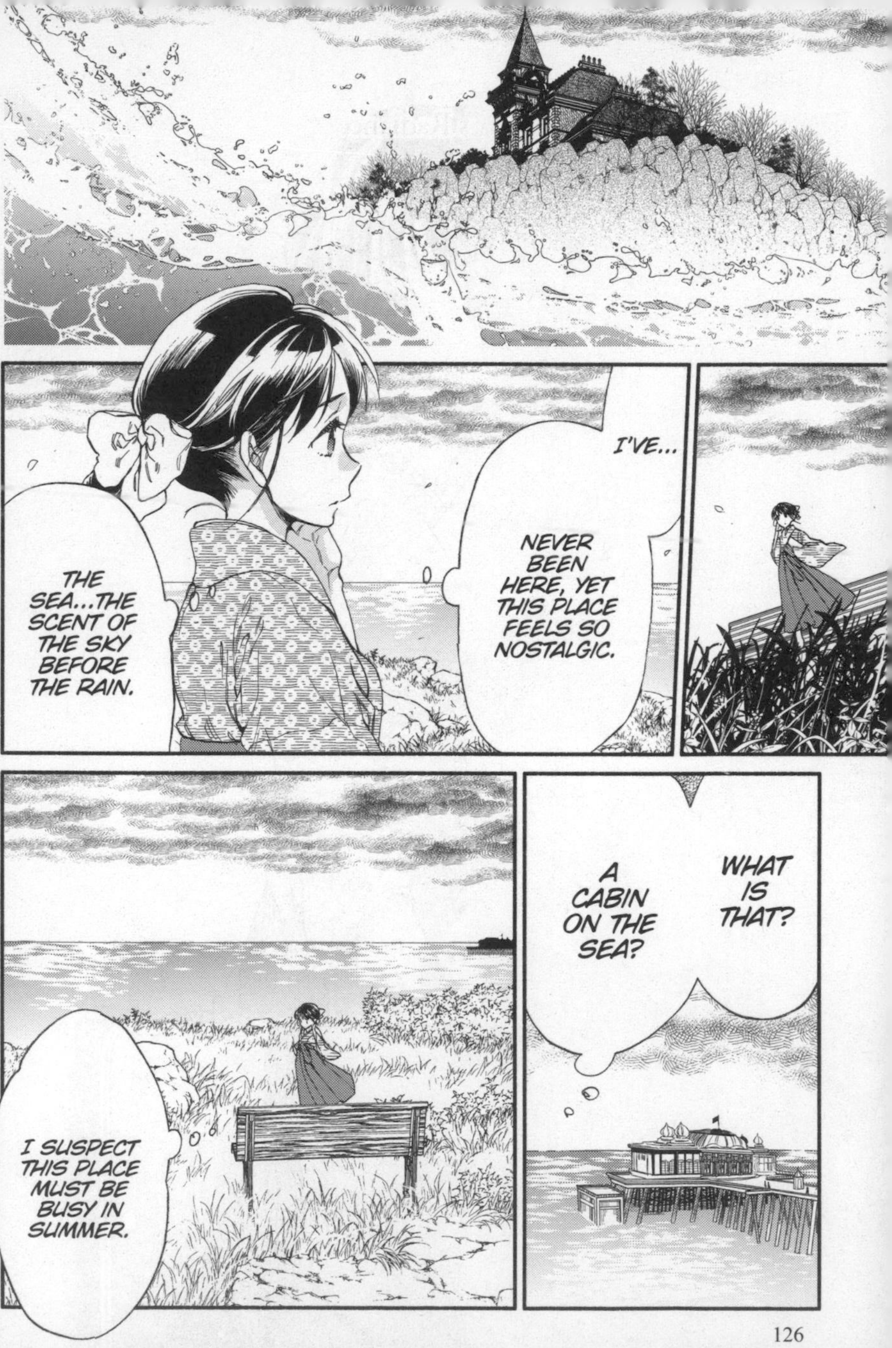
I'VE...
NEVER BEEN HERE, YET THIS PLACE FEELS SO NOSTALGIC.
THE SEA...THE SCENT OF THE SKY BEFORE THE RAIN.
WHAT IS THAT?
A CABIN ON THE SEA?
I SUSPECT THIS PLACE MUST BE BUSY IN SUMMER.

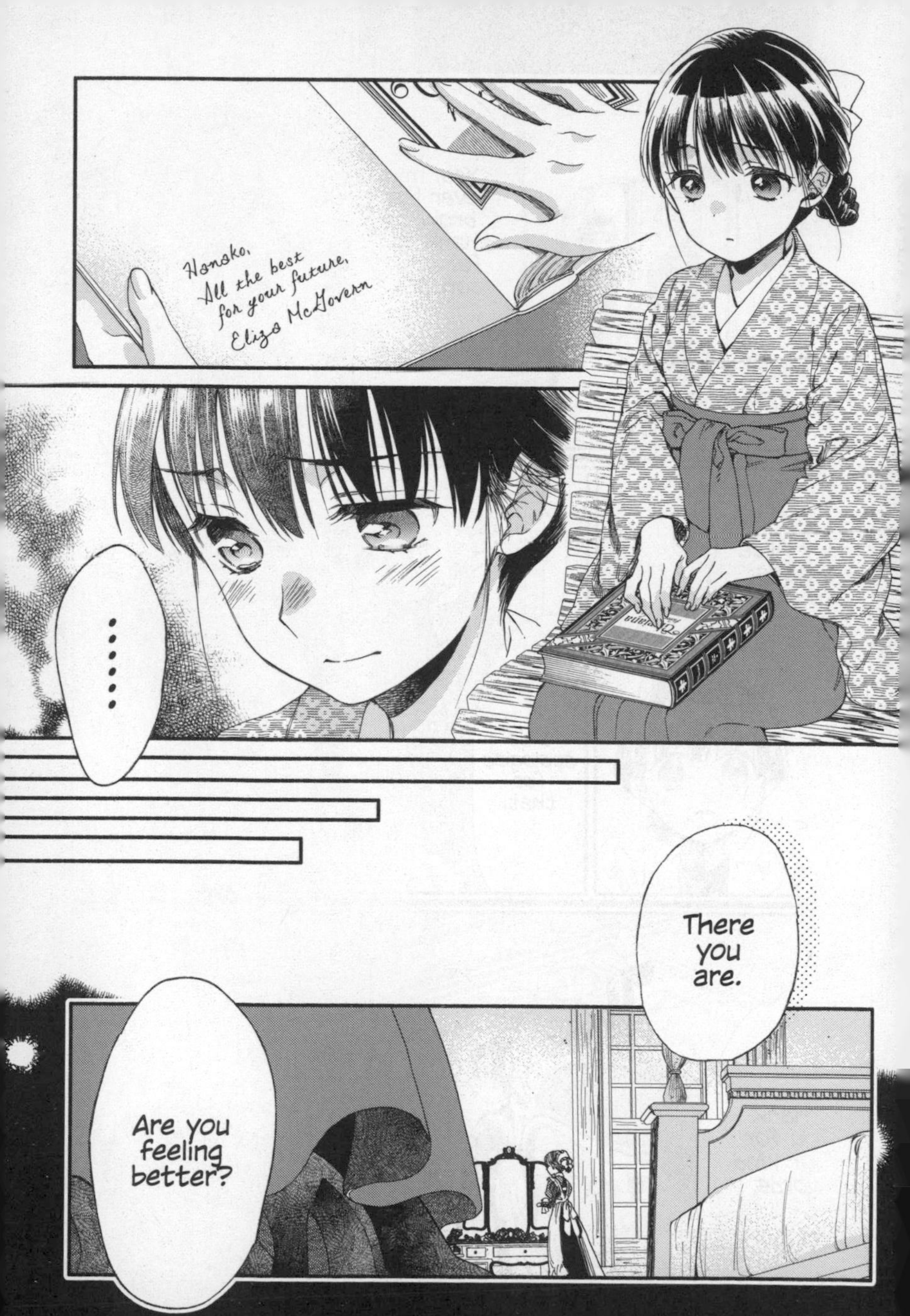
Hanako,
All the best
for your future,
Eliza McGovern
......
There you are.
Are you feeling better?

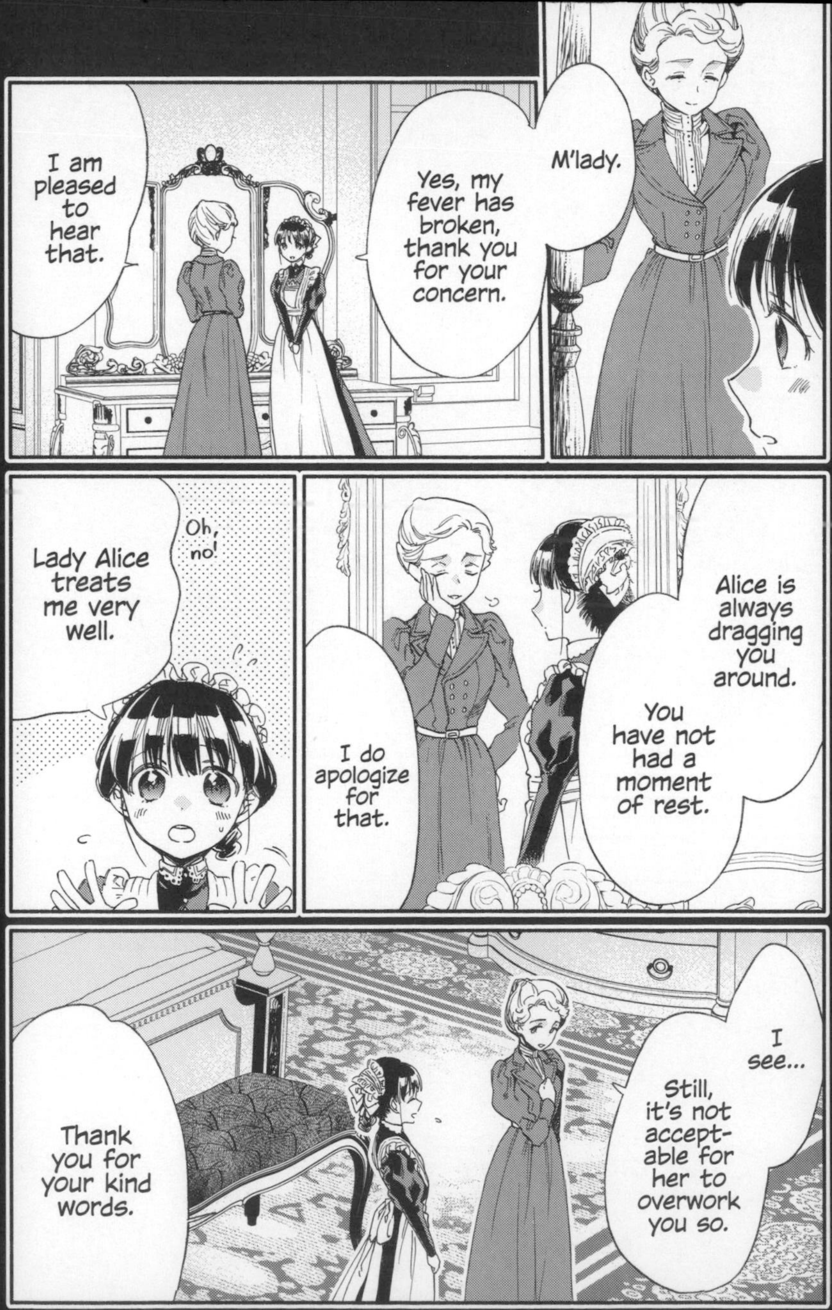
M'lady.
Yes, my fever has broken, thank you for your concern.
I am pleased to hear that.
Alice is always dragging you around.
You have not had a moment of rest.
I do apologize for that.
Oh, no!
Lady Alice treats me very well.
I see...
Still, it's not acceptable for her to overwork you so.
Thank you for your kind words.

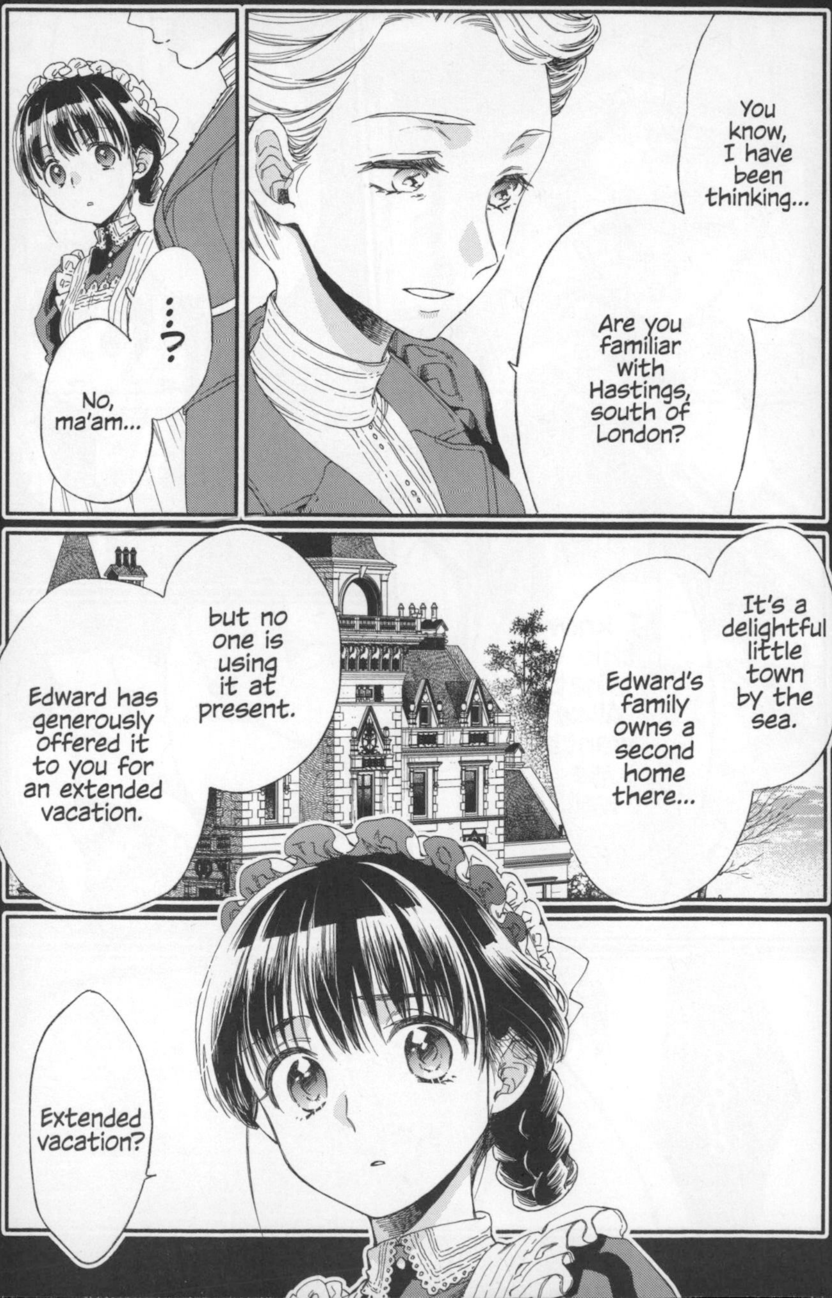
You know, I have been thinking...
Are you familiar with Hastings, south of London?
...?
No, ma'am...
It's a delightful little town by the sea.
Edward's family owns a second home there...
but no one is using it at present.
Edward has generously offered it to you for an extended vacation.
Extended vacation?

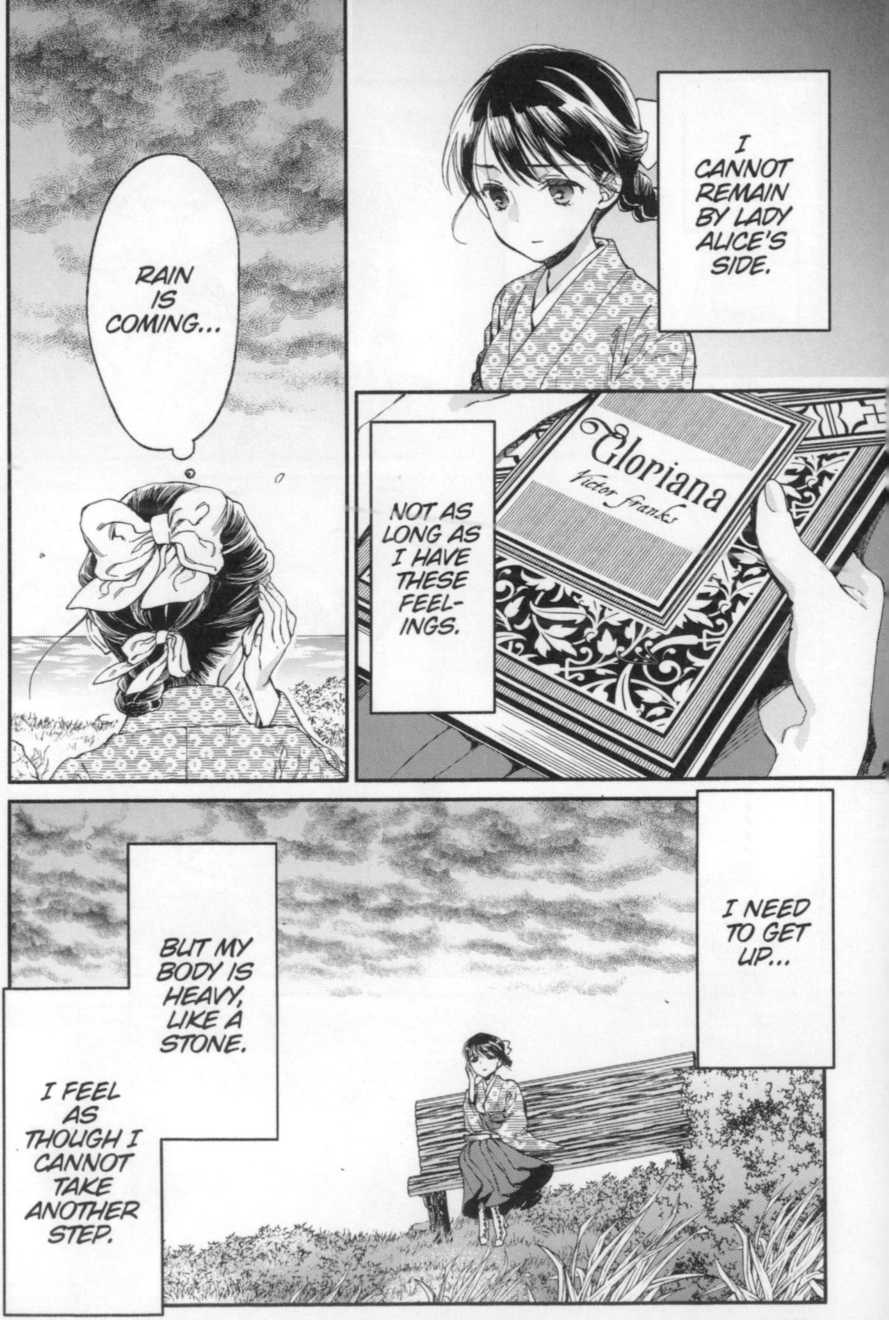
I CANNOT REMAIN BY LADY ALICE'S SIDE.
Gloriana
Victor franks
NOT AS LONG AS I HAVE THESE FEEL-INGS.
RAIN IS COMING...
I NEED TO GET UP...
BUT MY BODY IS HEAVY, LIKE A STONE.
I FEEL AS THOUGH I CANNOT TAKE ANOTHER STEP.

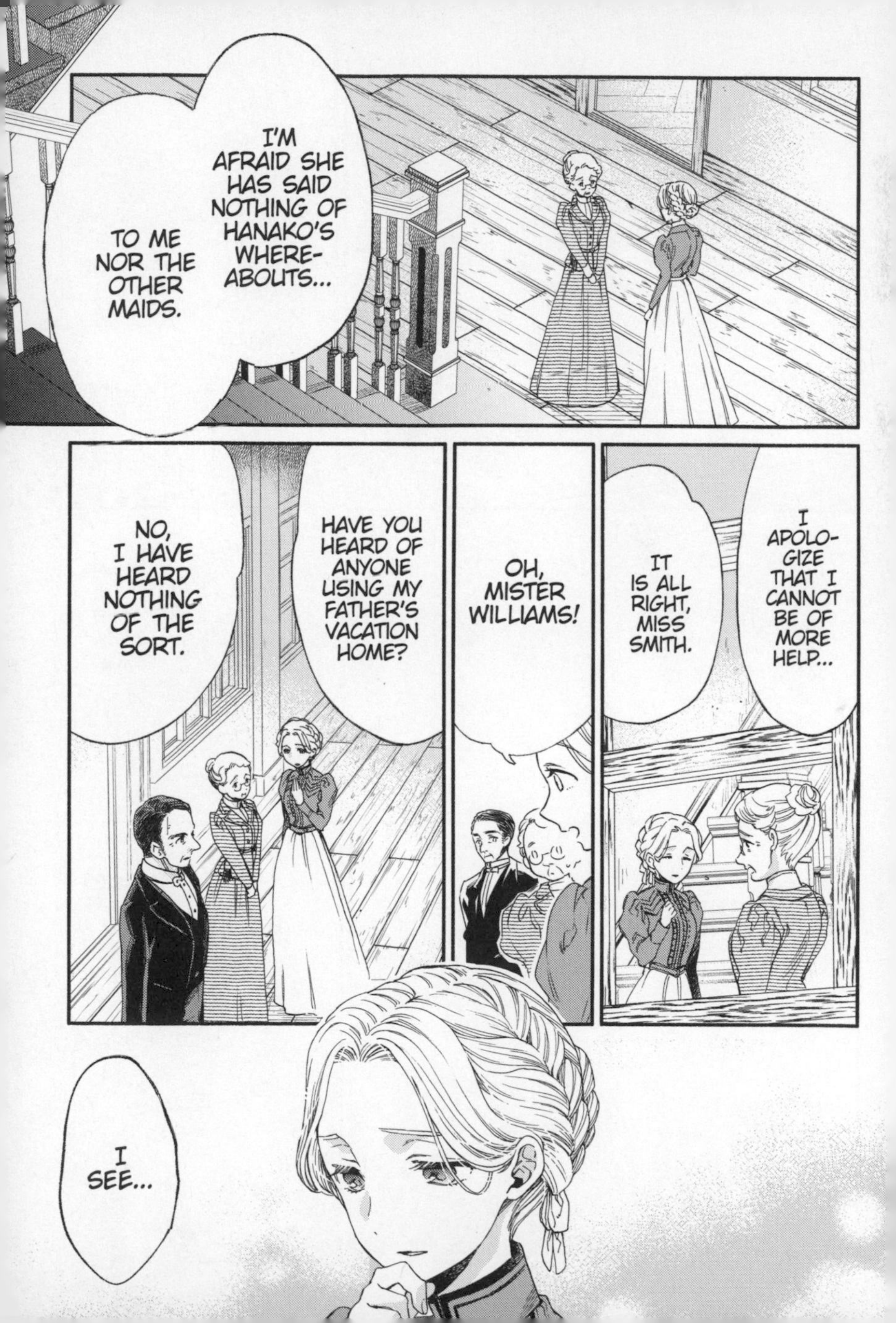
I'M AFRAID SHE HAS SAID NOTHING OF HANAKO'S WHERE-ABOUTS...
TO ME NOR THE OTHER MAIDS.
I APOLO-GIZE THAT I CANNOT BE OF MORE HELP...
IT IS ALL RIGHT, MISS SMITH.
OH, MISTER WILLIAMS!
HAVE YOU HEARD OF ANYONE USING MY FATHER'S VACATION HOME?
NO, I HAVE HEARD NOTHING OF THE SORT.
I SEE...

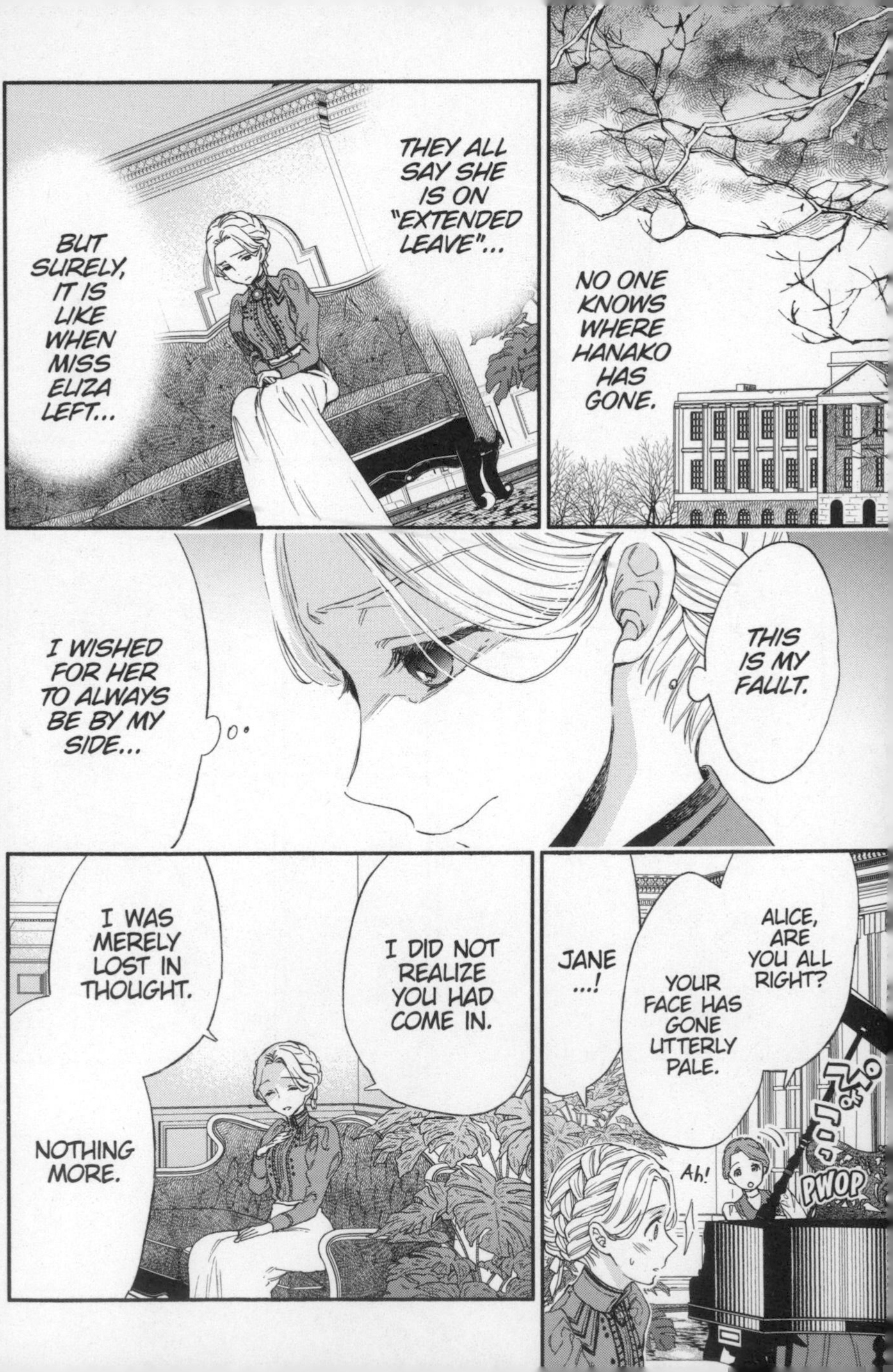
NO ONE KNOWS WHERE HANAKO HAS GONE.
THEY ALL SAY SHE IS ON "EXTENDED LEAVE"...
BUT SURELY, IT IS LIKE WHEN MISS ELIZA LEFT...
THIS IS MY FAULT.
I WISHED FOR HER TO ALWAYS BE BY MY SIDE...
ALICE, ARE YOU ALL RIGHT?
YOUR FACE HAS GONE UTTERLY PALE.
JANE ...!
Ah!
PWOP
I DID NOT REALIZE YOU HAD COME IN.
I WAS MERELY LOST IN THOUGHT.
NOTHING MORE.

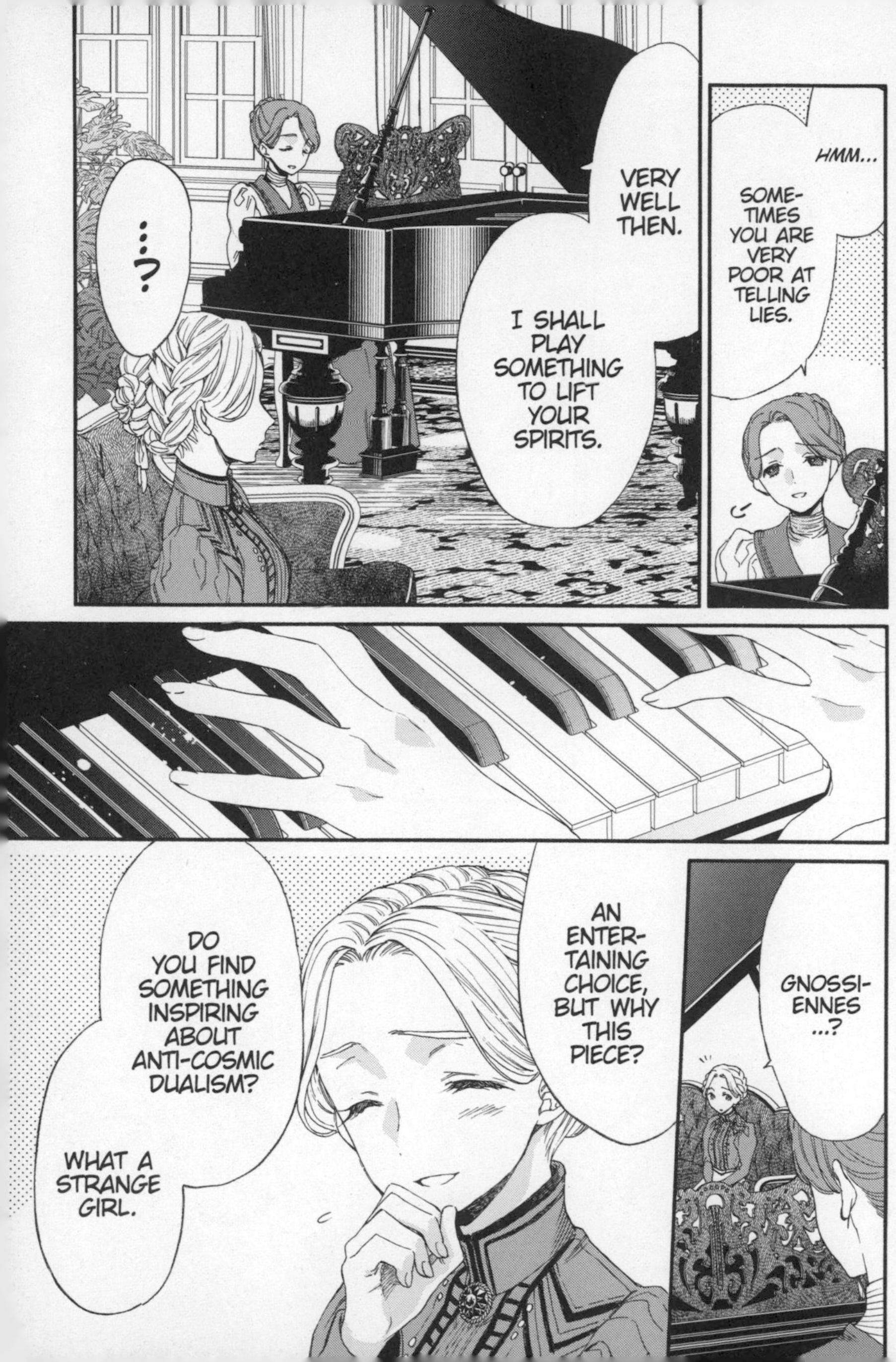
HMM...
SOME-TIMES YOU ARE VERY POOR AT TELLING LIES.
VERY WELL THEN.
I SHALL PLAY SOMETHING TO LIFT YOUR SPIRITS.
...?
GNOSSI-ENNES ...?
AN ENTER-TAINING CHOICE, BUT WHY THIS PIECE?
DO YOU FIND SOMETHING INSPIRING ABOUT ANTI-COSMIC DUALISM?
WHAT A STRANGE GIRL.

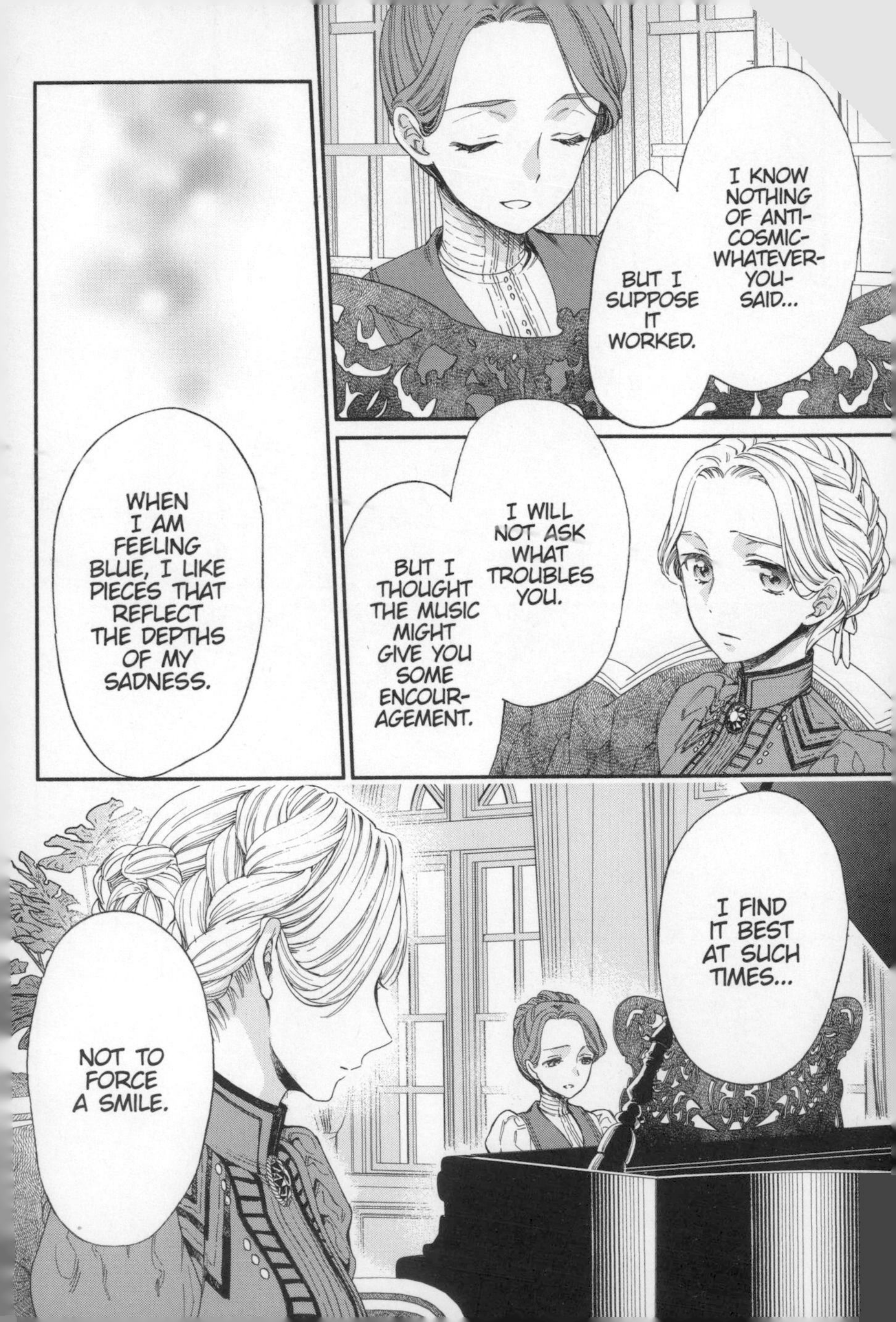
I KNOW NOTHING OF ANTI-COSMIC-WHATEVER-YOU-SAID...
BUT I SUPPOSE IT WORKED.
I WILL NOT ASK WHAT TROUBLES YOU.
BUT I THOUGHT THE MUSIC MIGHT GIVE YOU SOME ENCOURAGEMENT.
WHEN I AM FEELING BLUE, I LIKE PIECES THAT REFLECT THE DEPTHS OF MY SADNESS.
I FIND IT BEST AT SUCH TIMES...
NOT TO FORCE A SMILE.

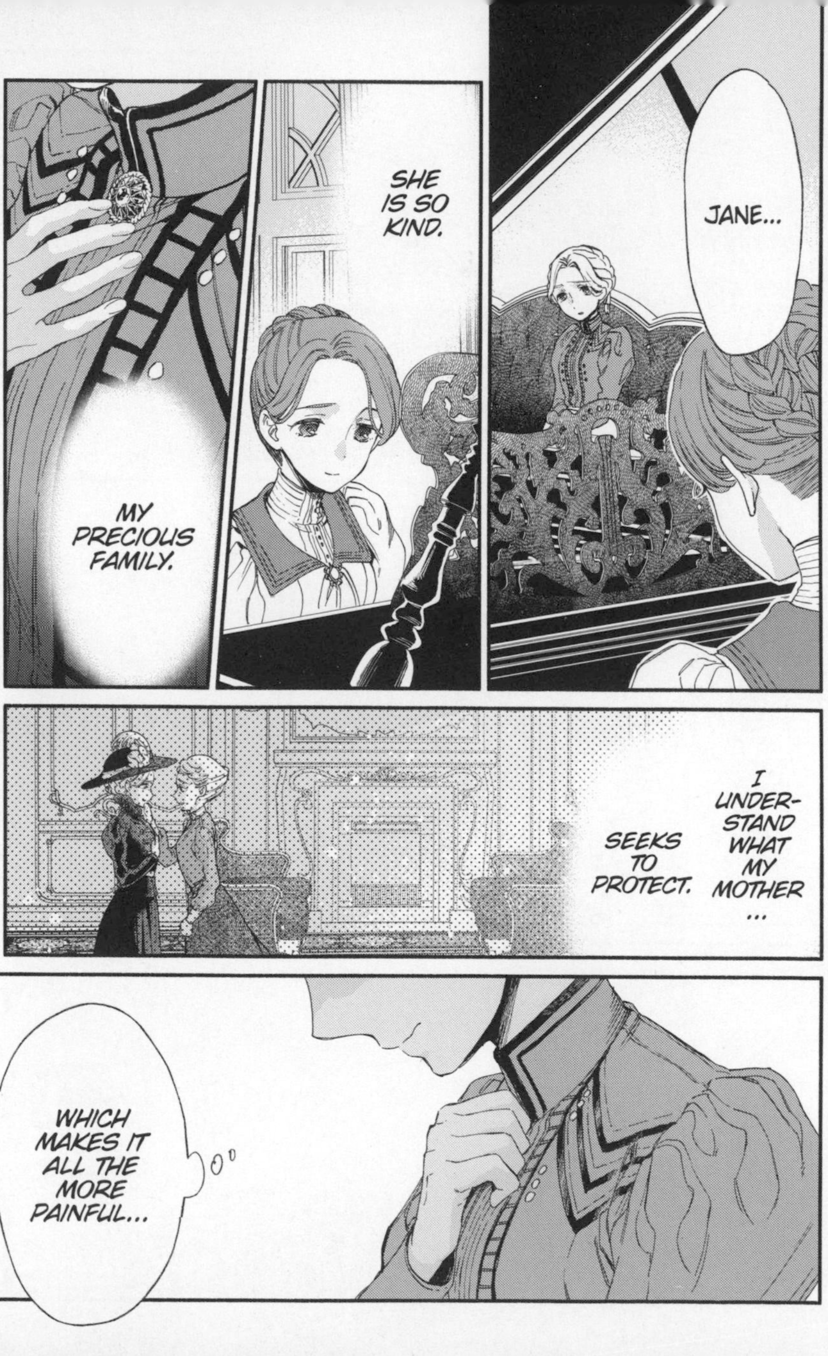
JANE...
SHE IS SO KIND.
MY PRECIOUS FAMILY.
I UNDER-STAND WHAT MY MOTHER...
SEEKS TO PROTECT.
WHICH MAKES IT ALL THE MORE PAINFUL...

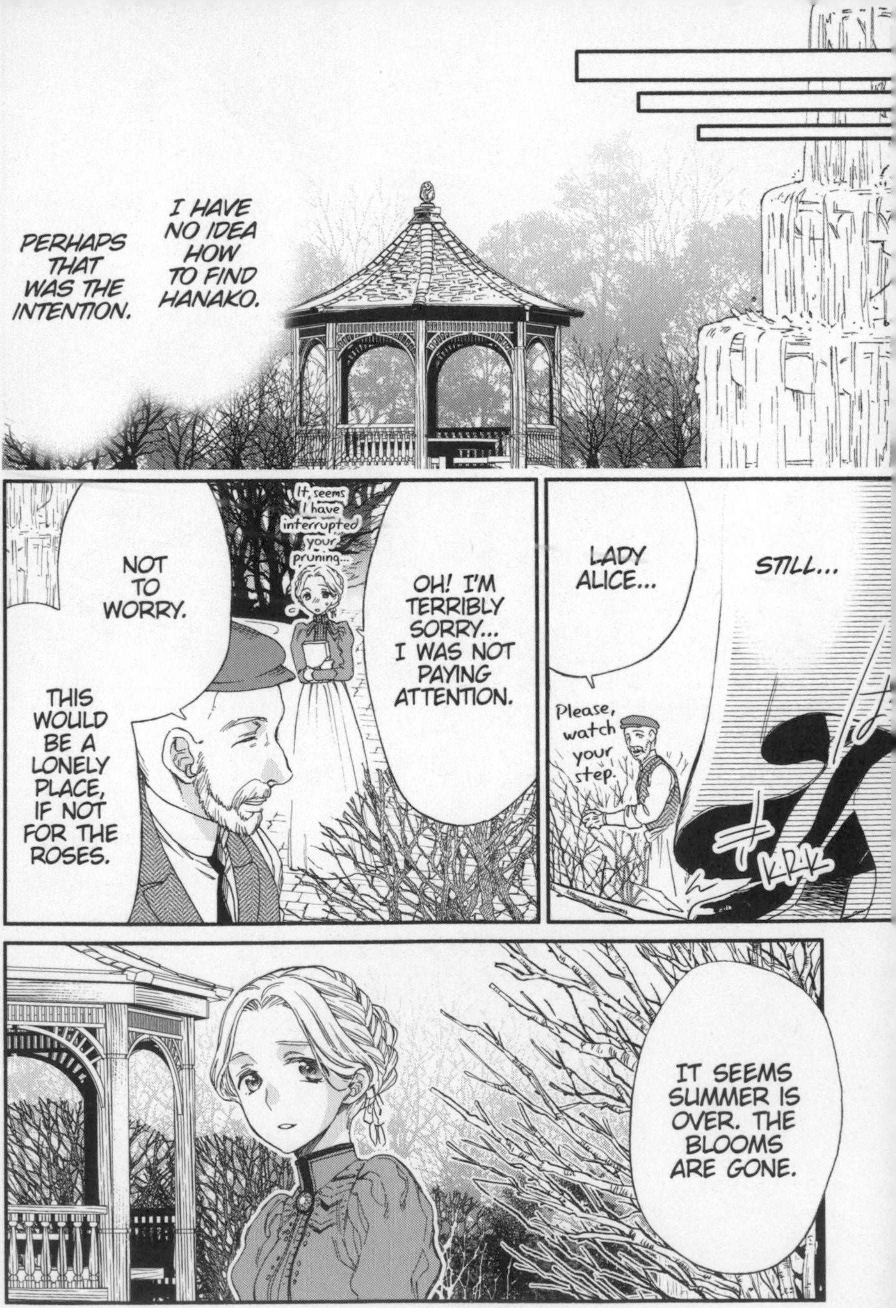
I HAVE NO IDEA HOW TO FIND HANAKO.
PERHAPS THAT WAS THE INTENTION.
STILL...
LADY ALICE...
Please, watch your step.
OH! I'M TERRIBLY SORRY... I WAS NOT PAYING ATTENTION.
It seems I have interrupted your pruning...
NOT TO WORRY.
THIS WOULD BE A LONELY PLACE, IF NOT FOR THE ROSES.
IT SEEMS SUMMER IS OVER. THE BLOOMS ARE GONE.

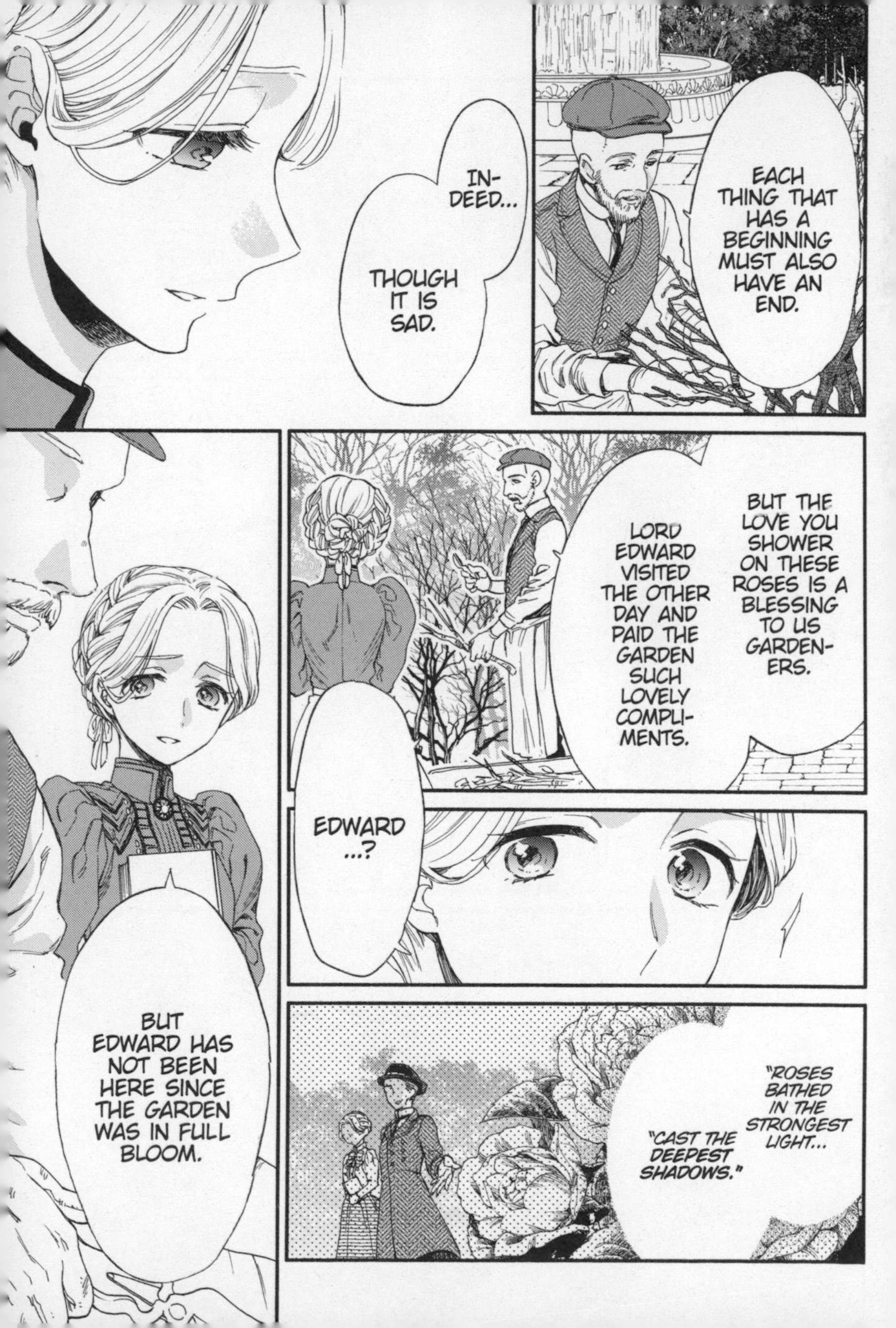
EACH THING THAT HAS A BEGINNING MUST ALSO HAVE AN END.
IN-DEED...
THOUGH IT IS SAD.
BUT THE LOVE YOU SHOWER ON THESE ROSES IS A BLESSING TO US GARDEN-ERS.
LORD EDWARD VISITED THE OTHER DAY AND PAID THE GARDEN SUCH LOVELY COMPLI-MENTS.
EDWARD ...?
"ROSES BATHED IN THE STRONGEST LIGHT...
"CAST THE DEEPEST SHADOWS."
BUT EDWARD HAS NOT BEEN HERE SINCE THE GARDEN WAS IN FULL BLOOM.

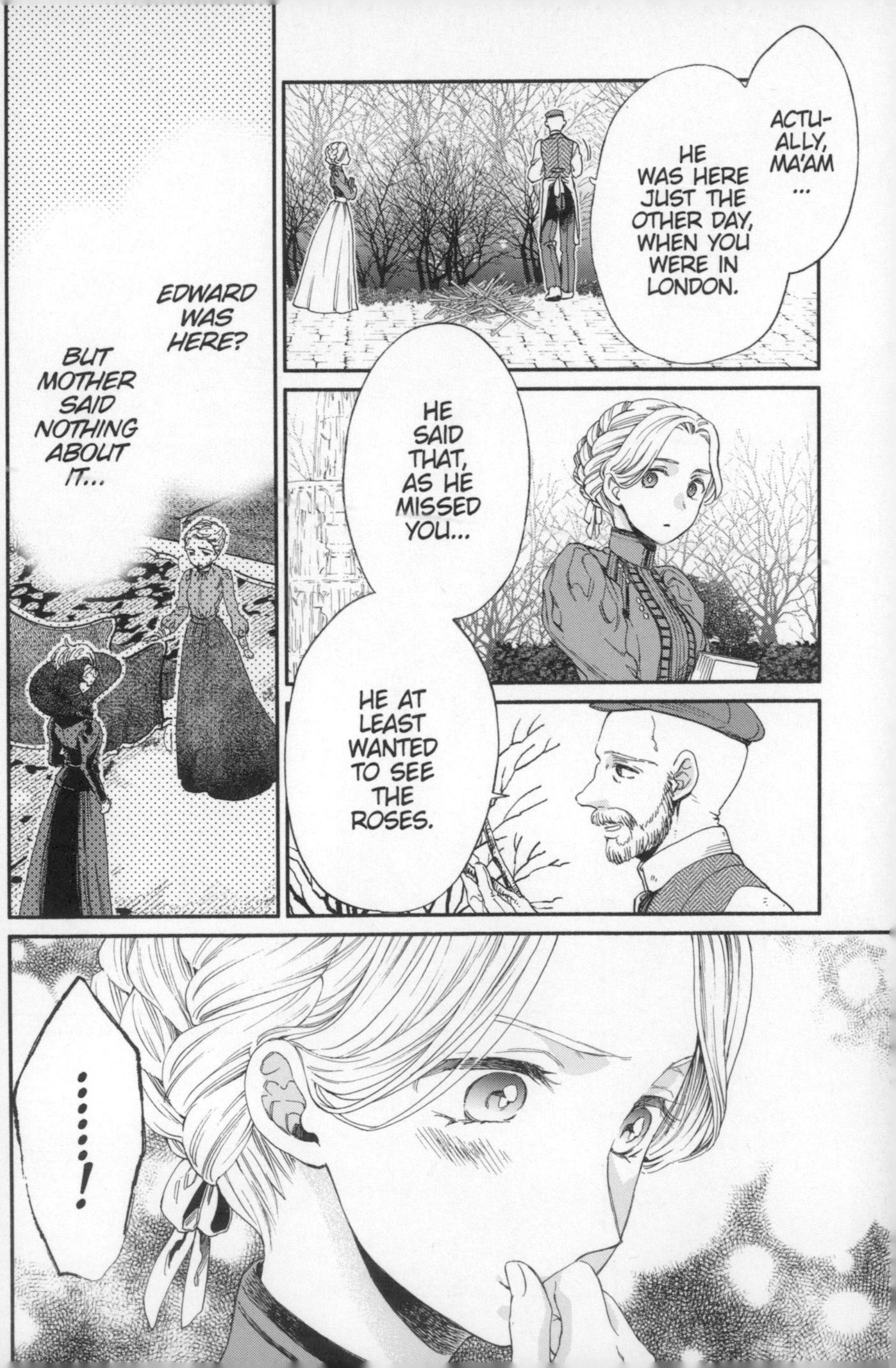
ACTU-ALLY, MA'AM ...
HE WAS HERE JUST THE OTHER DAY, WHEN YOU WERE IN LONDON.
HE SAID THAT, AS HE MISSED YOU...
HE AT LEAST WANTED TO SEE THE ROSES.
EDWARD WAS HERE?
BUT MOTHER SAID NOTHING ABOUT IT...
......!

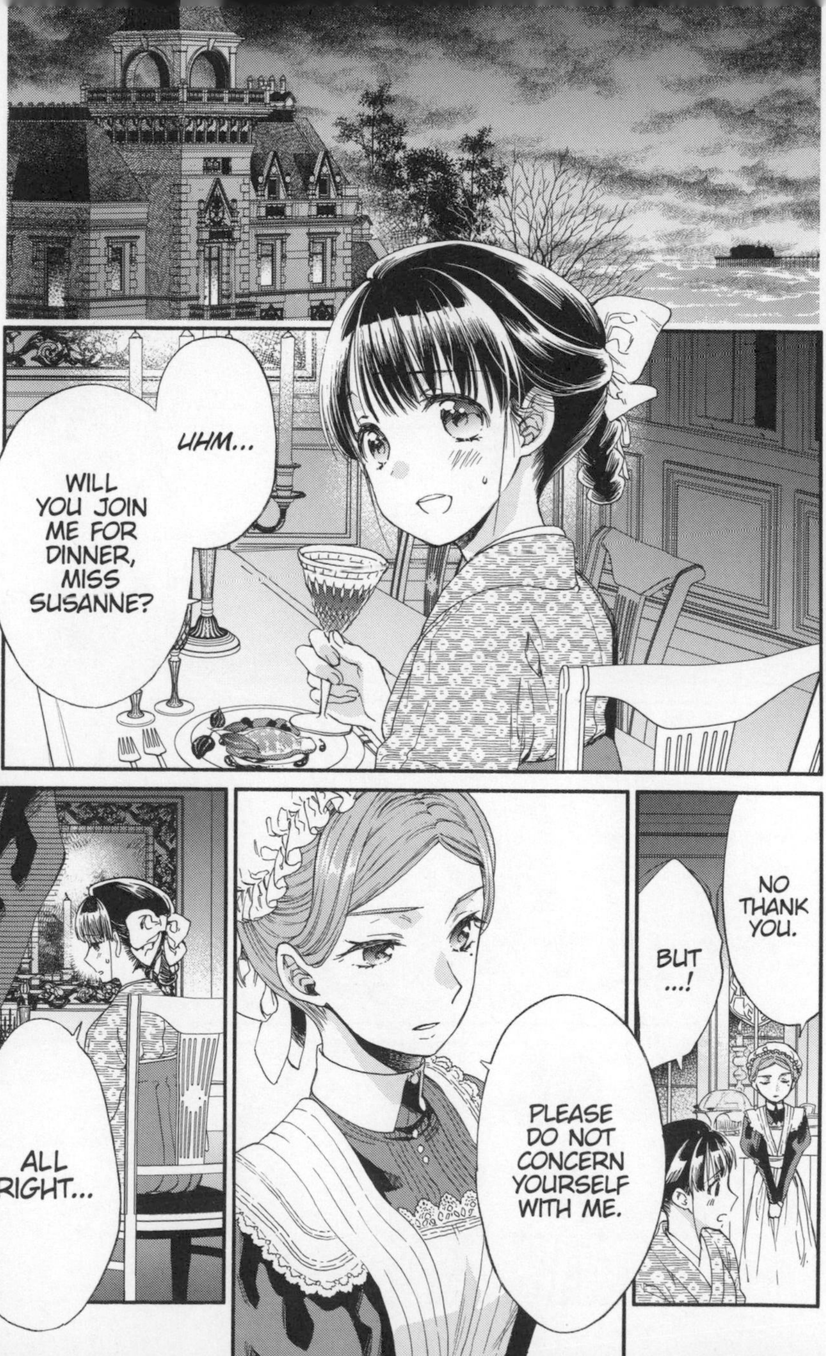
UHM...
WILL YOU JOIN ME FOR DINNER, MISS SUSANNE?
NO THANK YOU.
BUT ...!
PLEASE DO NOT CONCERN YOURSELF WITH ME.
ALL RIGHT...

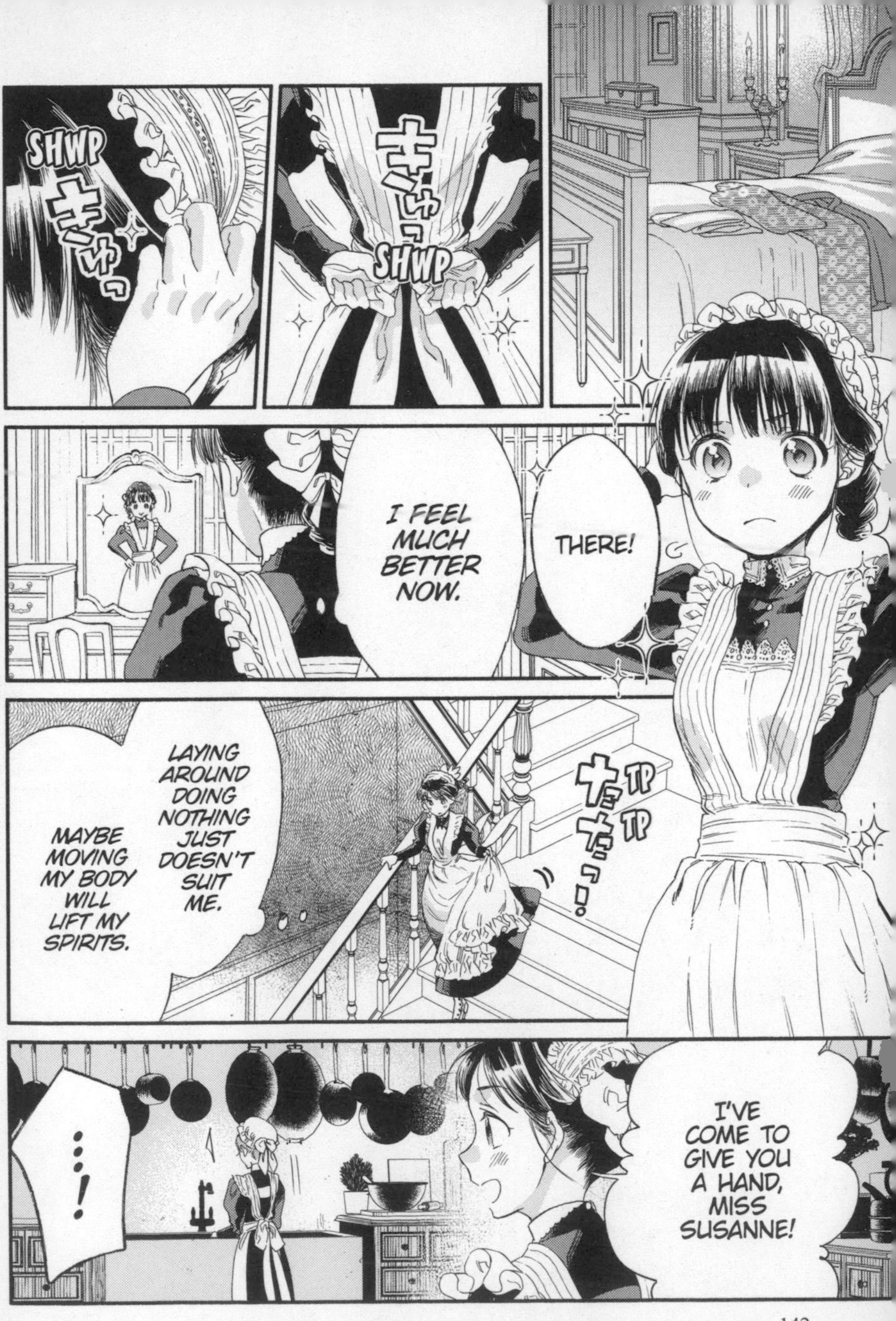
THERE!
SHWP
きゅっ
SHWP
きゅっ
I FEEL MUCH BETTER NOW.
TP TP
LAYING AROUND DOING NOTHING JUST DOESN'T SUIT ME.
MAYBE MOVING MY BODY WILL LIFT MY SPIRITS.
I'VE COME TO GIVE YOU A HAND, MISS SUSANNE!
...!

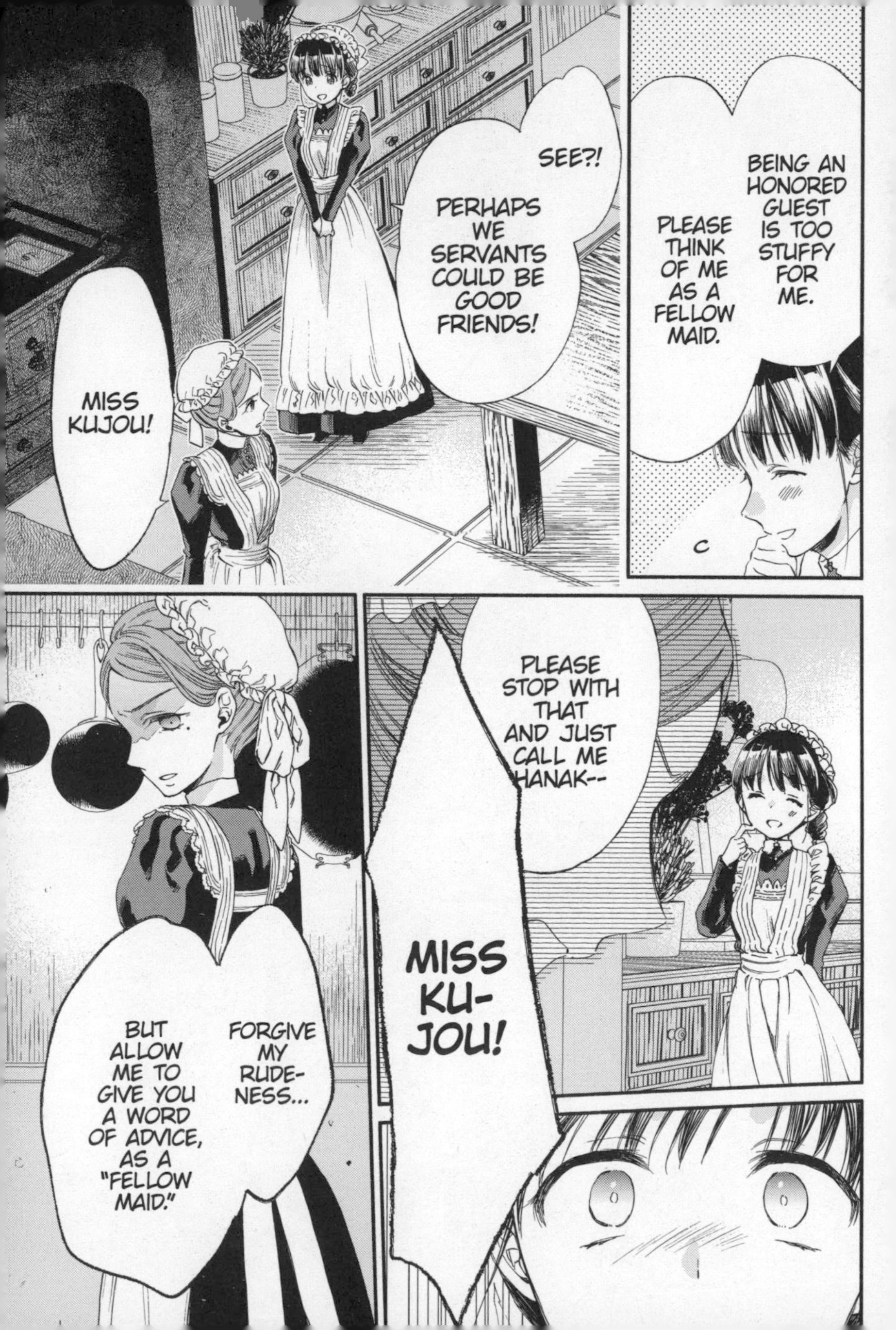
BEING AN HONORED GUEST IS TOO STUFFY FOR ME.
PLEASE THINK OF ME AS A FELLOW MAID.
SEE?!
PERHAPS WE SERVANTS COULD BE GOOD FRIENDS!
MISS KUJOU!
PLEASE STOP WITH THAT AND JUST CALL ME HANAK--
MISS KU-JOU!
FORGIVE MY RUDE-NESS...
BUT ALLOW ME TO GIVE YOU A WORD OF ADVICE, AS A "FELLOW MAID."

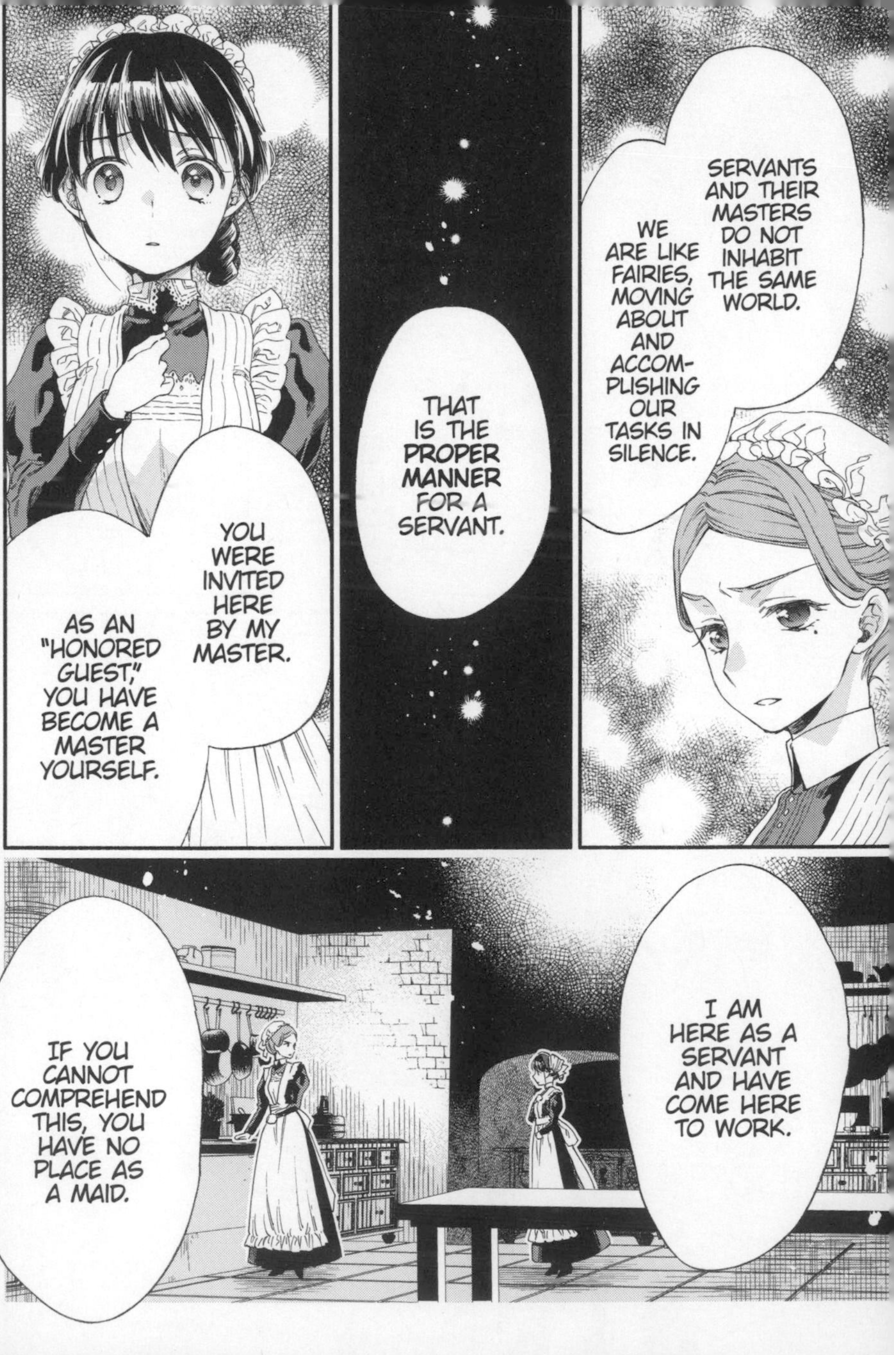

SERVANTS AND THEIR MASTERS DO NOT INHABIT THE SAME WORLD.
WE ARE LIKE FAIRIES, MOVING ABOUT AND ACCOMPLISHING OUR TASKS IN SILENCE.
THAT IS THE PROPER MANNER FOR A SERVANT.
YOU WERE INVITED HERE BY MY MASTER.
AS AN "HONORED GUEST," YOU HAVE BECOME A MASTER YOURSELF.
I AM HERE AS A SERVANT AND HAVE COME HERE TO WORK.
IF YOU CANNOT COMPREHEND THIS, YOU HAVE NO PLACE AS A MAID.

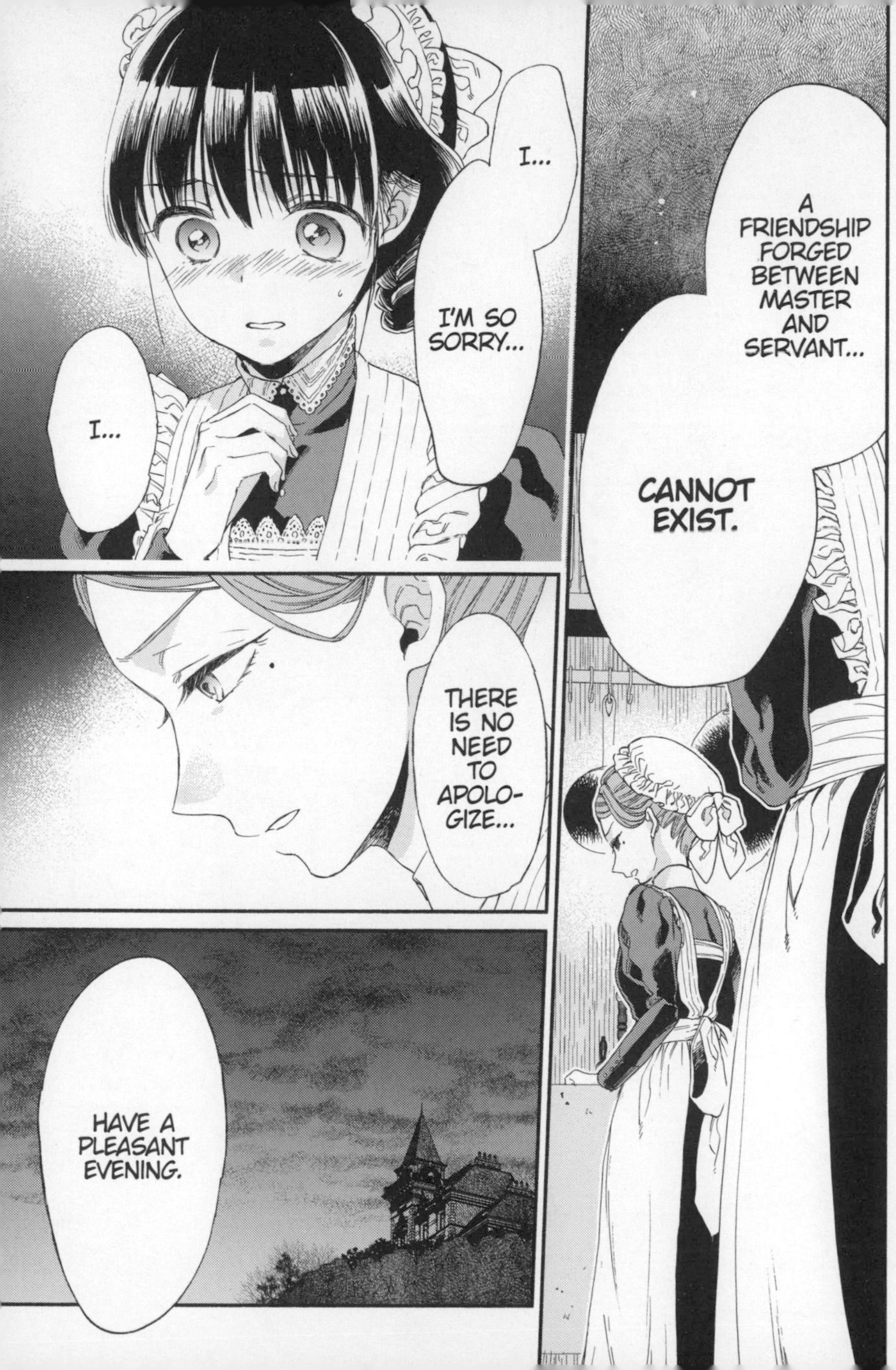
A FRIENDSHIP FORGED BETWEEN MASTER AND SERVANT...
CANNOT EXIST.
I...
I'M SO SORRY...
I...
THERE IS NO NEED TO APOLOGIZE...
HAVE A PLEASANT EVENING.

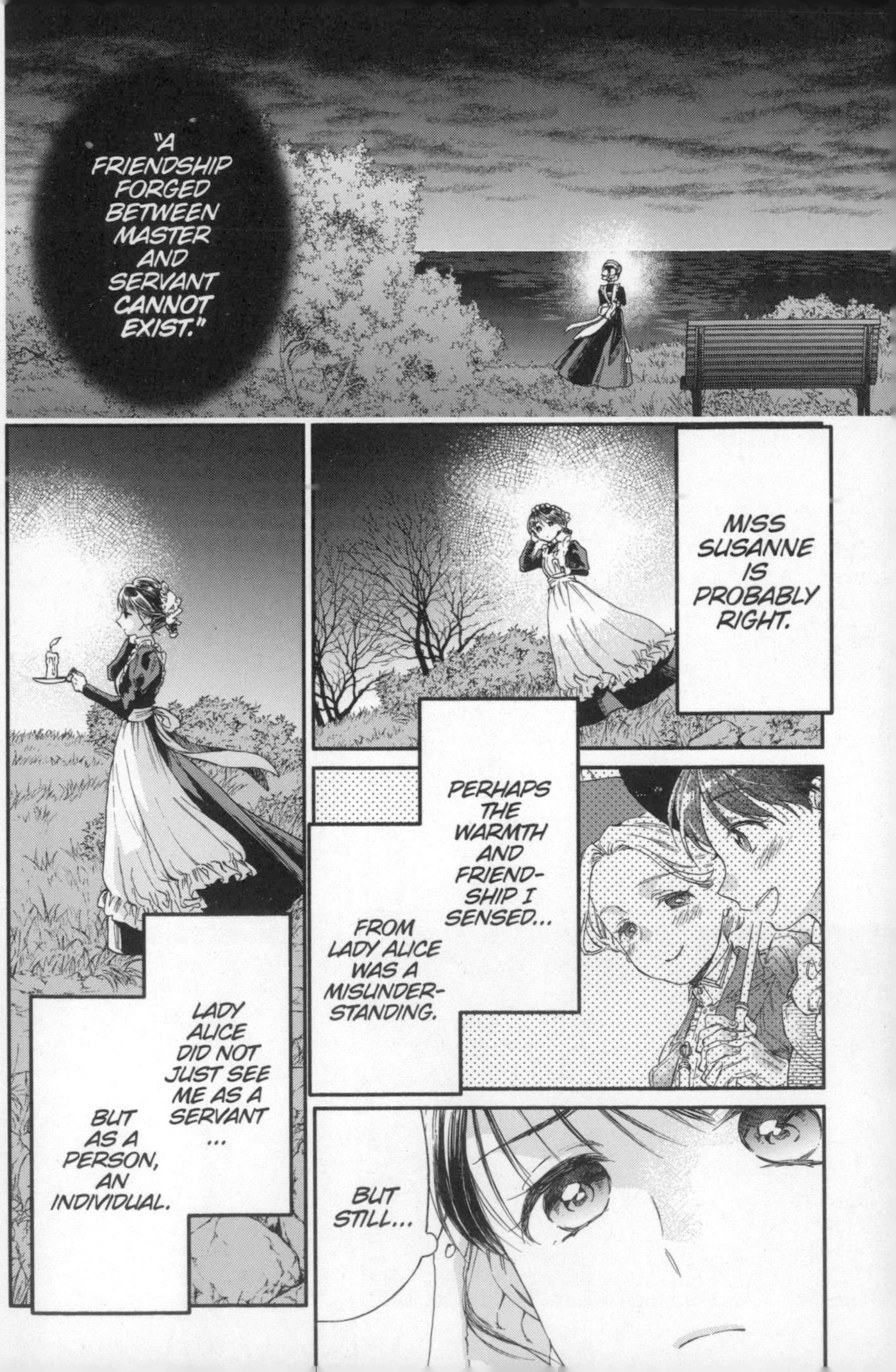
"A FRIENDSHIP FORGED BETWEEN MASTER AND SERVANT CANNOT EXIST."
MISS SUSANNE IS PROBABLY RIGHT.
PERHAPS THE WARMTH AND FRIEND-SHIP I SENSED...
FROM LADY ALICE WAS A MISUNDER-STANDING.
BUT STILL...
LADY ALICE DID NOT JUST SEE ME AS A SERVANT...
BUT AS A PERSON, AN INDIVIDUAL.

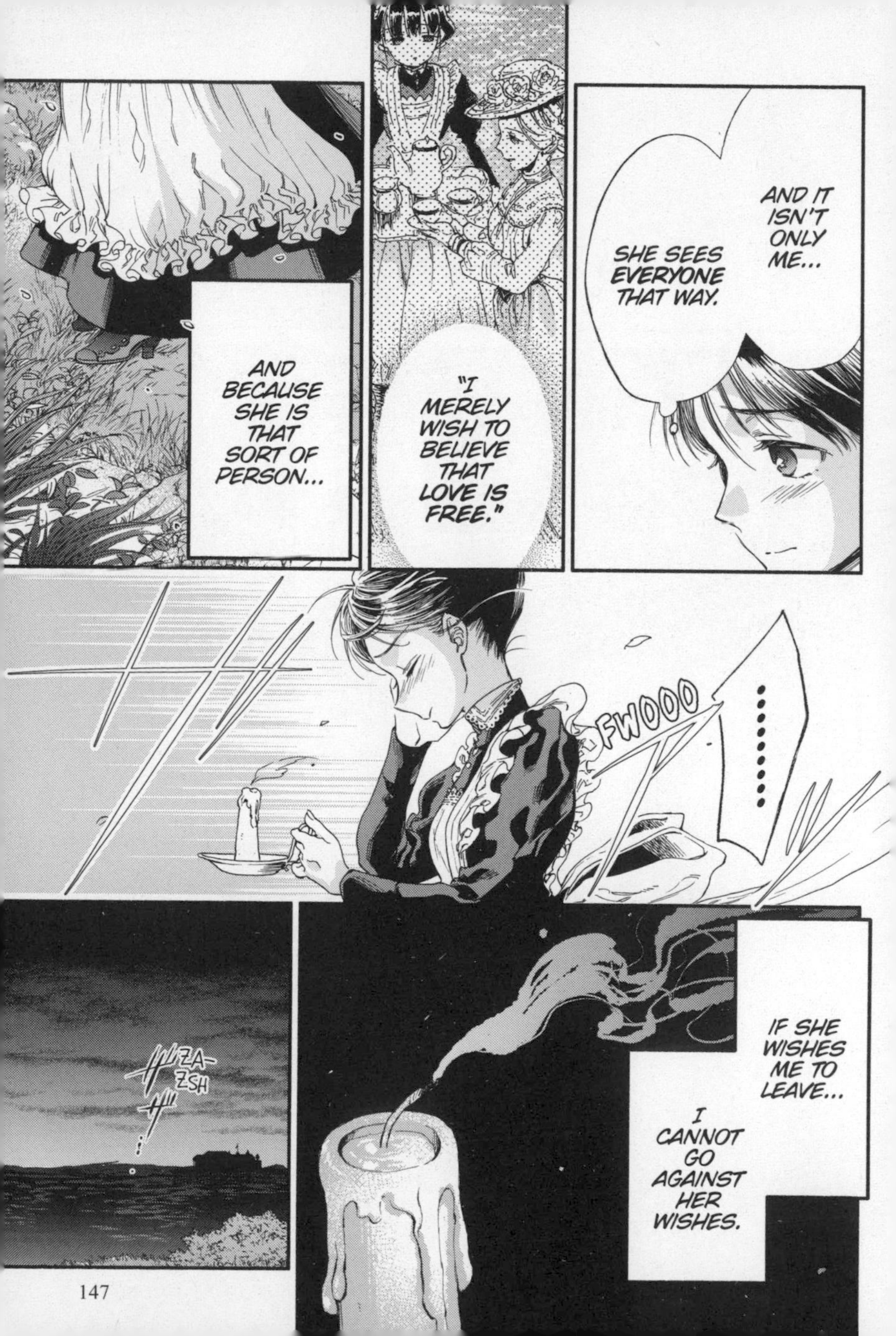
AND IT ISN'T ONLY ME...
SHE SEES EVERYONE THAT WAY.
"I MERELY WISH TO BELIEVE THAT LOVE IS FREE."
AND BECAUSE SHE IS THAT SORT OF PERSON...
......
FWOOO
IF SHE WISHES ME TO LEAVE...
I CANNOT GO AGAINST HER WISHES.
ZA-ZSH

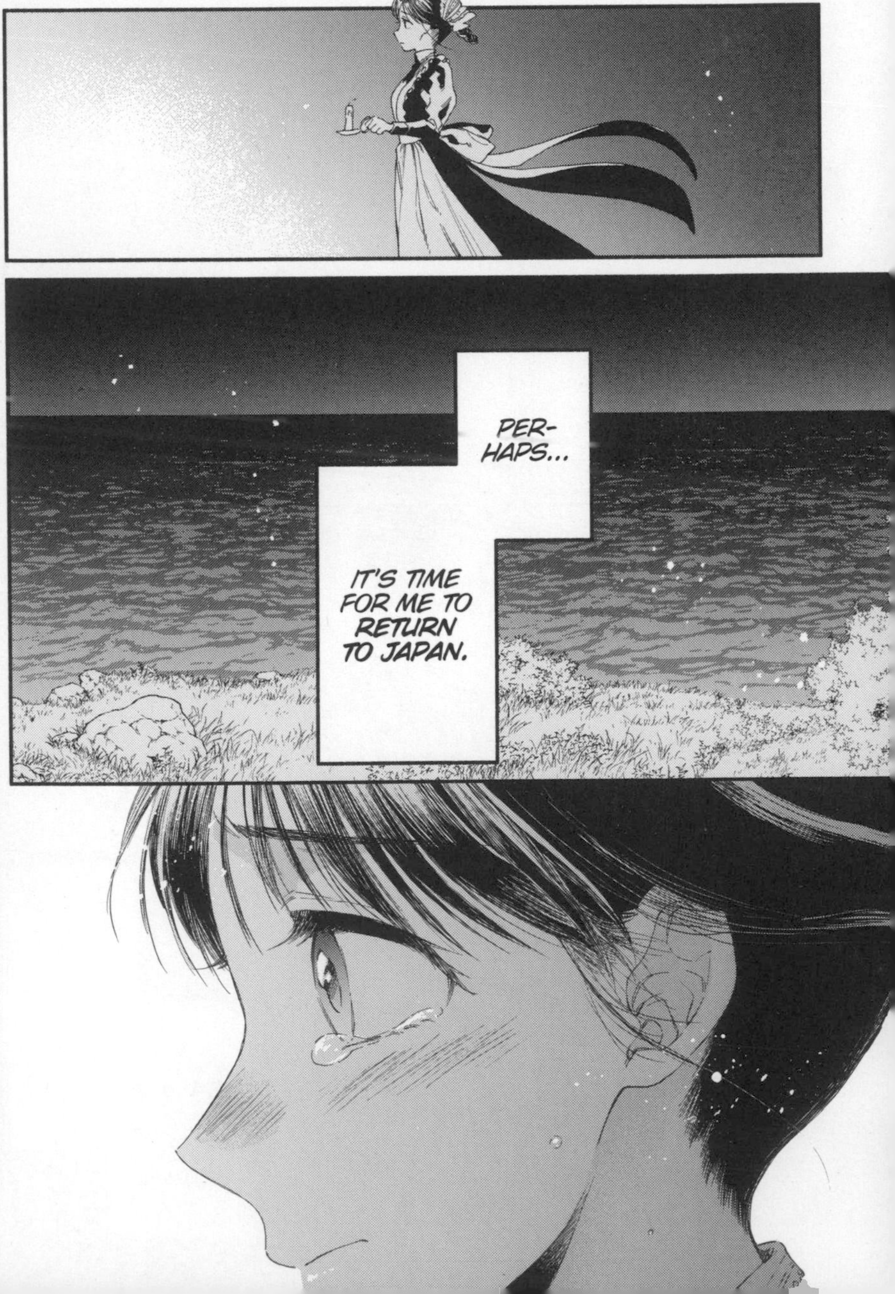
PER-HAPS...
IT'S TIME FOR ME TO RETURN TO JAPAN.

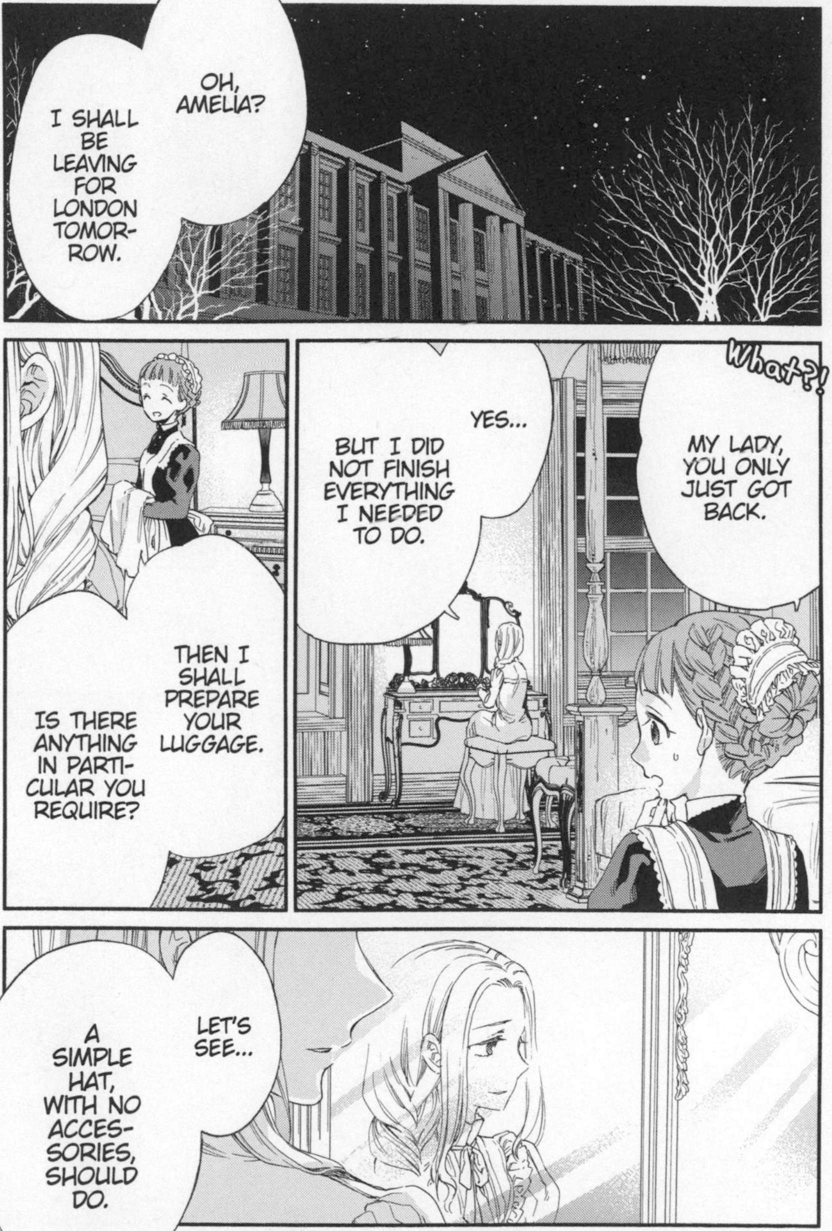
OH, AMELIA?
I SHALL BE LEAVING FOR LONDON TOMORROW.
What?!
MY LADY, YOU ONLY JUST GOT BACK.
YES...
BUT I DID NOT FINISH EVERYTHING I NEEDED TO DO.
THEN I SHALL PREPARE YOUR LUGGAGE.
IS THERE ANYTHING IN PARTICULAR YOU REQUIRE?
LET'S SEE...
A SIMPLE HAT, WITH NO ACCESSORIES, SHOULD DO.

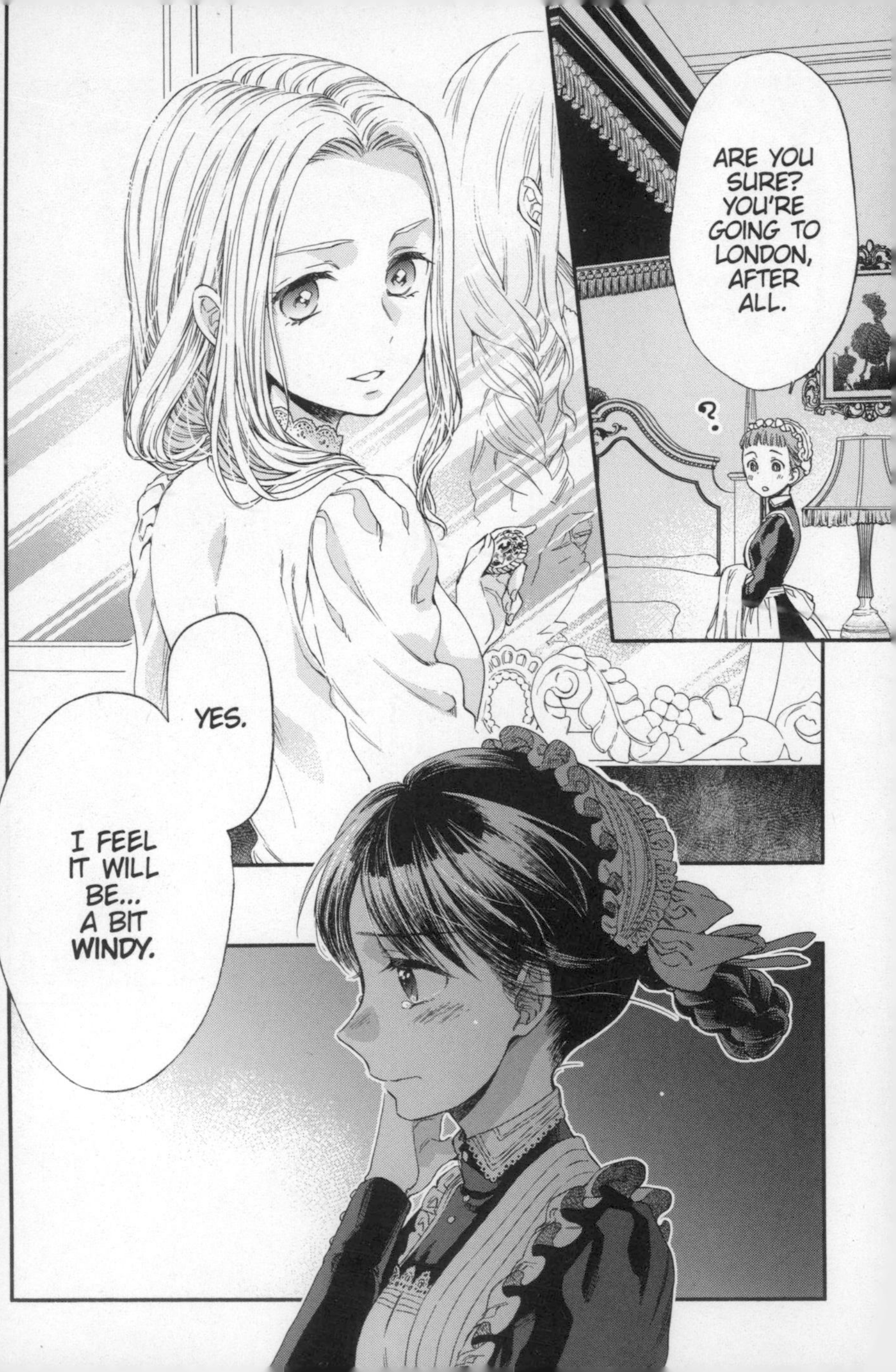
ARE YOU SURE? YOU'RE GOING TO LONDON, AFTER ALL.
?
YES.
I FEEL IT WILL BE... A BIT WINDY.

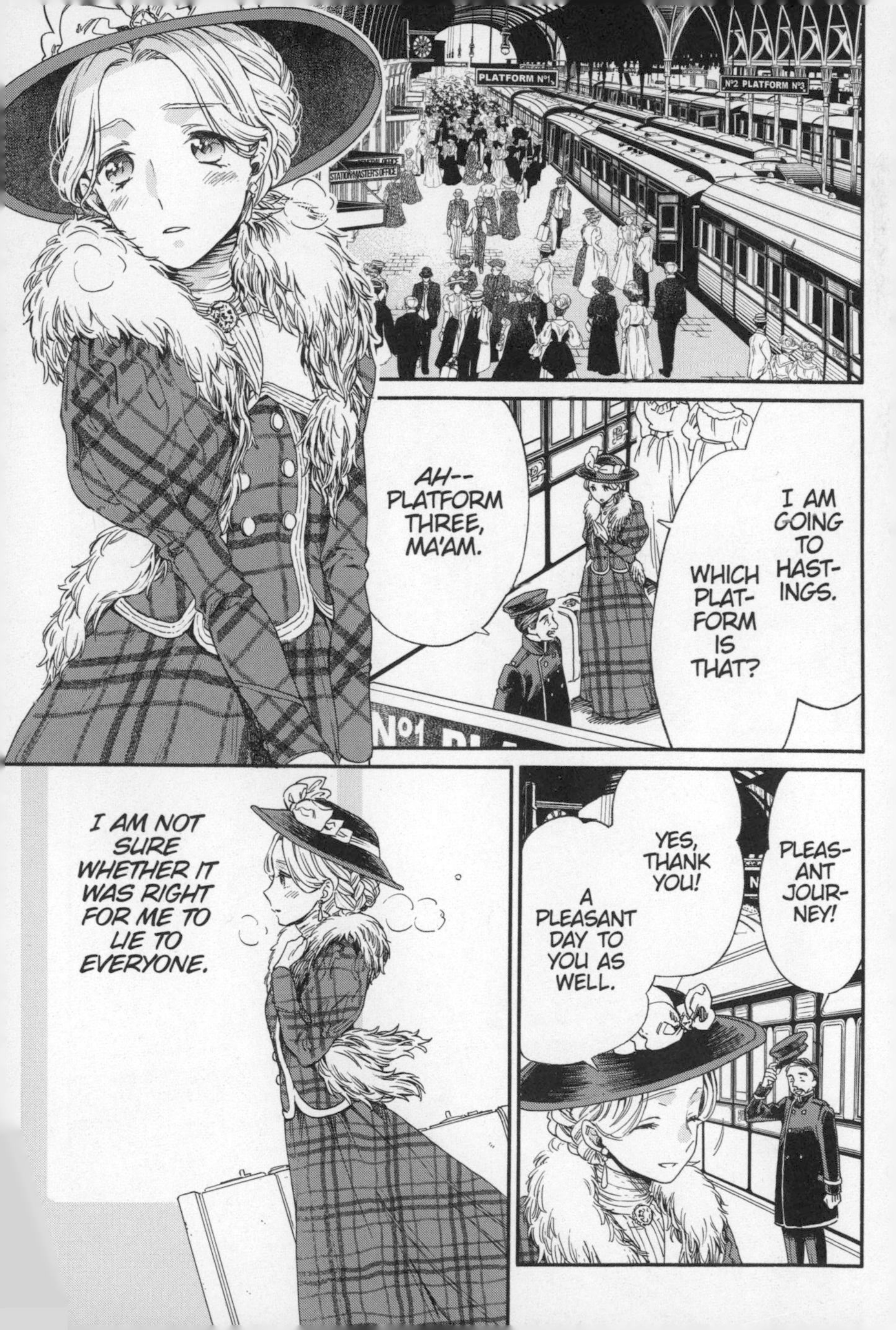
PLATFORM No1
No2 PLATFORM No3
STATION-MASTER'S OFFICE
I AM GOING TO HASTINGS.
WHICH PLATFORM IS THAT?
AH-- PLATFORM THREE, MA'AM.
No1
PLEASANT JOURNEY!
YES, THANK YOU!
A PLEASANT DAY TO YOU AS WELL.
I AM NOT SURE WHETHER IT WAS RIGHT FOR ME TO LIE TO EVERYONE.

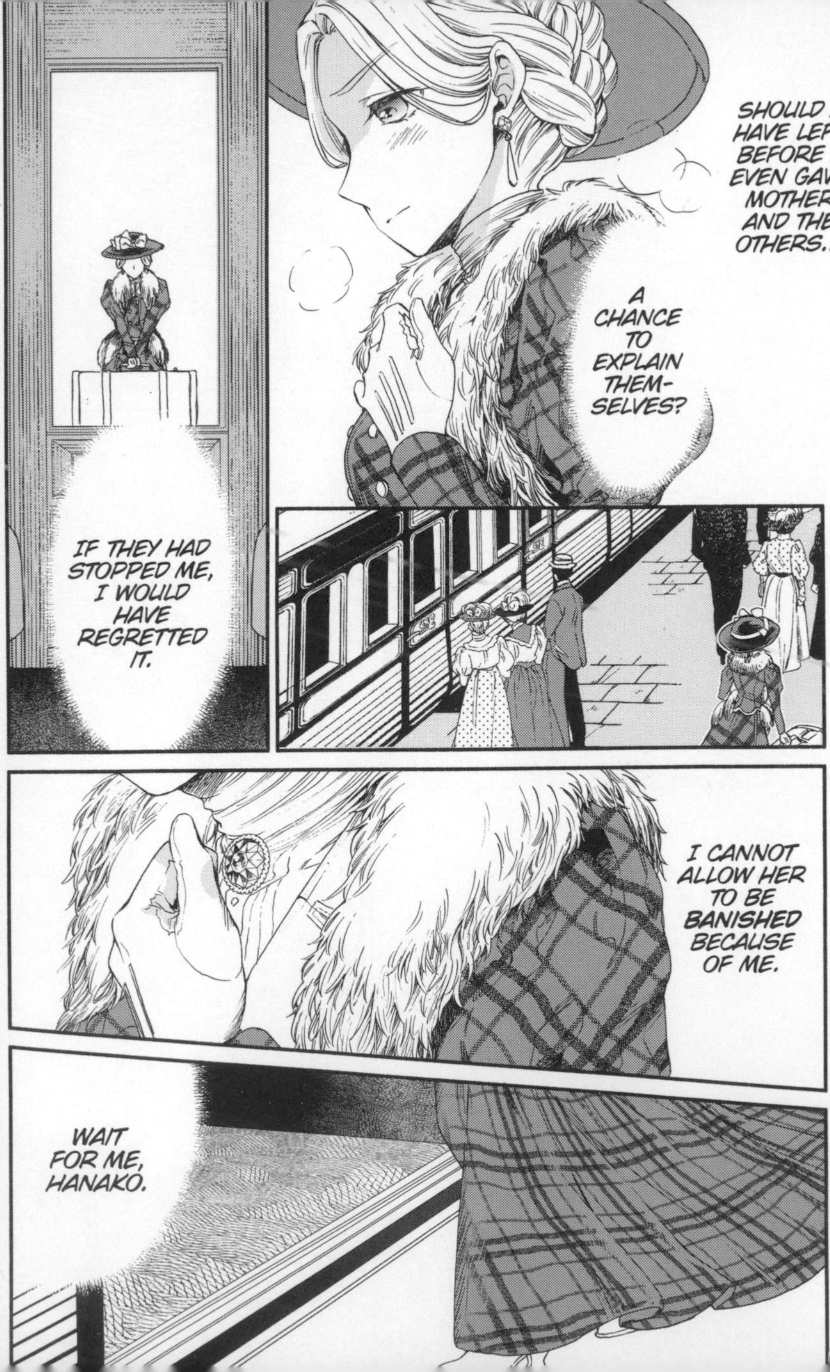
SHOULD I HAVE LEFT BEFORE I EVEN GAVE MOTHER AND THE OTHERS...
A CHANCE TO EXPLAIN THEM-SELVES?
IF THEY HAD STOPPED ME, I WOULD HAVE REGRETTED IT.
I CANNOT ALLOW HER TO BE BANISHED BECAUSE OF ME.
WAIT FOR ME, HANAKO.

{ Chapter 11 }
The Sunlight Between Clouds and the Opening Bud

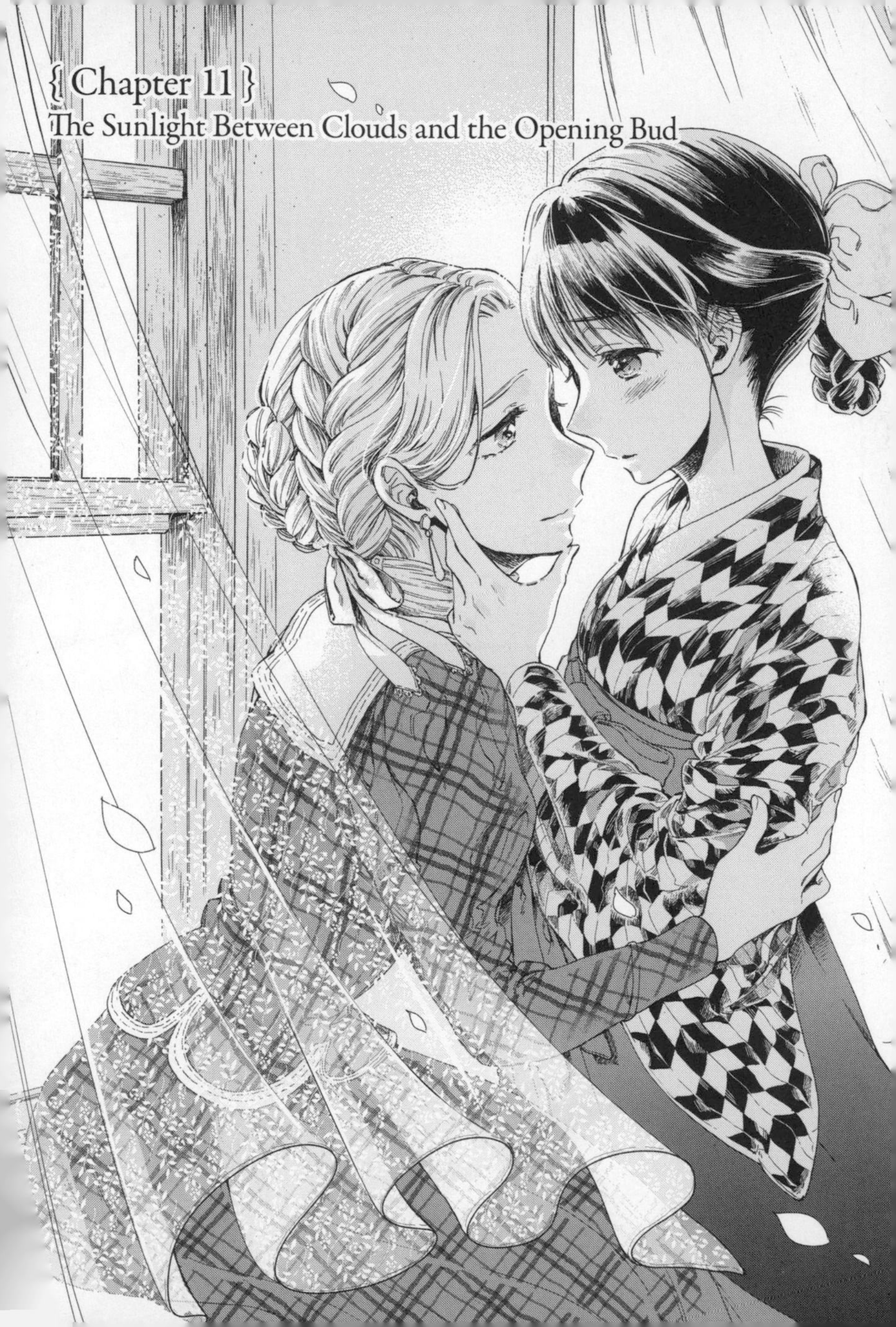

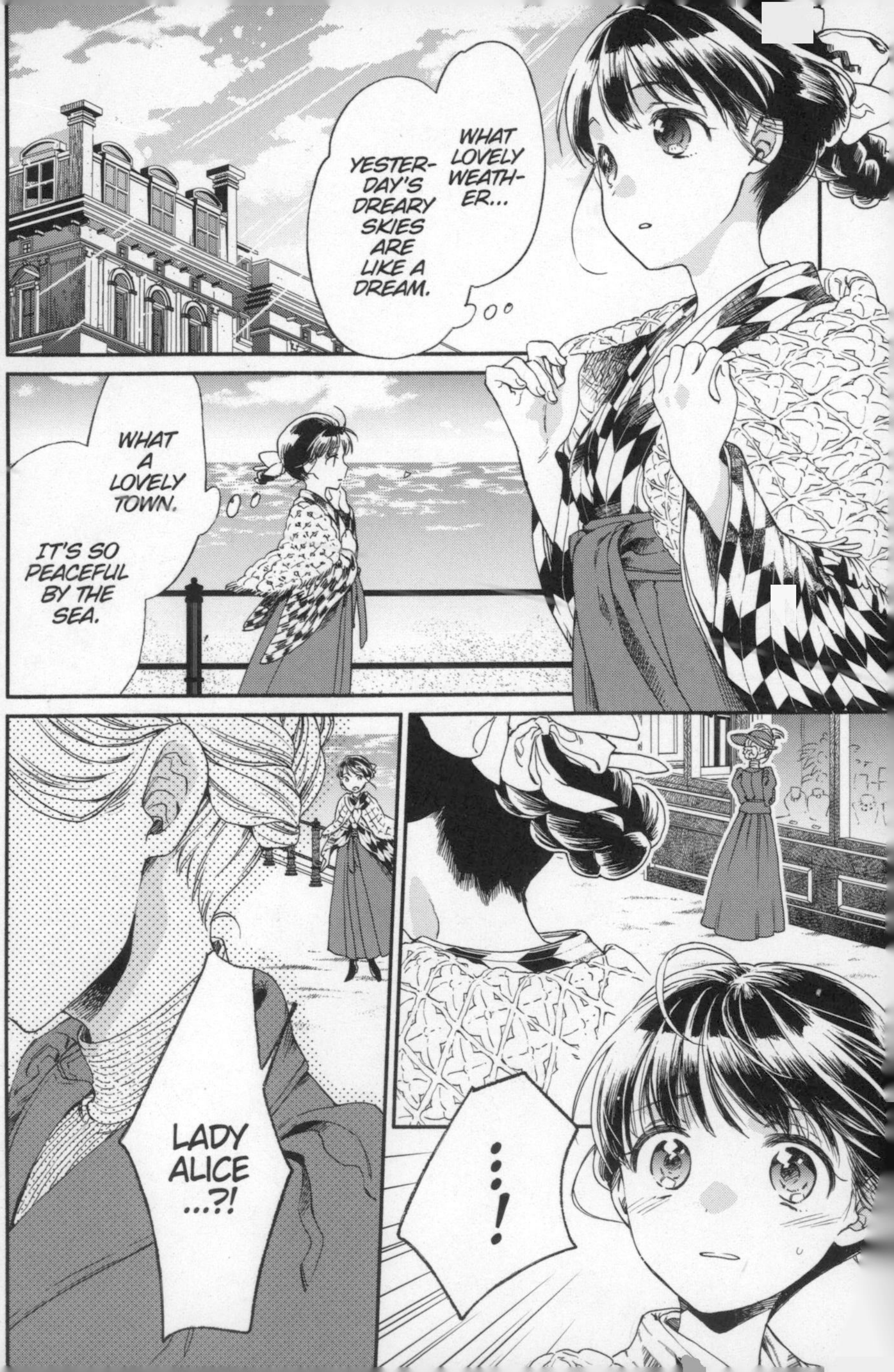
WHAT LOVELY WEATHER... YESTERDAY'S DREARY SKIES ARE LIKE A DREAM.
WHAT A LOVELY TOWN. IT'S SO PEACEFUL BY THE SEA.
...!
LADY ALICE ...?!

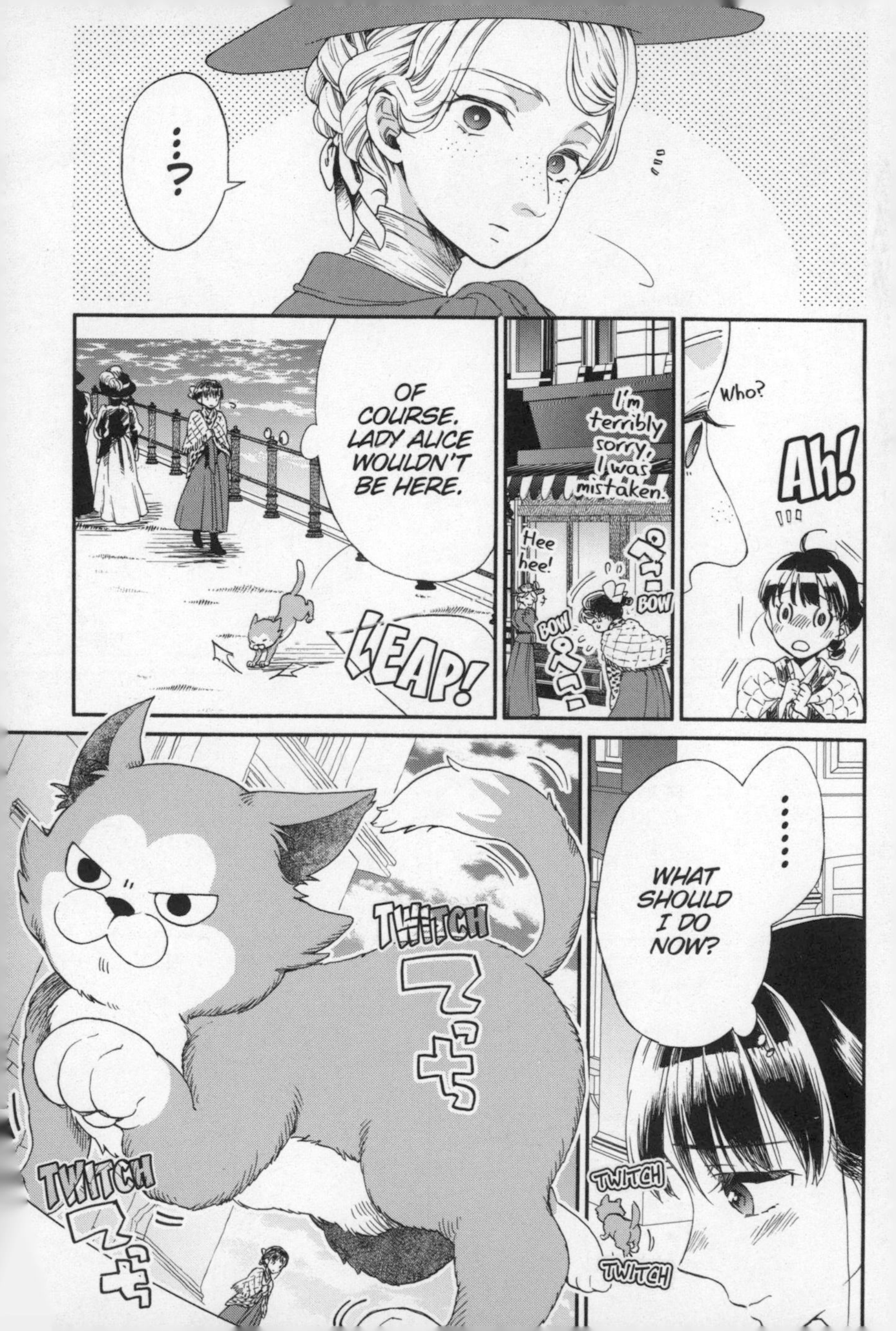

…っ?
Who?
Ah!
I'm terribly sorry, I was mistaken.
Hee hee!
BOW
BOW
OF COURSE. LADY ALICE WOULDN'T BE HERE.
LEAP!
...... WHAT SHOULD I DO NOW?
TWITCH
TWITCH
TWITCH
TWITCH

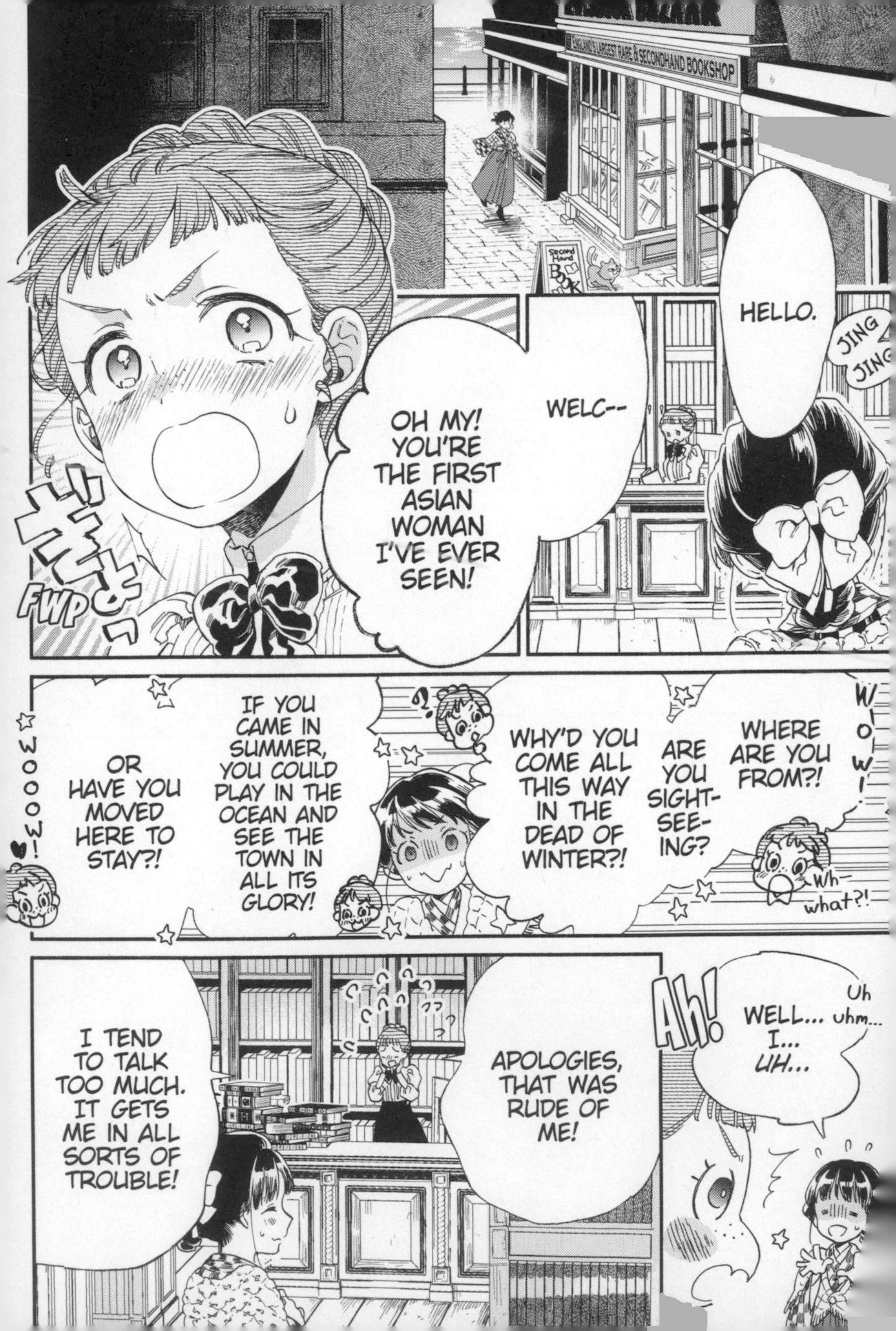
ENGLAND'S LARGEST RARE & SECONDHAND BOOKSHOP
Second Hand BOOK
HELLO.
JING JING
WELC--
OH MY! YOU'RE THE FIRST ASIAN WOMAN I'VE EVER SEEN!
FWP
WOW!
Wh- what?!
WHERE ARE YOU FROM?!
ARE YOU SIGHT-SEE-ING?
WHY'D YOU COME ALL THIS WAY IN THE DEAD OF WINTER?!
IF YOU CAME IN SUMMER, YOU COULD PLAY IN THE OCEAN AND SEE THE TOWN IN ALL ITS GLORY!
OR HAVE YOU MOVED HERE TO STAY?!
WOOOOW!
Ah!
Uh WELL... uhm... I... UH...
APOLOGIES, THAT WAS RUDE OF ME!
I TEND TO TALK TOO MUCH. IT GETS ME IN ALL SORTS OF TROUBLE!

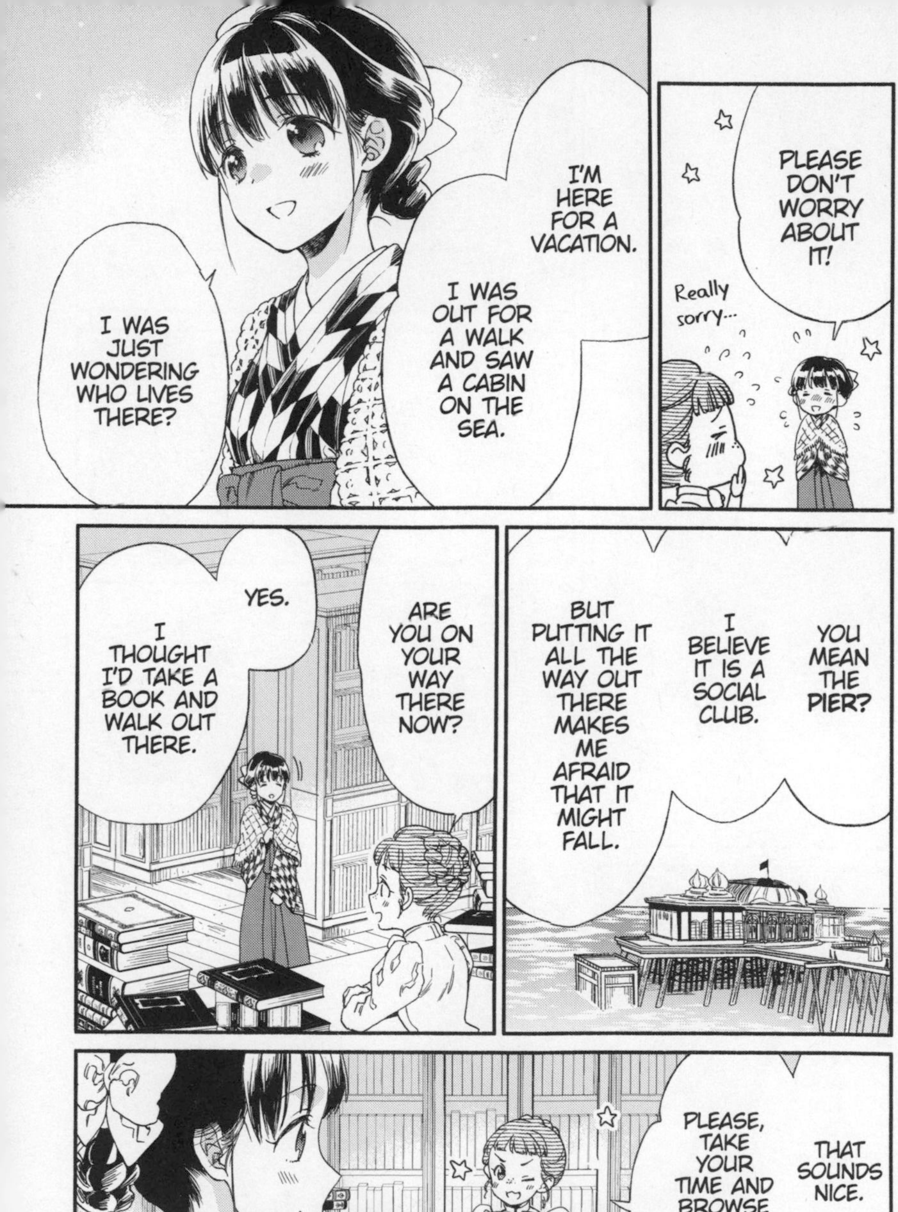
PLEASE DON'T WORRY ABOUT IT!
Really sorry...
I'M HERE FOR A VACATION.
I WAS OUT FOR A WALK AND SAW A CABIN ON THE SEA.
I WAS JUST WONDERING WHO LIVES THERE?
YOU MEAN THE PIER?
I BELIEVE IT IS A SOCIAL CLUB.
BUT PUTTING IT ALL THE WAY OUT THERE MAKES ME AFRAID THAT IT MIGHT FALL.
ARE YOU ON YOUR WAY THERE NOW?
YES.
I THOUGHT I'D TAKE A BOOK AND WALK OUT THERE.
THAT SOUNDS NICE.
PLEASE, TAKE YOUR TIME AND BROWSE ALL YOU LIKE.

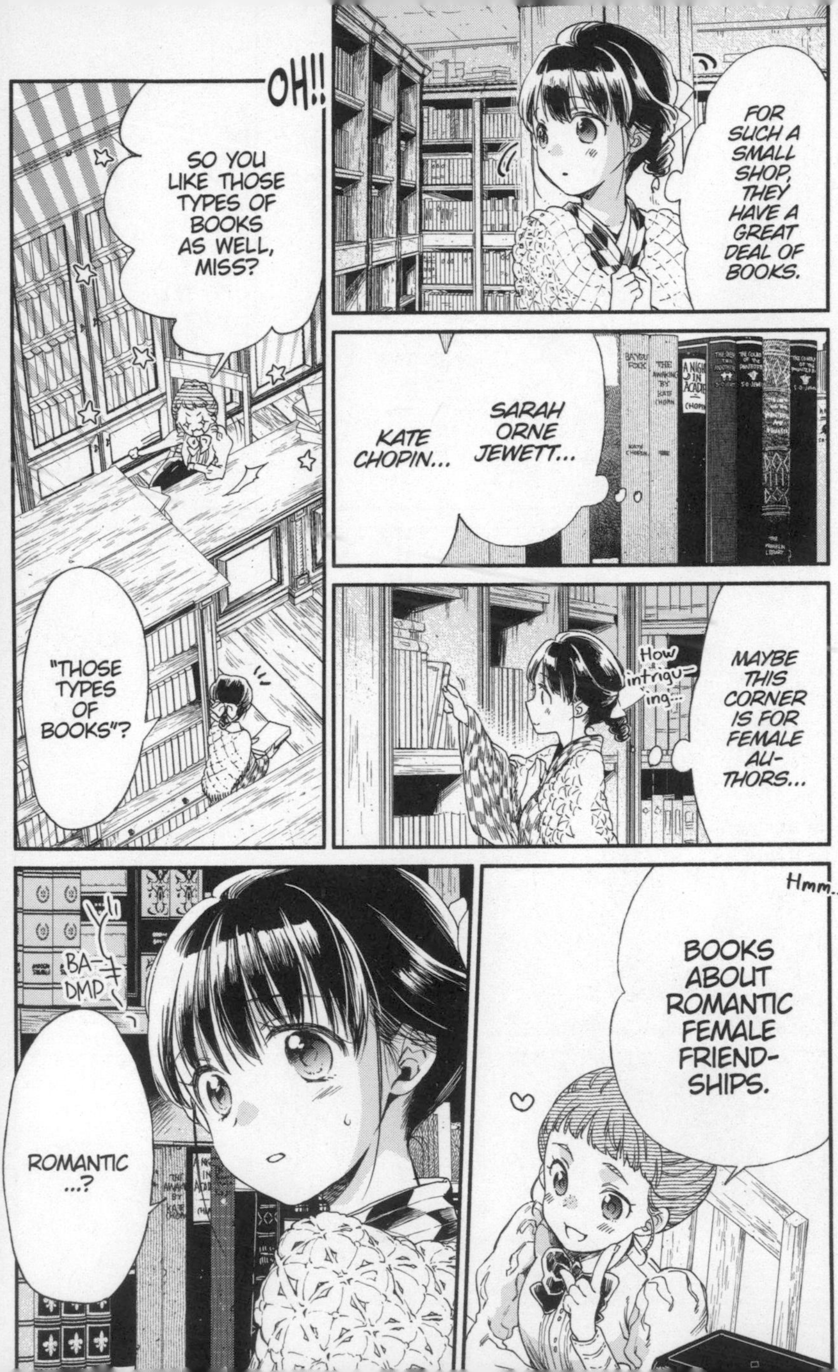
FOR SUCH A SMALL SHOP, THEY HAVE A GREAT DEAL OF BOOKS.
SARAH ORNE JEWETT...
KATE CHOPIN...
MAYBE THIS CORNER IS FOR FEMALE AUTHORS...
How intriguing...
OH!!
SO YOU LIKE THOSE TYPES OF BOOKS AS WELL, MISS?
"THOSE TYPES OF BOOKS"?
Hmm...
BOOKS ABOUT ROMANTIC FEMALE FRIENDSHIPS.
BA-DMP
ROMANTIC ...?

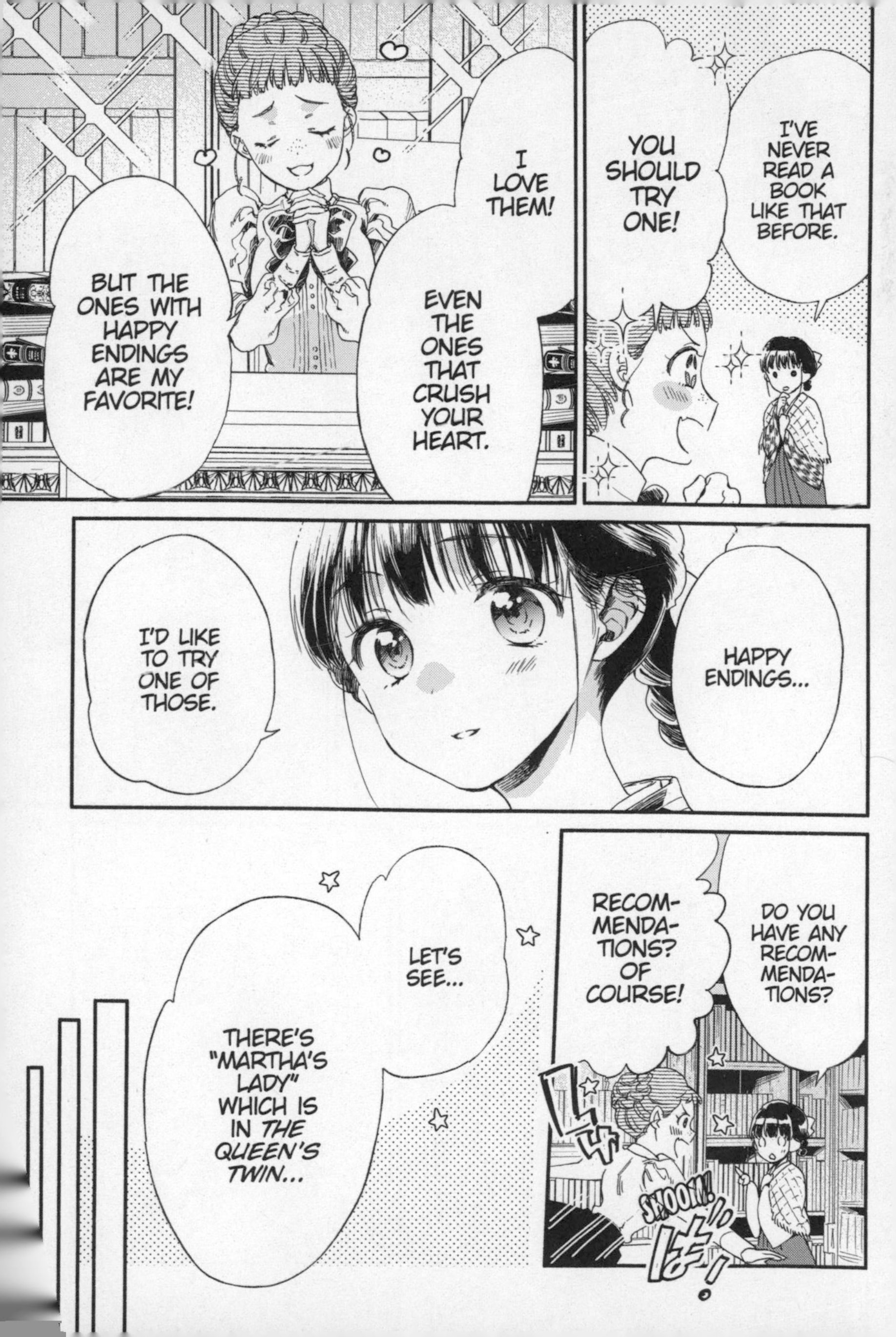
I'VE NEVER READ A BOOK LIKE THAT BEFORE.
YOU SHOULD TRY ONE!
I LOVE THEM!
EVEN THE ONES THAT CRUSH YOUR HEART.
BUT THE ONES WITH HAPPY ENDINGS ARE MY FAVORITE!
HAPPY ENDINGS...
I'D LIKE TO TRY ONE OF THOSE.
DO YOU HAVE ANY RECOMMENDATIONS?
RECOMMENDATIONS? OF COURSE!
SHOOM!
LET'S SEE...
THERE'S "MARTHA'S LADY" WHICH IS IN *THE QUEEN'S TWIN*...

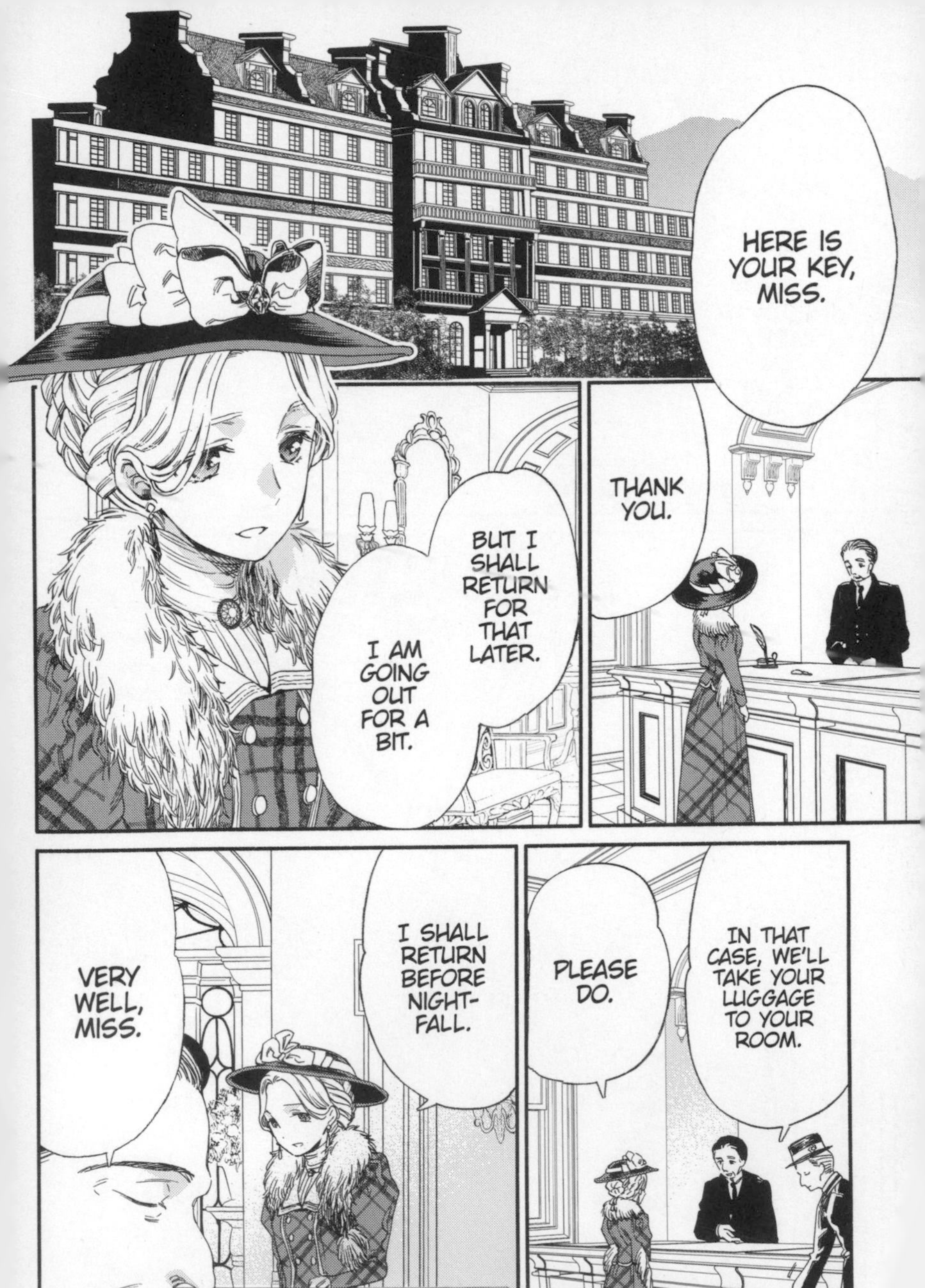
HERE IS YOUR KEY, MISS.
THANK YOU.
I AM GOING OUT FOR A BIT.
BUT I SHALL RETURN FOR THAT LATER.
IN THAT CASE, WE'LL TAKE YOUR LUGGAGE TO YOUR ROOM.
PLEASE DO.
I SHALL RETURN BEFORE NIGHT-FALL.
VERY WELL, MISS.

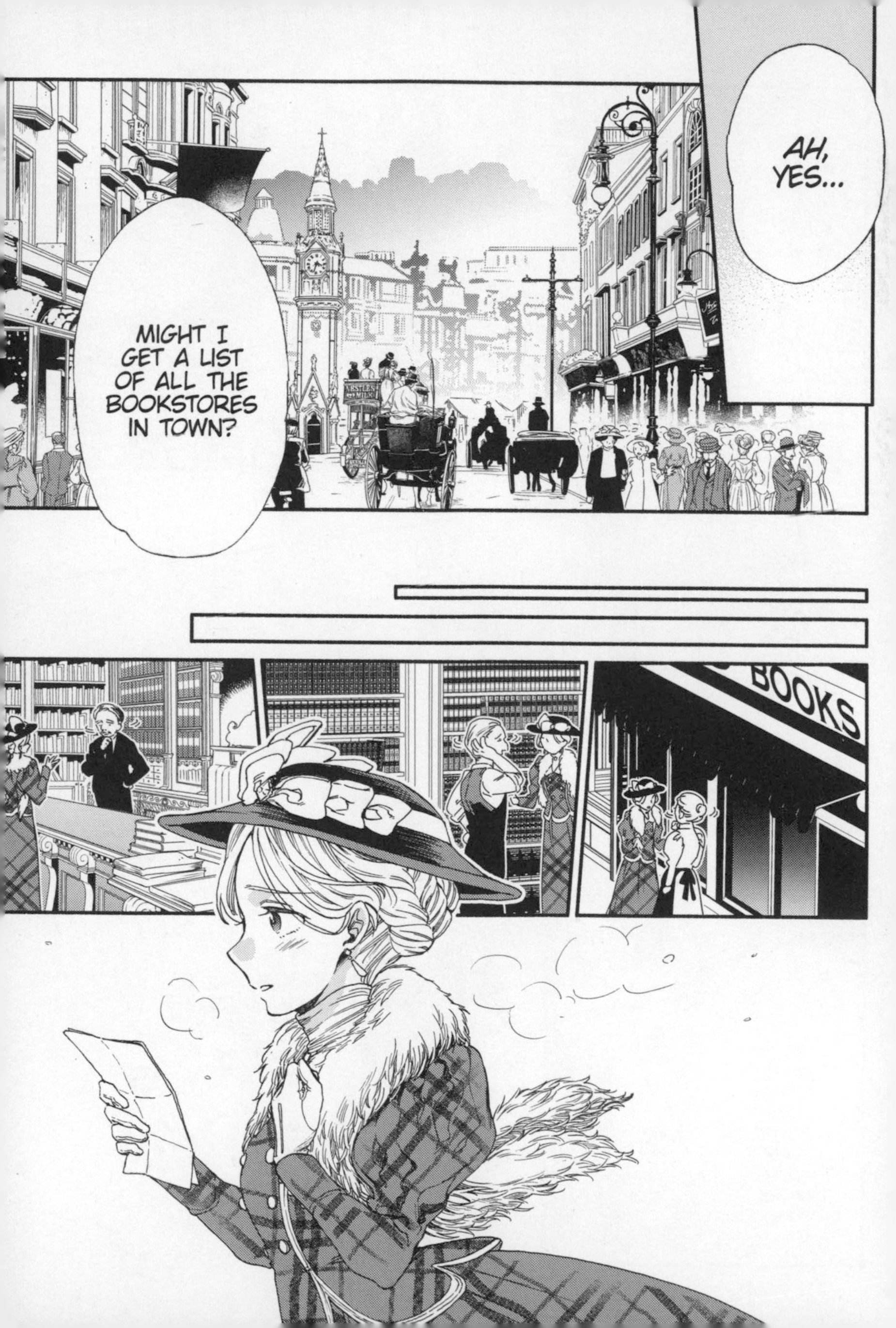
AH, YES...
MIGHT I GET A LIST OF ALL THE BOOKSTORES IN TOWN?
BOOKS

NO, THANK YOU FOR YOUR TIME.

I'M SORRY I CAN'T BE OF MORE HELP.

I'VE NEVER SEEN ONE BEFORE.

A JAPANESE WOMAN?

NOT ONE PERSON HAS SEEN HER.

BUT IF I WERE TO GO STRAIGHT TO EDWARD'S HOUSE...

THEY WOULD FIND OUT THAT I LIED. THAT I CAME HERE.

PERHAPS SHE HAS NOT COME INTO TOWN.

BUT IF HANAKO REALLY HAS COME TO HASTINGS...

THEN SURELY SHE WOULD HAVE VISITED A BOOKSHOP BY NOW.

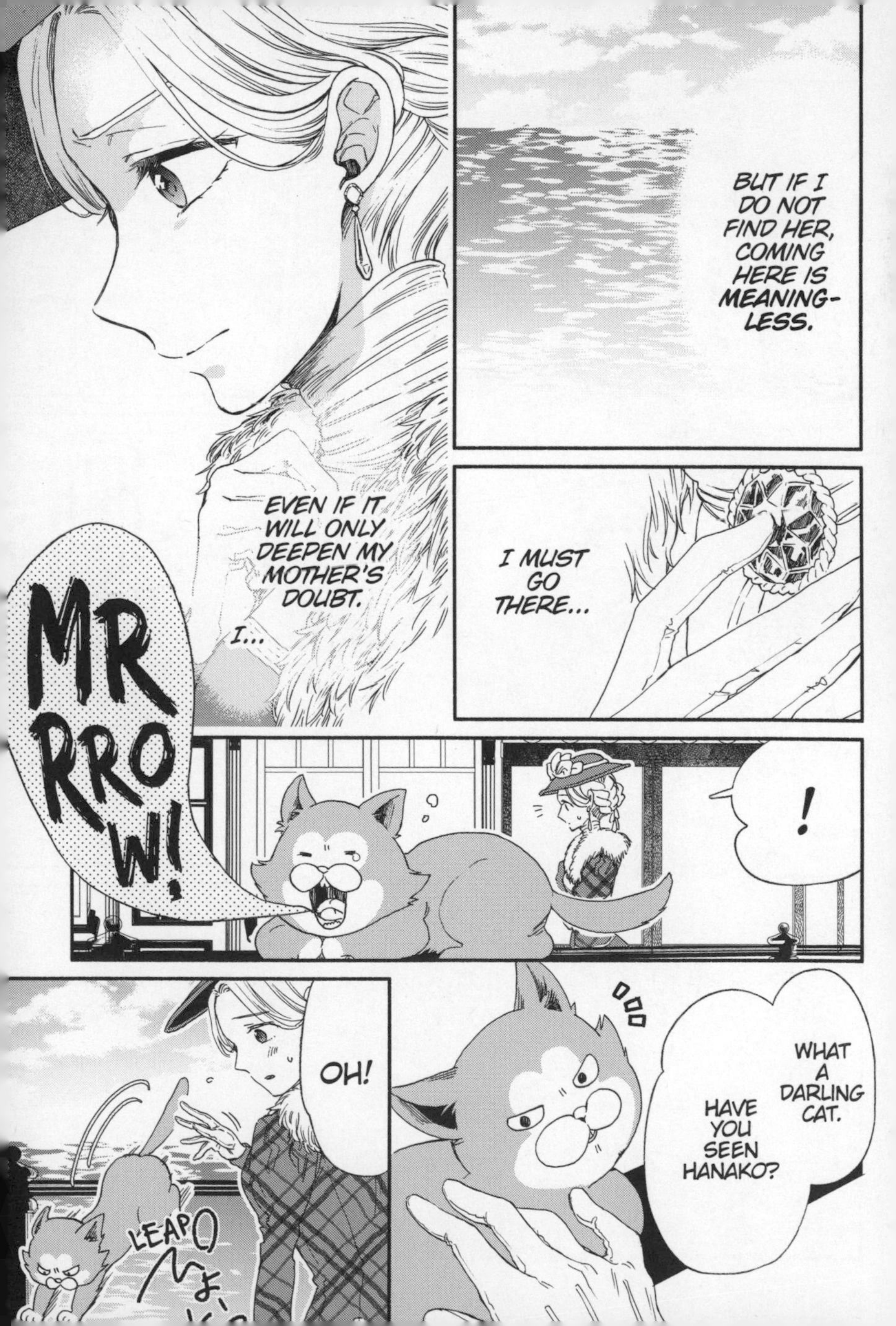
BUT IF I DO NOT FIND HER, COMING HERE IS MEANING-LESS.
I MUST GO THERE...
EVEN IF IT WILL ONLY DEEPEN MY MOTHER'S DOUBT.
I...
!
MRRROW!
WHAT A DARLING CAT.
HAVE YOU SEEN HANAKO?
OH!
LEAP

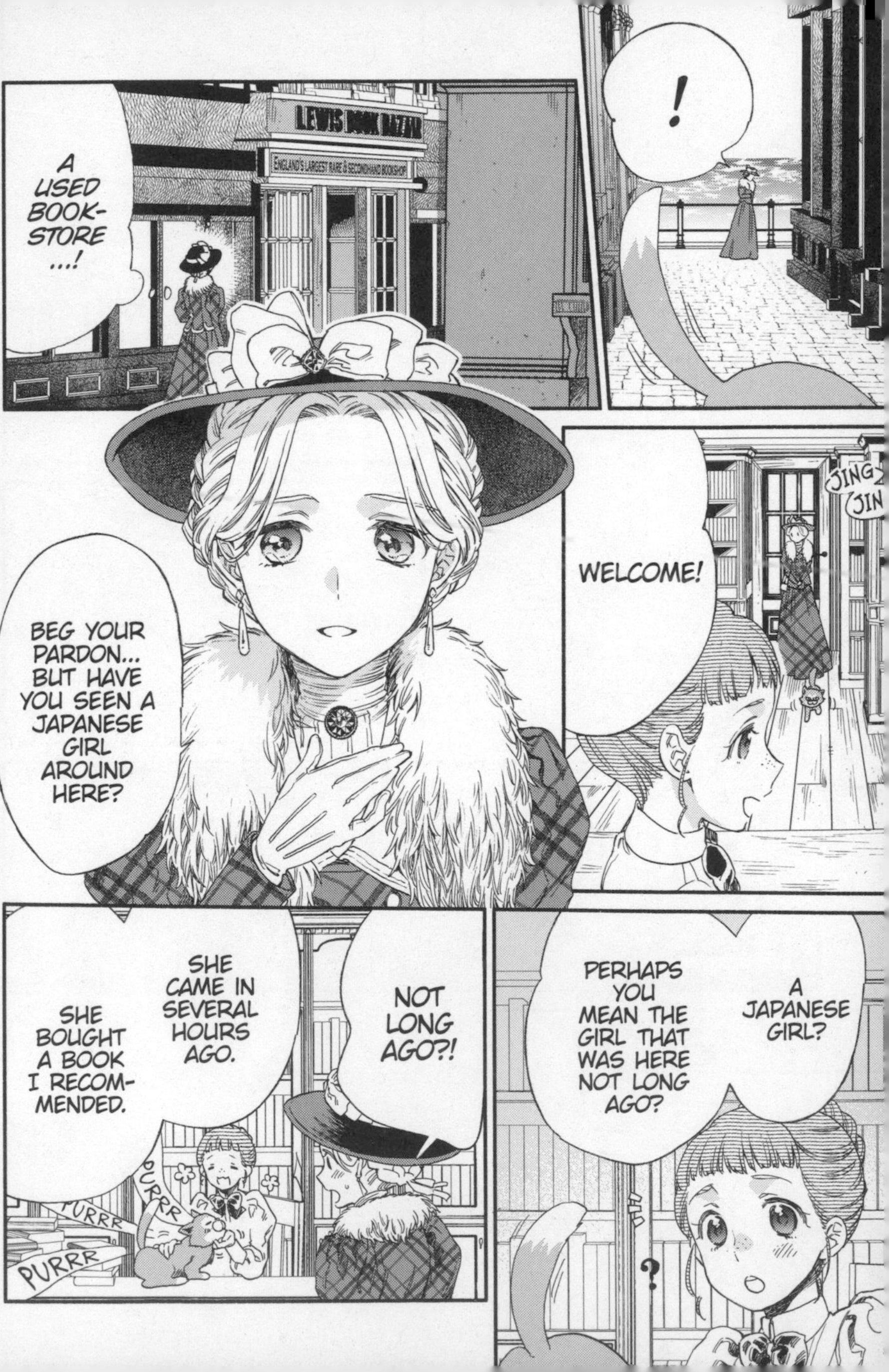
!
LEWIS BOOK BAZAAR
ENGLAND'S LARGEST RARE & SECONDHAND BOOKSHOP
A USED BOOK-STORE ...!
JING JIN
WELCOME!
BEG YOUR PARDON... BUT HAVE YOU SEEN A JAPANESE GIRL AROUND HERE?
A JAPANESE GIRL?
PERHAPS YOU MEAN THE GIRL THAT WAS HERE NOT LONG AGO?
?
NOT LONG AGO?!
SHE CAME IN SEVERAL HOURS AGO.
SHE BOUGHT A BOOK I RECOMMENDED.
PURRR
PURRR
PURRR

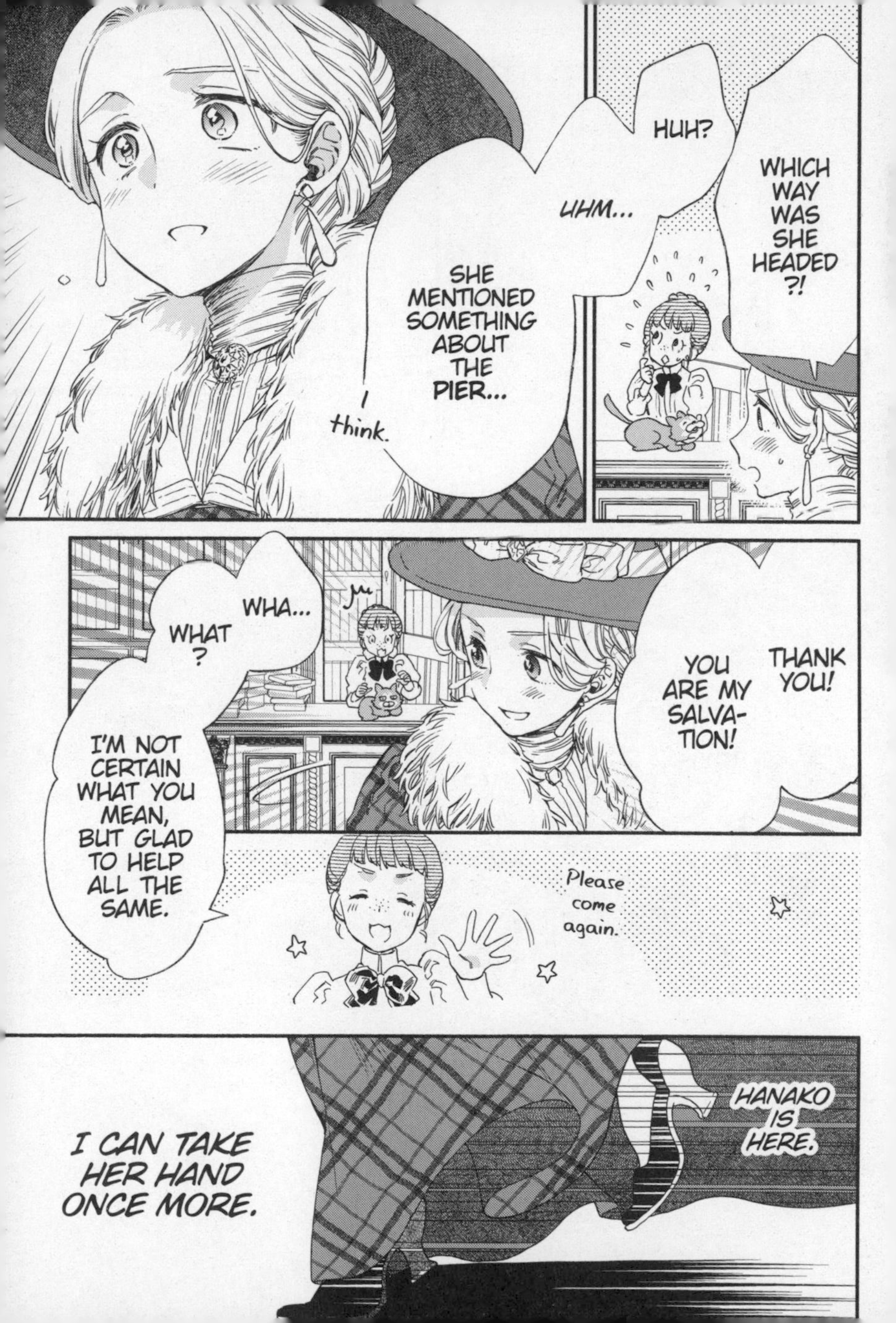
WHICH WAY WAS SHE HEADED?!
HUH?
UHM...
SHE MENTIONED SOMETHING ABOUT THE PIER...
I think.
THANK YOU!
YOU ARE MY SALVATION!
WHA... WHAT?
Please come again.
I'M NOT CERTAIN WHAT YOU MEAN, BUT GLAD TO HELP ALL THE SAME.
HANAKO IS HERE.
I CAN TAKE HER HAND ONCE MORE.

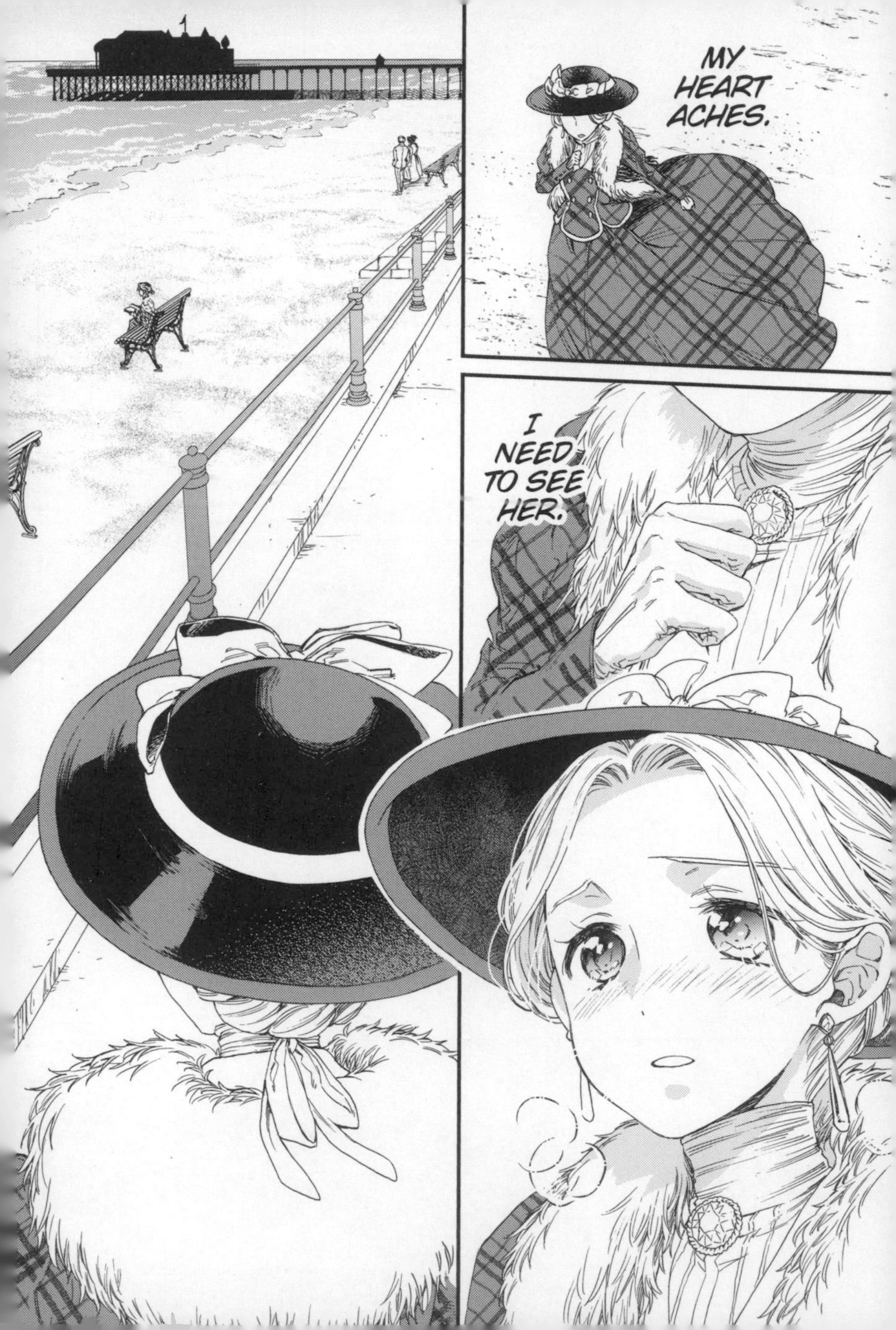
MY HEART ACHES.
I NEED TO SEE HER.

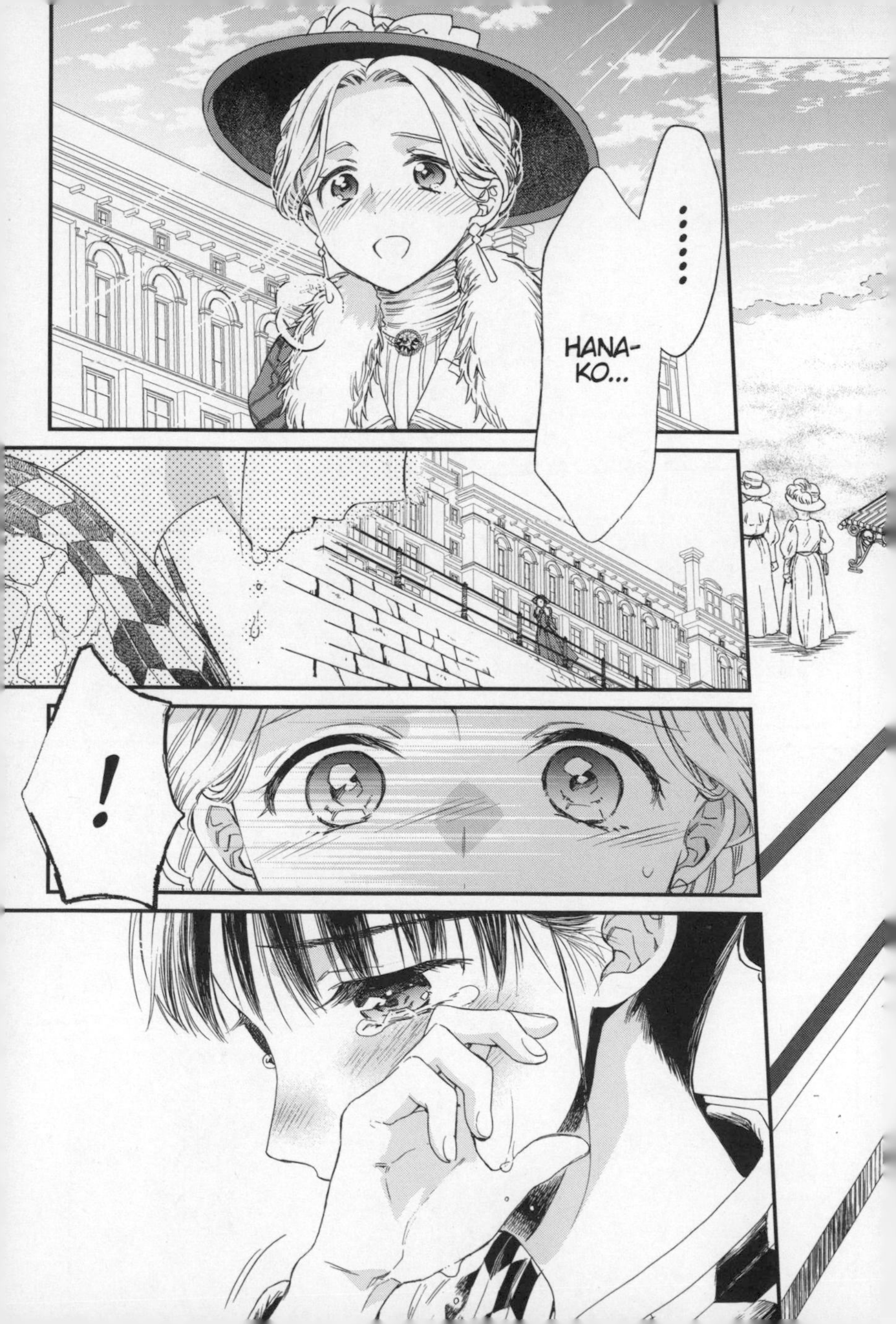
......
HANA-KO...
!

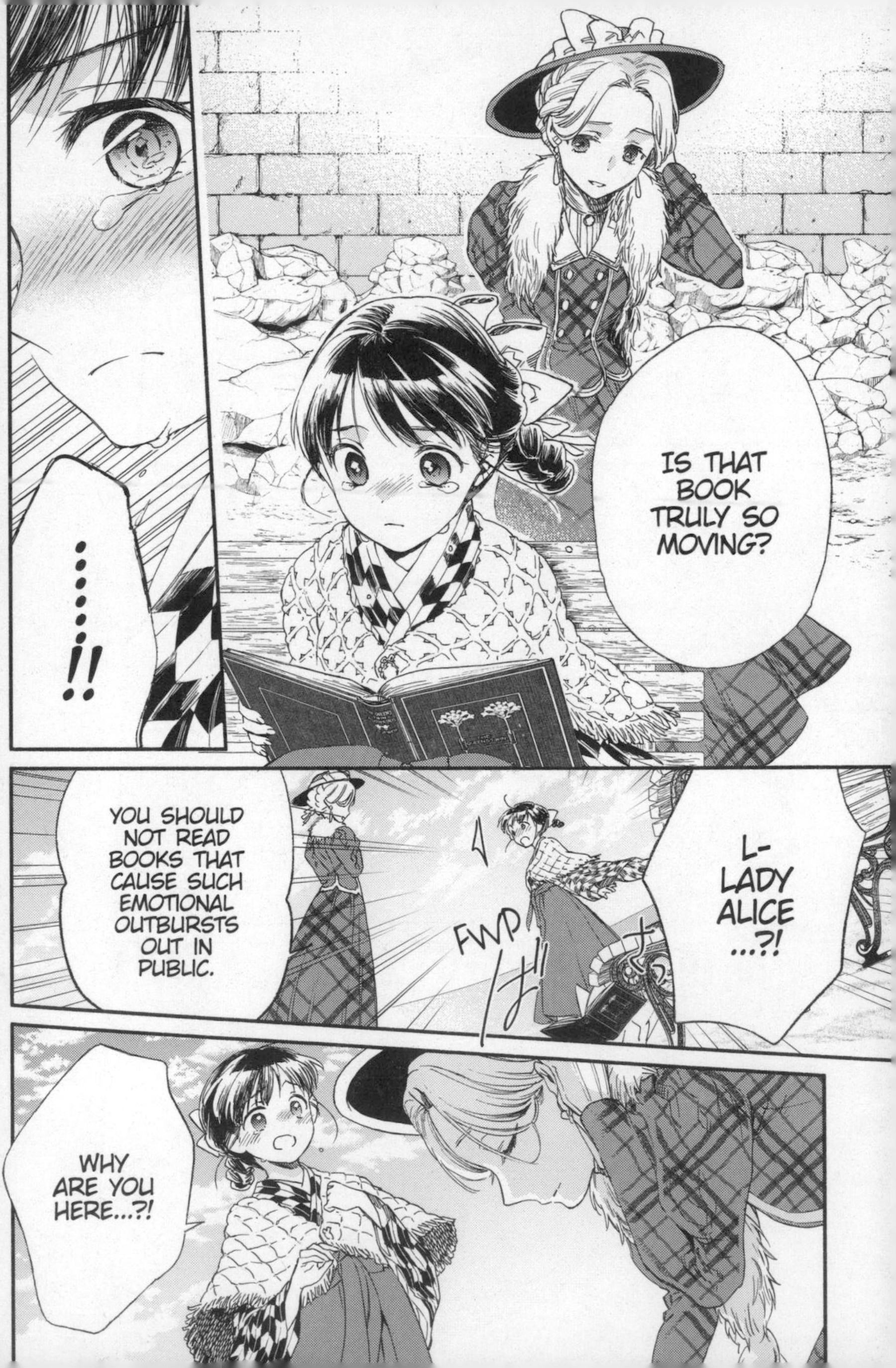
IS THAT BOOK TRULY SO MOVING?
......!!
L- LADY ALICE ...?!
FWP
YOU SHOULD NOT READ BOOKS THAT CAUSE SUCH EMOTIONAL OUTBURSTS OUT IN PUBLIC.
WHY ARE YOU HERE...?!

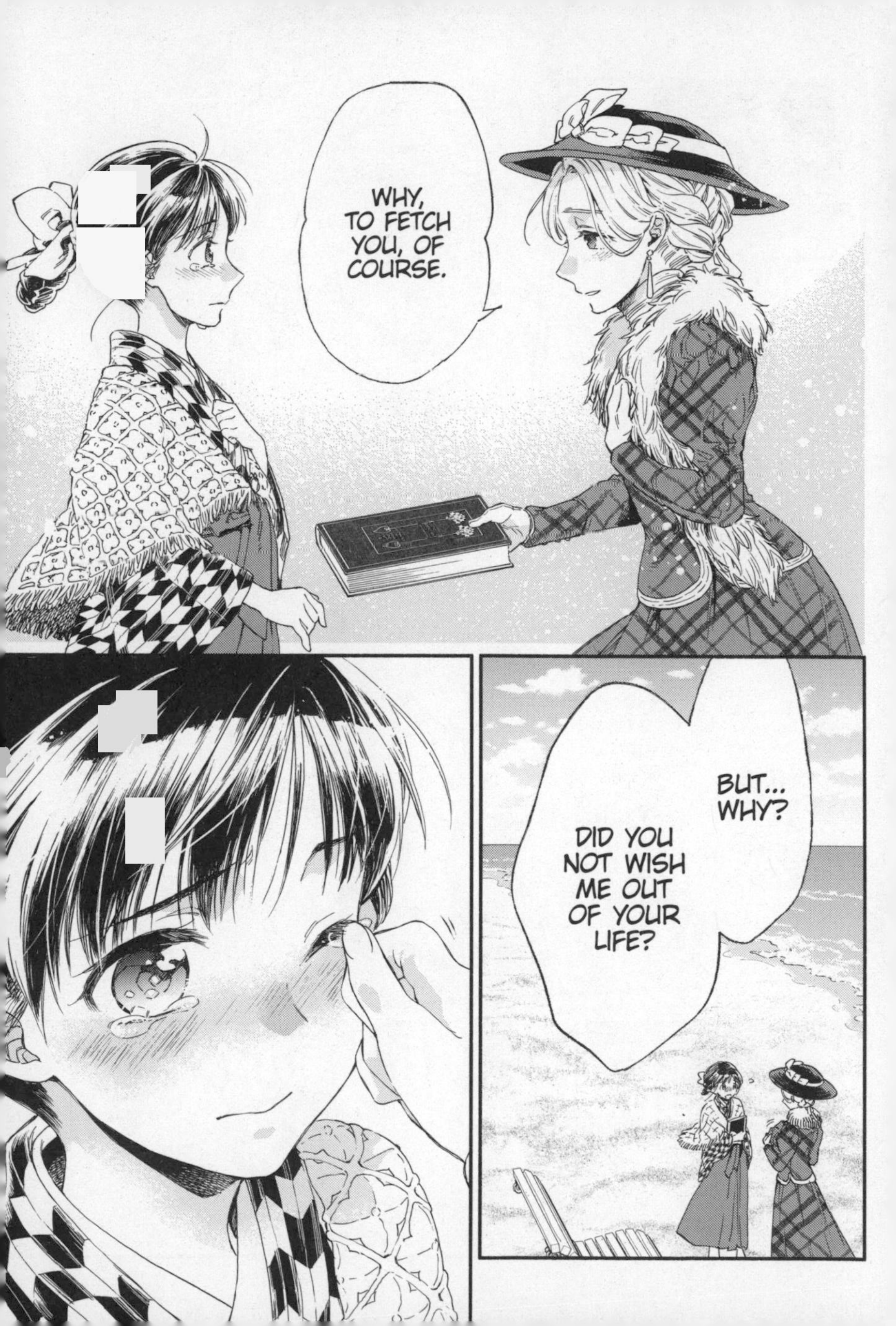
WHY, TO FETCH YOU, OF COURSE.
BUT... WHY?
DID YOU NOT WISH ME OUT OF YOUR LIFE?

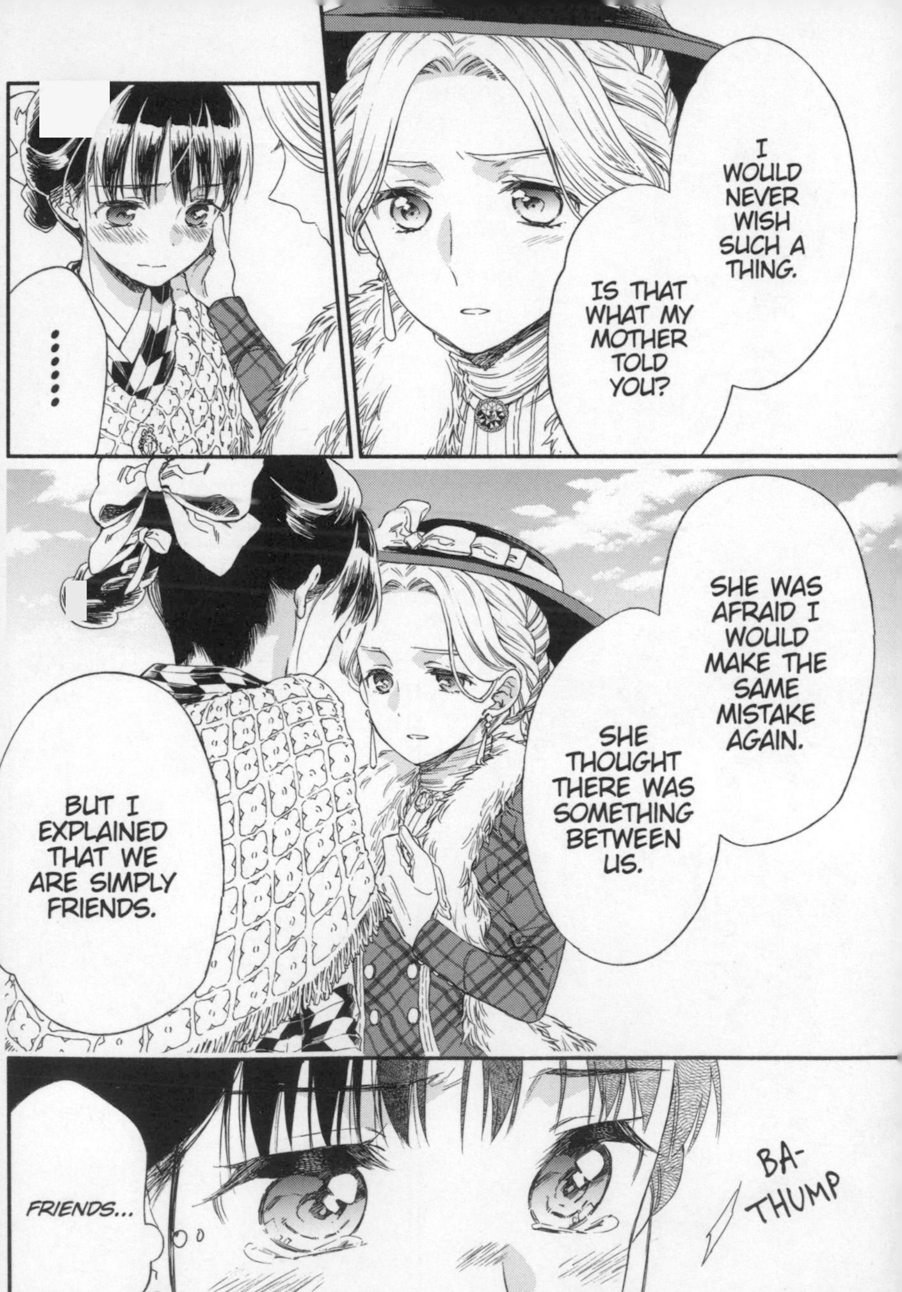
I WOULD NEVER WISH SUCH A THING.
IS THAT WHAT MY MOTHER TOLD YOU?
......
SHE WAS AFRAID I WOULD MAKE THE SAME MISTAKE AGAIN.
SHE THOUGHT THERE WAS SOMETHING BETWEEN US.
BUT I EXPLAINED THAT WE ARE SIMPLY FRIENDS.
BA-THUMP
FRIENDS...

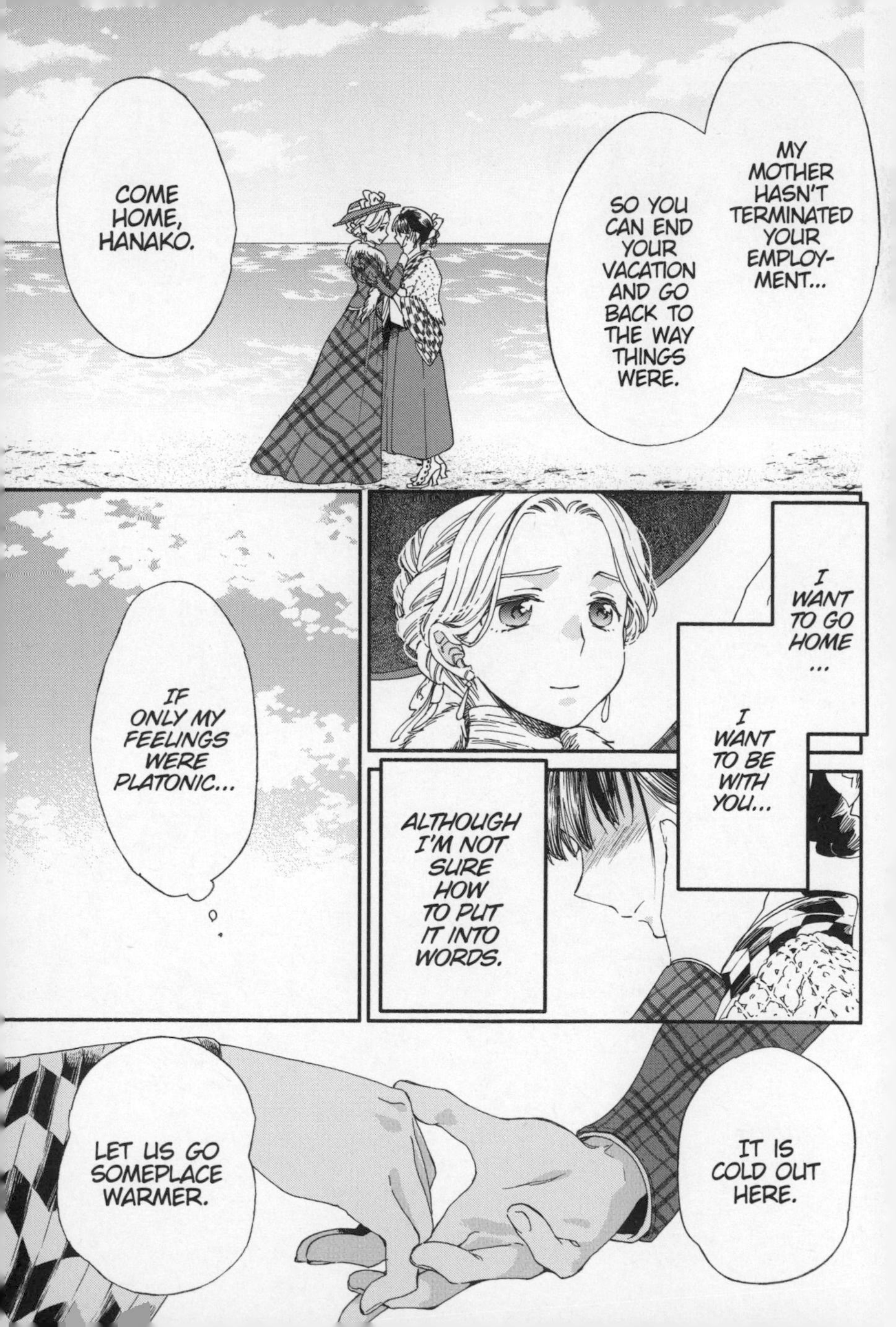
MY MOTHER HASN'T TERMINATED YOUR EMPLOYMENT...
SO YOU CAN END YOUR VACATION AND GO BACK TO THE WAY THINGS WERE.
COME HOME, HANAKO.
I WANT TO GO HOME ...
I WANT TO BE WITH YOU...
ALTHOUGH I'M NOT SURE HOW TO PUT IT INTO WORDS.
IF ONLY MY FEELINGS WERE PLATONIC...
IT IS COLD OUT HERE.
LET US GO SOMEPLACE WARMER.

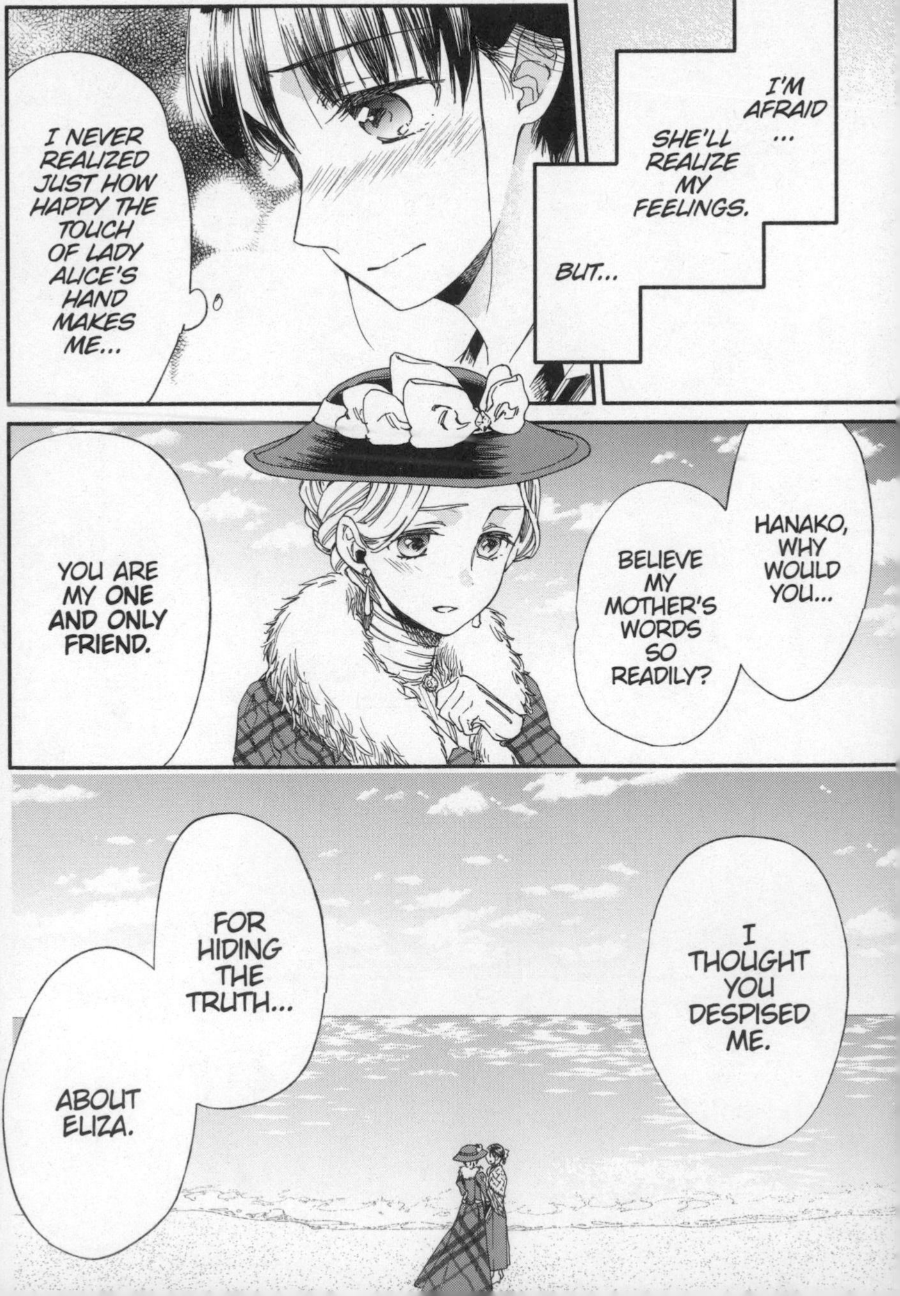
I'M AFRAID...
SHE'LL REALIZE MY FEELINGS.
BUT...
I NEVER REALIZED JUST HOW HAPPY THE TOUCH OF LADY ALICE'S HAND MAKES ME...
HANAKO, WHY WOULD YOU...
BELIEVE MY MOTHER'S WORDS SO READILY?
YOU ARE MY ONE AND ONLY FRIEND.
I THOUGHT YOU DESPISED ME.
FOR HIDING THE TRUTH...
ABOUT ELIZA.

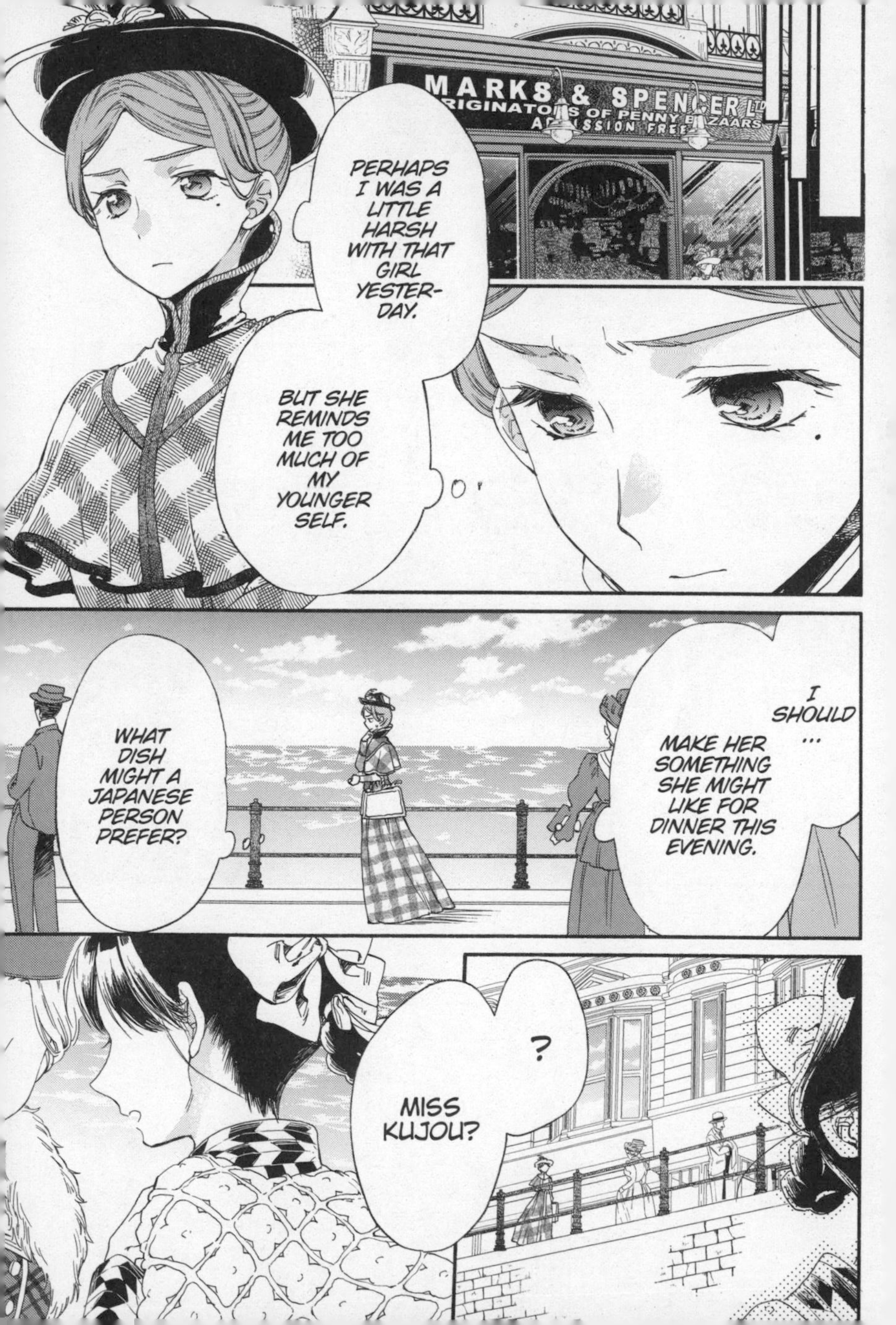
MARKS & SPENCER LTD
PERHAPS I WAS A LITTLE HARSH WITH THAT GIRL YESTER-DAY.
BUT SHE REMINDS ME TOO MUCH OF MY YOUNGER SELF.
I SHOULD ...
MAKE HER SOMETHING SHE MIGHT LIKE FOR DINNER THIS EVENING.
WHAT DISH MIGHT A JAPANESE PERSON PREFER?
?
MISS KUJOU?

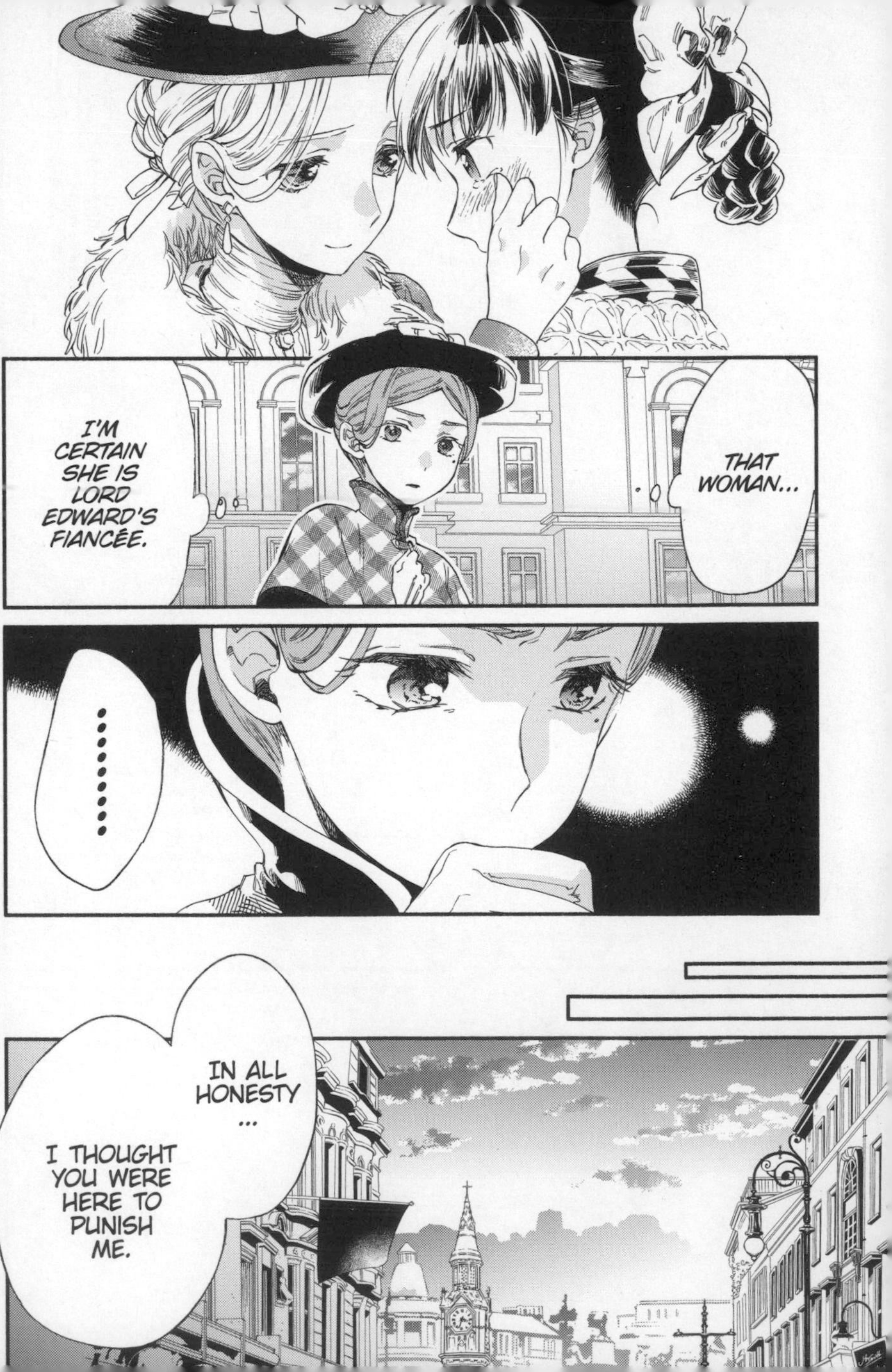
THAT WOMAN...
I'M CERTAIN SHE IS LORD EDWARD'S FIANCÉE.
....
IN ALL HONESTY ...
I THOUGHT YOU WERE HERE TO PUNISH ME.

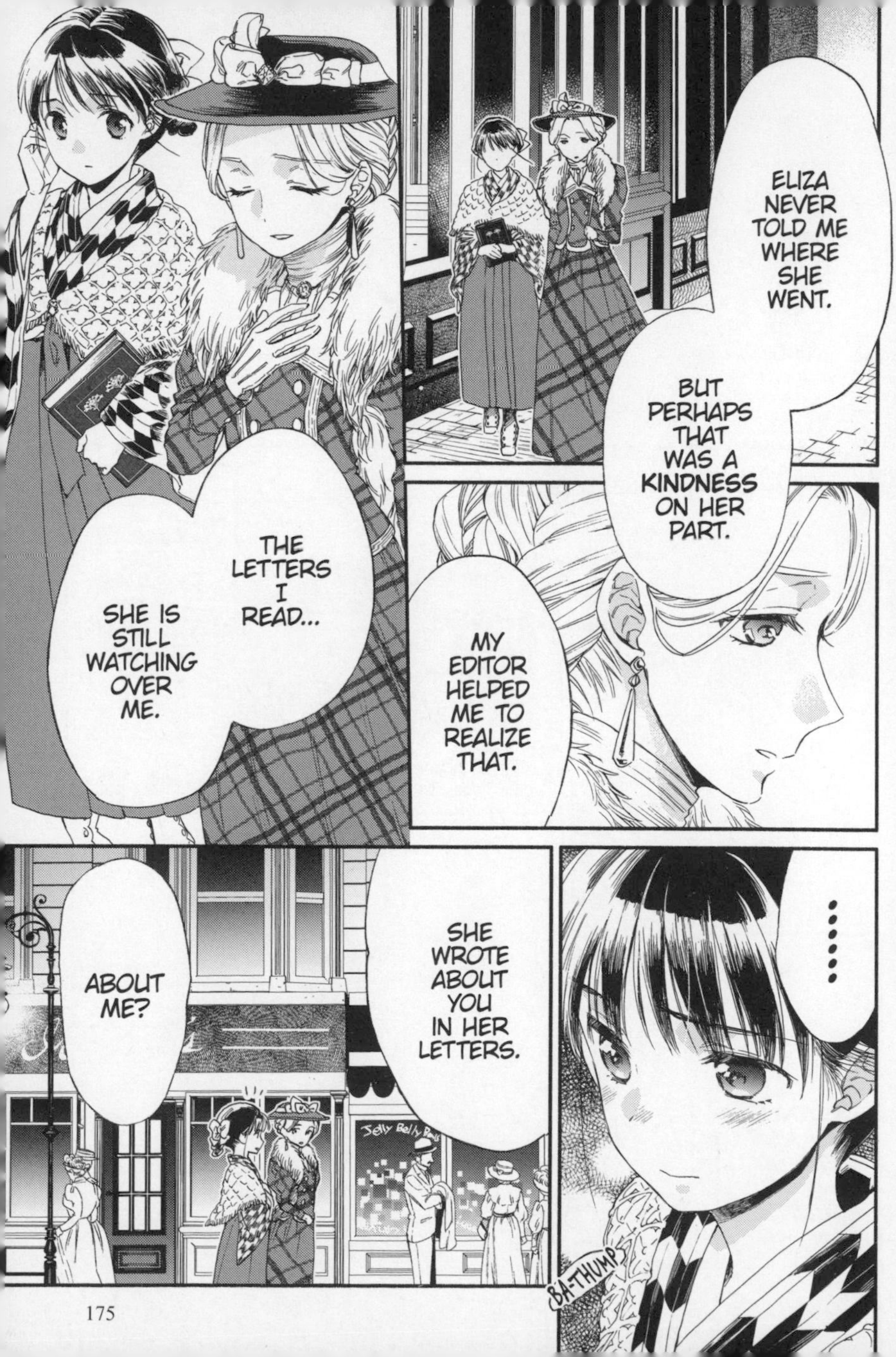
ELIZA NEVER TOLD ME WHERE SHE WENT.
BUT PERHAPS THAT WAS A KINDNESS ON HER PART.
MY EDITOR HELPED ME TO REALIZE THAT.
THE LETTERS I READ...
SHE IS STILL WATCHING OVER ME.
......
BA-THUMP
SHE WROTE ABOUT YOU IN HER LETTERS.
ABOUT ME?
Jelly Belly

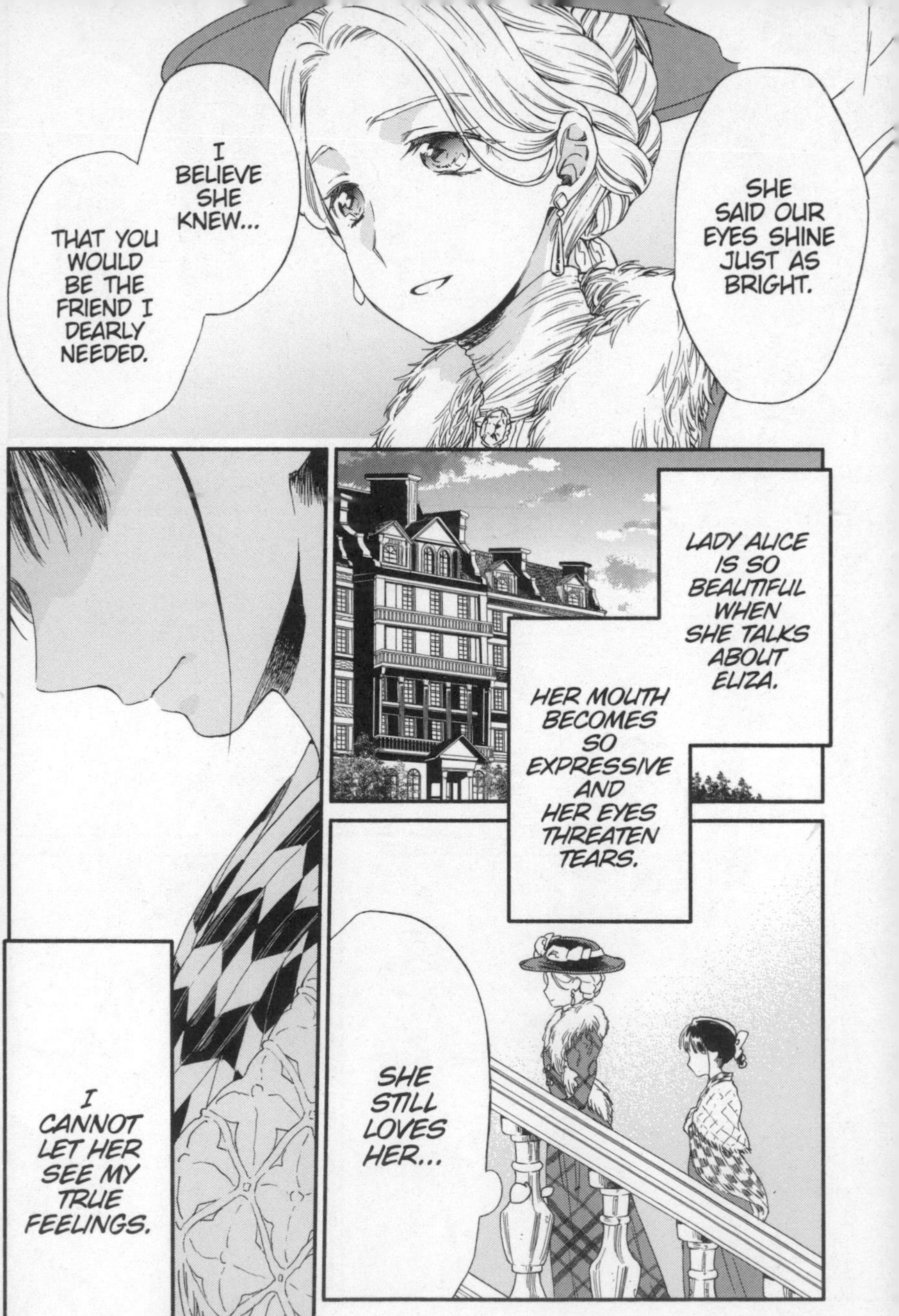
SHE SAID OUR EYES SHINE JUST AS BRIGHT.
I BELIEVE SHE KNEW...
THAT YOU WOULD BE THE FRIEND I DEARLY NEEDED.
LADY ALICE IS SO BEAUTIFUL WHEN SHE TALKS ABOUT ELIZA.
HER MOUTH BECOMES SO EXPRESSIVE AND HER EYES THREATEN TEARS.
SHE STILL LOVES HER...
I CANNOT LET HER SEE MY TRUE FEELINGS.

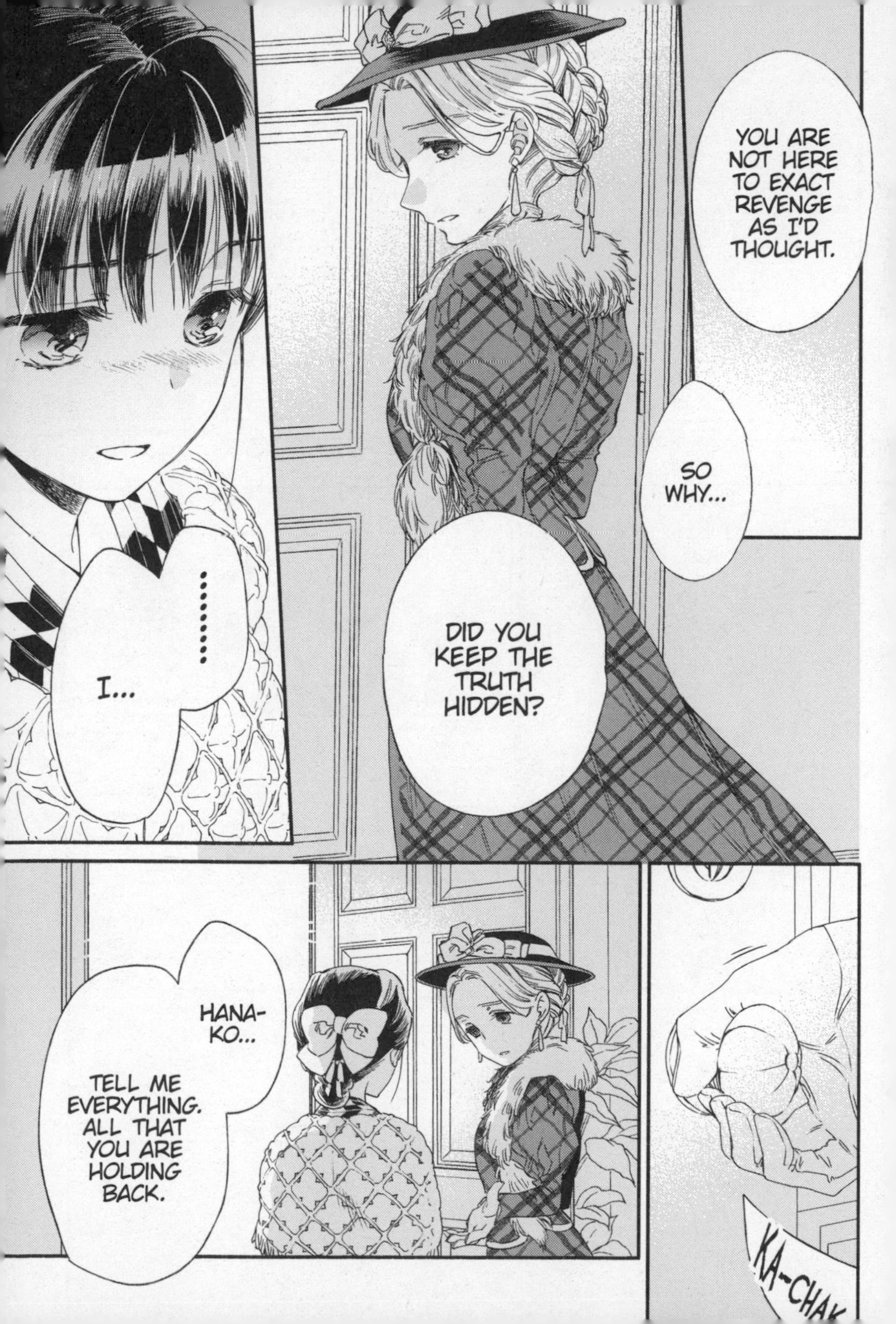
YOU ARE NOT HERE TO EXACT REVENGE AS I'D THOUGHT.
SO WHY...
DID YOU KEEP THE TRUTH HIDDEN?
......
I...
KA-CHAK
HANA-KO...
TELL ME EVERYTHING. ALL THAT YOU ARE HOLDING BACK.

HANA-
KO...?

I CANNOT
ALLOW
HER TO
SEE MY
JEALOUSY.

I
CAN'T...

ESPECIALLY
NOT AFTER
SHE SAID
THAT WE
ARE ONLY
FRIENDS.

WH-
WHY
NOT?

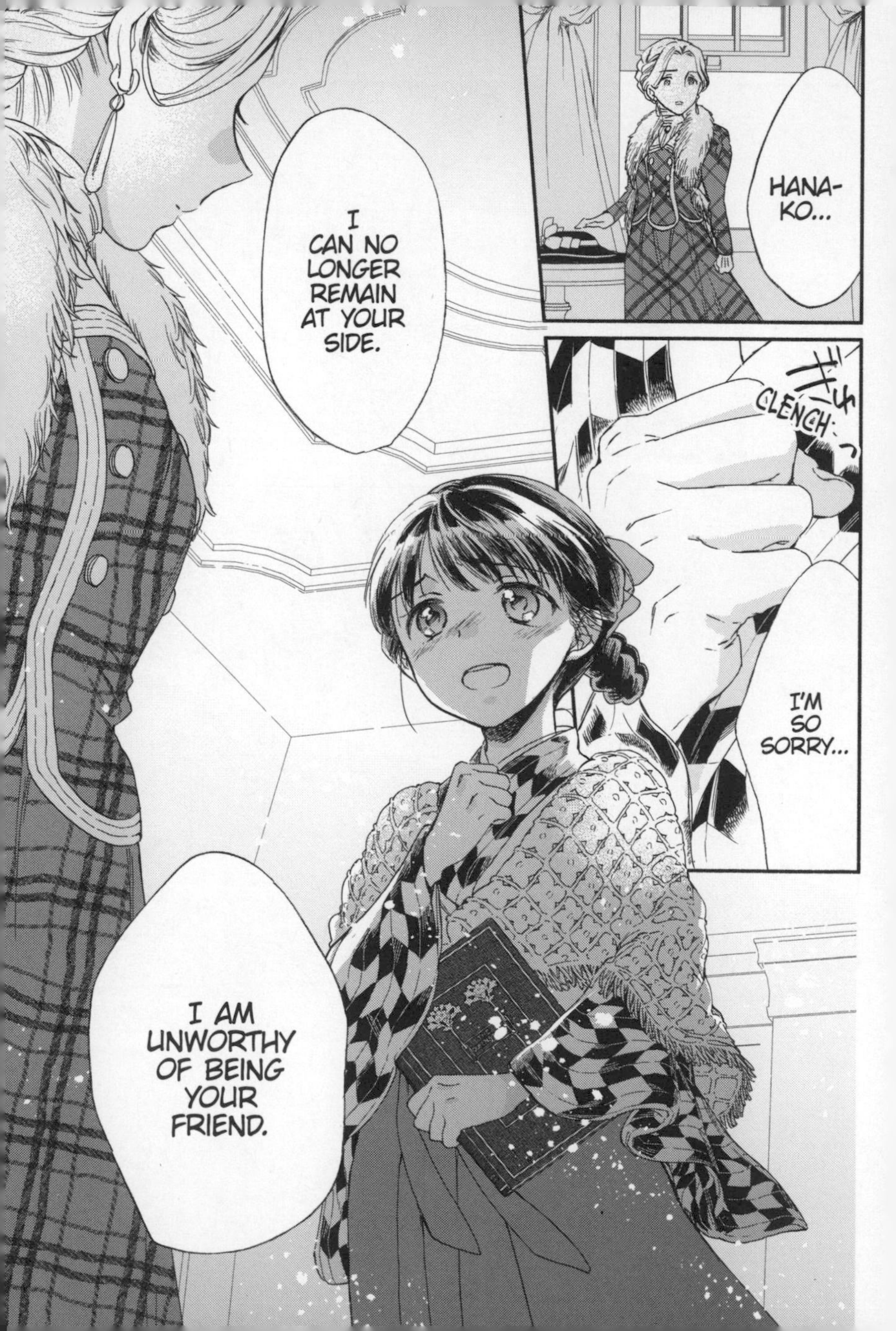
HANA-KO...
CLENCH
I'M SO SORRY...
I CAN NO LONGER REMAIN AT YOUR SIDE.
I AM UNWORTHY OF BEING YOUR FRIEND.

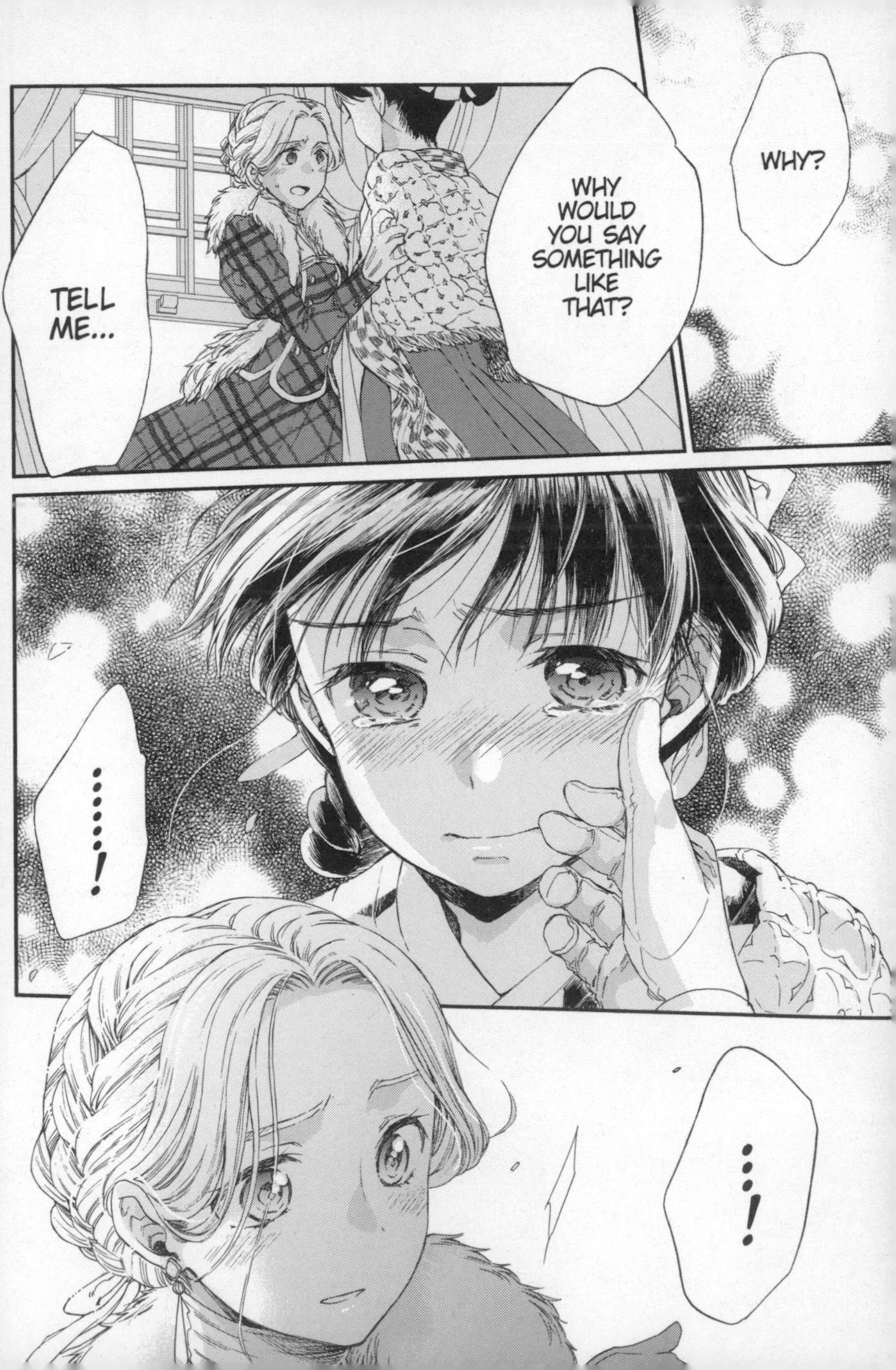
WHY?
WHY WOULD YOU SAY SOMETHING LIKE THAT?
TELL ME...
.....!
...!

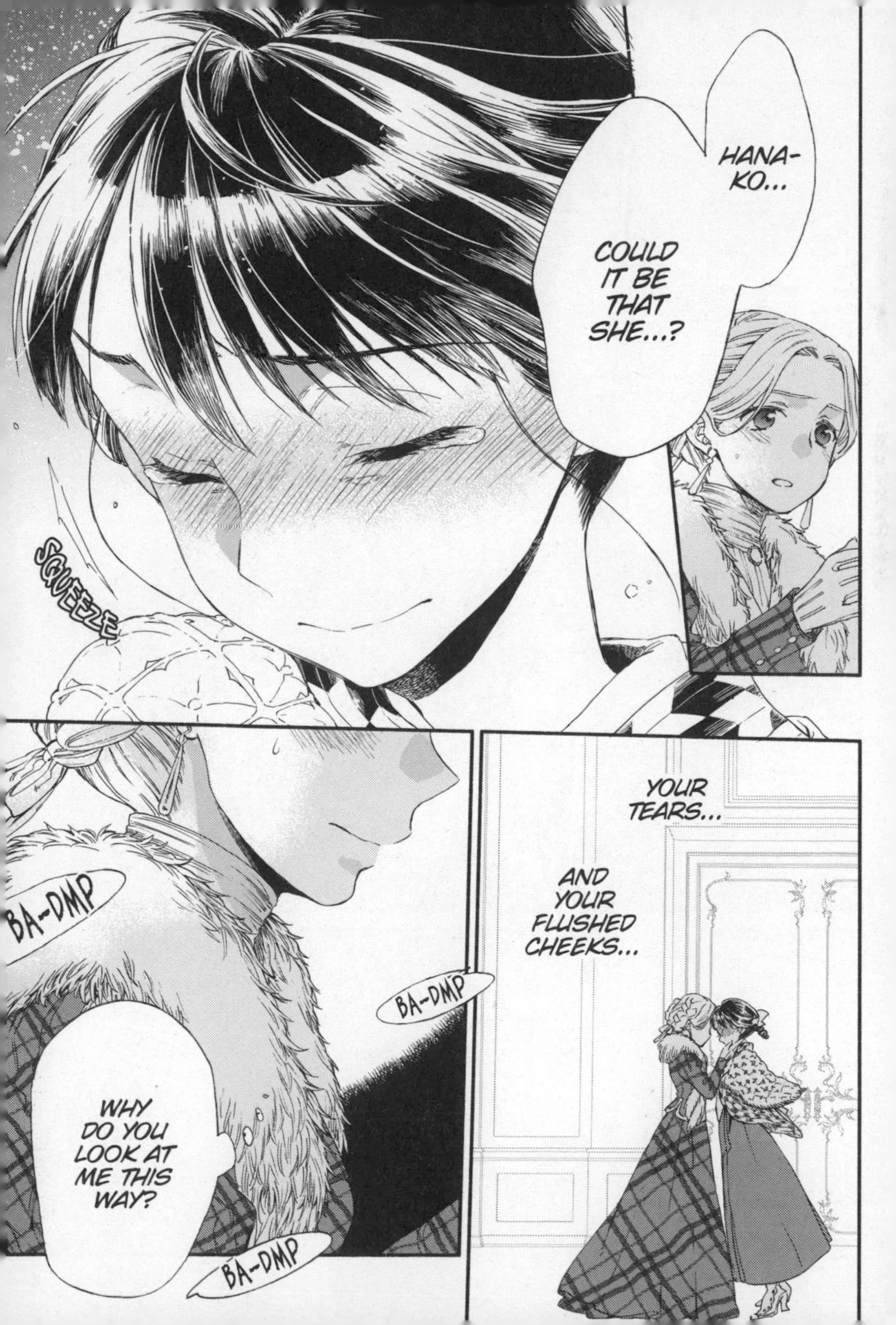
HANA-KO...
COULD IT BE THAT SHE...?
SQUEEZE
YOUR TEARS...
AND YOUR FLUSHED CHEEKS...
BA-DMP
BA-DMP
WHY DO YOU LOOK AT ME THIS WAY?
BA-DMP

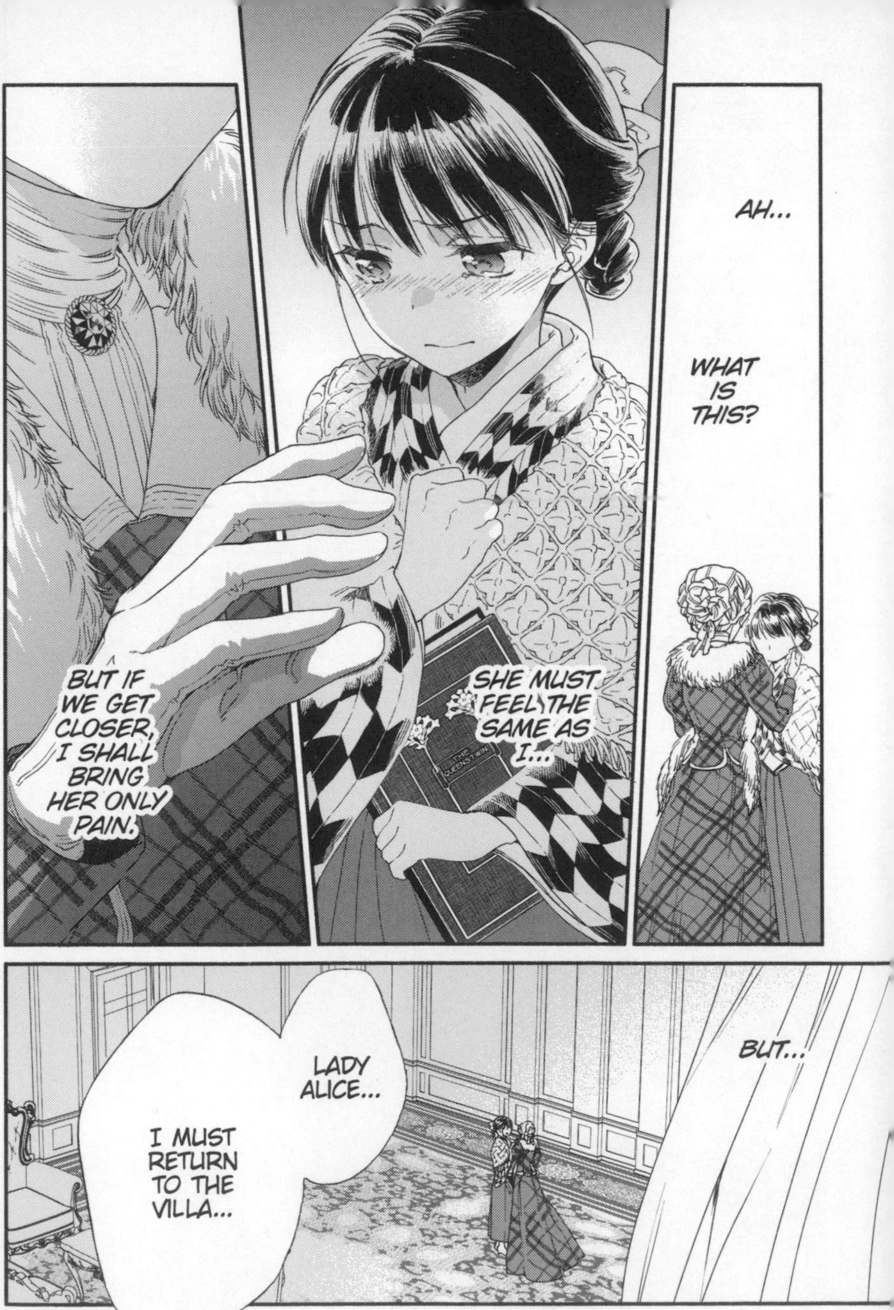
AH...
WHAT IS THIS?
SHE MUST FEEL THE SAME AS I...
BUT IF WE GET CLOSER, I SHALL BRING HER ONLY PAIN.
BUT...
LADY ALICE...
I MUST RETURN TO THE VILLA...

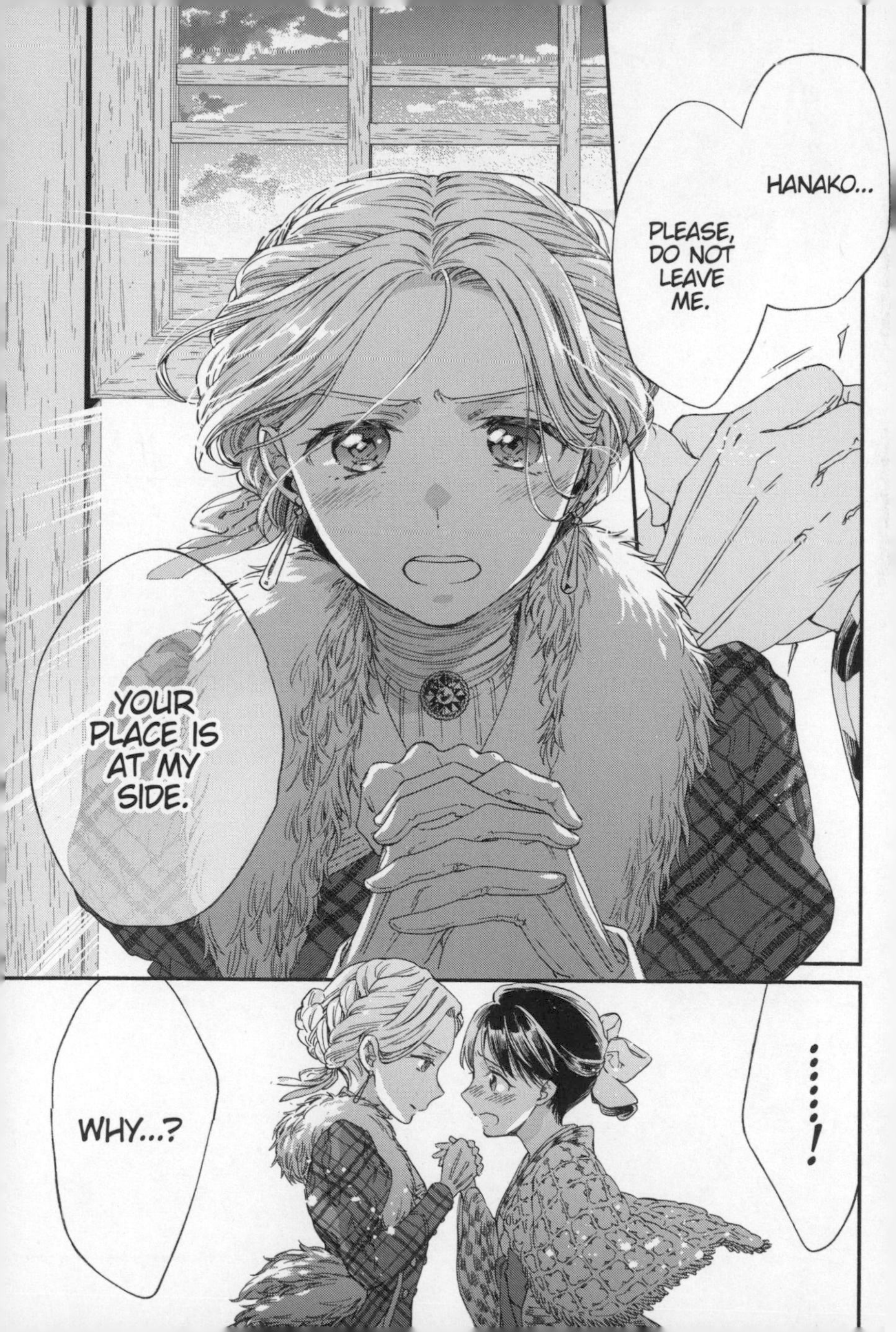
HANAKO...
PLEASE, DO NOT LEAVE ME.
YOUR PLACE IS AT MY SIDE.
......!
WHY...?

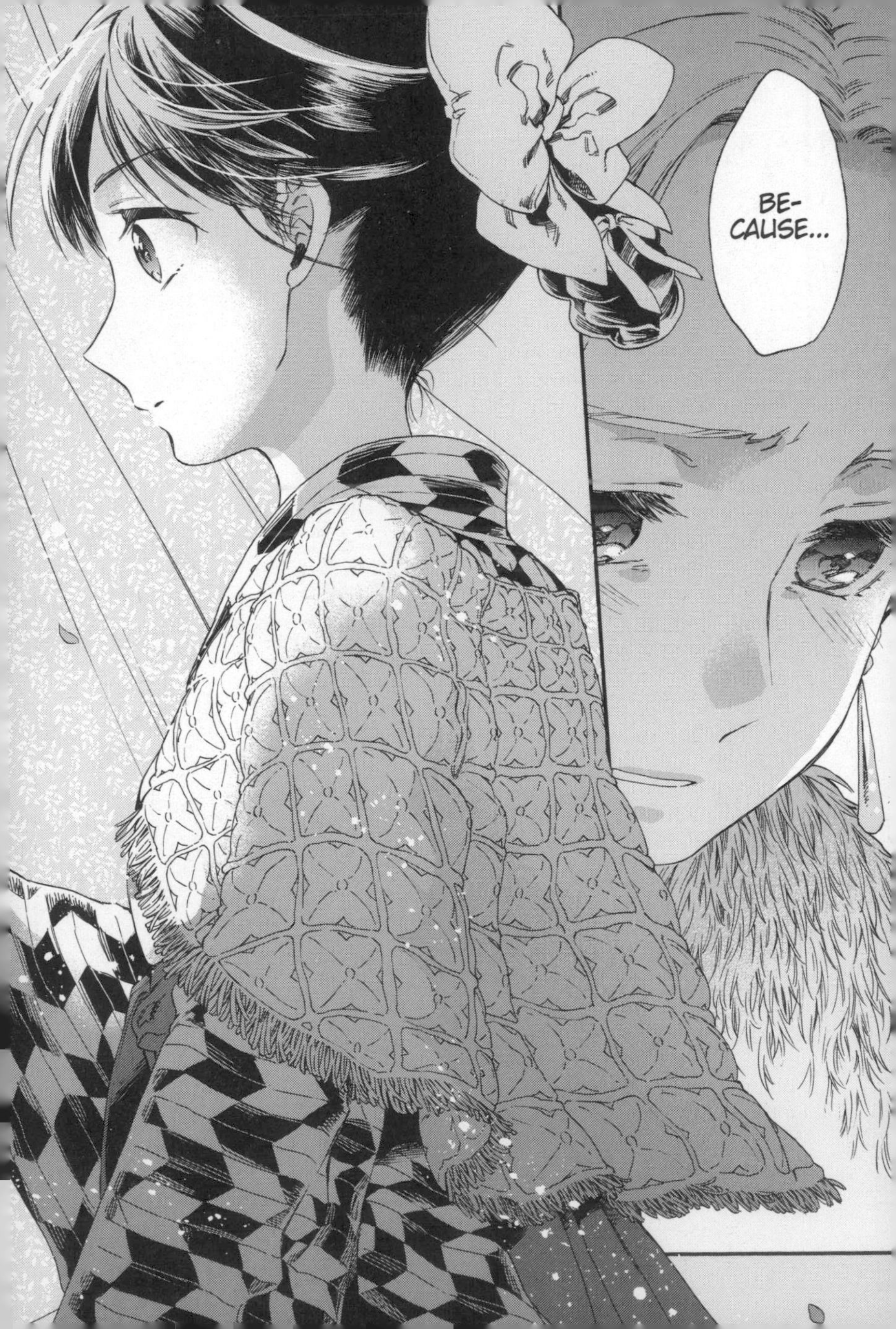
BE-
CAUSE...

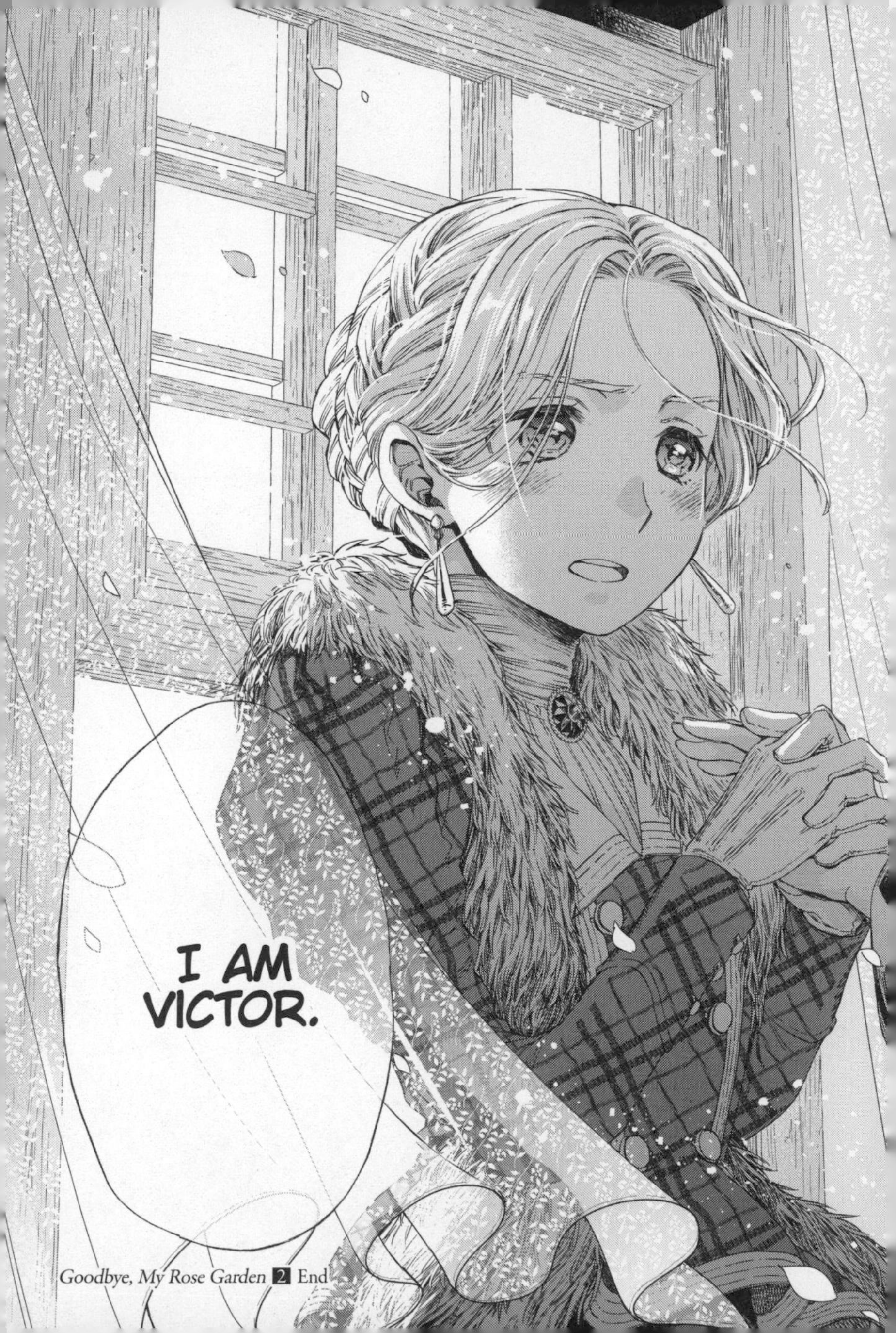
I AM VICTOR.

Goodbye, My Rose Garden 2 End

Goodbye,
my Rose Garden

Intermission: Toffee for You

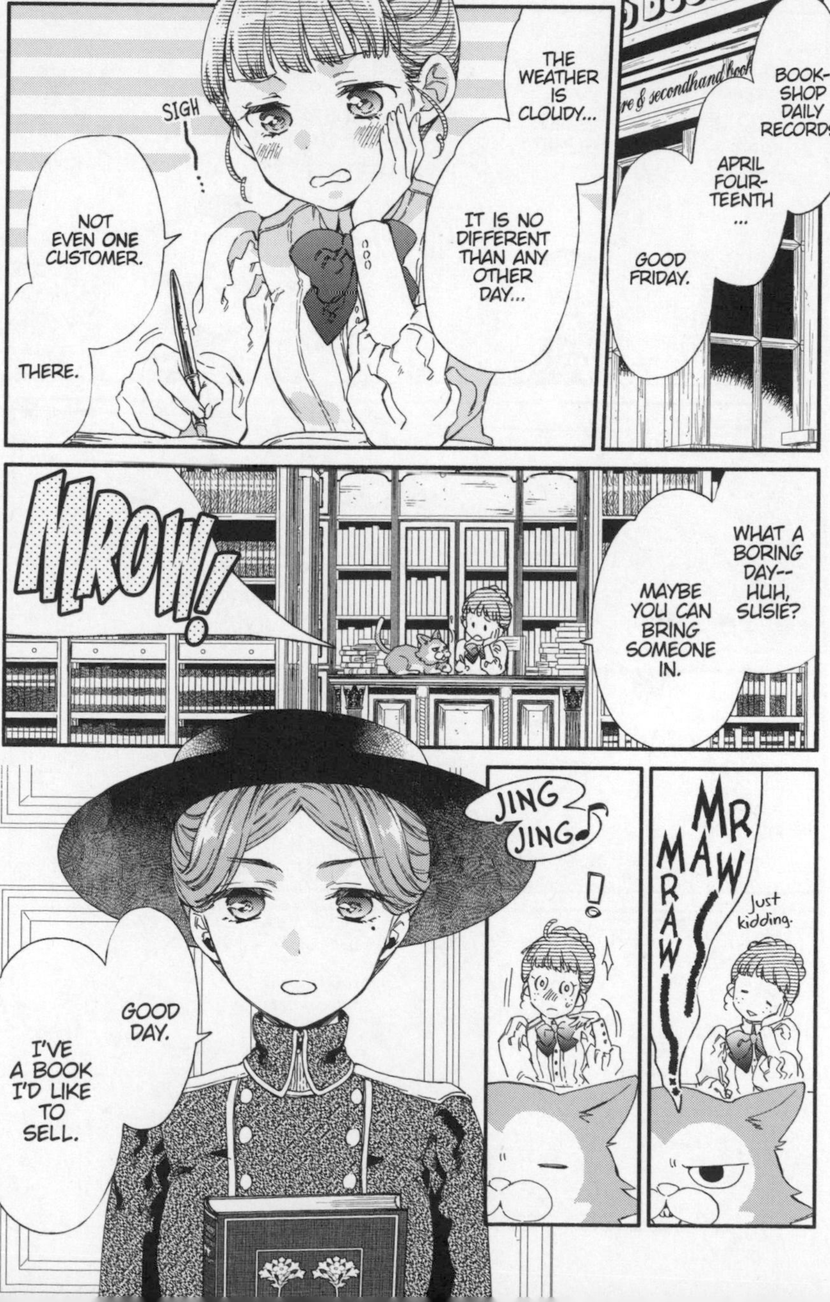
BOOKSHOP DAILY RECORDS.
APRIL FOURTEENTH...
GOOD FRIDAY.
THE WEATHER IS CLOUDY...
IT IS NO DIFFERENT THAN ANY OTHER DAY...
SIGH...
NOT EVEN ONE CUSTOMER.
THERE.
WHAT A BORING DAY--HUH, SUSIE?
MAYBE YOU CAN BRING SOMEONE IN.
MROW!
MR MAW
MAW MRAW
Just kidding.
JING JING
!
GOOD DAY.
I'VE A BOOK I'D LIKE TO SELL.

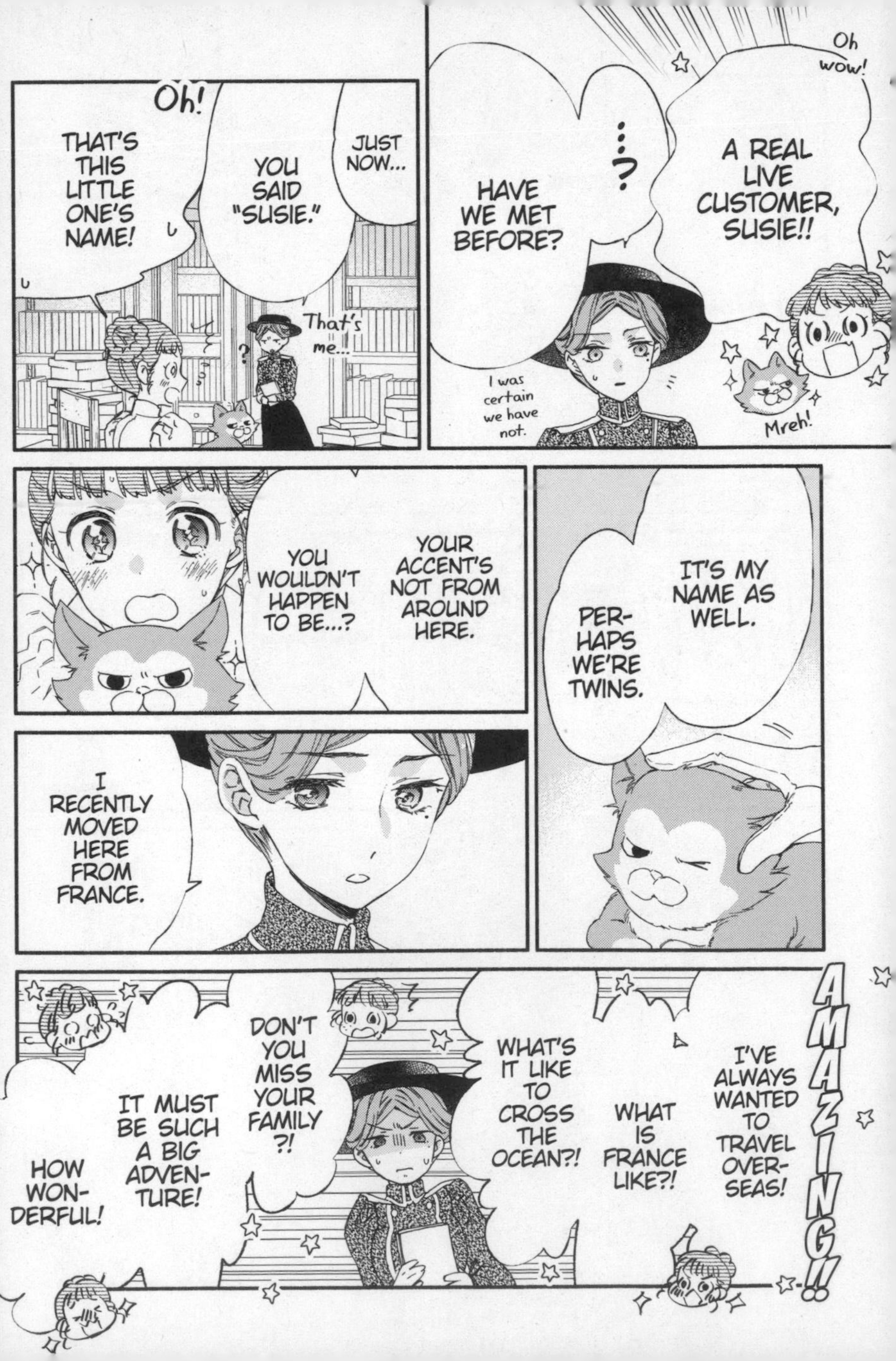
Oh wow!
A REAL LIVE CUSTOMER, SUSIE!!
...?
HAVE WE MET BEFORE?
Mreh!
I was certain we have not.
JUST NOW...
YOU SAID "SUSIE."
Oh!
THAT'S THIS LITTLE ONE'S NAME!
That's me...
IT'S MY NAME AS WELL.
PER-HAPS WE'RE TWINS.
YOUR ACCENT'S NOT FROM AROUND HERE.
YOU WOULDN'T HAPPEN TO BE...?
I RECENTLY MOVED HERE FROM FRANCE.
AMAZING!!
I'VE ALWAYS WANTED TO TRAVEL OVER-SEAS!
WHAT IS FRANCE LIKE?!
WHAT'S IT LIKE TO CROSS THE OCEAN?!
DON'T YOU MISS YOUR FAMILY?!
IT MUST BE SUCH A BIG ADVEN-TURE!
HOW WON-DERFUL!

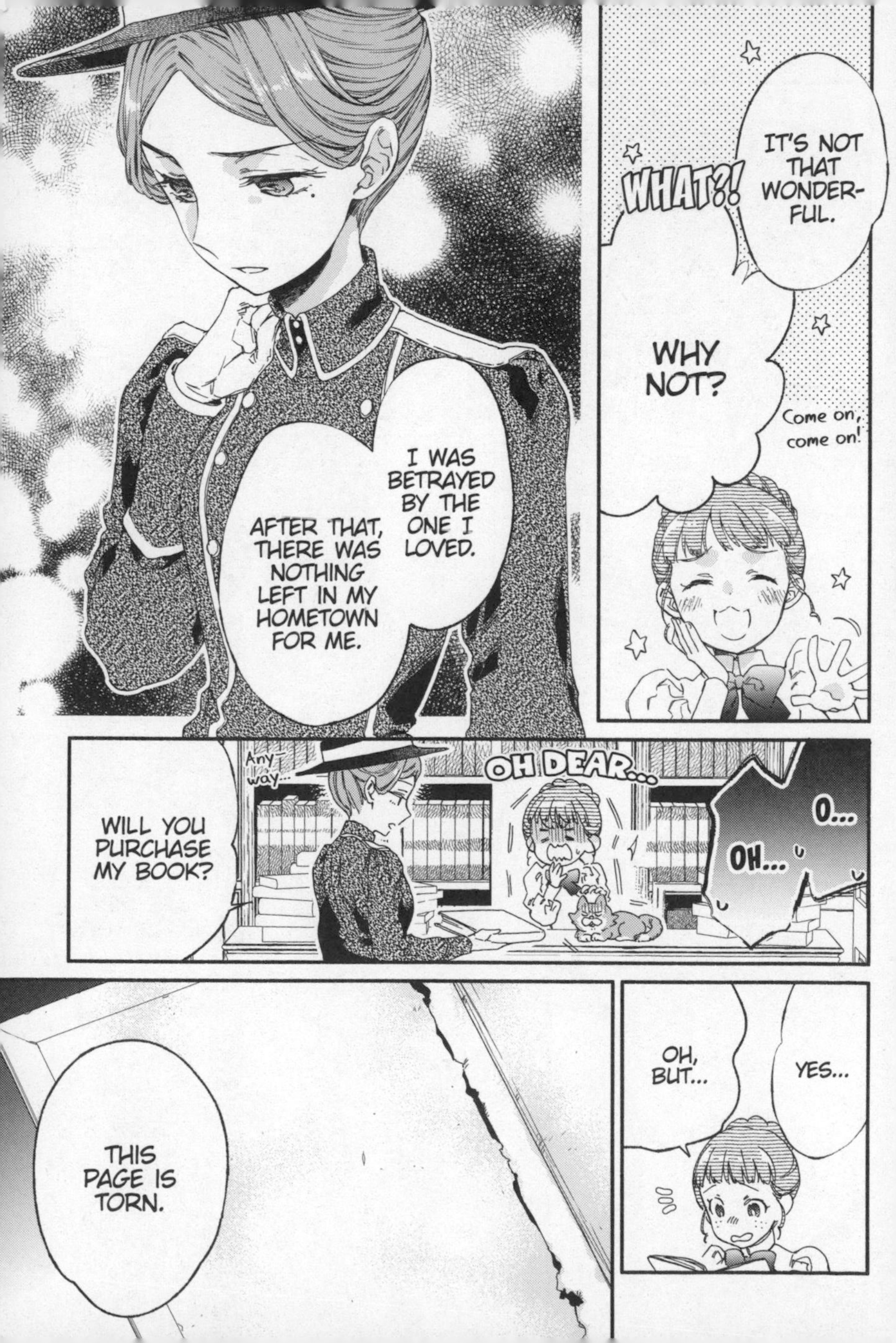
IT'S NOT THAT WONDER-FUL.
WHAT?!
WHY NOT?
Come on, come on!
I WAS BETRAYED BY THE ONE I LOVED.
AFTER THAT, THERE WAS NOTHING LEFT IN MY HOMETOWN FOR ME.
O... OH...
OH DEAR...
Any-way...
WILL YOU PURCHASE MY BOOK?
YES...
OH, BUT...
THIS PAGE IS TORN.

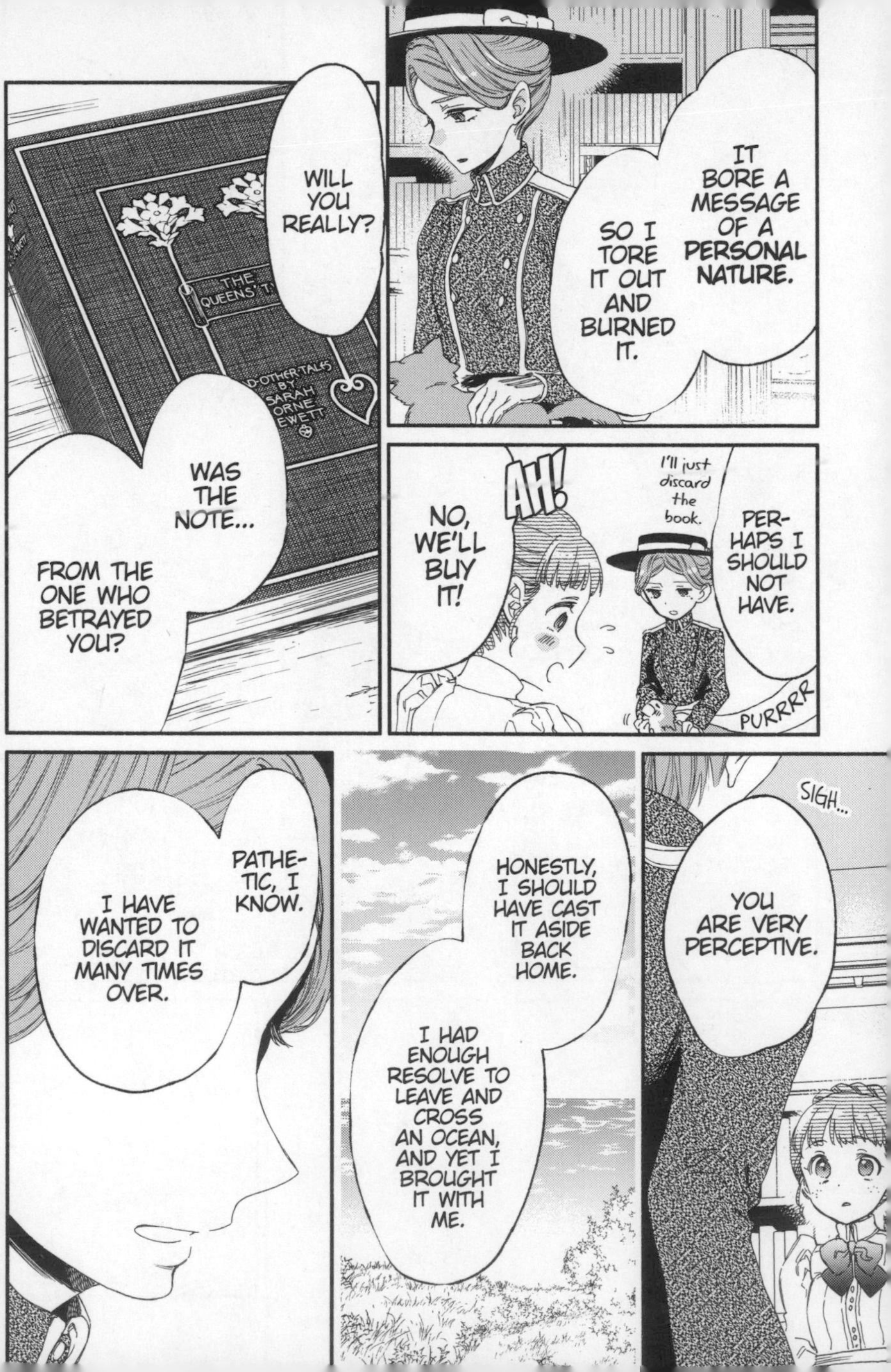
IT BORE A MESSAGE OF A PERSONAL NATURE.
SO I TORE IT OUT AND BURNED IT.
PER-HAPS I SHOULD NOT HAVE.
I'll just discard the book.
AH!
NO, WE'LL BUY IT!
PURRRR
WILL YOU REALLY?
WAS THE NOTE...
FROM THE ONE WHO BETRAYED YOU?
SIGH...
YOU ARE VERY PERCEPTIVE.
HONESTLY, I SHOULD HAVE CAST IT ASIDE BACK HOME.
I HAD ENOUGH RESOLVE TO LEAVE AND CROSS AN OCEAN, AND YET I BROUGHT IT WITH ME.
PATHE-TIC, I KNOW.
I HAVE WANTED TO DISCARD IT MANY TIMES OVER.

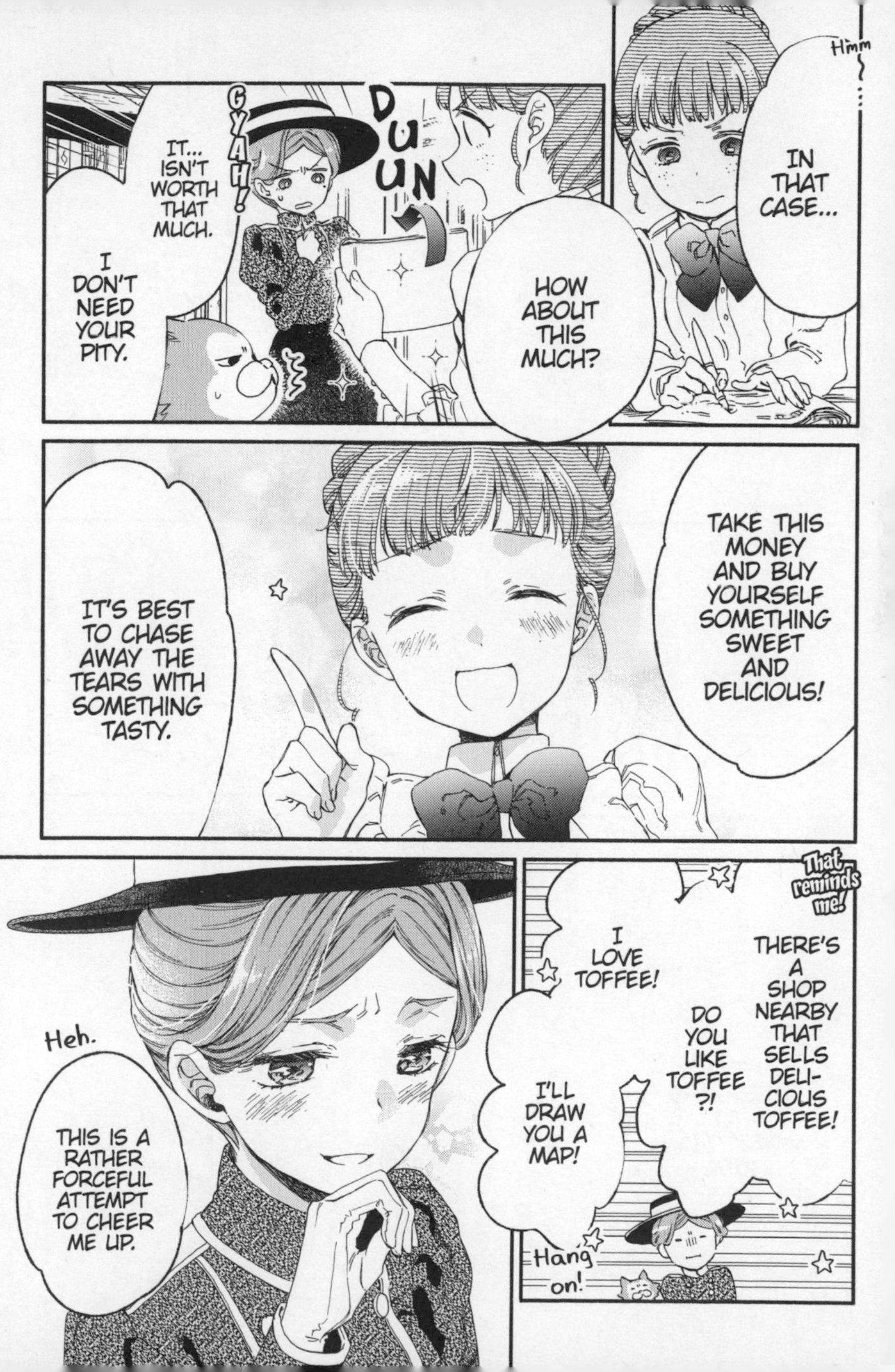
Hmm~...
IN THAT CASE...
HOW ABOUT THIS MUCH?
DUUN
GYAH!
IT... ISN'T WORTH THAT MUCH.
I DON'T NEED YOUR PITY.
TAKE THIS MONEY AND BUY YOURSELF SOMETHING SWEET AND DELICIOUS!
IT'S BEST TO CHASE AWAY THE TEARS WITH SOMETHING TASTY.
That reminds me!
THERE'S A SHOP NEARBY THAT SELLS DELICIOUS TOFFEE!
DO YOU LIKE TOFFEE?!
I LOVE TOFFEE!
I'LL DRAW YOU A MAP!
Hang on!
Heh.
THIS IS A RATHER FORCEFUL ATTEMPT TO CHEER ME UP.

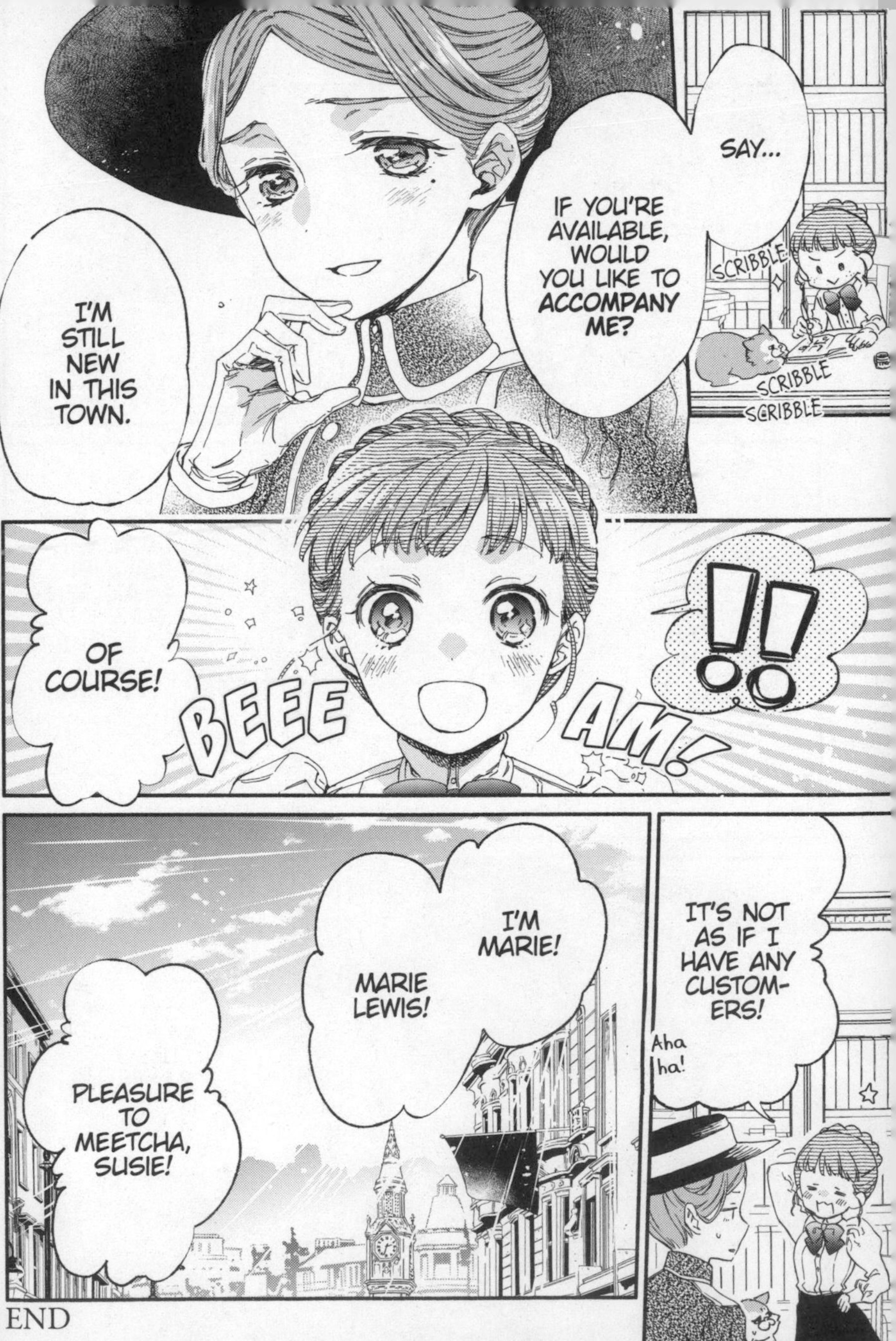
SAY...
IF YOU'RE AVAILABLE, WOULD YOU LIKE TO ACCOMPANY ME?
SCRIBBLE
SCRIBBLE
SCRIBBLE
I'M STILL NEW IN THIS TOWN.
!!
BEEEAM!
OF COURSE!
IT'S NOT AS IF I HAVE ANY CUSTOM-ERS!
Aha ha!
I'M MARIE!
MARIE LEWIS!
PLEASURE TO MEETCHA, SUSIE!

END

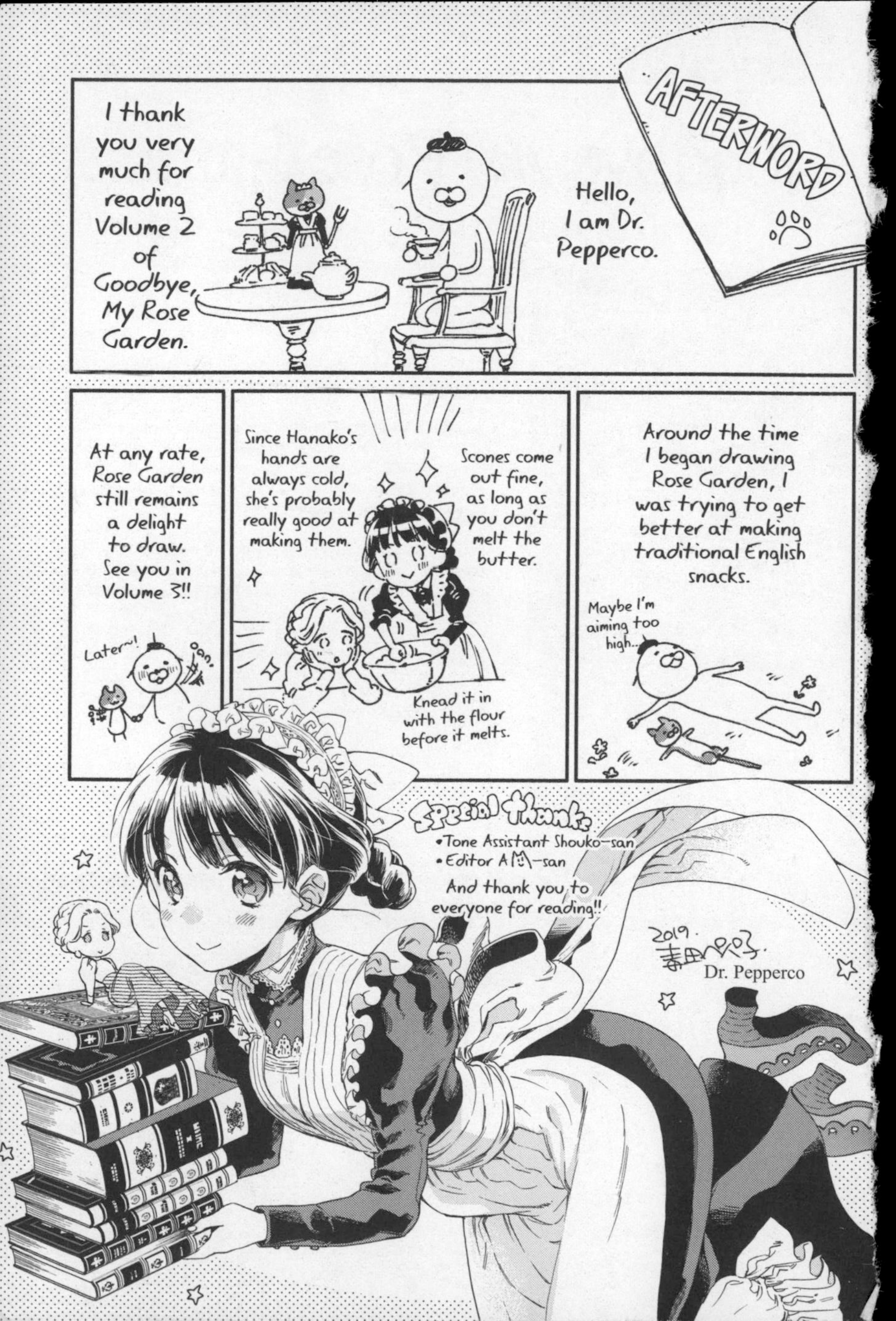
AFTERWORD
Hello, I am Dr. Pepperco.
I thank you very much for reading Volume 2 of Goodbye, My Rose Garden.
Around the time I began drawing Rose Garden, I was trying to get better at making traditional English snacks.
Maybe I'm aiming too high...
Scones come out fine, as long as you don't melt the butter.
Since Hanako's hands are always cold, she's probably really good at making them.
Knead it in with the flour before it melts.
At any rate, Rose Garden still remains a delight to draw. See you in Volume 3!!
Oan!
Later~!
Special thanks
•Tone Assistant Shouko-san
•Editor A山-san
And thank you to everyone for reading!!
2019.
Dr. Pepperco

SEVEN SEAS ENTERTAINMENT PRESENTS

Goodbye, *my* Rose Garden

story and art by **DR. PEPPERCO**

VOLUME 2

TRANSLATION
Amber Tamosaitis

ADAPTATION
Cae Hawksmoor

LETTERING AND RETOUCH
Kaitlyn Wiley

COVER DESIGN
Nicky Lim
(LOGO) **George Panella**

PROOFREADER
Danielle King

EDITOR
Jenn Grunigen

PREPRESS TECHNICIAN
Rhiannon Rasmussen-Silverstein

PRODUCTION MANAGER
Lissa Pattillo

MANAGING EDITOR
Julie Davis

ASSOCIATE PUBLISHER
Adam Arnold

PUBLISHER
Jason DeAngelis

Seven Seas press and purchase enquiries can be sent to Marketing Manager Lianne Sentar at press@gomanga.com. Information regarding the distribution and purchase of digital editions is available from Digital Manager CK Russell at digital@gomanga.com.

ISBN: 978-1-64505-506-8

Printed in Canada

First Printing: July 2020

10 9 8 7 6 5 4 3 2 1

FOLLOW US ONLINE: ***www.sevenseasentertainment.com***

READING DIRECTIONS

This book reads from ***right to left***, Japanese style. If this is your first time reading manga, you start reading from the top right panel on each page and take it from there. If you get lost, just follow the numbered diagram here. It may seem backwards at first, but you'll get the hang of it! Have fun!!

1
2
3
4
5
6
7
8
9

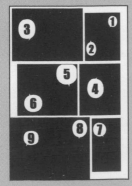